ISLAMIZING INTIMACIES

Islamizing Intimacies

Youth, Sexuality, and Gender in Contemporary Indonesia

NANCY J. SMITH-HEFNER

 University of Hawai'i Press ◈ Honolulu

Printed in the United States of America
25 24 23 22 21 20   6 5 4 3 2 1

Library of Congress Cataloging-in-Publication Data

Names: Smith-Hefner, Nancy Joan, author.
Title: Islamizing intimacies : youth, sexuality, and gender in contemporary
    Indonesia / Nancy J. Smith-Hefner.
Description: Honolulu : University of Hawai'i Press, [2019] | Includes
    bibliographical references and index.
Identifiers: LCCN 2018038442 | ISBN 9780824878030 (cloth ; alk. paper)
Subjects: LCSH: Muslim youth—Indonesia—Yogyakarta—Attitudes. | Muslim
    youth—Sexual behavior—Indonesia—Yogyakarta. | Islam and
    secularism—Indonesia—Yogyakarta.
Classification: LCC BP188.18.Y68 S65 2019 | DDC 306.70835/0959827—dc23
LC record available at https://lccn.loc.gov/2018038442

ISBN 978-0-8248-8425-3 (pbk.)

Cover art: College student friends, Yogyakarta
(courtesy of Watini Khairi Syilasyafi).

For William Francisco Hefner

CONTENTS

ACKNOWLEDGMENTS

This book is the product of a very long journey involving many people to whom I owe a huge debt of gratitude. First and foremost are the many Indonesians—young people and their parents, friends, and teachers; administrators and religious leaders; intellectuals and activists—who so generously shared their lives and stories with me. I cannot list their individual names here because I have promised them confidentiality; nonetheless I offer them my heartfelt thanks. I can, however, mention by (given) name some of the many individuals who acted as my research assistants over the years of my study and who will recognize their input in its pages: Ade, Agus, Astri, Dian, Farha, Fuji, Ida, and Tini. Very special thanks are owed to Iin Setiaji and her lovely extended family; to Prasetiyo Utomo ("Pak Tomo") and family; and to Laode Arham, Wahyu Kustiningsih, Eko Prasetyo, and Iip Wijayanto for their generous help and friendship over many years. I am particularly grateful to friends and colleagues associated with the Sunan Kalijaga State Islamic University and Gadjah Mada University: Bernard and Farsijana Adeney-Risakotta, Najib Azca, Zainal Abidin Bagir, Jeanny Dhewayani, Leonard Chrysostomos Epafras, Nina Mariani Noor, Dicky Sofjan, Siti Syamsiyatun, Nihayatul Wafiroh, and Mark Woodward. Hindun Anisah, Fauziyah Tri Astuti, and Siti Ruhaini Dzuhayatin have been consistently gracious and welcoming. A special thanks also goes to Kathleen Adams, Andrée Feillard, Byron and Mary Jo Good, James Hoesterey, Marcia Inhorn, Carla Jones, Joel Kuipers, Michael G. Peletz, and Nelly van Doorn-Harder, with whom I spent many productive and enjoyable hours in Indonesia, France, and the United States discussing our mutual interests and projects.

At Boston University I have appreciated and learned from conversations with faculty and affiliates of Boston University's Institute on Culture, Religion, and World Affairs. I have also benefited from stimulating discussions with my graduate student reading group on gender, sexuality, and romance: Feyza Burak Adli, Hafsa Arain, Paniz Edjlali, Jessica Garber, Jennifer Koester, Jessica Lambert, Dat Nguyen, and Laura Tourtellotte—and especially from conversations with Mehrdad Babadi.

Finally, and most importantly, I must thank my family, especially my parents, Joan D. and William T. Smith, who have been steadfast models of hard work and accomplishment and a lifelong source of inspiration. Robert Hefner, my husband and research partner, is my constant supporter, interlocutor, and sounding board. We have shared our experience and deep appreciation of Indonesia since graduate school at the University of Michigan. He has carefully critiqued multiple drafts of this work over the years, offering his invaluable expertise and support. The book would not have come into being without his love, encouragement, and patience. Our daughter, Claire-Marie, has been involved in my project from the start, first as an adolescent engaged in Yogyakarta's youth scene, and later as an accomplished scholar, ethnographer, and artist in her own right. Her input and keen observations over the years have been invaluable, and I am deeply thankful. Her brother, William Francisco, grew up during the writing of this book and likely does not recall a time when I was not working on it. A ready supplier of warm hugs and words of encouragement, this book is dedicated to him.

My project was generously supported by a number of grants and fellowships over the years. Research funding came from a Fulbright-Hays Faculty Research Fellowship, a Spencer Foundation Grant for Research, and a National Endowment for the Humanities Fellowship. A truly transformational year of collegial exchange and intensive writing was supplied by a fellowship at Radcliffe's Institute for Advanced Study, which allowed for the completion of a large portion of the manuscript. For all, I am deeply grateful.

Some material in chapter 6 previously appeared in "Reproducing Respectability: Sex and Sexuality among Muslim Javanese Youth," *RIMA (Review of Indonesian and Malay Affairs)* 40(1): 143–172 (2006). Portions of the argument made in chapter 7 appeared in "The New Muslim Romance: Changing Patterns of Courtship and Marriage among Educated Javanese Youth," *Journal of Southeast Asian Studies* 36(3): 441–459 (2005).

ISLAMIZING INTIMACIES

Approaching Java in a Time of Transitions

Zaman sudah berubah. Ini zaman moderèn.
"The times have changed. This is the modern era."

"Kebo nyusu gudèl," orang tua harus ikut anaknya sekarang.
" 'The water buffalo nurses from the calf,' nowadays, parents must follow their children's lead."

Yogyakarta

In 1999, on the cusp of the new millennium, the city of Yogyakarta in south-central Java, Indonesia, gave evidence of having undergone intriguing physical as well as social changes since my last extended visit in the 1980s.[1] Approaching the metropolitan area from the newly remodeled Adisucipto Airport on the eastern outskirts of the city, I found the landscape barely recognizable. Where once there had been lush green paddy fields and lazy, winding streams, there were now busy highways, cluttered shops, and four-star hotels. New suburban developments (*perumahan*) and rental properties (*rumah kontrakan*) filled much of what, fifteen years earlier, had been agricultural land. Between the remaining swaths of yellow-green rice paddy, modern cement-and-tile houses with tinted louvered windows and fancy wrought-iron gates had sprouted up like so many pastel mushrooms. Upscale residential compounds were set off from their poor neighbors by thick cement walls topped with jagged glass, similar to their counterparts in the nation's capital, Jakarta. Older homes boasted awkward additions—second stories with large silver satellite dishes perched on top of glistening red tile roofs, their shuttered balconies looking down on the more modest, yet-to-be updated houses of their neighbors.

The city's center had also been transformed from what in the 1980s had been a sleepy assortment of dusty shops, narrow roads, and open-fronted restaurants. Taxis had replaced many, though not all, of the town's three-wheeled pedicabs (*becak*) even on the main tourist drag, Jalan Malioboro (Malioboro Street). The now helmeted drivers of a sea of noisy motorbikes jostled shoulder to shoulder for space on the congested thoroughfares. Evidence of an unforeseen economic globalization, Dunkin' Donuts shops and Kentucky Fried Chicken restaurants had sprung up on many of the larger intersections in the city's northern middle-class neighborhoods, and it seemed as if every other corner featured an ATM machine or an Internet café (*warnet*). Yogyakarta also had several new, modern supermarkets and, in 1999, three expansive, air-conditioned, multistory shopping malls where cash registers were computerized and one could pay for a cappuccino and a croissant with a credit card. All these changes did not mean that the city's mass of poor and barely-getting-by had disappeared; on a per capita basis, the city lies in what remains one of Java's poorest districts. What it does mean, however, is that the poor are now scattered within a landscape visibly more varied and linked, in some perceivable way, to a new global order of things.

Now in the evenings and especially on weekends Yogyakarta's streets and shopping areas fill with throngs of young people, many in small, same-sex groups. Young women stroll arm in arm, make inexpensive purchases, and take discrete sidelong glances at the crowds of passersby. Young men hang out in the coffee shops and game rooms, eat snacks, and smoke cigarettes while less discretely sizing up the female shoppers. Married couples with small children in tow make it a family outing, eat a light meal at a food stall or, if they can afford it, at McDonald's or California Chicken, and enjoy the noisy, festive bustle Indonesians refer to as *ramai*. On Jalan Malioboro, the shopping district celebrated in tourist guides, the crowd becomes so dense and the sidewalks so full of hawkers with their mountains of wares—batik shifts and sarongs, leather belts and wallets, watches and jewelry, clothing and shoes, and handbags and handicrafts—that the flow of sidewalk traffic often comes to a stop. The peddlers take advantage of the crowd's snail's pace to call out to the passersby to stop and take a look. Western tourists in batik beachwear stand out above the crowd, becoming a special target for the street sellers, aspiring tour guides, and teenaged males eager to try out their textbook English.

Yogyakarta's social landscape gave evidence of other intriguing changes in 1999 that have only intensified in the years since. There were now many more women, especially young women, wearing some variety of Muslim head covering (*jilbab*). Many wore theirs modestly with a long-sleeved tunic and loose pants (*busana Muslim;* "Muslim garb"); others wore the headscarf with makeup and form-fitting blue jeans.[2] Women drove motorbikes in *jilbab* with their helmets precariously perched on top, the long ends of their headscarves fluttering out behind them. Throngs of female high school students lined the streets, laughing and chatting while waiting for public buses in their school uniform: white *jilbab* and long-sleeved blouses, long light grey skirts, and high-top sneakers. Occasionally, a woman walked by completely covered from head to foot in brown or black robes (*cadar*) with only a small slit for her eyes in the heavy veil covering her face. Also remarkable was that, at least in Yogyakarta's public sphere, one saw surprisingly few women, even very old women, clad in what for most of the twentieth century had been the preferred everyday fashion for Javanese females: a long, tightly wrapped batik sarong (*kain*) and fitted jacket (*kebaya*). Those who still wore the older, ethnically marked dress were found mainly at the frayed margins of Yogyakartan society: in the marketplace, in small food stalls, and among the poor beggar women in the streets. Middle-aged housewives, who in the 1980s invariably wore traditional Javanese dress, now did their errands in dresses, skirts, or slacks, with or without an accompanying *jilbab* or knit hat covered with a loose headscarf (*kerudung*). Among the city's new middle class, traditional Javanese dress was increasingly reserved for special and official occasions such as weddings, National Women's Day (Hari Kartini), graduations, and funerals.

Equally striking by comparison with the 1980s was the large number of women working in shops and in offices, waiting on the streets for public transportation, or navigating the traffic on their own motor scooters or at the wheel of a car. They were housemaids, factory workers, shopgirls, bank employees, teachers, and government workers (*pegawai negeri*). Among them, too, were the many female students who attend Yogyakarta's numerous public, private, nonconfessional or religious high schools, universities, and trade schools. In a city of some 600,000 on the cusp of the new millennium, the number of women students was fast approaching one-half of the over 100,000 university students in residence.

By 1999 and all the more over the years that followed, the city's traffic was heavier, people were busier, and, at least in the public sphere, they seemed less preoccupied with the refined etiquette for which the city has long been famous. On streets and in stores and offices, I heard much less of the formal Javanese, known as *kromo*, the speech style through which people a generation earlier had shown respect, demonstrated refinement, and otherwise grasped and enacted a complex and ethnically imagined social world (Errington 1999; Koentjaraningrat 1989; Wolf and Soepomo 1982). More often I discerned strains of the more rapid staccato of the national language, Bahasa Indonesia, drifting above the crowds. In a city where everything was once slow, refined, and deliberate, things seemed more rushed, and interactions more brusque and impersonal. My impression in 1999 and the years since, then, was of a Yogyakarta and a Java unhesitatingly more modern. Equally important for the argument of this book, both milieus were also far more visibly Muslim.

In returning to Java in 1999—this time to south-central Java—I planned to build on my research some years earlier on religion, gender, and language sociali-zation conducted in East Java[3] to look at young people and the forging of mod-ern subjectivities and new relational intimacies in the context of rapid social and political change. Certainly, this was a significantly different Java than I had encountered fifteen years earlier, and one vastly different from the Java of the 1950s described by Hildred Geertz (1989 [1961]) in her pathbreaking study of the Javanese family. I planned to explore those changes through the optics of education, gender, the new middle class, and the resurgence of interest among young Javanese in a more authoritative and normative Islam. My original inten-tion was to conduct an intensive eight-month study, but the changes were so vast and the pace of the transformation so rapid, that I continued to return to Yogyakarta at regular intervals over the fifteen years that followed. While the data I collected in 1999 provides a critical foundation for my analysis and for understanding the depth and direction of the changes taking place, subsequent research conducted on visits between 2000 and 2015 offers an important longi-tudinal perspective on those changes.

I had chosen Yogyakarta for this research for several reasons. Renowned as a center of both traditional Javanese culture and new culture-in-the-making, the city has always been a pioneer of the new styles of consumption, middle-class identity, politics, and religiosity that have swept Indonesia since the founding of the republic in 1945. The urban landscape itself reflects something of the complex mix that has made this city and its surrounding regencies—some three and one-half million inhabitants[4]—such a powerful force in a country of almost 260 million.[5] Yogyakarta extends outward from its traditional town center, located around the Sultan's vast palace complex (*kraton*) in what is today the south of the city, northward through the Malioboro business district, past the still-vibrant train station, through the Dutch-built "New Town" (Kota Baru), and on to and beyond the neat and impressive buildings that make up the campus of Gadjah Mada University, or UGM. The university is Indonesia's oldest and second largest, established in the early independence era on land donated to the republic by the Sultan of Yogyakarta. The Sultan's gesture in the early years of Indonesia's revolutionary struggle was one of many that helped to solidify his reputation as a champion of Indonesia's independence and social progress. Having played a courageously supportive role in the Indonesian war of independence (1945–1949), the Yogyakarta sultanate was the only traditional royal polity to be recognized and officially maintained by the new republic's progressive-minded leaders. It is for this reason that the greater Yogyakarta region today still enjoys an autonomous status as a "Special Region" (Daerah Istimewa) in the otherwise unitary Indonesian state.

In addition to Gadjah Mada University, there are scores of other schools in the city, some also public, but many private, technical, or religious. Prominent among them are the Universitas Islam Negeri Sunan Kalijaga (Sunan Kalijaga State Islamic University—until 2001 known as the Institut Agama Islam Negeri), one of Indonesia's most distinguished state Islamic universities; Universitas Negeri Yogyakarta (Yogyakarta State University, previously known as the Yogyakarta Teachers' College); several privately owned Muslim universities, including Universitas Muhammadiyah Yogyakarta (Yogyakarta Muhammadiyah University), Universitas Ahmad Dahlan (Ahmad Dahlan University), and Universitas Islam Indonesia (the Islamic University of Indonesia); and a well-regarded Catholic and an equally esteemed Protestant university. Yogyakarta's schools attract young people from all corners of the archipelago and increasingly (though still in relatively small numbers) from abroad. Graduates go on to fill important professional and political positions locally and in Jakarta, the nation's capital. As an Indonesian cultural center, Yogyakarta has long been regarded as second only to Jakarta in trendsetting influence. In part as a result of its still-functioning sultanate and its large university population, it has also played a disproportionately large role in Indonesian politics. In May 1998, just eight months before my arrival in Indonesia at the beginning of this study, students and activists from the city were at the forefront of the democracy movement that toppled the long-serving and authoritarian Suharto regime (cf. Bubalo and Fealy 2005; Rakhmat and Najib 2001).

Important too, Yogyakarta is the birthplace and (along with Jakarta) national headquarters of Muhammadiyah. With an estimated twenty-five million members, Muhammadiyah is one of the largest Muslim social welfare organizations in the world. In Indonesia it is second in size only to the Nahdlatul Ulama, or NU (Renaissance of Islamic Scholars), which has some thirty to thirty-five million members, the single largest concentration of which is found in East Java. Established in 1926, the Nahdlatul Ulama is commonly regarded as a "traditionalist" Muslim social welfare organization, in the sense that it is officially subject to the guidance of a board of classically trained religious scholars (*ulama*) (see Bush 2009; Dhofier 1999 [1982]; Fealy and Barton 1996; Feillard 1997a). It is also traditionalist in the sense that NU is dedicated to the preservation and transmission of the classical commentaries of the Shafi'i legal school (*madhab*) long regarded by most Southeast Asian Muslims, as well as Yemeni Arabs, Egyptians, and others, as authoritative. By contrast, Muhammadiyah (established in 1912) is an Islamic reform organization of a broadly "modernist"[6] variety (see Alfian 1989; Nakamura 1983; Peacock 1978a). Muhammadiyah's modernism is seen in its emphasis on the Qur'an and traditions of the Prophet rather than a commitment to a particular school of law or the medieval commentaries through which the law is taught and understood, as well as in its dedication to providing an impressive array of modern religious and social services through its well-coordinated network of schools (including universities), hospitals, orphanages, and associations for the propagation of the faith (Njoto-Feillard 2012).

With between 3 and 4 percent of its population Christian,[7] Yogyakarta is also home to a wide variety of Protestant and Catholic institutions, many of

Islamic high school girls, Yogyakarta. Photo by Claire-Marie Hefner.

Boys' Islamic high school graduation, Yogyakarta. Photo by Claire-Marie Hefner.

which date from the late colonial era. What is more, as an intellectual center, Yogyakarta boasts a large number of publishing houses, nongovernmental organizations, social and professional associations, and other institutions deeply involved in the shaping of modern Indonesian culture. Less auspiciously, and in part because of its prominent national role, Yogyakarta in the late 1990s was chosen to serve as the national headquarters for two of the country's more militant Islamist groupings, the Communication Forum for Followers of the Prophet (Forum Kommunikasi Ahlus Sunnah Wal-Jema'ah) and the Indonesian Council of Jihadi Fighters (Majelis Mujahidin Indonesia). Both of these groups sponsored paramilitaries that played a central role in the Muslim-Christian communal violence that swept the eastern Indonesian province of Maluku from 1999 to 2002, in which thousands died (van Klinken 2007; C. Wilson 2008). The presence of their male followers in white tunics and turbans on the streets of Yogyakarta during those same years was a source of embarrassment for moderate and liberal Muslims, and of considerable anxiety for non-Muslims.

Because I was interested in the effects of modern education—including new forms of religious education—on the middle class in general and middle-class youths' aspirations and identifications, Yogyakarta was the ideal site for my research. Moreover, in the politically and socially uncertain climate of the spring of 1999 and the early 2000s, the city appeared calm and peaceful compared to other Indonesian cities. In the view of many ordinary residents, the calm was a function of Yogyakarta's long-standing reputation as an important city of learning

Coeds between classes, Gadjah Mada University, Yogyakarta.
Photo by the author.

(*kota pelajar, kota pendidikan*). Others saw it as an unflagging effect of the spiritual potency and political acumen of Yogyakarta's sultan, Hamengkubu- wono X, the son of the sultan who had played such a prominent role in the struggle for Indonesian independence.

Into the Postmodern

Although it is becoming more difficult, it was still possible in 1999 to discover examples of Javanese gender, family, and interpersonal relations similar to those so vividly described by Hildred Geertz in *The Javanese Family* (1989 [1961]), a book based on research conducted in the 1950s that has long been regarded as the standard in the field. There are still—even today—older Javanese who speak refined "high" Javanese, or *kromo*, when the occasion requires it, although most young Javanese either cannot or choose not to. And despite the new bustle in the streets, one can still find families that conform to the patterns of formality, hierarchy, and avoidance that had once more widely characterized Javanese social relations. However, whereas earlier these and other "traditional" patterns had enjoyed a confidently hegemonic status as models of being Javanese, by 1999 they had become just one among a swirling postmodern mix of interpersonal possibilities. The traditional patterns have been fragmented and recast by the growth of a new middle class, new forms of education and employment, heightened physical and social mobility, a far more ethnically diverse urban landscape, and an Islamic resurgence that, from the 1980s on, has challenged many features of Javanese tradition.[8] The spread of these new social forms remains uneven and unfinished, and is certainly not embraced equally by all members or groups within Javanese society, even in a university town such as Yogyakarta. In these and other examples, one is reminded that modern social change in Java has brought not social or cultural homogenization but a pluralization and contestation of ways of being Javanese and Indonesian. This pluralization and contestation has deepened over the past thirty-five years, although, as the eminent historian of Java, Merle Ricklefs, has shown, its religious roots were set in place during the tumultuous changes of the late nineteenth and early twentieth centuries (Ricklefs 2006, 2007, 2012).

Some earlier ethnographic depictions of the family and gender roles in Java downplayed this pluralism and contestation, assuming a high measure of continuity in these cultural conceptions and practices from the 1950s (or even earlier) to today. Sometimes this continuity has been seen as the product of a relatively fixed and unchanging set of Javanese values, the key characteristics of which are a concern for hierarchy, spiritual potency, and controlled reserve associated in particular with the example set by the Javanese courts and traditional aristocracy, known as *priyayi*. Others have seen this ostensible continuity in gender roles and family relations as the result of the powerful New Order regime of President Suharto. Suharto's New Order ruled Indonesia and reshaped Javanese culture from 1966, when the regime came to power in the bloody aftermath of the destruction of the Indonesian Communist Party, until May 1998. In that month, President Suharto was ousted by a complex and largely middle-class alliance of high-minded democracy activists and reformist Muslims, as well as old-regime opportunists who realized it was in their interest to desert the embattled president.[9] The New Order regime was indeed authoritarian, and at least during its early years it was strongly committed to a singularly conservative and repressive interpretation of Javanese culture. As anthropologists Suzanne Brenner and Kathryn Robinson (among others) have emphasized, gender and family ideals were key components of the New Order's attempted culture making, and many of the models imposed on the nation as a whole were based on this conservative and essentialized model of Javanese culture.[10] Some Western scholars and journalists assumed that this politicized and "official" version of Javanese values was, in fact, the real essence of Javanese culture. However, just as there were always "other Javas away from the *kraton*" (R. Hatley 1984), there were also other Javas apart from those conveyed in New Order representations. Even before the collapse of the New Order, it was clear that the state and its cultural policies were never as pervasively hegemonic as the Suharto government had intended. Their failure is nowhere clearer than in matters of Islam and gender.

For these and other reasons, many accounts of Javanese and Indonesian culture from this earlier period overlooked Muslim discourses and practices as aspects of family, gender, and interpersonal relations, including major survey volumes published in the 1990s (cf. Atkinson and Errington 1990; Sears 1996a). It is equally striking that, although youth (*pemuda*)—particularly university students—have long been at the forefront of social and cultural innovation in Indonesia, and have been recognized as a key category in Indonesian politics (see Anderson 2006 [1972]; Aspinall 2005), they have received surprisingly little attention in sustained ethnographic studies of Indonesian and Javanese culture.[11] A new focus on young people began to emerge in the early 2000s with the publication of several edited collections on adolescent and youth sexuality, among them, *Coming of Age in South and Southeast Asia* (Manderson and Liamputtong 2002) and a volume of the journal *RIMA* (*Review of Indonesian and Malay Affairs*), *Youth, Sexuality and Personal Life in Indonesia* (Robinson, Utomo, and Campbell 2003), along with an important study of adolescent sexuality and sexual health in Lombok (Eastern Indonesia) by Linda Rae Bennett (2005), *Women, Islam, and Modernity*. Several more recent projects on youth have resulted in a number of articles and book chapters, as well as a special journal issue, and a comparative study of the social and sexual lives of adolescents in Solo and West Sumatra (see Nilan 2006; Nilan et al. 2011; Parker and Bennett 2008; Parker and Nilan 2013; Robinson 2016).[12] But the overwhelming focus on adolescents (*anak remaja*) in this work has resulted in a somewhat lopsided or at any rate incomplete picture of evolving religious identifications, family relations, and gender roles among young Indonesians. Although certainly adolescents are an important segment of Indonesia's burgeoning population, it is in fact among college-aged youth—those facing pressing decisions having to do with careers, dating, marriage, and family—that social change, religious normativization, and contested subjectivities have had their most visible effects.

It was among this segment of the youth population, too, that in the fifteen years following the New Order one encountered endless examples of young people wrestling with some of the most deeply personal and public effects of globalization, democratization, the growth of the middle class, and the resurgence of Islam—and it was here that I focused my study. The questions of gender, person, and family in which I was interested, then, had a kind of immediacy and simplicity to them, but they speak to a larger world of ongoing gender and religious change. These questions included but were not limited to: To what extent and in what ways has the Islamic resurgence affected youth identifications? How do the contemporary identifications, orientations, and aspirations of Muslim Javanese youth differ from those of an earlier generation? What impact has the Islamic resurgence had on young people's views of marriage, family, sexuality, and gender roles? What do these young people hope to become and what kind of future do they envision for themselves? Most generally but importantly, what does it mean to be modern, Javanese-Indonesian, and Muslim?

As these questions indicate, I hoped that Yogyakarta's Muslim youth would provide a window into their own lives as well as those of the previous generation, a window into shifting norms, values, and aspirational identifications. Because Yogyakarta's youth have long been trendsetters for the nation, I sensed that these young people, educated in some of Indonesia's finest institutions, would both illustrate and influence key aspects of Indonesian culture and identity in the unsteady aftermath of Suharto's New Order.

Ethnography and Subjectivity

I arrived in Yogyakarta with my husband and two children for an initial eight-month period of research in early January 1999 toward the end of Ramadan, the Muslim fasting month. Public billboards and street banners urged increased piety and announced religious study sessions and prayer meetings. The old black-and-white console television set that came with our rental house broadcast a continuous stream of programming showing young girls and boys praying, chanting, singing religious songs, and reciting the Qur'an. Even the female news anchor wore a headscarf and a modest, though stylish, Muslim tunic. By comparison with the Yogyakarta of the 1980s, I was struck by the normalization in the media of something that had been far from normal, even suppressed, previously: Islamic styles of greeting, interaction, and dress.

The changes in dress styles were most conspicuous with regard to young women. I had arrived with a suitcase full of knee-length skirts and short-sleeved blouses, which throughout the 1970s and into the 1980s, had been considered the appropriate "uniform" for female professors. Although some older professional women still wore similar styles, I felt conspicuously uncovered among my student respondents and quickly arranged to have some loose-style slacks (*kulot*) and longer "maxi" skirts and long-sleeved blouses made. At the time of our arrival, of course, it was the fasting month—something we were reminded of not only by the proliferation of religious information on the streets and television and the expanded religious activities in our neighborhood but also by the sluggish pace at which government and university offices moved. It took us several weeks to settle in, arrange for our house to be repaired and repainted, rent a car, hire household help and research assistants, and find schools for our children. As soon as possible, however, with the assistance of a bright and engaging young woman who was just finishing her bachelor's thesis (*skripsi*), I began interviewing young Javanese women students on the nearby campus of Gadjah Mada University.

I was quickly reminded that urban anthropology requires an adjustment in ethnographic methods from those of my earlier, village-focused ethnography in East Java. It is not possible in urban settings such as Yogyakarta to collect systematic information by dropping in unannounced on one's neighbors in the evening to chat informally or by hanging out in the front of one's house calling out to passersby to stop in for coffee—methods upon which I could easily depend during my research in East Java's rural uplands. Urban Javanese themselves refer to the relaxed style and rhythms of Javanese village life with nostalgia. "Stress" (borrowed into Indonesian from the English as *setrès*) is now part of Javanese public discourse and everyday life. University students are no exception to the attendant anxieties of the hectic urban rat race. In addition to their studies, most students are engaged in an array of social and religious activities; many also have part-time jobs and family obligations. Although ethnographic and participant observation—taking part in various campus events, club meetings, and study groups; visiting students at their boarding houses and homes; attending weddings, circumcisions, and religious celebrations; and simply hanging out in malls, coffee shops, and bookstores—remained an important part of my research, in 1999 and the fifteen years that followed I relied heavily on in-depth interviews, informal individual and small group discussions, and detailed surveys.

Some of the richest materials from my research came from in-depth interviews, often conducted over the course of several face-to-face meetings. During the initial eight months of my research (January–August 1999) I completed some 125 of these interviews, each lasting between one and one-half and three hours. All interviews were tape recorded, transcribed, and coded. Transcriptions were done by Javanese research assistants, the majority of whom were between the ages of twenty-two and twenty-five and were students themselves. Assistants also helped in identifying willing respondents, arranging times and places for meetings, and offering respondents an initial explanation of my project's ambitions.

Although in my earlier Javanese research I had relied sparingly on taped interviews, seeking instead more "natural" sociolinguistic interactions, in urban Yogyakarta these became a key element in my research methodology. I had initially been concerned that the presence of a tape recorder might make some interviewees uncomfortable or encourage them to offer less than candid responses. However, I soon discovered that with the proliferation of NGOs and research institutes that had appeared in Yogyakarta beginning in the 1980s, surveys and interviews had become commonplace. I found to my relief that interviewees quickly came to ignore the tape recorder and talk animatedly and freely. This candor was also related to the focus of my questions: questions of life choices and social intimacies were issues in which most young people were themselves personally interested and about which most had strong opinions. In the heady and optimistic era of Reformasi (the period of democratic reform that began with the fall of Suharto) and throughout the years that followed, students seemed to regard research of this sort as important, even critical.

The research advantages of taped, fully transcribed, and annotated in-depth interviews are multiple. Taped interviews permit the researcher to capture respondents' narratives in their own words, often with a precision and—notwithstanding my earlier concerns—experience-near detail impossible in ordinary field notes. Taped and transcribed interviews offer a wealth of data not easily captured by handwritten notes. There were occasions when, tired and frustrated by the pace of an interview, I felt I was getting little new insight from a particular interaction. In reviewing interview transcripts later, however, I would discover some fascinating point of cultural or personal revelation that had completely slipped by me at the time of the discussion. At other times I have been so excited to hear what I thought was confirmation of some current hypothesis that I completely missed the markers of hesitancy or irony in the respondent's commentary until reviewing the taped interaction. While in the chapters that follow I have changed personal names and certain details of individual stories, and in a handful of cases collapsed various accounts together, so as to maintain the anonymity of my respondents, I have nonetheless attempted to remain faithful to the young people's own words and interpretations by citing directly from interviews as much and as often as possible.

Taped interviews allow not only for close attention to *what* people say but also to *how they say it.* Code-switching between Javanese and Indonesian and the use of borrowings from Arabic and English are important indices of young people's cultural attitudes and identifications. Patterns of English borrowings, such as *pacaran backstreet* (dating/meeting on the sly), *lebih enjoy* (more enjoyable), *having fun saja* (just having fun,) and *traoma* (traumatic), for example, appear regularly in young people's discussions of relationships with the opposite sex, and reveal a widespread association between "dating" and what are perceived as modern, Western-influenced models of behavior. By contrast, the Arabic terms *alim* (religious, devout) and *saleh/solehah* (pious, virtuous) frequently appear in descriptions of desirable marriage partners. Similarly, the English borrowings *mengaktualisasi diri* (self-actualization), *independen* (independence), and *egois* (egotistical) are often used in contrast to the Indonesian concepts *mengorbankan diri* (self-sacrifice) and *kekeluargaan* (family obligations/values), or the Javanese *mbalas budi* (to repay the debt of gratitude [to one's parents]). These varied and sometimes contradictory usages underscore points of tension in young people's attitudes toward family and gender relations, cosmopolitan and local understandings of the self, and, more generally, modern social developments and Islam. The balancing of concerns with relatedness and autonomy, of social embeddedness and independence, hinted at in these terms are consistent themes in the stories students tell.

Detailed transcriptions of taped interviews allow respondents to tell their own stories in their own words, and I have included them here. Some of the stories I include because they are representative of the kinds of things young people say about their lives or the way they view a particular topic, and others because they are exceptional, radical or eccentric; both kinds of stories are important and necessary. These stories, in respondents' own words, supply the reader with a measure of verification for ethnographic generalizations beyond the ethnographer's imposed interpretation or the more general and totalizing "logic of the system." They express not only commonly held views but inconsistencies, contradictions, and tensions as well.

Of course the kinds of stories I was able to elicit and the responses to questions posed were influenced by my own status and role. This was not unproblematic, especially with regard to the exploration of topics relating to relationships with the opposite sex and sexuality. Although I was occasionally addressed by young people as *mbak* (older sister) rather than as *bu* (mother/Mrs.)—a more accurate reflection of my relative age and status—there was no getting around the fact that I was a foreign university professor interviewing students much younger than myself.[13] I addressed this limitation in a variety of ways. One method was through inviting respondents to comment on the experiences and behavior of friends and acquaintances or even celebrities or public figures currently in the news, rather than talk about themselves.[14] I also invited my young assistants and any friends, classmates, or housemates who happened to be present during interviews to add their own views and experiences to the discussion. This often led to conversations that took place between several young people rather than being addressed specifically to me. Interestingly, and rather unexpectedly, I found discussions about sex generally caused much less embarrassment than did discussions of *pacaran* (relationships, fiancé/es). Equally interesting, respondents were in some cases more comfortable speaking about romantic interests with me than they were with my Javanese research assistants, who—after all—might possibly know the individuals being discussed. When this appeared to be a cause of concern, my assistant would find some pretext to excuse her or himself from the room and would return after we had finished that portion of the interview.

While my position, age, and gender made some types of data more difficult to obtain, it made other sorts of data more accessible. I discovered early on that having my family with me opened up a wealth of experiences and insights to which otherwise I would not have had access. One very early example of this type of insight occurred our first week in Yogyakarta during our first period of research in 1999, while in a department store shopping for household goods. While my husband and I looked for sheets, towels, and kitchenware, my then thirteen-year-old daughter, Claire, was in charge of watching her three-and-one-half-year-old brother, William. Will was enthralled with the displays of glassware and china and made a determined beeline to inspect and, inevitably, handle these delicate items. His older sister saw it as her duty to restrain him. Soon there were several small groups of uniformed shopgirls hanging over their display counters, eagerly fixated on the unfolding sibling drama. Blocked by his older sister from handling everything in his line of vision, Will began to cry in protest. Claire made repeated attempts to distract his attention and to get him to stop crying, but nothing worked; Will was now in the throes of a full-blown tantrum. In desperation, Claire finally resolved to drag her brother kicking and screaming away from the fragile housewares. The shopgirls were aghast. One of them mustered her best English to gently admonish Claire saying, "You should love your brother. He's being good. *Actif* [active] is good. *Nakal* [naughty] is good." It was now Claire's turn to be aghast. She had, after all, expected to be praised for her heroic efforts to restrain her undisciplined brother and keep him from toppling the store's attractively arranged displays of highly breakable household goods.

The shopgirls' reprimands provided an early lesson on new or newly emphasized aspects of Javanese socialization and subjective experience. We would hear similar refrains repeatedly over the following months. The constant indulgence and attention that William received from virtually everyone we met in Indonesia exacerbated his typically unruly three-year-old behavior and provided us with more than sufficient opportunities to receive kind assurances from friends and total strangers alike that *laki-laki wajar nakal* (it's appropriate/normal for little boys to be naughty) and *aktif, nakal, berarti pintar* (active, naughty, means intelligent).

This positive emphasis on "modern" and more assertive personality characteristics such as inquisitiveness and activity (particularly but not only in boys) rather than the self-effacing shyness (*malu, isin*) and restraint traditionally associated with Javanese culture repeatedly surfaced in my discussions with older as well as younger Javanese. The newly popularized personal ideals for youth—active, energetic, curious, and outspoken—were touted on school banners and in textbooks, in television ads and on packaging for powdered milk, nutritional supplements, and vitamins. They were further underscored by the frequently heard admonitions of parents and teachers, *Jangan malu!* (Don't be shy/hang back!) and *Ojo minder!* (Don't feel insecure/inferior!). The cultivation of self-confidence (*percaya diri*) and ever-at-ease sociability (*pintar bergaul*) have been identified as essential elements of new cosmopolitan youth styles and an important focus of the tidal wave of youth publications that began to flood the bookstores beginning in the late 1990s and early 2000s as well as the subject of endless radio and television talk shows and seminars for young people and their parents. This concern with the development of new, "modern" subjectivities, that is, new modes of being, of self-understanding, and of interacting with the world, was widely shared by the young people in my study and is a central focus of the present work.[15]

Interview respondents were located largely through the use of a modified snowball technique. I began by first interviewing my assistants, and then their classmates and acquaintances, and continued by interviewing *their* housemates, classmates, and acquaintances. I began by interviewing women but quickly extended my net to include young men as well. Over the course of the fifteen years of my research, I worked with close to a dozen male and female assistants, the majority of whom were either students or recent graduates of local universities, and from a variety of different disciplines. As my assistants graduated from college or married and moved away or got jobs, I hired new ones—inevitably their circles of contacts varied considerably. Some respondents preferred to come to my home, to sit on our screened verandah and talk while drinking sweet tea and eating snacks. Others invited me to their rented rooms, where we sat on chairs or mats spread out on the floor while I tried to make out their responses over the roar of traffic just outside the window or their housemates' laughter in the next room. Some invited me to their parents' homes; others I invited to student cafés or local restaurants for more privacy or better recording conditions.

I conducted all interviews and discussions in Indonesian, interspersed with Javanese. English terms and borrowings have become common in middle-class

Indonesian; however, in only one case—a young woman who was preparing to leave for an international conference in India—did a respondent request that I conduct the interview in English, and I was happy to oblige. During interviews, I asked students about their family background, educational history, marital and family plans, career aspirations, and religious attitudes. The interviews, however, were always deliberately open-ended. Their loose structure was intended to encourage respondents to expand freely and spontaneously on issues of particular concern to them. The result was that the discussion in many interviews meandered in unexpected but often profoundly interesting directions. At the end of each interview I asked the respondent if he or she could suggest other students who might be willing to talk to me. My only requirement was that respondents be college-aged, Muslim (whether observant or not), and Javanese.[16] Often times I returned again to the same respondents—if they were willing—one or more times to ask additional questions. In a number of cases, I returned to interview their parents or teachers. Some respondents were themselves interested in pursuing the discussion further and became regular visitors to our house, stopping by frequently to chat about social life, politics, and educational programs in the United States.

In the initial eight-month phase of my research I focused my attention mainly on students associated with two universities: Gadjah Mada University (Universitas Gadjah Mada or UGM) and the nearby Sunan Kalijaga State Islamic University (Universitas Islam Negeri Sunan Kalijaga or UIN). I chose these two schools because they are representative of two very different types of tertiary educational institutions available in Yogyakarta, and, as a result, they attract rather different types of students. In terms of their size and student body, Gadjah Mada University is sprawling and large, with some 55,000 students in graduate and undergraduate programs, while the Sunan Kalijaga State Islamic University has some 28,000 students and a much more concentrated campus.[17] Gadjah Mada is officially nonconfessional (although, as in all Indonesian universities, a course is required each year in one's professed religion), while the State Islamic University is a state-supported Muslim university. As far as numbers and types of fields of study offered, Gadjah Mada offers a wide range of liberal arts and science programs; until the early 2000s the State Islamic University offered diverse programs of study but concentrated its offerings in the fields of Islamic studies, including Islamic law, education, and religious predication. At the most general level, Gadjah Mada's students tend to come from somewhat more economically secure, urban backgrounds; among those who hail from religious families, the larger proportion show "modernist Muslim," that is, Muhammadiyah orientations. Those from the State Islamic University tend, by contrast, to come from more modest economic conditions and from more rural backgrounds, often from religious communities and *pesantren* (Islamic boarding schools) associated with the "traditionalist" Muslim social welfare organization, the Nahdlatul Ulama.

I completed 125 in-depth interviews in this initial phase of research. In August 1999, the month before I left Yogyakarta, I enlisted a team of ten students from Gadjah Mada and another ten from the State Islamic University to help me conduct a detailed written survey on issues that paralleled those addressed in interviews. Two hundred college students were surveyed: one hundred from each campus, evenly divided between males and females, and from a wide variety of academic disciplines.

Between 2000 and 2015 I made thirteen subsequent several-weeks-long visits to Yogyakarta. During that period I conducted an additional 125 semistructured interviews with student religious leaders, feminists, political activists, and Muslim intellectuals and explored changing attitudes toward marriage, family life, shari'a (Ar. Islamic law), and gender roles in more depth. I also carried out several additional, small, topically focused surveys. These subsequent visits yielded important additional material and contacts, but the longitudinal character of my research has had another substantial if initially unplanned benefit. It has allowed me to follow a number of young individuals over a critical period of their lives, as they have navigated their university educations, contemplated careers, negotiated questions of courtship and dating, entered the workforce, married, and started families of their own. These relationships—ones that I developed with this core group of female and male respondents from Gadjah Mada and the State Islamic University in the initial eight-month phase of my project—remained at the center of my fifteen-year study.

Islam, Social Intimacies, and the New Middle Class

This book examines the tensions Javanese young people face in navigating between the new opportunities offered by modern social change—expanded educational opportunities, greater social mobility, and increased personal autonomy—and the increasingly Muslim tenor of Javanese society. I focus particular attention on the impact of recent trends in public life and popular culture on the shaping of Muslim middle-class subjectivities. Drawing on over 250 extended narratives of young people's everyday lives, as well as surveys and countless informal discussions and interviews, the book examines issues of gender and sexuality, education and marriage, and new forms of sociability and self-expression.

While the core of the students in my study was associated with either Gadjah Mada University (UGM) or the State Islamic University (UIN), in following the social networks of these students and interviewing their friends, acquaintances, and family members, my study eventually and inevitably included students associated with many of Yogyakarta's other universities as well. And while the overwhelming majority of my respondents were Muslim, among their friends, acquaintances, and family members were those who were not. No matter what their institutional affiliation or background, students all voiced a similar and anxious concern: how to navigate Yogyakarta's increasingly cosmopolitan social scene with its expanded opportunities, amusements, and temptations and somehow secure a foothold in Indonesia's new middle class.

Higher education is widely considered to be a prerequisite to Indonesian middle-class status; however, economic and social success is by no means automatic, particularly in the uncertain political climate of post-Suharto Indonesia. Indeed, not all of the individuals that I followed over the fifteen years of my research succeeded at achieving the secure class standing to which all aspired. Moreover, and very importantly for the individuals whose life histories I examine in the chapters that follow, middle-class membership requires not only an academic degree and a stable career but also an appropriate marriage. The marriage should ideally take place as soon as possible after graduation, but not before—a balancing act that has many young people, particularly young women, feeling quite anxious. A plethora of organizations, specialists, and experts of various sorts have emerged in recent years to offer advice and guidance to young people on how to overcome the perceived obstacles to middle-class status. Many, indeed the majority, of these sources are Islamic in tenor. Muslim service providers are based in the middle class and largely serve the middle class. A central theme of the book is that, for growing numbers of Muslim Indonesians, Islam and public piety have increasingly come to be identified with and a vital prerequisite of middle-class status (see George 2010; Haenni 2005; Hoesterey 2012; C. Jones 2003, 2010a).

In Indonesia as elsewhere in the Muslim world, the resurgent interest in Islam and new forms of religious education have resulted in a proliferation of religious authorities and multiple and competing interpretations of Islam (Eickelman and Piscatori 2004 [1996]; Mandaville 2007; Zaman 2002). Although the resurgence has greatly diminished the public presence of the more pantheistic and heterodox variants of mysticism for which Java was once famous, it has not done away with the pluralism long characteristic of Indonesian Islam.[18] What the revitalization of Islam has done is heighten public piety and deepen arguments among Javanese and other Indonesians about how to be a good Muslim, and what the implications of that are for politics, personal style, and, no less significant, gender.

One of the challenges of modernity for young people then, is whether to embrace this diversity, including religious diversity (that is, diverse ways of being religious), or to reject it—or something in between. Should religion be privatized, as more assertively secularist actors in the liberal West and some portions of the Muslim world recommend (cf. Kuru 2009)? As elsewhere in the contemporary Muslim world, the stronger tendency among Muslim Indonesian youth of even moderately Islamic persuasion has been to insist that the assertively secularist privatization of religion, whereby religion is to be made a matter of individual personal belief and no more, is inconsistent with a pious profession of Islam. But just how Islam is to "go public" is a matter on which there is anything but a consensus. Some youth insist that a properly public profession of the faith is one that is consistent with a broad and highly generalized set of ethical values and activities—values often seen as convergent with, if not identical to, the "Western" democratic values of liberty, equality, and social justice. However, Muslim youth of a more self-consciously "Islamist" persuasion insist not only that Islam should not and cannot be reduced to private observance but that its influence has to be both comprehensive (Ar. *kaffah*) and highly specific, so that it encompasses and regulates all domains of life in a strictly prescribed and generally uniform manner.[19]

In Western academic literature, and indeed among more self-consciously political Islamists, the more widely discussed expression of these contests touches on questions of state, politics, and society. Does Islam require an "Islamic" state? Must God's law, the shari'a, be applied in all spheres of social life? Is Western-style democracy compatible with Islam? Although these questions have been the subject of raging debates in Indonesia from the 1990s to today, they are *not* the more pervasive concerns of the majority of the youth whom I came to know over the course of this research. For most youth (with, perhaps, the notable exception of a small activist minority), the debates over Islam and modernity are felt most compellingly with regard to questions of more immediate, quotidian, and intimate provenance, including those of courtship and marriage, relations with one's parents and kin, career and family, and, most generally, everyday inter-actions and patterns of sociability. Many among the latter concerns correspond in a broad manner to what the anthropologist Saba Mahmood has referred to as "religious sociability" (2005, 3)—styles of speech, dress, bearing, and interaction subject in some complex manner to the norms or ideals of Islamic authenticity (see also Deeb 2006; Deeb and Harb 2013a, 2013b). Though often overlooked in the literature on Islam and resurgence, it is not in the realm of politics but in these tangibly intimate spheres that most youth experience the tensions and attractions of Islamic ideals and real-world practices, God's ethical pathway for the world (shari'a), and lived realities. The diverse and sometimes contradictory ways in which Muslim youth assess and engage these issues speaks to larger questions of selfhood and subjectivity in the experience of Islam (Schielke 2009a, 2009b, 2015; see also Kloos 2018).

A particular focus throughout the book is that of women and of women's shifting roles. In Indonesia, as in other areas of the Muslim world, women's roles have been more vividly and profoundly reshaped than men's roles by recent social and political changes. As elsewhere in the Muslim world, it is women's bodies that have become a major battleground in the ongoing struggle between modernism and tradition (Ahmed 1992, 2014; Hasso 2010; Mir-Hosseini 1999, 2003). It is Indonesian women who have made the most radical adjustments in their dress, demeanor, and public behavior. It is women too, particularly young women, who have been the major focus of heated public debates and moral "panics" concerning gender roles, youth sexuality, and an alleged decline in moral standards (see Bennett 2005; Brenner 1996; Blackburn 2004; Parker and Nilan 2013; Smith-Hefner 2006, 2009a; van Doorn-Harder 2002; Webster 2016).[20] If youth are in the forefront of social and political change in Indonesia, it is women who are very much in the forefront of youth. This book focuses on the challenges these and other developments pose for young Muslim women torn between, on one hand, new life paths and career opportunities, and, on the other, public efforts to rescript women's lives to bring them in line with more scripturally informed interpretations of Islam (cf. Feillard 1997b; Nurmila 2008; Syamsiyatun 2008; van Doorn-Harder 2006, 2007).

Among the book's aims, then, is to contribute to the growing and important literature on Islam and gender.[21] While there is now a significant volume of scholarship on the topic from Muslim-majority countries, in the case of Indonesia, the currently available literature has primarily adopted either of two approaches: a top-down approach that focuses on institutions, state politics, and feminist resistance, or a textual approach, rooted in the analysis of the Qur'an and hadith or in *fiqh* (Islamic jurisprudence).[22] By contrast, the point of departure for the present book is the everyday hopes, dreams, and experiences of Muslim youth. Although emphasizing the perspectives of young women, it also takes seriously those of young men, recognizing their essential coimbrication (cf. Ghannam 2013). It underscores the pluralized, contested, fluid nature of gender and sexuality in Indonesia's Muslim middle class and attempts to situate Javanese youth within the larger theoretical debates concerning public ethics and sexual morality in the modern period. The book asks what it means to be both "modern" and Muslim. It examines the everyday life experiences of young people with regard to intimacy and education, family and relationships, and career and religion. Through all these explorations, the book focuses on the efforts of Muslim Javanese youth to strike a new balance between religious piety, intimate relationships, and new forms of personal achievement and public activity.

Islam, Youth, and Social Change

Indonesia is the world's most populous Muslim-majority nation, with some 87.3 percent of its 260 million citizens officially professing Islam. Almost half of the country's Muslims live on the densely settled island of Java.[1] Although Indonesian government statistics no longer record ethnicity, it is estimated that about 85 million of Java's 124 million residents are ethnic Javanese; more than 95 percent of Javanese are, in turn, Muslim (Indiyanto 2013). Until the early New Order period, however, the majority of Javanese subscribed to varieties of Islam best known for integrating Sufi, folk Javanese, and Javanese court traditions within a broadly Islamic frame that the historian Merle Ricklefs has aptly described as a "mystic synthesis" (Ricklefs 2007; see also Beatty 1999; C. Geertz 1976 [1960]; Headley 2004; Woodward 1989).

This chapter positions Javanese youth within the broader historical context of religious and sociocultural change in Java. I begin by outlining the classic categories and models of Muslim modernity put forth by anthropologists Clifford Geertz and James Peacock, which, although contested, remain important reference points for the understanding of Indonesian Islam and Muslim youth today. I then turn to the programs and policies of the New Order government that inadvertently supported the renewed interest among young people in more normative and textually informed forms of Islam. Against this backdrop, I consider how these and other factors have led to the weakening of sectarian divides within Indonesian Islam, to the recent pluralization of Islamic identifications and groupings among Muslim Javanese youth, and to the emergence of a new education-based Muslim middle class—now expanding at a rapid rate.

Santri and Abangan

Writing in the 1960s, Clifford Geertz describes the most culturally salient divide in Javanese society as lying between the socioreligious groups he labeled *santri* and *abangan*. Santri (lit. "students of a traditional Islamic boarding school") are, in a conventional sense of the term, observant Muslims who orient their profession of the faith toward the scriptural and ethico-legal standards of Islam as learned through formal religious education, whether in modern Muslim day schools (*madrasah*) or in religious boarding schools that are in Indonesia referred to as *pesantren* (a place or residence for *santri*).[2] Students in *pesantren* schools study the Qur'an, the hadith, religious jurisprudence (*fiqh*), and a host of other more or less classical Islamic sciences, the major texts of which are known in

Indonesia as the *kitab kuning* (lit. "yellow texts," a reference to the color of the paper upon which they were written; see van Bruinessen 1994).

In the late 1950s, Geertz estimated that *santri* comprised perhaps only one-third of the Javanese population. According to his estimate, as well as that of many other scholars working on Islam at that time, the great majority of Javanese in this period were *abangan*, which is to say, practitioners of a syncretic Islam that blended Sufi, pantheistic, and Javanese folk beliefs (including some Indonesian-Hindu elements) into an indigenized synthesis of religious practice and belief. In his pioneering work, *The Religion of Java* (1976 [1960]), Geertz seemed to imply that the division between *santri* and *abangan* Muslims in Java was a primordial opposition that took shape from the first years of Islam's arrival in Java. But the rivalry between *santri* and *abangan* varieties of Islam became more self-conscious, polarized, and politicized over the course of the late nineteenth and twentieth centuries, culminating in the bitter political contest of the 1950s and 1960s (Ricklefs 2007, 2012; see also Woodward 1989).

The initial conversion of small numbers of Javanese to Islam goes back to the fourteenth and fifteenth centuries, when trade and population movement across the greater Indian Ocean realm drew growing numbers of people to Islam. In Java, the process of conversion accelerated in the sixteenth century after the collapse of Java's last great Hindu-Buddhist kingdom of Majapahit (Ricklefs 2006). By the end of the eighteenth century, most of the ethnic Javanese population had converted at least in name to Islam, with the notable exception of a Hindu enclave in Java's eastern salient and a few small pockets of Hindu settlement in the uplands of Central Java (see Hefner 1985). As the historian Merle Ricklefs has shown, during these same centuries, Java's imperial courts achieved a "mystic synthesis" in which "Islam was the core religious element in Javanese senses of identity, while also accommodating older spiritual forces" (Ricklefs 2006, 217)—including various guardian spirits of the air, mountain, and seas. Absent or underdeveloped in Java were the Islamic boarding schools that, in the Muslim Middle East and South Asia, had played such a central role in the promotion of more "shari'a-minded" varieties of Islam; that is, varieties of Islam that placed more emphasis on the forms of Islamic normativity associated with jurisprudence, or *fiqh* (see Berkey 2003; Hefner 2009a; Makdisi 1981).

According to Ricklefs (2006, 89), the first major Muslim boarding school (*pesantren*) was only established in Java in the early eighteenth century. But a culturally transformative network of schools emerged significantly later in the aftermath of the Java War (1825–1830) and the effective displacement of the Javanese monarchs and aristocracy from the pinnacle of Islamic society. As a result of the expansion of *pesantren* with their *fiqh*-focused legal curriculum, the late nineteenth and twentieth centuries saw heightened interest in Islamic jurisprudence and related disciplines (van Bruinessen 1994). The greater shari'a-mindedness of *santri* Islam also reflects the fact that, from the late nineteenth century onward, Indonesian Muslims were traveling in vastly greater numbers to centers of religious study in Arabia and Egypt, and religious study at those centers was marked by a growing emphasis on Islamic law and jurisprudence, and a relative displacement (but *not* an extinction) of the Sufi-inflected spiritualism (Ar. *tasawwuf*), that had exercised a significant influence on the *abangan* variety of Javanese Islam.[3]

The rise of a more shari'a-minded normative Islam beginning in the late nineteenth century did not win the hearts and minds of all Javanese Muslims.[4] A far greater proportion of ethnic Javanese in the 1950s and 1960s remained nominal Muslims of the *abangan* variety. In fact, as Merle Ricklefs (2012) has demonstrated, the divide between *abangan* and *santri* probably widened during this time, as a result of the politicization of religious disputes. During these years, adherents of the *abangan* variety of Islam were often willfully indifferent or opposed to the normative standards of shari'a-oriented Islam. *Abangan* Muslims might perform congregational prayer at the mosque on occasion (although many did not), and some performed the annual fast. But theirs was a syncretic Islam, one that placed as much emphasis on the performance of village and household rituals (Jv. *slametan*) that involved the presentation of food offerings to ancestral and guardian spirits as it did the fulfillment of daily prayers or, least of all, formal study in an Islamic boarding school.[5] A result is that there is or was once considerable regional variation in *abangan* ritual and traditions across Java (Beatty 1999; Hefner 1985).

The more shari'a-minded *santri* were by no means uniform in their profession of Islam either; scholars of Islam in Java typically distinguish two major groupings of *santri* Islam. Clifford Geertz referred to these groupings as "traditionalist" *santri* (*santri kolot*, lit. "old-fashioned *santri*") and "modernist" *santri* (*santri modéren*). At the time of Geertz' research, modernist *santri* were broadly associated with urban merchant and trading classes, whereas, at least in Java (especially Central and East Java) the traditionalists had their base among the rural landholding elite and the network of Islamic scholars and boarding schools they supported. Modernists were active in several religious organizations. The most important of these in Geertz' day and still today was the Muhammadiyah, which had been established in Yogyakarta in 1912 (Alfian 1989; Nakamura 1983). By contrast, traditionalist *santri*, with their roots in *pesantren* boarding schools, had a variety of regional and national organizations. By far the largest of these on the island of Java was the organization of traditionalist religious scholars and their followers established in East Java in 1926 and known as Nahdlatul Ulama (see Bush 2009; Feillard 1995).

Prominent among the traditionalist *santri* are classically trained religious scholars who have dedicated a good portion of their lives to studying the Qur'an, the hadith (the sayings and deeds of the Prophet as recorded in authenticated texts), and an array of Islamic sciences. From the mid-nineteenth century onward, a growing number of these scholars also made the pilgrimage to and spent time studying in or near Mecca. The returned male pilgrim is given the title *haji*, a status of considerable standing in the traditionalist community. In a pattern that played a major role in the deepening Islamization of Java in the late nineteenth and early twentieth centuries (see Laffan 2003; Ricklefs 2007), upon returning to Java it was common for these scholars to establish their own religious boarding schools, typically with a *fiqh*-focused curriculum (van Bruinessen 1994). The schoolmaster or head teacher in a *pesantren* school is referred to as a *kyai,* a charismatic as well as educational role similar to that of the classically trained religious scholars (*ulama*) in the Middle East and South Asia.[6]

Secular Nationalists and Islamists

At the time of Geertz' research in the early 1950s, Indonesia had one of Asia's most open and competitive parliamentary systems (Feith 2007). In Java, the new party organizations were harnessed to the already existing rivalry between *abangan* and *santri,* politicizing the religious division, and supercharging politics with religious passions. Although there was a host of political parties operative on the national scene, the main division in Java pitted *santri*-based parties against secular nationalists and communists; the latter two groupings recruited primarily from the *abangan* community. While the *santri* parties tended to unite in the face of communist and secular nationalist agitation, they were internally divided, *madrasah*-educated modernists against *pesantren*-trained traditionalists. The secular nationalists and the Muslim modernists tended to regard rural *santri* teachers and their students as "old-fashioned" (*kolot*), because of their focus on the study of classical religious texts and their emphasis on a system of religious education that both modernist Muslims and their nationalist rivals regarded as out of step with the demands of the modern age (C. Geertz 1976 [1960]; see also Hefner 2009b).[7]

In Clifford Geertz' view, there was a class and status dimension to *abangan*-ism as well. At the upper end of the *abangan* social hierarchy he positioned the Javanese elite known as the *priyayi.* In the early nineteenth century, before Dutch colonialism transformed the native ruling class, the *priyayi* were people of aristocratic pedigree with ties to the various courts and principalities operating at that time across Java (C. Geertz 1976 [1960]; also Ricklefs 2006; Sutherland 1979; Van Niel 1984). According to Geertz' system of categorization, as well as historical studies from this period (Ricklefs 2006; Sutherland 1979), the *priyayi* were a cultural as well as a political elite. Their preferences in matters of speech, the arts, ceremony, and religion exercised a great influence on the broader Javanese population, especially the *abangan* (Errington 1985; Smith-Hefner 1989). As a result of the incorporation of this indigenous political elite into the Dutch colonial administration in the aftermath of the Java War, the *priyayi* gradually lost much of their commanding cultural influence in Javanese society, at the same time that the religious scholars associated with *santri* Islam were gaining in influence. During this same period, however, the term *priyayi* was generalized so as to include all government bureaucrats or civil servants (*pegawai negeri*), only some of whom had ties to Java's indigenous courts.

In the years since Clifford Geertz' early research, many scholars have pointed out that Geertz' inclusion of *priyayi* within the nominally Islamic category of the *abangan* is misleading. In Weberian terms, the *priyayi* are a status group and social class (which is how the term is still used by many Javanese youth in Yogyakarta). While some *priyayi* subscribe to an elite variant of *abangan* belief, others do not, professing a thoroughly *santri* variety of Islam (cf. Bachtiar 1973; Dhofier 1999 [1982]; Woodward 1989). In light of this criticism, most scholars have acknowledged that the critical socioreligious divide in twentieth-century Java was not tripartite but dualistic, between an increasingly shari'a-minded *santri* community and the more or less syncretic *abangan*.

Although Geertz saw these socioreligious categories as an enduring feature of Javanese social life, his writings from the late 1950s and early 1960s make clear that he recognized that the categories were highly unstable. Attracted as they were to organizations of a secular nationalist and socialist variety (including the Indonesian Communist Party, Partai Komunis Indonesia, PKI), the *abangan* in his view seemed well on their way to becoming modern in a more or less secularized manner. Traditionalist Muslims (the *santri kolot*), Geertz believed, were also in transition if not outright decline because, in his view, the future lay with those Javanese who were the beneficiaries of modern education either in secular or mixed secular and religious schools (cf. Lukens-Bull 2001, 2005). In the town in East Java where he conducted his research, pseudonymously referred to as "Mojokuto" (Pare, East Java), Geertz noted that in 1930 there had been six large Islamic boarding schools, as well as many smaller boarding schools. However, by the time of his research, there were only two large boarding schools and eleven smaller ones (C. Geertz 1976 [1960], 185). He predicted that along with this shift in focus to modern education the *kyai*, or rural religious teacher, would lose his authority.[8]

Both in his Java research and in his later comparison of Islam in Java and Morocco (C. Geertz 1971 [1968]), Geertz made clear that he believed that the core values of Javanese culture lay with the relativistic and tolerant syncretism of the *abangan*. He also hinted that the secular nationalists/*abangan* would likely remain at the center of Indonesian society and politics; modernism and moderation would win out over traditionalism. Influenced by Weberian variants of secularization theory popular in his youth, Geertz did not foresee the global or Indonesian resurgence of Islam, nor did he anticipate that, as would be the case, the relative influence and cultural vitality of *abangan*-ism was to experience a precipitous decline.

In the late colonial and early independence period, the divide between practicing *santri* and *abangan* Muslims lax in their profession of the faith became a key fault line for political mobilization (Hefner 2000, 15; see also Feith 2007; C. Geertz 1976 [1960]). *Santri* Muslims rallied to political parties and civic associations linked to Nahdlatul Ulama, Muhammadiyah, and other Muslim organizations (Ricklefs 2007). *Abangan* Muslims, secular nationalists, the Christian Javanese minority, and Javanese mystics who had repudiated Islam entirely rallied to a variety of nationalist and leftist parties, the two largest of which were the Indonesian Nationalist Party (PNI), secular-nationalist in orientation, and the Indonesian Communist Party (PKI). In the years just prior to the New Order's rise to power, the religious divide was bitterly politicized. Under President Sukarno, the PKI transformed itself into the largest of Indonesia's political parties, and the largest Communist Party in the noncommunist world (Hefner 2000, 16; see also Ricklefs 2008). Muslim parties and organizations also developed their social and political organizations. As the political rivalry between secularists and Muslim parties heated up in the late 1950s and early 1960s, the variety of Muslim social organizations came to include paramilitaries made up of dedicated Muslim youth—some of which had ties to the Indonesian armed forces (Fealy and McGregor 2010; Sidel 2006).

On September 30, 1965, a group of young left-wing army officers in the capital city of Jakarta staged a coup against their right-leaning rivals in the armed forces, ostensibly (they claimed) to preempt what they alleged was a rightest military plot against President Sukarno (who at the time was cooperating extensively with the communists). Ineptly organized, the left-wing officers' coup was suppressed in a matter of days. However, in the months following, Muslim groups joined forces with the conservative army leadership to destroy the PKI. An estimated one-half million people were killed in the violence that followed. Another half million were imprisoned without trial, many for a decade or longer (Cribb 1990; Roosa 2006). On Java the great majority of those killed or imprisoned were people of nominal or *abangan* Muslim persuasion.

A little-known Javanese army general by the name of Suharto stepped in to take control and coordinate the campaign against the Communist Party. Over the months that followed, he sidelined Sukarno, eventually taking up the presidency and instituting his own "New Order" regime (Hefner 2000; Sidel 2006). Although in his early years most Indonesia observers regarded him as a nominally Islamic *abangan*, Suharto was above all a skilled if authoritarian tactician. As Merle Ricklefs (2012) has observed, the destruction of the Communist Party and the domestication of the country's nationalist party in the early years of the New Order era in fact greatly undermined the social and institutional supports for Java's *abangan* community.

Beginning in the late 1970s and early 1980s, Indonesia, following many other countries in the Muslim world, underwent a far-reaching Islamic resurgence (Eickelman and Piscatori 2004 [1996]; Hefner 2000). The resurgence gradually depleted the ranks of the *abangan* and greatly boosted the social fortunes of Muslim social organizations, especially the mass-based organizations, Nahdlatul Ulama and Muhammadiyah. Its organizational dynamics aside, the Islamic resurgence in Indonesia also had a powerful effect on the lifestyles and aspirations of Javanese youth. Rather than leaving the *santri* community unaltered, however, the broad social changes that underlay the resurgence were to bring about a transformation in the profession of normative-minded Islam as well. In the span of a quarter century, the observant Muslim community was to go from being a minority to a majority of ethnic Javanese. But even as Javanese Islam became more visibly "*santri*," the culture and social practice of Islamic observance would itself be transformed.

Muslim Puritans

One of the few sociocultural anthropologists to carry out ethnographic research focused specifically on Muslims and Muslim Javanese youth in the early 1970s,

James L. Peacock drew heavily on the social categories and dynamics captured in Geertz' research from the 1950s. However, because the Java in which he carried out his studies had changed, and because he was interested in painting a more intimate portrait of the educational and socialization dynamics in Javanese and Indonesian Islam, Peacock ultimately provided an alternative understanding of Muslims and modernity in Java and Indonesia. Peacock's work (1978a, 1978b) is of particular interest for the present study because he attempted to link religious groupings to specific psychological orientations and patterns of sociability. His analysis provides an unusually rich vantage point for assessing the nature and scale of the changes in—and anthropological paradigms for the understanding of—Javanese Islam and youth subjectivities over the past generation (cf. Hoesterey 2015).

Just as Geertz had forecast a generation earlier, Peacock suggested that modern schools (whether secular or religiously based) that included general studies in their curricula were likely to displace Indonesia's traditionalist boarding schools. More generally, and as Geertz had also forecast, Peacock hinted that traditionalist Islam was bound to lose ground to movements of a modernist Muslim orientation. However, on one very important point, Peacock staked out a different position than that of his predecessor. Writing in the 1950s, Geertz had implied that the *abangan* and some variety of secular nationalism would likely remain at the heart of Indonesian and, especially, Javanese society.[9] Writing a half-generation later, Peacock distanced himself from this prognosis. Based on his research, he projected the growing ascendance of the Muslim reformists associated with groups such as the mass organization of modernist Islamic reform, the Muhammadiyah.

Muhammadiyah was founded in 1912 by a Central Javanese merchant of minor aristocratic pedigree known as Kyai Haji Ahmad Dahlan. In 1890 Dahlan had traveled from Yogyakarta to Mecca, where he studied with a leading Islamic reformist of Minangkabau-Sumatran background, Syeikh Ahmad Khatib. Khatib himself had been influenced by the modernizing ideas of the great Egyptian Muslim reformist Muhammad Abduh (see Alfian 1989; Laffan 2003; Noer 1973; Peacock 1978a). When Dahlan returned to Java after his studies in the Middle East, he immediately set out to promote the new ideas of modern Islamic reform in Indonesia, beginning in his hometown of Yogyakarta in south-central Java in the neighborhood known as Kauman, where the elite among Yogyakarta's *santri* population resides, adjacent to the sultan's palace (Noer 1973, 74; see also Mulkhan 2010; Peacock 1978b).

The Muhammadiyah organization Dahlan established had many of the trademark features of reform-minded modernist organizations in other parts of the Muslim world. Muhammadiyah reformists made extensive use of new print technologies, disseminating their message in pamphlets, journals, and books (Eickelman and Anderson 1999; Feener 2007; Laffan 2011). The reformists also borrowed extensively from new Western models of volunteer civic and social-welfare associations. Rather than relying on the informal and hierarchical networks of classically trained *ulama* and their students, Muhammadiyah had a centralized bureaucracy, membership lists, and centrally coordinated and ledger-book rationalized finances. Rather than developing schools for the study of jurisprudence and the classical Islamic sciences, Muhammadiyah set out to develop a centrally managed system of modern Islamic schools, complete with classrooms, blackboards, and a curriculum devoted to both religious and general education. By the early 1950s, the organization had spread to Muslim regions across the archipelago, constructing not only hundreds of Islamic schools but also modern clinics, hospitals, nurseries, and orphanages.

During the period of Suharto's New Order, Muhammadiyah continued to develop its extensive network of high schools and colleges, the best of which boast extensive libraries, scientific laboratories, and up-to-date computer facilities. Today this well-run and educationally sophisticated organization has some twenty-five million followers, making it the largest modernist-reformist Muslim organization in the world. It manages no fewer than 12,000 schools, 167 colleges or universities, 421 orphanages, 345 polyclinics and hospitals, and a nationwide bank (Bank Pengkreditan Rakyat; see Njoto-Feillard 2012). Along with the Nahdlatul Ulama, the Muhammadiyah has been and continues to be an important pillar of Indonesia's Muslim civil society (Hefner 2000).

Conducting his research in the early 1970s, Peacock was interested in the question of what reformism as a cultural and religious movement implied for psychological rationalization and expressive behavior. In his 1978 book *Muslim Puritans*, he explored these questions, examining the implications of Islamic reform for child socialization, personality development, and religious understanding. Peacock identified modernist-reformists as those who favored independent interpretation (*ijtihad*) of the Qur'an and the Sunnah (the sayings and deeds of the Prophet as recorded in the hadith) rather than deferential conformity (*taqlid*) to the commentaries and authority of classically trained Islamic teachers. Reformists also insisted on the purification of both local culture and religious practice, so as to purge them of syncretistic accretions and bring them into greater alignment with reform-minded notions of Islam (Peacock 1978b, 18). In the research he conducted in Yogyakarta in the 1970s, Peacock discovered that the psychological rationalizations of reformism were most clearly and consistently evidenced among members of Muhammadiyah and its training corps, Darol Arqom (188).

Reformist Psychology and Child Socialization

Peacock found that Muslim reformists rationalized religious practice in order to make it more coherent as well as to more efficiently focus on the achievement of religious ends such as salvation. They curtailed the traditionalist habit of presenting Friday sermons in Arabic rather than the local vernacular and streamlined the practice of prayer, focusing on normatively recognized prayers and rejecting prayers not specifically prescribed in the Qur'an and Sunnah (Peacock 1978b, 203). Reformists also looked with disfavor on a number of traditional Javanese Islamic practices, including the preservation of sacred heirlooms

(*pusaka*) such as ceremonial daggers (*keris*) and the appeal to the various autoch-
thonous (place) spirits long at the heart of the "mystic synthesis" of courtly and
popular Islam (see Ricklefs 2006, 161–174).

For similar reasons, reformists rejected traditional Javanese *slametan* (ritual
meals). According to Geertz, *slametan* formed the core of the Javanese (*abangan*)
religious system by affirming the social and cosmic order and keeping participants safe from spiritual and other disturbances (C. Geertz 1976 [1960], 14).[10]
Slametan are held to celebrate life stages, to mark important dates on the Muslim
calendar, to reinforce bonds of village solidarity, and to address special or unusual
occurrences such as sorcery, illness, building a new home, or departing for a long
trip (C. Geertz 1976 [1960], 30). Not surprisingly, reformists viewed *slametan* as
bid'ah, "illegitimate innovations." For similar reasons they rejected the system of
numerological divination called *pétungan* that was used to determine the most
auspicious date for holding *slametan* and other important events.

One cannot emphasize too strongly that *slametan* were not merely ritual
matters or random aspects of a syncretic variety of Islam; they were, in fact,
part and parcel of an entire system of Javanese socialization, sociability, and
subjectivity (see Beatty 1999, 2002). Traditional practices of Javanese socialization included many routines that encouraged the child's passivity, dependency,
and sociocentric identification with a hierarchical social world. Very young
infants were massaged, for example, so their bodies would remain pliable and
could later be molded into appropriate postures. Babies and toddlers were
nursed on demand and never left alone but held close to the mother's body in a
shawl or *slendang*. Facing outward from the mother's left hip, much of the young
child's socialization focused on interactions with third parties, in contrast to
the largely dyadic exchanges more characteristic of much child socialization in
the middle-class West (Smith-Hefner 1988a; see also Ochs and Schieffelin
2001). In these interactions, emphasis was placed on drawing the child's attention to the relative status of the interlocutor and on gently encouraging the
cultivation of a properly polite demeanor. Most generally, however, care was
taken not to frustrate the desires of young children,[11] who were allowed to eat
and sleep on their own schedule and to "excrete almost anywhere and anytime,
indoors or out" (Peacock 1978b, 55).

Peacock identified two important Javanese values underlying traditional Javanese practices of socialization. Drawing on Hildred Geertz' (1989 [1961]) work
on the Javanese family and sociability, he identified these values as *rukun* (Jv.; In.
rukun), "social cooperation and harmony, emphasizing solidarity," and *urmat*
(Jv.; In. *hormat*), "respect, emphasizing hierarchy" (Peacock 1978b, 59). Peacock
noted that *slametan* rituals reinforced traditional Javanese ideals of social cooperation and harmony and served to locate the child in a supernaturally grounded
cosmic order. "The swaddling, cuddling, and protectiveness encourage[d] passivity, and the push-pull and continuous advice [of Javanese socialization], stifle[d]
initiative" (59). Peacock argued that these Javanese practices that encouraged
passivity and inhibition functioned to instill the restraint prized by Javanese and
required for maintaining respect and social consensus (59).

Showing once again that the socialization practices at work here were part of a rich psycho-socio-religious complex, these attitudes were further reinforced through interactions with the father. Ethnographic studies have shown that, while Javanese fathers were generally indulgent and attentive when the child was young, the relationship shifted dramatically when the child reached the age of around five (Peacock 1978b, 57, citing H. Geertz 1989 [1961]; see also Smith-Hefner 1988b). At this point the father would become distant and begin to demand appropriate speech and demeanor. Through these interactions the child learned proper manners and the responsiveness to the social hierarchy (Jv. *sungkan*) that marked a mature, refined Javanese (Peacock 1978b, 57). To "become Javanese" (Jv. *dadi jowo*) was to learn to see oneself as embedded in a network of relationships and a style of sociability that had a social logic, pleasure, and compellingness that was thought to be consistent with Islam, but was not in any simple sense directly grounded on the stipulations or norms of Islamic law, at least as understood in modern times.

Peacock found that these traditional Javanese practices of subject formation and sociability contrasted with those preferred by parents from Muslim reformist backgrounds. Here again Peacock was ahead of his time in demonstrating that religion is not just a matter of doctrine or even social practice but woven into public and intimate behavior. By comparison with non-reformists, for example, toilet training of children in reformist families took place considerably earlier. Reformists also restricted practices such as *kuloni*, the child sleeping next to its mother, and *gendong*, the child being carried close to the mother's body in a shawl. In reformist families, the child's eating, sleeping, and excreting were more often tightly scheduled. Moral tuition differed as well. Instead of the push-pull of kinetic training and verbal instruction (*tuturi*) preferred by the non-reformists (common techniques used, for example, to teach traditional Javanese dance and the arts, and, more generally, appropriate deferential postures), reformist parents offered their children moral advice and direction based on scriptural reference (Peacock 1978b, 58–60).

With regard to life cycle rituals, Peacock found a similarly stark divide between Muslim reformists and the proponents of Javanized varieties of Islam. Whereas non-reformists tended to focus on birth and birth rituals (*slametan*), reformist parents focused more of their attention on later childhood, in large part because childhood itself was understood as a period marked by the urgent need to provide instruction in Islam (Peacock 1978b, 66). *Slametan* used to celebrate pregnancy, birth, and early childhood, were rarely observed by reformists (60). Reformists did, however, perform those life passage rituals with a clear Islamic reference—such as circumcision and marriage—but they did so in a manner that, at least relatively speaking, restricted both their cost and their social ostentation; they therefore rejected court-inspired finery and dispensed with the elaborate ceremony and lengthy celebration of the non-reformists. *Wayang* shadow-puppet theater and Javanese dance,[12] both common entertainments at traditional Javanese *slametan*, were disapproved of and rarely included in the life cycle celebrations of reformists.

Reducing the ritualization and indulgence of childhood, reformists focused their attention instead on both practical and moral education. Peacock found, for example, that reformist parents typically eschewed the traditional Javanese practices of entrusting the care of the child to a relative for a short time or child lending for a longer period of time, taking instead more personal responsibility for their children's upbringing and religious training (Peacock 1978b, 61, 66). Javanese child lending takes a wide variety of forms; it can occur quite early in the child's life (with the arrangements sometimes made while the child is still in the mother's womb) or after a precipitous event such as an illness. It can last for a matter of days or for the life of the individual (see Beatty 2002). A child may be entrusted to an older relative who is deemed a better caretaker for the child or a relative who can offer the child certain social or economic advantages, such as schooling. (Because preferred schools may be located in an urban area far from home, a young child may be entrusted to a relative or teacher who lives in that location.) These practices are thought to reinforce the development of refined manners and sensitivity to hierarchy (Jv. *sungkan*), as children are required to be especially respectful to surrogate parents.[13]

Reformist parents, however, avoided such practices, on the grounds that they were contrary to a proper pattern of Islamic socialization and family organization. Virtually none of the reformists in Peacock's survey had lent out a son to relatives or sent him to a *pesantren* boarding school (thereby entrusting the child's care and training to a religious teacher, or *kyai*). Instead, reformists kept their sons at home and sent them to government-style day schools, taking greater responsibility for the child's religious training themselves (Peacock 1978b, 66).[14] And, while not completely rejecting the hierarchical relationship of father and son, reformists nonetheless minimized the veneration of the father, emphasizing instead the (relatively) more egalitarian tendencies of reformist Islam (107). During the celebration of Lebaran (Idul Fitri), which comes at the end of the fasting month, for example, Javanese children ask forgiveness from their parents by kneeling before them and bowing. Peacock writes that among other things the rite expresses "a deep veneration of the father by the child, who relates to the father formally and hierarchically" (106). Among reformists, however, he found that sons more often simply shook hands with the father (*salaman*) "rather than bowing the head (*sungkem*) and kneeling at the father's feet (*sembah*)" (106).

Peacock suggested that these social and psychological practices had rich implications for what is today called ethical subject formation (see Mahmood 2003, 2005). In particular, he showed that the practices resulted in a greater focus and continuity in the child's identifications (Peacock 1978b, 73). The modernist-reformist pattern of socialization, Peacock concluded, contributed to the development of a more "Protestant like personality," marked by a number of psychological dispositions. Among them were a clearer sense of self (because of internalizing identity from the parents only rather than from multiple caregivers) and a tendency toward self-blame (that is, guilt rather than shame) because responsibility is identified as located within the self. Peacock speculated further that these dispositions supported an ethical disposition to *tauhid*, the belief in and dedication to the "unicity" of God, rather than the diffusion of God's or supernatural power into a disparate assortment of animistic entities, as among non-reformists (61, 98). In these and other cultural patterns, Peacock found that reformists veered away from an emphasis on the values of social harmony and hierarchy characteristic of Javanese tradition, and "toward the ideal of the seeker of salvation who is both self-reliant and self-disciplined and who is motivated by distant objectives rather than enmeshed in the sociocosmic nexus" (60). The distinctive traits of life-world and subjective rationalization characteristic of reformists led Peacock to conclude that the reformists could be appropriately described as "Muslim Puritans."

This, then, is the crux of a fundamental difference between Clifford Geertz' and James Peacock's observations on cultural currents in Javanese society. Whereas Geertz had implied that the *abangan* (in some modernized, and likely more secular, variety) would remain the dominant socio-religious grouping in Indonesian society, Peacock's descriptions left little doubt that, whatever their current demographics, Muslim reformists such as those in Muhammadiyah were in the ascendency, in both Java and Indonesia as a whole. Peacock thus diverged more fully from the secularization-theory assumptions of Geertz' work; he also came much closer than Geertz to anticipating the Islamic resurgence of the late 1970s and 1980s. Although he didn't fully forecast all aspects of the great revitalization that was to come, his work is infused with a sense of reformist Islam's progress and promise in contrast to the secular modernist pessimism with regard to religion that was especially pronounced in Geertz' later work, *Islam Observed* (1971 [1968]).

But social change has a tendency to transform not one neatly demarcated cultural variable but many, and often in an uneven or ambivalent way. Here in Indonesia, the Islamic resurgence of the 1980s and 1990s would introduce a new dynamic into the religious identifications and subject formation of contemporary Muslim Javanese youth. This momentous event greatly complicated the categories and social influence of *abangan*-ism and *santri* Islam. More generally, it has forever changed the varieties and cultural substance of Javanese Islam by ushering in new forms of Muslim piety and experiences of Muslim—and "modern"—subjectivity (see Hefner 2011; Machmudi 2008b).

Setting the Stage for a Resurgent Islam

Muslim groups that joined forces with the army and conservative nationalists to destroy the Communist Party in 1965–1966 had expected to be given a prominent role in Suharto's New Order government. However, they soon found themselves sorely disappointed. Having dealt with the Communist threat, Suharto kept the Muslims at arm's length and quickly moved to restrict independent political parties, particularly Islamic ones. The new president focused his attention on the restoration of social order and made a conservative program of political and economic stabilization his first priority (Hefner 2000, 16; Liddle 1996; Ricklefs 2008).

Social stability and economic growth under Suharto eventually resulted in an expansion and diversification of urban employment. After the Middle Eastern oil embargo of 1973, Indonesia entered a period of sustained economic expansion fueled initially by the rise of oil prices on the world market. The country experienced twenty years of growth rates averaging in excess of 6 percent per annum (Hill 1994). Improvements in roads, transport, and communications brought formerly remote areas of the country into extensive contact with national life, while also accelerating the pace of urbanization (G. Jones 1994a, 19–22; see also Hefner 1990, 2000). In the 1950s Indonesia had been primarily a rural society with fewer than 20 percent of its population living in cities and town. By the 1990s, almost a third of the country's population resided in urban areas (G. Jones 1994a, 23; today more than half of all Indonesians live in urban areas), and villages across the republic were more closely linked to urban culture and networks than ever before.[15]

During this period, new employment opportunities opened up in government as well as in small manufacturing and service industries. Between the years 1974 and 1981, for example, Indonesia's civil service (*pegawai negeri*) expanded from 1.67 million to 2.79 million people, an increase of 66 percent (G. Jones 1994a, 39). Hundreds of factories sprang up on the outskirts of major cities, especially on densely populated Java, creating thousands of low-paying assembly jobs. Many of these new opportunities were open to female workers. In fact, factories often preferred to hire young, unmarried women because of their assumed dexterity, diligence, and, most important, docility (Wolf 1996, 150; see also G. Jones 1994b; Ong 2010 [1987]).[16] Although senior managerial positions in industry and manufacturing remained overwhelmingly male, elsewhere there were new white-collar employment opportunities for educated women as well, in everything from teaching and clerking to government service (Blackburn 2004; G. Jones 1994b; Sen 2002). However troubled its political circumstances, Indonesian society was on the move, and the widespread socioeconomic changes were to have enormous implications for Javanese youth, Javanese Islam, and the long-standing contest over how to be Muslim.

In the 1970s and 1980s the New Order government also expanded educational opportunities throughout Indonesia by instituting an ambitious program of school construction under the Inpres (Presidential Instruction) program (G. Jones 1994a, 31). There was a dramatic increase in the number of public, nonconfessional schools (referred to as "general schools" or *sekolah umum*) as well as state-supported and private Muslim day schools (*madrasah, sekolah Islam*). Identifying education as crucial for human resource development as well as national development (*pembangunan nasional*), the government made primary education compulsory through grades one through six and later through grade nine.[17] The expansion of educational programs under the New Order, along with parents' willingness to sacrifice to send their children to school in hopes of stable employment, resulted in near universal primary school education by 1983. By the 1990s illiteracy had virtually disappeared among Indonesian youth (Jones and Hagul 2001, 207).

During this same period, school enrollment at upper and lower secondary levels also increased sharply. Female rates of educational participation rose even more dramatically than did those of males, dramatically decreasing the gap in female-to-male school enrollment ratios (G. Jones 1994b). These patterns were true not only with regard to "general" schools but for Islamic schools as well. By the mid-1980s the number of female students attending Muslim schools came to equal or even exceed the number of males, particularly at the secondary levels (Oey-Gardiner 1991, 58; see also Jackson and Parker 2008; G. Jones 1994a).

As noted briefly above, Muslim schools are of two basic types: Muslim boarding schools (*pesantren*) and Muslim day schools (*madrasah* and *sekolah Islam*, or Islamic schools; see Azra, Afrianty, and Hefner 2007; Hefner 2009a; Jackson and Parker 2008; van Bruinessen 2008). *Pesantren* boarding schools are for the most part private institutions run by individuals or foundations, many under the auspices of Muslim mass organizations such as the NU or Muhammadiyah. These schools emphasize study in the Islamic sciences, beginning with the Qur'an and hadith, but including also jurisprudence (*fiqh*), Arabic grammar, principles of religion, the sources of the law, didactic theology, and mysticism (Hefner 2009b, 60). Originally restricted to males, growing numbers of *pesantren* opened their doors to female students beginning in the 1930s.[18]

Contrary to Clifford Geertz' forecasts in the 1950s and 1960s, *pesantren* did not die out with the development of modern state schools and the expansion of secondary and tertiary education (Lukens-Bull 2005). Although competition with state schools and the perception that state education offered better employment opportunities led to the collapse of many smaller Islamic schools in the 1950s, they also led to reforms in the larger schools. By the 1970s only a relatively small number of *pesantren* continued to provide instruction exclusively in religious subjects. Responding to parental demand for marketable skills as well as religious piety, the majority of Islamic schools had expanded their curriculum so as to provide instruction in general or "secular" subjects as well. The schools made this accommodation in any of several ways: by building *madrasah* day schools on the *pesantren* complex grounds; by making arrangements with *madrasah* located nearby where their students studied both religion and general studies following the national curriculum guidelines; or by introducing general studies into the *pesantren* curriculum itself (Hefner 2009b; van Bruinessen 2008; Zuhdi 2006).

Like *pesantren*, most *madrasah* are privately run. However, since 1989, all *madrasah* and *sekolah Islam* desiring state certification are required to use the national curriculum provided by the Department of Religion (for *madrasah*) or the Department of Education (for *sekolah* Islam), thereby ensuring that, aside from their religious studies, students in Islamic schools adhere to the same general curriculum as students in general schools (see Azra, Afrianty, and Hefner 2007).[19] As in general schools, *madrasah* have age-based grades that are organized into primary, middle, and upper levels, and graduation to a higher level is based on test results (Jackson and Parker 2008).

The aggregate result of all these far-reaching developments in the Islamic educational field is that, under the New Order, a diploma from a Muslim school became officially equivalent to one from a general school (*sekolah umum*) and Muslim school graduates could sit for the state college entrance exam (SNM-PTN) along with general school graduates. These developments in the formal educational field have had profound implications for the everyday aspirations and experiences of Muslim youth (Parker and Nilan 2013, 81).

Islam and the New Middle Class

The educational advances and unprecedented pace of socioeconomic change during Indonesia's New Order period also, and no less significantly, contributed to the growth of Indonesia's middle class (see Heryanto 1999, 2003; Hull and Jones 1994; Tanter and Young 1990). The general contours of this new middle stratum were already broadly apparent in the early 1980s, but their details and cultural dynamics were to develop more clearly over the next quarter century. A product of New Order social and educational development, the new middle class is different from the old Muslim middle class in several important respects. The single most important difference is that the primary social and cultural capital for the new bourgeoisie (especially its large Muslim wing) is no longer based in the bazaar trade or large landholdings about which Clifford Geertz had written, but in higher education and the social credentials and connections it facilitates. The primary fields of employment for this group are, in turn, not market commerce or petty trade but government, education, new information services, and the professions. While in the late 1990s and early 2000s the new middle class was still relatively small—perhaps only between 5 percent and 15 percent of the Indonesian population—its development has nonetheless been of enormous social and political significance (Hefner 2000; Heryanto 1990, 2003; Tanter and Young 1990).[20]

With its newly expanded consumptive capacity, Indonesia's new middle class has also become a primary producer and consumer of new cultural trends in media, leisure, fashion, and entertainment (Heryanto 1999, 2008, 2014; C. Jones 2003; van Leeuwen 2005). In the early years of the New Order these trends had a regionally varied and loosely "ethnic" air, consistent with the state's emphasis on a depoliticized, aestheticized, and standardized version of ethnicity as the government took over the role previously played by political parties in cultivating cultural forms (B. Hatley 1994; Heryanto and Lutz 1988).[21] The government's intervention in regional performing arts, literary traditions, and the media was intended to encourage the formation of a national cultural identity that would replace the populist-nationalist political vision of earlier years and counter what New Order officials regarded as the corrosive influences of a liberal and capitalist West (B. Hatley 1994, 224; see also Daniels 2009).

But the New Order state's ability to drive and direct the emerging national cultural scene proved to be less comprehensive than the state or many Western observers believed. Even as the New Order government sought to impose its own hegemonic model of national and ethnic cultures, many in Indonesia's new middle class became increasingly uncomfortable with the rarefied nature of these ethnic portrayals and the government's heavy-handed manipulation of "culture" and "tradition." For growing numbers of Indonesians in the 1980s and 1990s, especially educated Javanese youth, Islam was becoming an important and alternative source of social identity—and an alternative, if not openly resistant, modernity (cf. George 2010).

Just as it had done with ethnicity, Suharto's New Order government moved to control and contain religious diversity through programs of religious education and social and cultural standardization. During its first twenty years, the state did so by, among other things, promoting a far more conservative interpretation of the nation's official philosophy, known as the Five Principles, or Pancasila. The five principles are belief in one God, a just and civilized humanity, national unity, and the rule of the people through consultation and representation, to achieve social justice for all Indonesians (Guinness 1994, 271; see also Bowen 1991). Although during the first two decades of the republic, nationalist Indonesians had tended to understand the first principle of the Pancasila as authorizing religious freedom for believers of all faiths in Indonesia, Muslim organizations and the Department of Religion had always insisted that the principle implied that only recognized monotheistic religions based on revelation were allowed (Kim 1998; Ropi 2012). During the polarized political circumstances of the Sukarno era, the issue of state recognition and religious freedom had never been decisively resolved, but, with the notable exception of the 1965 regulation on religious blasphemy (Bagir 2013), the national government made few systematic attempts to rein in religious freedoms. Under the tightly controlled circumstances of the New Order, however, this changed, and changed dramatically. For New Order officials, religion was to serve as one of the main instruments for preventing any revival of the much-vilified and now destroyed Communist Party. State officials thus reinterpreted the first principle of the Pancasila in line with the earlier Muslim understanding, eventually authorizing just five (monotheistic) religions: Islam, Catholicism, Protestantism, Hinduism, and Buddhism.[22]

In New Order government programs and publications, religion in the form of monotheism was associated with progress, literacy, power, wealth, and sophistication. By contrast, "traditional" religions that were not clearly monotheistic and had no authoritative scriptures were represented as "local custom" at best or irreligious paganism at worse (Guinness 1994, 296; see also Kim 1998). Pressure to become a member of one of the recognized world religions was reinforced by official suspicions that agnosticism and atheism provided fertile ground for the growth of communist ideology. State policies on religious affiliation, then, promoted conversion to Christianity, Hinduism, Buddhism, or Islam and resulted in the abandonment or suppression of local traditions deemed backward by the state, as well as by some reform-minded religious citizens in society (Hefner 2000, 18; see also G. Jones 1976; Kuipers 1998; Tsing 1993).

Through a greatly expanded program of compulsory religious education, Indonesia's national educational system played a powerful role in reinforcing affiliation with a government-recognized monotheistic religion. A program of religious education had been recommended during the early years of the Sukarno-led parliamentary period (1950–1958), but in most of the country the program was never put into place, owing to a dearth of instructional materials and trained teachers, as well as opposition from teachers' unions, many of which were *abangan* and secular nationalist in orientation. However, the New Order's interest in promoting religion as an antidote to communism, combined with its programs of school expansion and teacher training, allowed for the development of a nationally standardized and compulsory program of religious education in all Indonesian schools (Machmudi 2008b, 75). Beginning in the 1970s, all students, elementary through university level, were (and continue to be) required to have a minimum of two hours of religious instruction per week, with separate instruction for students of the various religions represented in each school (Hefner 2009b, 68). This instruction focuses on the fundamentals of religious belief and practice; for Muslims, these are the elements of doctrine (*aqidah*), worship (*ibadah*), and morals (*akhlak*).

The Suharto government also used the Pancasila as a means of control over social unrest and potential political challenges (Bowen 1991, 126). Students, government employees, community leaders, and business and private employees were required to attend Pancasila ethical courses. These courses encouraged ideological conformity and emphasized the inappropriateness of appeals to ethnic and religious solidarity as a basis of political organization (Mackie and MacIntyre 1994, 26; Nishimura 1995). In 1982–1984 the government implemented a series of laws requiring all social, religious, and political parties to accept the Pancasila as their ideological basis and "sole principle" (*asas tunggal*). Many Muslims found this requirement objectionable on religious grounds, as it implied that Pancasila took priority over Islam. Muslim groups that refused to accept the Pancasila as their ideological foundation, however, were stripped of their legal standing and thus effectively banned (Hefner 2000, 17).[23]

In the face of these and similar repressive state policies, most of the larger Muslim organizations adopted a strategy of abjuring direct political action and turned their energies instead to proselytizing activities (*dakwah*) and social outreach (Machmudi 2008b; Rosyad 2007). On university campuses such as that of Gadjah Mada in the late 1970s and early 1980s, Muslim student groups turned their efforts to religious education and Islamic social activism. Government policies enacted in 1978 that aimed at "campus normalization" and prohibited all forms of explicit political activity on campus in fact worked to the benefit of Muslim religious organizations, since state controls weighed less heavily on religious groups than they did social and political ones (Hefner 2000). Barred from overt political activity, campus religious organizations threw themselves into a flurry of educational and social welfare activities. These included setting up study groups that grappled with questions of Islam and modernity; raising funds for scholarship programs for poor village youth; sending predication or *dakwah* teams into nearby neighborhoods and villages; and, most generally, training disciplined cadres of student activists to promote a deeper Islamization of campus life (Bubalo and Fealy 2005; Hefner 2000; Machmudi 2008b; Madrid 1999).

By the late 1980s, on campuses in Yogyakarta, Jakarta, Bandung, Surabaya, and other university towns, a broad and significant division had begun to emerge among these Muslim groups. There were, on the one hand, the more or less "Muslim nationalist" organizations, which promoted *dakwah* proselytization and religious piety, but which also remained committed to a Muslim interpretation of Indonesia's Pancasila-based multiconfessional nationalism. These groups included the Himpunan Mahasiswa Islam (HMI, Association of Muslim University Students) and the NU-linked Pergerakan Mahasiswa Islam Indonesia (PMII, Indonesian Muslim University Student Movement), as well as the Ikatan Mahasiswa Muhammadiyah (IMM, League of Muhammadiyah University Students). Most of these groups promoted a more "ethicalized" rather than literalist understanding of Islamic law (shari'a).

On the other hand, the late 1980s and early 1990s also saw the emergence of student groupings of a more internationalist and self-consciously Islamist orientation (cf. Bubalo and Fealy 2005; Machmudi 2008a). The most influential of these was a loosely organized network of moderate Islamist students known as the Jema'ah Tarbiyah, or Religious Education Movement (lit. "Religious Education Community"). This relatively moderate but Muslim Brotherhood–influenced group drew on two constituencies in its recruitment efforts: the growing number of Muslim students returning from studying in the Middle East, and more conservative *dakwah* student groups on campus.

Although their presence was rare in the late 1970s and early 1980s, by the late 1980s and early 1990s these conservative Muslim activists had established a visible presence on campuses across Indonesia—particularly "secular" state colleges and universities, rather than the country's system of state Islamic institutes (IAIN/UIN). The new Islamists stood apart from the general student body in their dress and interactional styles. Male members sported short beards or goatees and wore collarless long-sleeved tunics and ankle-length pants. Female members wore the "tight headscarf" (*jilbab*), a large, expansive head covering tightly pinned under the chin and extending over the chest and hips, worn with long-sleeved blouses and long skirts or long, loose pants and tunics. A much smaller number of women wore dark, shapeless, full-length robes or *cadar* (Brenner 1996; Feillard 1999; Smith-Hefner 2007). These styles contrasted with the clothing styles worn by the general student population on nonconfessional campuses such as that of Gadjah Mada, where until the late 1980s, a modest version of Western-style dress was the norm: short-sleeved shirts and dress pants for males, and short-sleeved blouses and knee-length skirts or slacks for females. The habitus and patterns of social interaction among the *tarbiyah*-linked groups were also distinctive. Members refused to shake hands with individuals of the opposite sex. Putting aside long-established Indonesian greetings, they exchanged the Arabic greeting and response *"Assalam alaikum/Warahmatullohi wabaraktuh."* No less significant, they carefully avoided "inappropriate proximity" (*khalwat*) and even direct eye contact with the opposite sex. Stridently and repeatedly, they also condemned dating as utterly inconsistent with Islamic values, insisting that "there is no dating in Islam."

Although in the early 1980s Islamist student groups had an only nominal presence on Indonesian campuses, by the early 1990s, the *tarbiyah*-linked groups had used their superior organization and moral dedication to win control of student senates on most "secular" university campuses across the country. *Tarbiyah* groups also controlled the Lembaga Dakwah Kampus (Campus Institution for [Islamic] Propagation), the state-sanctioned body responsible for providing university students with the religious lessons all students are obliged to take (Bubalo and Fealy 2005; Hefner 2009b; Machmudi 2008b). In taking the lead in state-mandated religious education in this way, *tarbiyah* activists were able to recruit newcomers to their movement and subtly undercut the state's ability to define the terms of the religious education all university students were supposed to receive (Hefner 2000). Perhaps most significantly, *tarbiyah*-linked groups broke with the long-standing and heretofore neat divide between modernist and traditionalist Muslims. Although closer in some normative matters to Indonesia's modernists, the new *tarbiyah* Islamists regarded both of Indonesia's main Muslim constituencies as not fully authentic in their profession of Islam.

These campus developments were all part of a broader, if highly variegated resurgence in Islamic piety and devotion that took place in the last two decades of the New Order period. During this time Indonesia saw an upsurge in mosque construction, Friday worship, organized religious study, alms collection, and pilgrimage to Mecca (Hefner 2000, 17; see also Feillard and Madinier 2011; van Bruinessen 2013). As the resurgence gained momentum, the government itself caught wind of the change and began to make accommodations to Muslim social groupings and cultural interests. Set in place in the late 1980s and early 1990s, these new accommodations of Muslim interests included the creation of a codified compilation of Islamic law (Bowen 2003; Feener 2007; A. Salim 2008), the expansion of the authority of the Muslim courts (Cammack 2003), the establishment of an organization of Muslim intellectuals (ICMI), and the founding of the country's first Islamic bank, the Bank Muamalat Indonesia (Hefner 2000, 128–166; see also Hefner 1993; Ramage 1995). These and similar moves were an attempt in part to counterbalance Suharto's worsening relationship with powerful military commanders and to court Muslim support; however, they also reflected Suharto and his advisers' awareness of the growing social and political influence of the Islamic resurgence (Effendy 2004; Hefner 2000; Porter 2002).

The state's efforts did not quell Muslim criticisms of government corruption and nepotism. An open and increasingly assertive repoliticization of Indonesian campuses began in 1993 with a wave of student activism, both Islamist and nationalist (Aspinall 2005). The activism escalated to unprecedented levels after the clampdown on the Indonesian Democratic Party (Megawati Sukarnoputri's party) in July 1996. The final blow to the regime came in the wake of the Asian financial crisis from mid- to late 1997. With the radical devaluation of the rupiah and sharp price increases in late 1997 and early 1998, the anti-Suharto movement gained momentum. In the spring of 1998, Muslim student organizations, those from Yogyakarta's campuses most notably among them, were instrumental in forcing the president's resignation. These young activists were part of the aspiring new, Muslim middle class. They were part of a generation that was vastly more well educated than previous generations, better informed about national and world events, and more socially connected. Most important for the present study, they were also considerably more interested than previous generations in more normative and textually based forms of Islam.

Muslim Youth: Plural Identifications, Plural Subjectivities

In the aftermath of the New Order, Islamic identifications and groupings among Muslim Javanese youth have become visibly stronger but also more pluralized. Unanticipated by Geertz and many of his generation, the Islamic resurgence has introduced a new dynamic into the shaping of young people's religious identifications and subjective experience. The resurgence has transformed and effectively erased the neat social polarity of Geertz' categories of *santri* and *abangan* and reconstructed the varieties of Javanese Islam. No less significant, whereas two generations ago Islamic piety was the monopoly of Islamic *santri*, today it is an aspiration and reality—a pluralized reality—among most segments of the Muslim public. The long-standing distinction between modernist and traditionalist Muslims has also been greatly changed and pluralized, not least as a result of the rise of *tarbiyah*-linked Islamist groups. Still marginal in terms of their overall numbers, but exercising a normative influence greater than their proportions in society, Indonesia has, in addition, witnessed the growth of Saudi-influenced Salafiyyah. Like their counterparts elsewhere in the world, Salafis aspire to model their practice of Islam on the example of the first three generations of pious Muslims (Ar. *ahl al-salaf*). They also reject democracy, enforce radical gender segregation, and advocate far stricter patterns of Islamic dress and sociability (Wahid 2014; Hasan 2006). Whereas much scholarly attention has been devoted to examining the national-level "political" consequences of the new Islamic scene, the chapters that follow suggest that these broad social and political changes have been paralleled by an important but less systematically studied pluralization and contestation of forms of intimate relations, sociability, and subjectivity—not least with regard to gender. Styles of dress and greeting, interactions with the opposite sex, dating, and marriage patterns among youth continue to be the subject of intense public debate.

Varieties of Muslim Youth

Educated youth have been in the forefront of Indonesia's Islamic resurgence, and students at nonconfessional state universities—as opposed to those at Islamic colleges—have been the origin points of the many new Islamic movements that have proliferated since the fall of the Suharto regime (Anwar 1995; A. G. Karim 2009; Machmudi 2008b). These new Islamic movements, sometimes referred to as "new *santri*" movements, include moderately conservative predication or *dakwah* groups such as the Jema'ah Tarbiyah (Religious Education Movement) and the Kesatuan Aksi Mahasiswa Indonesia (KAMMI, Indonesian Muslim University Student Action Union) as well as more radical, caliphate-promoting and internationally oriented organizations such as the Hizbut Tahrir Indonesia (HTI, Indonesian Party of Liberation) (Osman 2010). In the late 1990s and early 2000s, these groups emerged as a visible and growing presence on campuses such as Gadjah Mada University and other nonconfessional state universities across Indonesia. Although their organizations' ethical and political programs vary, most activists in these new Islamic movements pride themselves in working to "correct" Islamic practices and to banish illegitimate and unfounded innovations (*bid'ah*).

The "new *santri*" movements played a significant role in the student wing of the campaign to oust President Suharto in 1997–1998, but they did not dominate the effort (cf. Madrid 1999). Since the early 2000s, however, these more conservative Islamist groups have taken the lead in many campaigns for campus morality, often displacing their more well-established moderate Muslim and Muslim nationalist rivals. Most of these long-standing Muslim student associations—the Himpunan Mahasiswa Islam (HMI, Association of Muslim University Students), the Pergerakan Mahasiswa Muslim Indonesia (PMII, Indonesian Muslim University Student Movement), and the Ikatan Mahasiswa Muhammadiyah Indonesia (IMM, League of Muhammadiyah University Students)—have some measure of official linkage to Indonesia's existing mass-based Muslim social welfare associations, Muhammadiyah or Nahdlatul Ulama. In terms of membership, most of these mainstream student organizations are as large as or larger than their Islamist counterparts. But the "new *santri*" movements bring greater social discipline and a higher-pitched activism to their efforts to introduce more rigorous campus moral standards, qualities that have allowed them to achieve an influence disproportionate to their actual numbers (cf. Hasan 2010, 2012; A. G. Karim 2009; Machmudi 2008a, 2008b). The more long-standing Muslim student organizations have had to adjust their programs to respond to the challenge posed by the upstart arrivals claiming normative superiority.

This chapter explores the shifting social and religious identifications of Muslim Javanese youth as they emerged in the late 1990s and early 2000s on the campuses of Gadjah Mada and the Sunan Kalijaga State Islamic University in Yogyakarta, as well as the role of Muslim student organizations and other, less formal, student groups in shaping young people's experience. While many of the university students I interviewed reported being actively involved in campus activities and organizations, the reorientations in young people's religious identifications do not necessarily involve participation in an organization or group. For many young people this religious reorientation is expressed more generally—in a greater self-consciousness regarding the understanding and practice of Islam, in their concerted efforts to eschew those customs and traditions deemed un-Islamic, and in the widely articulated desire to simply lead a more pious life (cf. Nilan 2006, 91). Nonetheless, Muslim student organizations have played a key role in setting the tenor of campus religious life and in offering young people social and ethical models for emulation. These models and the discourses that accompany them have spread far more widely as young people have graduated and taken on influential roles in government and public religious life or have simply returned to their hometowns and villages to help "develop their communities."

I begin by sketching out the broad contours of the socioeconomic and religious family backgrounds of students from Gadjah Mada (UGM) and the State Islamic University (UIN). I then describe the Muslim organizations and identifications as they emerged on the campuses of UGM and the UIN in the years just after the fall of the Suharto regime. I use students' life historical and interview material from this period to flesh out the description of youth affiliations and to illustrate the development and directions of new youth groups in the years that followed. An important theme begins to emerge from young people's interviews and life historical data presented here that will be developed throughout the following chapters. Despite—in fact in some ways as a result of—the trend toward greater normativity in the understanding and practice of Islam, the lives, aspirations, and religious affiliations of young people reveal ongoing processes of individuation, contestation, and pluralization (cf. Bowen 2003; Eickelman and Piscatori 2004 [1996]; Mahmood 2005; Schulz 2011). Although there are young people who aspire to practice Islam as a complete and comprehensive way of life (*Islam kaffah*)—one based on a scripturalist understanding of religion as a clear set of commandments and prohibitions that leaves little room for different interpretations or negotiation—in their everyday practice, the vast majority of youth express other, often contradictory, concerns and seem responsive to not one but a variety of moral registers (cf. Nilan 2006; Schielke 2009).

Varieties of Neo-reformist Youth

Yogyakarta's Gadjah Mada University is Indonesia's second-oldest public university and its largest in terms of numbers of students and academic programs.

A nonconfessional state school, in 1999 the university enrolled over thirty-eight thousand students in eighteen faculties and more than one hundred departments.[1] The school has a diverse and heterogeneous student population, drawing young people from all over the archipelago and even from abroad. The largest proportion of its students, however, is ethnic Javanese. They come from the Special District of Yogyakarta and the much larger surrounding province of Central Java, as well as from Jakarta and East Java. A small but nonetheless significant percentage of local students comes from families and neighborhoods linked to the Yogyakartan court, areas that were historically known as strongholds of a Javanized profession of Islam, like that which Merle Ricklefs refers to as Java's "mystic synthesis" (Ricklefs 2007, 5–6). Others grew up in the neighborhoods of Kauman and Karangkajen, which surround the palace in the city's old center, neighborhoods that for several generations have been identified with the variety of modernist Islamic reform associated with Muhammadiyah.

Despite the diversity of the student body, students attending Gadjah Mada share certain general characteristics. A majority come from well-educated middle-class or rising middle-class Indonesian families. About half of students' fathers and one-quarter of mothers surveyed in 1999 and again later in the mid-2000s had one or more years of college. This is to say, the student population comes from families notably better educated than the average Indonesian family.[2] No less striking, many of the parents of Gadjah Mada's students were state employees or civil servants (*pegawai negeri*). Others were professionals who worked in the private sector as teachers or headmasters, journalists, lawyers, dentists, or doctors. Fewer were involved in business (*wiraswasta, pedagangan*), and fewer still obtained a significant percentage of their income from farming. An indication of their families' relatively comfortable economic situation, a majority of students attending Gadjah Mada, even in the early 2000s, reported owning a motorcycle and a computer. Most also received a monthly allowance from their parents that permitted them to buy books and school supplies. Yet despite their parents' generally higher levels of education and relative economic security, more than half of Gadjah Mada's students indicated they would be the first in their families to receive a college degree.

Gadjah Mada University is regarded as one of Indonesia's finest universities, and its students are typically graduates of the nation's best secondary schools. Many students come from highly ranked "favorite"[3] state or Muhammadiyah schools or from well-regarded Catholic high schools. Although college acceptance depends largely on one's performance on the state college entrance exam (the SNM-PTN),[4] Gadjah Mada's students report consistently high class rankings throughout their school careers. Another index of their more middle-class standing, many students had also attended college-preparatory classes after school or worked with private tutors to ensure strong test results. Significantly, very few of Gadjah Mada's students come from *pesantren* backgrounds,[5] and in general young people who had studied in Islamic schools reported having a difficult time competing with students coming from schools that focused entirely on "general" (nonreligious) subjects (see also Thomas 1988, 911).[6]

Many Gadjah Mada students came from families that, two generations ago, were adherents of Javanist or *abangan* Islam, sometimes also referred to as *Islam Jawa* or "Javanese Islam." Their grandparents and even some among their parents had sponsored *slametan* ritual meals at times of life passage; a smaller but still significant percentage had prepared offerings for ancestral and guardian spirits and still believed in the supernatural powers of the Goddess of the South Java Sea, Nyai Rara Kidul (cf. Daniels 2009; Wessing 1997). But for most of these youth the great shift in popular Islamic culture had begun with their parents' generation. Their parents had been the beneficiaries of New Order programs of compulsory religious education in all schools. Those who were Muslim had received instruction in the fundamentals of Islam, learning how to pray, perform the annual Ramadan fast, and pay *zakat* alms.

Notwithstanding their parents' experience, in interviews, students typically described their parents' knowledge of Islam as "basic" (*dasar*), "minimal" (*minim*), or "not that strong" (*tidak begitu kuat*). But while some young people used the term *abangan* or, even more commonly, *Islam Jawa* to describe their parents' religion, almost no student in this group referred to his or her own religious orientation in this way. Rather, these students took pains to distance themselves from their parents' profession of Islam, insisting they would not follow aspects of their parents' religious practice they recognized as polytheistic or heretical (*musyrik, bid'ah*). Most described their own profession of Islam simply as "regular" (*biasa*) or "general" (*umum*) but went on to immediately signal their commitment to a higher religious standard, commenting that they were still working to deepen their knowledge and piety through religious study and practice.

When asked about the reasons for this generational shift in religious self-identification, students unhesitatingly cited the years of required religious education they had received in school as a particularly critical influence. Across Indonesia in the 1980s this instruction had become more rigorous and standardized as a result of improved levels of teacher training and the development of higher-quality instructional materials.[7] The effects of such religious instruction have been cumulative. Translations of religious literature from Muslim majority countries such as Egypt, Yemen, and Saudi Arabia have become more widely available in bookstores and in electronic form, and a significantly higher percentage of religion teachers, even those who teach in nonconfessional, general schools, now receive religious training in the Middle East (Machmudi 2008b). Although students commonly described this instruction as "still insufficient" (*masih kurang*) for what is required to be a good Muslim, they nonetheless argued that it had made them more aware of their religious responsibilities (*lebih sadar akan kewajiban*) than was the case for previous generations. Many also emphasized that school religious instruction made them far more cognizant of those customary Javanese practices properly deemed irreligious "association" (In. *syirik*; Ar. *shirk*), "that which duplicates God" (*yang menduakan Tuhan*) and that should, therefore, be abandoned. Religious instruction in the schools has also encouraged students to seek greater religious knowledge outside of the classroom through regular religious study (*pengajian*),[8] seminars, tapes, books, and pamphlets that proliferated beginning in the late 1980s.[9] Moreover, during religion classes, many teachers required female students to dress modestly and to wear the headscarf (*jilbab*) and urged them to commit to wearing the headscarf continuously as an aspect of their responsibility (*kewajiban*) as a Muslim woman.[10] Beginning in the late 1990s and early 2000s, many young women took this instruction to heart and began wearing the *jilbab* consistently in high school or more often in college (Smith-Hefner 2007).

Diah's[11] family background and life story exemplify many of the characteristics of Gadjah Mada University students outlined above. At the time of our first meeting, Diah was in her third year of medical school at Gadjah Mada. Pretty and petite, she wore a fashionable print silk headscarf pinned tightly under her chin, a long-sleeved blouse, and dark slacks. Her feet were in open-toed sandals with low heels and flesh-colored socks. Her clothing style hinted at slightly modernist Muslim leanings, though she shied away from explicitly identifying with either Muhammadiyah or Nahdlatul Ulama. Her outfit and self-presentation were modestly fashionable and up-to-date, though just a bit severe. She wore a dusting of pale face powder and a barely discernible hint of lipstick and dabbed the perspiration off of her face with a neatly folded handkerchief with lace trim. Diah had three sisters and a brother, all of whom had already graduated from college and married. At twenty-one, she was the youngest in her family and the only one still living with her parents.

Diah's home was located in a comfortably middle-class neighborhood on the outskirts of Yogyakarta where many of the houses were being remodeled and expanded to include second-story additions. Her father was a doctor, and her mother was a housewife. Both of her parents had emphasized the importance of higher education not only for their son but for their four daughters as well. Diah recounted that she had wanted to study economics, but her father was disappointed that none of his older children had gone into medicine. He convinced Diah to list medical school as her second choice on her entrance exam. She had acquiesced, invoking what is a very widespread and "traditional" ideal of generational obligation (Jv. *balas budi*) while applying it to an opportunity that two generations earlier would have been far less available to young women. She mused, "Maybe my parents' prayers were stronger than mine, because I was accepted into medicine and not economics. So, okay, I went along with it because I thought about everything I owe my parents. This was a way to repay them [*balas budi*] for all they have given me."

Despite their prayers being more efficacious than her own, Diah described her parents' religion as "common or lay Islam" (*Islam awam*) and "not very strong" (*tidak begitu kuat*). Indeed, to judge by her descriptions, her parents are striking examples of adherents to the variety of Islam that Merle Ricklefs (2006) has referred to as the "mystic synthesis" among Javanese. The key characteristics of that synthesis are a strong identification as Muslim but a willingness to accommodate a variety of ritual practices, social customs, and even supernatural agents identified with Javanese culture but not explicitly sanctioned (and, in fact, typically condemned) in more self-consciously reformist varieties of Islam.

Like most Javanese of mystic synthetic persuasion today, Diah's parents prayed and followed the fast. Her father even attended Friday prayers at the mosque and her mother participated in routine religious study (*pengajian*). Nonetheless, in Diah's reformist estimation, both of her parents were still "very Javanese" (Jv. *Jawa banget*). Diah's mother continued to put out offerings for the ancestors in the Javanese month of Ruwah (when the spirits of the deceased return to earth and must be appeased) and celebrated life cycle events with traditional *slametan* ritual meals (see Beatty 1999, 2002; Woodward 1989). Once a year her mother also took the family's heirloom dagger (*keris*) to a *dukun* (a traditional specialist of Javanese occult arts) to have it cleaned and blessed (cf. Daniels 2009). Diah recounted, "At Ruwah my mom always makes red and white porridge [*bubur*] and sets it out with coffee and flowers, bananas, cigarettes, and betel. She puts it out and then prays over it. She also bathes the family dagger [*keris*]. I should mention that my mom is actually a very distant relation of the Sultan. The *keris* is a family heirloom. She takes it someplace near the palace to a specialist [*dukun keris*] to have it washed and blessed every year."

Diah's attitudes about these long-maintained Javanese customs, however, showed the clear imprint of her religious education in school, as well as her extracurricular studies in which she had also engaged, albeit only intermittently.

Well, as for me, I don't believe in that stuff. I don't even want to know about it. None of my siblings wants to know either. Like the ritual meal [*slametan*] for seven months pregnancy and the *mitoni* when the baby's first born, and the *tingkeban* when it's seven months and *selapan*[12] . . . and when people die like at one thousand days, you know, for each of those times, there's a *slametan*. But I don't believe in any of it. I won't do it when I have a family of my own. I don't pay any attention when my mom does it either, so I don't know how to do it. It's a waste of time and money and it doesn't have anything to do with Islam. In fact it's like "duplicating god" [*menduakan Tuhan*]. . . . My mom knows I don't agree with her. She's okay with it. She just says, "Yes, kids these days. They aren't interested in custom [*adat*] anymore."

Like so many of the students at Gadjah Mada, Diah described her own religion as "regular or general Islam" (*Islam biasa, umum*), quickly adding that she felt her religious knowledge was still quite limited (*terbatas*). As a medical student, Diah didn't have much time for extracurricular activities, though she read religious literature on her own and attended religious seminars when she could. One of the lessons Diah learned from her religion classes at school and through self-study was that it is a Muslim woman's responsibility (*kewajiban*) to wear the headscarf (*jilbab*).

Diah was first "awakened" (*tergugah*) to the desire to wear the headscarf when in middle school in the early 1990s. Her parents, however, were initially opposed to her wearing it. They appealed to her saying that young people, particularly young women, are "susceptible to change" (*masih labil*), and so it was better to wait until college to be certain about her decision. Diah waited as her parents asked, but she didn't change her mind. In the second semester of her first year of college, she began wearing the headscarf consistently—as did 80 percent of the female students in her medical program—and has worn it consistently ever since. For her, she said, the headscarf was not an end point but a symbol of her desire to become a more pious person, a daily reminder to control her behavior. Veiling was part of a process, she explained, of becoming a more exemplary Muslim.

Rini's story further details and expands upon many of the same themes, particularly those relating to the contest of religious and ethnic identifications in the aftermath of Indonesia's Islamic revival. Like Diah, Rini's appearance and preoccupations identify her as more self-consciously "Islamic," even Islamist, than most of her parents' generation, although she too resisted identification with any particular campus-based or national Islamic organization. I first met Rini at a campus culture show; at the time she was a second-year student at Gadjah Mada studying English literature. She came from a small town in south Central Java where her parents were both civil servants (*pegawai negeri*). Her father worked at a government dam, and her mother was a secretary in a government office. Both had had some college education but left school before finishing their degrees. Rini had one younger sister, who was also a student at Gadjah Mada University, and several older half siblings from her father's two former marriages.

Rini came to our meeting at the campus canteen wearing loose slacks, a long and enveloping *jilbab* that covered her chest and was tightly pinned under the chin, and a long-sleeved blouse. It was an exceptionally hot August day, and beads of perspiration stood out on her forehead. But she politely declined my offer of snacks and a cold drink. She explained to me that she was fasting in an effort to make up for all of the times in middle school she had only pretended to fast during the month of Ramadan. "In middle school I was really rebellious. During the fasting month, I didn't fast. I just pretended to so that my friends wouldn't talk about me. Now I'm worried about all those sins I collected for not fasting. I want to erase the sins I collected in the past. I calculated how many days I missed, and I'm trying to pay back the days I didn't fast before."

Like Diah, Rini referred to her parents' variety of Islam as "common Islam" (*Islam awam*) but then went on to describe them more critically as "Javanese Muslims" and as "more Javanese than Muslim." A generation earlier, when I had first done research in East Java, on the Javanese family and Islam, a significant number of informants would use the phrase "Javanese Islam" to proudly refer to their religious identity, typically in contradistinction to Muslims they deemed too exclusive or "fanatical" (*fanatik*). However, in the case of Rini and many others among the offspring of "Javanese Muslims," being "too Javanese" is now regarded as an admission of intellectual and ethical deficiency—a cultural shortcoming that both explains and demands the redirecting of one's profession of the faith in a more normatively Islamic direction. It was in just this fashion that Rini explained that her parents had only recently begun to perform the daily prayer with any regularity; however, in their daughter's eyes, their Javaneseness still exceeded their Muslimness.

Like Diah's mother, Rini's mom still put out offerings for the spirits. Her father, though less directly involved, supported his wife's practices:

My parents are both more Javanese in their orientation than Muslim. Their religion is just *awam*. *Awam* means not fanatic or anything, not really even religious. For example, my father really only started praying with any regularity maybe seven or eight months ago. In my mom's case, just in the last two months. The process may have begun earlier, but, really, I saw my mom pray for the first time two months ago. She's still really into making offerings for the spirits, like putting out rice porridge and boiled water in a glass. And she wears a waist wrap with special things folded in it (I'm not sure what) to keep her safe. My dad believes in spirits, too, but he leaves it up to my mom to do the offerings.

Like Diah, Rini insisted that she had no interest in these Javanese customs and had no intention of continuing them once she had set up her own household. "I do what my mom tells me and prepare the rice porridge or whatever," she said, "but afterward, when she isn't looking, I just eat the offerings myself and throw the rest out."

Rini's parents were even more strident than Diah's in their opposition to their daughter's decision to wear the headscarf. For most of its history, the New Order government had banned Islamic headscarves in all public schools, finally lifting the prohibition only in 1991.[13] Despite the change in regulation, and despite a dramatic uptick in the number of schoolgirls wearing the headscarf, in the early 2000s many families of government officials (like Rini's)—in which one or both parents were employed as civil servants (*pegawai negeri*)—were still vigorously opposed to veiling (cf. Brenner 1996; Smith-Hefner 2007). During the early and middle years of the New Order, civil servants were neither rewarded for nor encouraged to exhibit public piety, and in Yogyakarta and adjacent areas of Central Java, many offices openly discouraged the headscarf. However, by the mid-2000s, attitudes in government offices even in areas such as Yogyakarta had changed, and allowed or even encouraged more visible displays of Muslim piety. Beginning in this period, too, local and provincial governments in some parts of Indonesia had implemented bylaws (*peraturan daerah, perda*) that had made the headscarf mandatory for schoolgirls and, sometimes, female government officials (Bush 2008; White and Anshor 2008). But in the early years of the post-1998 transition, a good number of parents still invoked the government's earlier suspicions of "radical" or "fanatic" Islam and, as a result, were vehemently opposed to the practice (Alatas and Desliyanti 2002; Brenner 1996; Smith-Hefner 2007).

Rini's parents illustrated this once-widespread view vividly. They regarded their daughter's veiling not as a step in the direction of a more normative profession of Islam but as a deviation away from a more sociable and inclusive "Javanese Islam" and toward religious and political fanaticism. Her parents were particularly worried that the change of faith would hinder their daughter's employment opportunities and possibly scare off potential marriage partners.

Rini first began wearing the headscarf consistently during her third year of high school. As a result of her religious study in secondary school, Rini explained, she had come to recognize the headscarf as a "requirement" (*kewajiban*) for Muslim women. She and her parents argued regularly and loudly about her decision. On two occasions, her parents actually chased her out of the house for wearing the headscarf at home. She said that she convinced them to accept her decision only by pointing out that Muslim dress could be fashionable and by allowing her mother to choose the styles and colors that her mother felt were particularly attractive and complimentary to her complexion.[14]

With their backgrounds in Javanese-Islamic families, Diah and Rini represent a new but important category of Muslim youth on Indonesian campuses. They are among the group that has been referred to by some observers as the "new *santri*." The Indonesian historian of Islam, Yon Machmudi, has described the group vividly as young people "differing from their own parents and the older generation in terms of political orientation, religious ideology, and attitude towards inherited traditions.... Some of them retain their links with traditionalist or modernist groups, some others keep their distance from them and yet still others show radical orientations" (Machmudi 2008a, 69; see also Anwar 1995; A. G. Karim 2009). Most importantly, the young people in this group are far less interested in signaling their allegiance to various aspects of Javanese culture and society and expressing their "Javaneseness," and far more concerned than their parents in expressing their identification with an Islam understood and enacted in a manner devoid of ethnic markers. In the case of those Gadjah Mada students like Diah and Rini, though their style and sensibilities hint at a somewhat more modernist orientation, they self-identify as religiously observant, but typically as neither traditionalist nor modernist.[15] However, their focus on educational achievement, religious norms understood in a nonethnic and "universal" way, and personal development makes them look very similar to Peacock's modernist-reformists, and for this reason they might also be described as "new reformists" or "neo-reformists."

Although "new *santri*" students of the neo-reformist stripe like Diah and Rini made up the single largest category of active Muslim youth on the campus of Gadjah Mada University, there was, however, a significant minority among the Gadjah Mada students who were raised in religiously observant families and did not feel that they needed to disidentify with their parents so as to enact a proper performance of Islam.[16] These young people had grown up in devout Muhammadiyah or, less frequently, NU families, and were comfortable with their identification as *santri* Muslims. As my interviews with parents of Gadjah Mada students confirmed, this earlier generation of observant Muslims had a sense of itself as a "community under siege" and discouraged from open demonstrations of their faith in many official, government contexts (Machmudi 2008a). Under the influence of Indonesia's Islamic resurgence, however, the ranks of the observant Muslim community began to swell in the late 1980s and 1990s. Young people who came from long-established Muhammadiyah, Nahdlatul Ulama, or other observant *santri* families and communities remained a minority—but a minority defined now in terms of their long-standing "Muslim" family background rather than conscious rejection of the variety of Islam professed by their parents.

Agung was one of those students who came from a strongly religious—in this case, Muhammadiyah—background. He had not, however, attended Muhammadiyah schools, explaining that as a male his parents had allowed him to make his own choices with regard to his education from the time he was young; he had chosen, then, to attend "general" schools. I first met him in 2001 when he was a fourth-year student at UGM studying archeology. He arrived for our interview dressed in black slacks and a crisply ironed white shirt. His hair was well cut and carefully combed, and he had a small, carefully trimmed mustache. Agung had come to Yogyakarta from a small town in East Java, originally to attend a better-quality high school than was available in his hometown. His mother had only finished grade school. His father had finished the equivalent of high school in a teacher training program. His parents were anxious to see Agung obtain a university degree and to "surpass their own achievements" (*melebihi orang tua*). Agung had actually failed to gain admission to Gadjah Mada in his first application, but after taking some private preparatory courses, he was eventually accepted. His parents were pleased and extremely proud; Agung was the first from his small town to be matriculated at a prestigious state school like Gadjah Mada.

Agung described his family background as "strongly" Muhammadiyah:

Almost everyone in my neighborhood and in my family is Muhammadiyah. My dad was a Muhammadiyah activist when he was younger. His education was all in Muhammadiyah schools. He was a branch organizer. He did that from the time he was in school until he became a teacher. Even as a new teacher, he was active.

When I was young, my family lived close to the mosque; it was just in front of our house. It belonged to my grandparents. The mosque was in the center of our neighborhood and surrounded by people who were also Muhammadiyah. Most of them were my relatives. I went to the mosque every day for regular prayers [*sholat*] and for *pengajian* every afternoon from Maghrib until Isyak. On weekends and holidays my friends and I would sometimes even sleep there on the floor.

Agung's mother sold small household necessities out of a store in the front of their house. His father worked as a grade school teacher. An exception to Peacock's general findings among *Muhammadiyah* reformists, Agung's father was also an accomplished shadow puppet master, or *dalang wayang*. Agung said he had never felt any interest in *wayang* while growing up, and in fact was dismissive of it. After all, *wayang* is associated with Javanese tradition; the stories are drawn from the Hindu epics, the Mahabarata and the Ramayana. Most Muhammadiyans avoid *wayang* because of those associations. Agung shared these attitudes, but had changed his mind, he said, when he came to Yogyakarta, where the

Javanese arts are more widely appreciated as an important aspect of Java's heritage and tradition. He began studying with a local puppet master—a distant friend of his father's—and performed shadow puppet shows (*wayang kulit*) with him on weekends and in the evenings to support his studies.

Sensitive to the issue of *wayang*'s associations with Java's syncretic past, Agung was at pains to explain that he had come to realize that there was no inherent conflict between *wayang* and Islam. (In this respect, one can note, Agung's personal views were close to those of the national Muhammadiyah leadership in the early 2000s, which had sought to promote a new accommodation with those aspects of ethnic culture that were not contrary to Islam).[17] In fact, he emphasized, *wayang* had historically been used to spread Islam. If the people who hired him to perform wanted to put on *slametan,* he said, it was up to them. If they wanted to make some kind of offering, it was their choice; he did not get involved and did not want to know about it. Actually, his father had told him much the same thing when he was younger, but Agung had refused to listen. Agung recounted,

My dad always said that *wayang* is a way to spread Islam, so there is no conflict with religion. But when I was younger I didn't listen to that. I didn't want to know about it. I thought it was *syirik*. But now I know that although it's true that there are puppeteers [*dalang*] whose beliefs are not Islam but Javanist, it isn't necessary to follow those practices. Neither my father nor I follow any spiritual practices like that, none whatsoever. For example, *dalang* are advised to fast and meditate before a performance. I do that, but I don't have a spiritual experience, just the usual, that's all. It's the same with my father. None of my family follows any *kejawen* [Javanist] practices anymore. We still do birth *slametan* and death *slametan*, but only the religious prayers and the meal [*kenduren*]; there are no offerings.

Despite his strong Muhammadiyah background, it is striking that Agung shared the narrative of students from nonobservant Muslim backgrounds and described his own religious understanding as "barely adequate." Here, as in these other cases, the idea that there is a single, correct understanding and practice of Islam is so pervasive in student circles, and yet so hard to realize in one's own life, that it results in a widespread denigration of one's own religious practice—even where, as with Agung, one hails from a devout reformist Muslim background. "I feel there are still real limitations to my religious knowledge," he said. "I still think my Islam is only 'regular Islam.' I follow the requirements of my religion. But as for the depth and understanding of al Qur'an, the *fiqh*, and all of that, I feel that I really don't know much."

The conviction that there was a single, proper profession of Islam, and that that profession requires a deeper knowledge and practice of Islam, was one of the most consistent themes of the narratives I collected among Gadjah Mada students between 1999 and 2015. Although "piety" can mean different things in different faith traditions, even within Islam (see Deeb 2011; Hassan 2003; Mahmood 2005), the most common feature of pietization among students on national campuses in Indonesia today has to do with this profound shift in what it means to be Muslim (now understood as having the knowledge of a set of normative ethical standards) and what those meanings should imply for behavior (understood as living in conformity with those standards, standards that require a critical distancing from earlier ethnic traditions; cf. Nilan 2006, 91). Many students framed their orientation as one of *kesadaran,* or "consciousness/realization," and described the foundation for their shift in orientation as developing out of this new awareness (Brenner 1996; Smith-Hefner 2007).

This shift in the culture and practice of personal piety is, of course, illustrative of a broader change taking place in Javanese society and Indonesia as a whole. In a conscious effort to improve their religious understanding, students said they regularly bought and read religious literature, listened to religious programming on television or the radio, or engaged in regular discussion of religious topics with friends. What is more, over one-third of Gadjah Mada students surveyed said that in addition to their personal efforts to upgrade their religious knowledge, they were involved in some variety of organized religious activity, such as weekly *pengajian,* tutoring or volunteering at a religious school or foundation, or membership in a Muslim student organization.

Muslim Student Organizations, Gadjah Mada

Whether or not Gadjah Mada University students were directly involved in Muslim student organizations as active members, these organizations had a disproportionate effect on campus life by setting the tone and parameters of campus religious discourse and activism. While there have been occasional conflicts between groups, organizers attempt to downplay their differences, insisting they are insignificant compared to the groups' shared religious focus. The groups nonetheless compete for campus leadership positions in the student senate and faculties. There are also notable differences in the groups' platforms and ethos. Perhaps most significant is the subtle but ongoing "competition in goodness" between groups—visibly expressed on campus through styles of dress and forms of sociability (see Gade 2004a, 2004b; van Doorn-Harder 2006).

In the early 2000s, the organizations with the largest representation among Gadjah Mada's students were the Himpunan Mahasiswa Islam (HMI) and the new but rapidly expanding Kesatuan Aksi Mahasiswa Muslim Indonesia (KAMMI). Groups with significantly smaller student numbers included the Pergerakan Mahasiswa Islam Indonesia (PMII); the Ikatan Mahasiswa Muhammadiyah (IMM); the Jema'ah Shalahuddin (JS, Shalahuddin Mosque Group); Forum Studi dan Dakwah (FOSDA, Forum for Religious Study and Propagation); and somewhat later to the scene, Hizbut Tahrir Indonesia (HTI).[18] I focus here on two groups that have been particularly influential in setting the religious tenor on Gadjah Mada's campus since the early 2000s—HMI and KAMMI.

The Himpunan Mahasiswa Islam, or HMI, has the longest and proudest history among Muslim student organizations in Indonesia. The HMI was initially established in Yogyakarta in 1947, only two years after Indonesian independence. At that time, the organization recognized that many university students were not consistent in or concerned about their daily worship, and it hoped to encourage students to attend to proper religious practice (Albar and Kurniawan 2009; see also Machmudi 2008a). From the 1950s to the 1970s, the HMI was regarded as religiously focused but, on political matters, broadly nationalist in orientation. In the early 1970s, the famous leader of the HMI, Nurcholish Madjid, had made a series of bold speeches in which he rejected the idea that an Islamic state or even Islamic parties were required by Islam. Indeed, he challenged Muslims to recognize that there were aspects of secularization that were not merely consistent with but essential to Islam (Barton 1995).[19] After Madjid's leadership, the HMI came under the direction of a variety of leaders—most less boldly liberalizing than Madjid.[20]

In the mid-1980s, under the constrictive pressures of a Suharto regime intent on "depoliticizing Islam," the HMI had split into two factions: the original HMI and a splinter group, the HMI-MPO.[21] The latter group was one of two major Muslim social organizations that refused to abide by the government's demand that they accept the Pancasila (Five Principles) as their foundation, insisting that their group's sole institutional foundation was Islam. Banned from campus by the government, the HMI-MPO organization went underground until Suharto's ouster.[22] Despite their officially illegal status, the group remained active and quite vocal in organizing demonstrations against the Suharto regime. The group managed to participate in antiregime activities by joining an umbrella organization, the Liga Mahasiswa Muslim Yogyakarta (LMMY, Yogyakarta League of Muslim University Students). With the end of the New Order regime, the HMI-MPO emerged from underground to become a leading voice for pro-democracy reform. Today, the majority of MPO cadres in the Yogyakarta chapter feel that rather than engaging in resistance against the state, the struggle to change society is most appropriately accomplished by working within the system itself (Albar and Kurniawan 2009).

Of the two branches of the HMI, in the years following the fall of Suharto, the MPO was the larger and more influential on Gadjah Mada's campus. Although the platforms of the two groups are in fact similar in many respects, by comparison with the original HMI, the MPO leadership has adopted somewhat more conservative policies particularly with regard to gender segregation and female dress, and some among its regional branches have flirted with Islamist ideologies.[23] Nonetheless, student members emphasized the organization's flexibility with regard to policies and its willingness to accept a variety of religious and political points of view. Despite their modernist foundations, the MPO leadership describes the group as neither modernist-reformist nor "fundamentalist," arguing, "Our refusal to accept the *Pancasila* as our basic foundation indicates that we are not modernist, while our willingness to embrace the Constitution of the Republic [rather than working for the establishment of Indonesia as an Islamic state] indicates that we are not fundamentalist" (Albar and Kurniawan 2009, 11; see also Aspinall 2005).

Arif, a student activist and MPO leader at Gadjah Mada, sketched out many of the organizations' basic tenets. We met for an interview in a coffee shop not far from his boarding house in the summer of 2004. He wore an untucked but neatly buttoned shirt and carefully pressed dark slacks, and immediately lit up a cigarette. Arif's background was somewhat unusual in the context of UGM; he was originally from Jombang in East Java, which he described as "NU territory." His mother was a religion teacher in a state grade school, and his father was a farmer and village head. Arif was the oldest of three children and the only son. He says of his early years,

> I grew up just outside of Jombang near the famous pesantren Tebu Ireng. It's famous because it's really big and its former head, Kyai Pak Hasyim Asyhari, was once Minister of Religion [and also one of the two founders of Nahdlatul Ulama in 1926]. So Tebu Ireng became famous. I actually didn't attend Tebu Ireng but stayed in a small pesantren nearby. But my formal education was all general [*umum*]. I went to state schools—general schools—growing up. It's kind of an accident that I ended up at Gadjah Mada. It was my parents' choice. I chose Airlangga University in East Java. But I got my second choice, which was Gadjah Mada.

Arif said he had joined the HMI after talking with friends and checking out a few other organizations. He said he found the inclusive culture of HMI-MPO the most appealing. His own cultural affiliation with NU speaks to the blurring of sectarian divides within Indonesian Islam:

> I think at MPO one of our most important tenets is the value of inclusivity. For example, most of my friends [MPO members] can't accept the idea of an Islamic state. If we ever had an Islamic state, we fear that we would lose or marginalize all non-Muslim people, or marginalize anyone who was not in agreement with Muslim leadership. I never went to a KAMMI meeting, but I did go to a meeting of the Jema'ah Shalahuddin,[24] where KAMMI types actualize themselves at the intracampus level. But I felt so limited in that context, like if I smoked they reminded me [that I shouldn't] even though I've been smoking since high school! In my mind we at MPO are much more flexible. I mean, Islamic principles are always the basis for action, and, yes, we have many individuals in our organization who are conservative—some prefer to wear the big headscarf and *Islami* clothing styles. But in the MPO, Islam is not automatically or inflexibly applied. It's applied contextually, not only textually. And its contextual interpretation is then placed within the current context. At least that's what I see from my friends at HMI-MPO.

A testimony to the HMI's "inclusivity" and flexibility is that the organization drew students from a variety of backgrounds and with a variety of orientations, including increasing numbers of those who were, as Arif notes above, religiously conservative. As if to underscore this trend, a female member wearing an enveloping and tightly pinned headscarf and a modest, loose tunic and long skirt joined us briefly during our interview and explained that she was initially attracted to the organization because she felt more comfortable with the *"Islami"* attitude of MPO members:

> I was drawn to MPO because I am rather *Islami*. I feel comfortable at the meetings because the atmosphere is polite and respectful, like I never hear swearing or anything like that. I think there's a real respect for women. For example, greeting doesn't exist at MPO; that is, no there's no shaking hands between guys and girls. We all follow that. The basic thing is that they respect me and don't touch me, so it makes me feel protected. And when we talk, the guys don't move the conversation to sexual topics or innuendos. So I don't feel like a sex object. That never happens, so I can just relax and enjoy myself there.

In fact, as early as 1966 the mainline HMI established a separate institute for women at the branch level called KOHATI, the Women's Corps of the HMI. The purpose of the institute was and is still today to offer women the freedom and space to discuss issues of particular interest and relevance to their members, recognizing that many young women—particularly but not only those from religious backgrounds—may be more comfortable speaking out in a same-sex environment (cf. Albar and Kurniawan 2009). The HMI-MPO has also made a concerted effort to encourage women to take on leadership roles in the organization, and a number of women have become heads of *komisariat*, the secretariats at the faculty level. But the major thrust of the organization's platform is, as Arif points out, its willingness to include those from a variety of backgrounds and Muslim orientations. An expression of that inclusive orientation, the HMI-MPO blends more casual, post-ethnic interactional styles with the careful concern for certain Islamic social markers. So, for example, while smoking is tolerated and conservative styles of *Islami* dress are not required of members, the free mixing of genders is negatively sanctioned and handshaking between men and women is rejected in favor of verbal greetings in Arabic.[25]

Considerably more conservative in terms of its social and gender policies is the student organization known as Kesatuan Aksi Mahasiswa Muslim Indonesia, or KAMMI. KAMMI is an organizational offshoot of the as yet informally organized "Religious Education Movement," or Jema'ah Tarbiyah, that first appeared on Indonesian campuses in the mid-1980s (Bubalo and Fealy 2005; see also Feillard and Madinier 2011). The Tarbiyah Movement was deeply influenced by the ideas and ethical aspirations of students who had returned from studying in the Middle East (particularly in Cairo), where they had come into contact with and been influenced by the ideas of the best-known of Middle Eastern Islamist movements, the Muslim Brotherhood (Machmudi 2008b). On Indonesian university campuses in the mid-1980s, members of the Tarbiyah Movement engaged in activities similar to their Muslim Brotherhood counterparts in the Middle East. They organized small groups or *usroh* (Ar. "families") that studied, prayed, and fasted together in an effort to Islamize Indonesian society in a gradualist way, starting with small communities of observant believers. They also organized *halaqah* (Ar. "study circles") that discussed the works of prominent Muslim Brotherhood authors, especially Hasan al-Banna and Sayyid Qutb (Machmudi 2008b).[26]

It is estimated that by the end of the 1990s some 10 to 15 percent of Indonesian students at major state universities were active in campus mosque and proselytizing (or *dakwah*) organizations, the majority of them associated with the Tarbiyah Movement (Bubalo, Fealy, and Mason 2008, 54). *Tarbiyah* activists quickly pushed aside other, more nationalist-minded Muslim student groups (such as the HMI and the PMII) to win control of leadership positions in student governing bodies. *Tarbiyah* activists also managed to take control of the state-sponsored but student-managed religion courses that all Indonesian university students are required to take during each year of their university program.

In February 1998, as the authoritarian Suharto government was teetering toward collapse following the Asian financial crisis, *tarbiyah* activists met in Malang, East Java, and established KAMMI to coordinate Islamist student opposition to the regime (Bubalo, Fealy, and Mason 2008, 54). The organization soon became the most influential and visible of the Muslim student activist groups on Indonesian campuses. In May 1998, when Suharto finally stepped down from office, *tarbiyah* leaders also moved to establish what would be one of the first parties of the post-Suharto era to be ideologically based on Islam, the Justice Party, or Partai Keadilan. Justice Party candidates entered the 1999 parliamentary race on a platform of clean government and social services for the poor. With just a few months to prepare their campaign, they won a respectable 1.4 percent of the vote. In the 2004 elections the party changed its name to the "Prosperous Justice Party" (Partai Keadilan Sejatera, PKS), and went on to win 7.3 percent of the vote, a share that gave the party forty-five seats out of five hundred in the national legislature (Machmudi 2008a, 4; see also Bubalo, Fealy, and Mason 2008).[27]

Although KAMMI claims independence from the Prosperous Justice Party, it shares the party's platform of clean government and social welfare services for the poor. Neither KAMMI nor the PKS overtly militate for an Islamic state or for the statewide implementation of Islamic law or shari'a. However, both groups insist that with proper education and religious understanding Muslim Indonesians will come to see the wisdom and justice of the law, and embrace it as their own. Equally important, in provinces in Indonesia where regional bylaws of an "Islamic" nature were implemented in the early to mid-2000s, PKS activists were among their enthusiastic proponents (Bush 2008; Lindsey 2012).[28]

Informed by the ideas of the Muslim Brotherhood and its founder, Hasan al-Banna, KAMMI activists present Islam as a complete and comprehensive way of life (*Islam kaffah*) (Bubalo and Fealy 2005; see also Eickelman and Piscatori 2004 [1996]). Rather than emphasizing the direct and top-down Islamization of the state, however, the movement focuses its efforts on the reform of the individual and lifestyle as an avenue to broader societal reform. In interviews, KAMMI student activists repeatedly emphasized that the first step toward this broader social and political change is with the reform of one's self, one's circle of friends, one's family, and one's neighborhood.[29] In other words, KAMMI is an organization dedicated to the reform and "Islamization" of society by way of, at least in the first instance, Muslim forms of sociability (cf. Mahmood 2005). KAMMI, however, is not and has never been an exclusively pietistic organization like the women's groups portrayed in Saba Mahmood's Cariene account (Mahmood 2005); they have always made clear their conviction that pietization is a necessary first step toward the broader Islamization of state and society (cf. Hasan 2012; Noor 2011).[30]

On the Gadjah Mada campus in the 2000s, KAMMI was best known among Islamist student organizations for its ability to attract middle-class youth from nominally Muslim (*abangan* or *Islam Jawa*) families and provide them with something of a Muslim "born-again" conversion experience. Like new or revitalized adherents to other faith traditions, many among these KAMMI recruits make clear that, in reaction against what they see as the moral chaos of campus life and Indonesian society, they were drawn to the organization and its vision of Islam because it seemed to offer an unambiguous and comprehensive set of moral guidelines. After an earlier period of non-Islamic living, many also bring to their faith the commitment and enthusiasm of a religious convert.

In the early 2000s, KAMMI organizers readily acknowledged that female participants were equal to or even surpassed the number of males (cf. Hasanudin and Nurrahman 2009). Somewhat higher rates of female participation relative to male participation are widely reported for the Prosperous Justice Party (the PKS) as well but are difficult to substantiate. Equally interesting, a disproportionate number of KAMMI activists are found at large and officially "secular" state universities like Gadjah Mada University rather than Muslim institutions like the Sunan Kalijaga State Islamic University, as well as from the exact sciences and technical fields, among them political science, economics, mathematics, medicine, pharmacy, dentistry, and engineering—fields in which women are typically a distinct minority.[31]

Mona's background and life story illustrate many of the general characteristics of KAMMI recruits and the KAMMI profession of Islam. Mona was an active member of KAMMI and had recently taken on an important leadership position in the group. At the time of our interview in 2006, she was a third-year student at Gadjah Mada in the Faculty of Math and Science. She wore a long loose tunic with gathered sleeves over a long, loose skirt. Her cream-colored and rather stark *jilbab* was voluminous, fully covering her chest down to her waist. So as not to allow the exposure of any skin, she also wore flesh-colored socks and flat sandals. Her tightly pinned headscarf and wire-rim glasses accentuated her round face, which showed no trace of makeup.

Mona said her family lived in Jakarta. When she was younger, they had lived in Yogyakarta, near her grandparents, and Mona had attended a rather conservative *madrasah*. But when she was in middle school her family moved to Jakarta, and from that time on Mona had attended only nonconfessional state schools. She described her parents as "very liberal" and "not very religious." Her dad was a general manager of a large corporation. Her mother had worked as a businesswoman for several years but had stopped at her husband's urging and now ran a small, part-time business out of her home. Mona explained,

My parents are very liberal. They said, "Go ahead, do what you want to as long as you're still a Muslim, choose your own path." They let us decide. They aren't very religious. They *sholat* only occasionally and my mom wears sleeveless dresses [*rok you-can-see*] that show the shape of her body when they go out with their business associates.

I love my parents and in the Qur'an it's very clear that you should save your parents from the flames of hell. But as a child, all you can do is let them know in a gentle way that they should change that behavior. Thanks be to God, since they went on the hajj this past year, my mom has begun to dress a bit more modestly.

It was in Mona's third year of high school that she decided to wear the head-scarf. She had worn it off and on in middle school, but because she played bas-ketball, she couldn't wear it all the time. The team uniform consisted of shorts and a short-sleeved jersey. Her coach had warned her, "If you take up the *jilbab* you won't be able to play sports, and if you don't play sports, you'll gain weight." Mona fought with the school for three months to allow her to continue to play basketball wearing long pants, a long-sleeved shirt, and a headscarf. The school refused. Finally, she said she had asked herself, "Will basketball get me into heaven?" Mona quit the team. Her coach was right, she said with a wry smile, "After I quit, I gained eight kilos!"

At Gadjah Mada, Mona had first become a member of the HMI. However, she explained, she found that the group was not sufficiently "clear and consis-tent" in the guidelines it provided; it did not provide the level of commitment to the Qur'an and the Sunnah that she was looking for. She consulted with friends, who urged her to try out KAMMI. She said she attended several meetings and found there the clear-cut set of life rules she felt she needed. So she decided to join: "In KAMMI our guides are truly the Qur'an and the Sunnah. The truth is in them and needs no translation. That's our commitment—to maintain the Qur'an and Sunnah and to apply their truth to all aspects of our lives [*secara kaffah*]. In KAMMI we aren't hoping that Indonesia becomes an Islamic state. We only want an Islamic system. When that system is applied in its entirety, not just partially, and there is no interpretation, then Islam will be merciful to all. That's what we work for."

Mona said she had struggled with some of the more conservative aspects of KAMMI's gender policies. During her training to become a leader within the organization she had argued with her trainers over what she perceived as certain gender inequalities with regard to the position of women:

I gave them a hard time because I really wondered why a woman was not allowed to lead a man, you know, like in prayer, and why a woman is not con-sidered an equal witness. I studied it for a long time, and I discussed it with my friends. And after a long time, maybe I was given a holy light/guidance by God, but I realized that my radicalness was the result of my lack of under-standing. I realized that it [the difference between male and female] has to do with woman's God-given nature [*kodrat*]. According to their nature, women are soft, meek, and gentle. So that no matter how hard or tough I am in governing this organization (you know, I just recently became general secretary), whenever I had a political opponent who approached me with a sad voice, it would crush my heart, and I would give in. No matter what you want to say, that's a fact. Women often use their feelings rather than their head. I have to admit that. I've only admitted that recently. I only admitted it after I studied it. So it makes complete sense that as a witness, you should have two women for each one man. This doesn't mean that God considers women to be somehow less reliable than men. But because of the types of cases they will be confronted with, they might become too emotional. Problems have to be dealt with in a rational way. Sometimes women, in fact, cannot use their reason. It's a reality I will accept. At this moment I accept it.

To bolster her argument (that there are no gender inequities in KAMMI), Mona pointed to the fact that unlike the HMI, KAMMI did not have a separate women's section. "This clearly indicates that Islam [and KAMMI] does not marginalize women." The issue, as she saw it, was not lack of leadership ability ("women are bright; why shouldn't they transmit their knowledge?") but how women could lead in a manner consistent with their "softer" and "less rational" feminine *kodrat*, or God-given nature.

With their distinctive dress and strict patterns of gender sociability, female members of KAMMI such as Mona are highly visible on the Gadjah Mada University campus. They wear far more enveloping headscarves than most Muslim women, ones drawn tightly around the face and pinned under the chin so that the hair and ears are completely covered. The fabric extends over the chest in the front and over the hips in the back. Like Mona, they prefer loose long-sleeved tunics and long skirts or layered jumpers over long dresses and wear opaque flesh-colored socks. (As Mona explained, the layers of clothing obscured the shape of the body—considered religiously correct, but also especially useful, she said, for women who had a few extra pounds like her). The colors of their clothing are typically restrained, limited to light solid-colored or pastel scarves and dark-colored tunics and skirts. While fashionable fabrics, eye-catching colors, and trendy prints and patterns have become popular for women's headscarves in Indonesia, KAMMI women prefer dark colors and limit decoration on their headscarves to a small edging of simple cotton lace.

KAMMI women say they cover themselves not only to identify themselves as pious Muslims but also to prevent men from becoming sexually aroused, an outcome for which women are regarded as largely responsible in mainline *fiqh* commentaries in Islam (cf. Ali 2006; Mir-Hosseini 2003). Their maximally modest dress is meant to discourage lust or sexual desire on the part of men and to guard against the possibility of *zina*, illicit sex or fornication. For similar reasons, KAMMI has instituted a variety of stringent gender rules for its members that serve to regulate cross-gender greetings, gaze, seating arrangements, and even modes of transportation. These rules forbid unrelated male and female members to touch, require the separation of male and female members at meetings by a cloth or barrier, and insist that members avoid being in close proximity with a member of the opposite sex who is not related (*muhrim*) without a chaperone present. In a manner consistent with Muslim Brotherhood adepts in other parts of the world, KAMMI members do not shake hands with members of the opposite sex but instead greet each other verbally, almost always with the Arabic exchange of blessings, "*Assalamualaikum.*" Prolonged eye contact or even furtive glances between the sexes are similarly discouraged because these acts too can arouse desire. Female members of KAMMI are also not allowed to ride on the back of an unrelated male's motorcycle—a situation that would necessarily place them in inappropriate proximity with a member of the opposite sex and a challenge for those young women who do not own their own mode of transportation.[32]

Since the early 2000s, KAMMI has grown rapidly and many observers state that it has become the largest Muslim student organization on UGM's campus. Estimates made by KAMMI leadership in the mid- to late 2000s were that KAMMI members comprised 10 to 15 percent of the student body at Gadjah Mada and similar (nonconfessional) universities, though exact numbers are hard to come by (Bubalo, Fealy, and Mason 2008, 54). Whatever the organization's actual size, KAMMI has had a disproportionate effect on campus life. KAMMI activists are highly visible and extremely well organized, and their styles of sociability set them apart from non-Muslims and secular Muslims quite clearly. Equally important as far as many recruits are concerned, in an environment that many new students find disorienting and ethically dangerous, KAMMI offers a model for Islamic living that is clear, consistent, and rule-bound rather than relativist. In this manner, KAMMI aspires to set the standard for *Islami* styles of sociability and gender interaction in a manner intended to be not only comprehensive but also in countercultural opposition to the standards and behaviors of other, even mainline, Muslim students.

Conservative Muslim groups such as KAMMI and the significantly smaller Hizbut Tahrir attract young people overwhelmingly from the ranks of the "new *santri*"—individuals whose lives and family backgrounds prior to their new Islamic affiliation tended to reflect the mixed influences of Javanese (or another regional) culture, Indonesian nationalism, global consumerism, and pop-culture media. "Converts" like Mona had often explored other organizations and found their moral guidance wanting. For Mona and others, a standard refrain is that these other Muslim organizations were insufficiently comprehensive in their interpretation and implementation of religious requirements as set forth in the Qur'an and hadith. However, precisely because so many of the KAMMI students come from nominal Muslim backgrounds, few really have the knowledge, training, or authority to say whether the approach to Islamic ethics foregrounded in Muhammadiyah or NU teachings is authentic or comprehensive at all. Moreover, even in the religious study circles (Ar. *halaqa*) in which KAMMI students relearn the principles of their faith, the emphasis is on not the in-depth study of Islamic traditions but a boot-camp-like immersion in what are said to be the core, clear, and easy principles of faith.

It is precisely because KAMMI's search for a "comprehensive" Islam proceeds by way of digest-like summaries and drills that Muslim students who come from traditionalist/*pesantren* backgrounds often find the religious training and lessons offered in KAMMI programs to be superficial and, in their eyes, distant from cherished and long-standing Islamic traditions. Rather than moving carefully and methodically through the hadith or classical commentaries under the careful guidance of a *kyai*, these students observe, KAMMI activists throw themselves into difficult texts and complex legal issues without the knowledge or history required to grasp the issues in question (see A. G. Karim 2009). *Santri* from the nearby Sunan Kalijaga State Islamic University who hailed from NU backgrounds—even those who took exception to the pluralist and democratic views of their NU friends—were among those who most consistently found the neo-*santri* approach to "authentic" Islam "thin" (*tipis*) and unconvincing. Trained in their *fiqh* studies to understand that there is always diversity in legal rulings, few among these NU youth were inclined to publicly castigate their KAMMI comrades. Instead they would good naturedly wonder aloud whether the fervor of their KAMMI friends wasn't an expression of an insecurity with regard to their mastery of Islamic sources and their identity as Muslims.

Varieties of Neo-traditionalist Youth

The Sunan Kalijaga State Islamic University, or UIN, in Yogyakarta is one of eighteen state Islamic institutes of higher education established throughout Indonesia just prior to or during the New Order period.[33] Unlike nonconfessional state universities such as Gadjah Mada University that are under the auspices of the Ministry of Education, the State Islamic Universities, as Islamic institutions, are under the Ministry of Religion. Yogyakarta's State Islamic University (UIN) is located in the northeastern portion of the city in the neighborhood known as Sapen. The campus centers on a large and impressive university mosque surrounded by gnarled shade trees and set at the top of a steep flight of tiled steps.[34]

In the early 2000s, the UIN had a modest enrollment of about fifteen thousand students. However, in the mid-2000s the school underwent a major restructuring to become a multifaculty general university with religious and nonreligious faculties, and the student body swelled to over twenty-eight thousand (see Azra, Afrianty, and Hefner 2007; Jamhari and Jabali 2002; Lukens-Bull 2013). By 2010, almost half of the students in the State Islamic University were majoring in nonreligious subjects, including business, general education, psychology, and sociology—though even nonreligion majors are still required to take a significantly larger number of courses in Islamic studies than their counterparts in the "secular" university system. A now scant majority of UIN's students continue to enroll in the religious faculties, the most popular of which are Islamic education (*tarbiyah*) and Islamic law (*shari'a*), followed by Islamic propagation (*dakwah*) and theology (*ushuluddin*).

Not surprisingly, many of the parents of State Islamic University students emphasized the importance of a religious education for their children (especially for their daughters), and said they chose to send their children to the UIN because of their expectation that the school would provide a safe, moral environment. Many said they hoped their offspring would use their education to secure employment of a religious or entrepreneurial nature or to combine both and establish their own religious school or foundation. In the early 2000s, some parents expressed ambivalence about the white-collar government jobs (*pegawai negeri*) often associated with a degree from a nonconfessional state university. However, despite this ambivalence associated with the civil service, there were always State Islamic University students who have taken advantage of the expansion of government positions involving the teaching of religion and the adjudication of religious law. State Islamic Universities such as that in Yogyakarta have long provided the lion's share of teachers of Arabic and of Islam required for government and private religion schools. The high enrollments of students in Islamic law (shari'a) reflect perceived employment opportunities in government service, particularly in the Office of Religious Affairs (Kantor Urusan Agama or KUA) and the Ministry of Religious Affairs (Kementerian Agama or MORA), which have jurisdiction over matters of marriage, divorce, and inheritance (Johnson, Gaylord, and Chamberland 1993, 79; Lindsey 2012).

As with the students at Gadjah Mada University, those attending the State Islamic University in Yogyakarta shared certain features of family background and religious formation. In contrast to the prevailing pattern among Gadjah Mada students, however, most UIN students were from the countryside and had grown up in traditionalist *santri* families. The great majority came from villages (*desa/dusun*) or rural subdistricts (*kecamatan*) in Central, West, and East Java—areas with a heavy concentration of NU *pesantren.* Their parents tended to be based in traditional middle-class and lower-middle-class professions, such as farming, trade, small-scale merchandising, and religious education. About 20 percent of the fathers of State Islamic University students surveyed were state or government employees (*pegawai negeri*); of these, however, the overwhelming majority served as religion teachers in state schools, a category of civil servant that is consistently differentiated from government officials in fields of nonreligious administration. Among the state employees were also a small number of fathers who filled positions in village or subdistrict (*kabupaten*) government. But the most striking background feature of UIN students was the considerable number of fathers and mothers who were involved in some capacity in teaching or administering Islamic boarding schools (*pesantren*), schools that are typically organized as private family enterprises or foundations (see Dhofier 1999 [1982]; Lukens-Bull 2005). Although this characteristic of UIN students has shifted somewhat with the establishment of nonreligious faculties and programs, it continues to exert an important influence on student attitudes, including their understanding of Islam.

Surveys from the initial period of my research (1999–2005) revealed that the educational profile of State Islamic students' families also differed markedly from that of students at Gadjah Mada University. Compared with their Gadjah Mada counterparts, parents of State Islamic University students had significantly lower levels of schooling, most of which had taken place in *pesantren* or the *madrasah* religious schools associated with them. Within the *madrasah* system, there are three educational levels that parallel the levels within the general (*umum*) school system (Johnson, Gaylord, and Chamberland 1993). At the primary school level is the *madrasah ibtidayah* (MI), which is roughly equivalent to elementary school. At the lower secondary level is the *madrasah tsanawiyah* (MT), which is roughly equivalent to middle school. Finally, at the upper secondary level is the *madrasah aliyah* (MA), equivalent to high school in the general school system (cf. Azra, Afrianty, and Hefner 2007). Some 40 percent of mothers and 25 percent of fathers of UIN students had received only a grade school education in a *madrasah ibtidayah,* and twice as many mothers as fathers had ended their education at *madrasah tsanawiyah* (middle school)—most often to marry. Very few mothers or fathers had any schooling beyond the secondary level (*madrasah aliyah*); those who did typically had only a year or two of teacher training. Many fathers of State Islamic University students, however, had spent as many as twelve years in a *pesantren* school engaged in in-depth religious study. In the overwhelming majority of cases, therefore, students who attended UIN would be the first members of their families to receive a university degree.

Like their parents, the majority of State Islamic University students in the early 2000s—fully 81 percent of men and 65 percent of women according to my surveys and interviews—had attended religious schools, rather than general, nonconfessional schools (*sekolah umum*). A majority of these schools were affiliated with the traditionalist Nahdlatul Ulama. Irwan, a student in his final semester at the State Islamic University in the Faculty of Education (Tarbiyah), is an example of this educational profile; his situation and life history share many features with those of other male students at the UIN. We were introduced by a mutual friend, and I arranged to meet him on the university campus. At the time of our meeting in 2002, Irwan was twenty-seven. Dressed in worn jeans and a T-shirt, he hardly looked his age. Irwan was originally from rural East Java, a province known as a "warehouse" for religious boarding schools (*gudang pesantren*). He was the third of seven children. His father was a fruit farmer, and his mother was a housewife. His mother had graduated from a middle school *madrasah* (*madrasah tsanawiyah*) and had then gone on to complete a two-year training program for religion teachers. His father had attended a general grade school until the age of twelve and then attended a Muslim boarding school (*pesantren*) for seven years. It was a small *pesantren,* run by a distant relative. His parents' background thus marked Irwan's formation as solidly traditionalist *santri.* Irwin described his family as follows: "My family is traditional santri [*santri kolot*]. My parents' Islam is very strong [*sangat ketat*]. My dad attended the general school in his village because it was close to his house. But my grandfather really hated the colonial government, and he equated the general education system with colonial education. So he didn't allow my father to go further than grade school and then he sent him to my great-uncle's *pesantren.* My dad really liked it there. He wanted to become a *kyai,* but it didn't work out."

Irwan's father had sent all of his own children to the same *pesantren* boarding school that he had attended. In the afternoons, they had studied general subjects in a nearby *madrasah*. Reflecting a changed perception now widespread in Nahdlatul Ulama and traditionalist Muslim circles, Irwan said that although his father shared some of his own father's mistrust of the state educational system, he had come to recognize the importance of a general education in today's economy. He had seen the children of a relative who had moved to Jakarta successfully graduate from state (nonconfessional) schools. They had all gone on to college and had found stable jobs. As a result, Irwan's father decided to urge his own sons to continue their schooling. With the exception of Irwan, they had enrolled in two-year degree programs. By contrast, none of Irwan's sisters had gone further than high school. Irwan explained, "I think my dad really did want to send my sisters to college, too, but he couldn't afford it. He realized that all of us [boys] had to work to help support ourselves while studying. He wasn't confident that the girls could do that, and he knew he couldn't support them."

Irwan would be the first in his family to receive a diploma from a four-year institution, and there was considerable pressure on him to finish. He was older than much of his cohort because he had had to wait to start college; his brother had been taking courses for a diploma in English at a private school, and his parents didn't have enough money to support them both at the same time. Now Irwan was struggling to complete his senior thesis (*skripsi*) while working full-time for Nahdlatul Ulama as a regional organizer. "My parents are really happy that I am involved with NU," he commented, "because they come from an NU background and they are all active in NU at the local level." Irwan said that he hoped to get a job with a nongovernmental organization (known in Indonesia as LSM, Lembaga Swadaya Masyarakat) after graduation and, like many State Islamic University students, said that he wanted to do something with his knowledge to help develop his community back home.

By comparison with many of their counterparts at Gadjah Mada, State Islamic University students like Irwan identified closely with their parents' profession of Islam. Perhaps not surprisingly given the numbers who had attended Muslim schools (*madrasah* and *pesantren*), very few identified their religious orientation as "regular" (*biasa*) or "general" (*umum*). For similar reasons, few State Islamic University students described their parents as *abangan*. Instead, students used terms like "traditional NU" (*NU tradisional*), "traditional santri" (*santri kolot*), or "very religious *santri*" (*santri yang sangat kental*) to describe their religious background and upbringing and in explaining their own religious identification. As mentioned briefly above, a result of the depth and consistency of their religious formation, State Islamic University students and their parents tended to be critical of the Islamist activism of the "new *santri*" variety, which they associated with nominal Muslims "converted to" a born-again profession of the faith—and with a lack of familiarity with the rich textual and jurisprudential commentaries of classical Islam.

Many of the themes that emerge from Irwan's background—in particular the emphasis placed on religious education and the personal identification with a religious community (that of NU) and an educational system (the *pesantren*) that mediates one's identification with Islam as a way of life and as a culture—also figured prominently in the life histories of women at the UIN. Nurul, a classmate of Irwan, was a second-year student in the Faculty of Ushuluddin (Theology), specializing in *tafsir hadith* (hadith interpretation). When I first met her in 2001 she was twenty-one and still adjusting to life in the urban environment of Yogyakarta. Nurul came from a rural area of Central Java about two hundred kilometers to the northeast of Yogya. She described her home village as a bastion of Nahdlatul Ulama activism, known for its many *pesantren salaf* (religious schools focused on the study of traditionalist Islamic subjects, including jurisprudence [*fiqh*] and Sufism [*tasawwuf*]). Dressed modestly but far less severely than KAMMI women like Mona, Nurul wore a scarf of a soft blue fabric draped loosely over her shoulders and chest and pinned under her chin. She had on a modest dark blue flower-print, long-sleeved tunic and a full-length skirt. She wore sandals but no socks—a not-so-subtle sign she was not of Islamist-reformist persuasion.

Nurul was the oldest of four children—all of them girls. Her father ran a small business selling construction material. He provided religious instruction at the local mosque each evening, and occasionally gave sermons and offered religious seminars. Nurul's mother had once been a religion teacher, too, but had stopped when her children were small. Now she helped her husband with the business, dealing with most of the financial issues.

Nurul's father had graduated from a religious upper school (a *madrasah aliyah*, the equivalent of high school) and had then studied at a *pesantren* for ten years. Her mother had also attended a *madrasah aliyah* but had gotten married before graduating. She was seventeen at the time; Nurul's father was twenty-seven. Nurul described her father as "moderate" in many of his viewpoints, not least of all his commitment to and pride in Indonesian nationhood. However, he was unstinting in his insistence that she attend religious schools and continue to practice her religion. Although Nurul had expressed an interest in "studying language or political science" from the time she was young and had begged her parents to allow her to attend general (*umum*) schools for middle school or high school, her father "put more emphasis on religion than general knowledge" and had sent her to a nearby *madrasah tsanawiyah* and then to a *madrasah aliyah*.

For Nurul and Irwan, like most of the students attending the State Islamic University, Islam was understood as a taken-for-granted aspect of their basic identity and as closely connected to their families and communities. For most, their Islam was not new or rediscovered but something that had been an integral and authentic part of their lives since they were young. Irwan, for example, said that he just couldn't imagine that any of his friends back home would *not* do their daily prayers or go to *pengajian* religious study. It was simply what everyone did, the foundation of family and community life. Similarly, when asked about the headscarf she wore, Nurul responded that for her it was never a conscious decision (to wear it or not to wear it); it was a comfortable part of her family life and upbringing. "For me, the headscarf is like a symbol or an identity. It was like that in *aliyah* [secondary school]; we all wore it, not because it was a guarantee of superior morality, but because of the culture."

Yet despite their devout religious backgrounds, State Islamic University students had also experienced the effects of the Islamic resurgence and expressed a renewed interest in religious normativity. Although many referred to their religious training and upbringing as "culturally NU," in their desire to rationalize and articulate their religious practice, these young people are more aptly seen as part of a new wave of religious culture and piety in Nahdlatul Ulama. It is an Islamic culture that aspires to preserve the identification and engagement with a long-established legacy of classical Islamic learning and practice, but hopes to do so with a more self-conscious and higher-education-mediated understanding of how those traditions should be experienced.[35] It is in this sense that these young people are perhaps more aptly referred to not as traditionalists (as many of their parents) but as "new" or "neo-traditionalists."

So, for example, although Nurul said that she considered veiling simply a comfortable part of her culture and socialization, through her coursework and through discussions with classmates at the State Islamic University, she said she had come to realize that it was more than just a cultural symbol: it was a religious requirement (*kewajiban*) for Muslim women. As a result, she had become more conscious of how she wore it, was now careful to cover all of her hair, ears, and neck, and pinned it more securely so that it would not slip off when she moved. Other UIN students, including Irwan, recounted how elements of Javanese tradition viewed as being at odds with Islamic norms—among them feasts and celebrations to commemorate the dead and community-wide *slametan* to appease ancestor spirits and bless the harvest—had gradually been abandoned by their families and communities. Other ceremonies, such as weddings and circumcisions, had become streamlined and more religiously focused. In some cases these shifts have been the result of the urgings of the recent generation of neo-traditionalist youth who have absorbed the discourses of their religious training and of the campus groups and organizations to which they have been exposed.

State Islamic University Organizational Life

As a relatively small, Muslim institution, the State Islamic University offers far fewer extracurricular activities than does Gadjah Mada. State Islamic University students also expressed a higher level of dissatisfaction with their coursework and professors. Though this dissatisfaction had lessened considerably by 2010 or so, many students in the early 2000s said they found their university courses were merely a repetition of materials they had already mastered in their years spent in religious study in *madrasah* or *pesantren* boarding schools. One result of this dissatisfaction was the very high rate of participation among State Islamic University students especially in the late 1990s and early 2000s in student-organized and student-led study circles (Ar. *halaqa*) and seminars. Student groups developed their own curriculum and study guides, and some occasionally even invited guest lecturers such as visiting anthropologists. Whether through reading great masters of Islamic theology such as the eleventh-century jurist and Sufi al-Ghazali (a figure enormously popular in NU university circles) or participating in *salawat* prayer meetings involving supplications to the Prophet Muhammad, however, these young students differed from their Islamist counterparts at Gadjah Mada University in their firm confidence that the traditionalist Islam to which they and their communities were heir is a rich and living civilizational tradition.

It was in large part through their involvement in these study groups and in Muslim religious organizations that UIN students had become more conscious of the traditions they had once taken for granted, and many strove to increase their understanding and improve their practice. Fully 74 percent of the State Islamic University students surveyed reported some level of involvement in a Muslim student organization. A reflection of their *pesantren* backgrounds, the largest number of students—over 40 percent of those surveyed and interviewed—were members of the NU-affiliated PMII (see Anis and Yahya 2009). Considerably smaller numbers indicated involvement with the HMI and the IMM.[36]

Although its star has dimmed a bit from the activist years of the late 1990s and early 2000s, the Pergerakan Mahasiswa Islam Indonesia or PMII is still today known as the most progressive and "plural" of the major Muslim student organizations. It is and was throughout the 1990s and early 2000s (when activism was still in the air) also among the most loosely organized, a quality that sometimes handicapped the leadership's ability to coordinate demonstrations—or respond to the challenge presented by rival Islamist groups. The PMII is also considered among the most progressive of the Muslim student organizations with regard to politics and gender issues. The organization has been open to working with outside foundations and various LSM/NGOs (many with funding from Western sources)[37]; as a result, its members are typically exposed to discourses of civil society, religious pluralism, and gender sensitivity (cf. Blackburn 2004; Schröter 2013; Syamsiyatun 2008; van Doorn-Harder 2006). Because the organization's membership is plural with regard to political and social/cultural orientations and encourages intellectual debate, however, there is also greater plurality and internal inconsistency in members' points of view than is the case among rival student organizations (cf. Saluz 2009).

Zaki was typical of the male activists associated with the PMII in the early years of the post-Suharto period of Reformasi. Originally from a rural area of East Java, Zaki was the fourth of seven children and the only one of the seven who had gone on to college. At the time of our interview, he was a third-year student at the State Islamic University in the Faculty of Shari'a (Islamic Law) specializing in *hukum pidana politik* (criminal law). I met him at the cramped student office of the PMII with three other male students. Zaki wore what he laughingly described as the PMII "male activist's uniform": worn jeans and a wrinkled T-shirt. He affected an interactional style that was deliberately casual, open, and, at times, brashly if jokingly direct. There were no polite formalities or small talk (*basa basi*) and no coffee or tea to accompany the doughnuts I had brought. He and the three other male students present proceeded over the course of our conversation to chain-smoke one cigarette after another until a foggy haze hung over the room. We sat on mats on the floor; there was little else in the room.

Zaki said he had become involved with the PMII because he was disappointed in the quality of his courses at UIN. He complained that teachers often didn't show up for classes, the materials they presented were often not sufficiently challenging, and the teaching methods were not up to date. Out of boredom, he said, he would look for additional readings outside of those listed on the syllabus, but his teachers would accept only information from their own lectures and handouts. He and his friends sought intellectual stimulation in activities outside of the classroom. As he described it, "Lots of my friends in the PMII learn everything from their outside activities and rarely go to their regular classes. Last semester I had two classes that I never attended. I just asked the professor for the review materials and took the final exam. For most classes, you just memorize the review materials anyway. Besides, I understood the material because I'm often involved in seminars or study groups on those topics. I've never had to retake a class because of a poor grade."

Zaki had worked with the PMII to organize study groups and seminars on topics such as critical discourses on religion, religious pluralism, feminism and religion, politics and religion, and English. Unlike students from Gadjah Mada, many State Islamic University students felt that they had received adequate religious education through their years spent in religious schools. Those like Zaki, who were in religious fields of study, were often less intent on adding to their religious knowledge than on critically reflecting on what they had been taught and considering more deeply how Islam might be applied to politics, social life, and to personal relationships.[38] While Zaki identified closely with his religious background and described his parents as "strongly Islamic," he, like many students from traditionalist backgrounds, was secure enough in his religious foundation to question some elements of that background.

In part as the result of the efforts of campus organizations such as the PMII, there emerged a small but vocal group of UIN students who staked out a critical or progressive Muslim-democratic position. Although one occasionally encountered a student of this sort who hailed from a Muhammadiyah or otherwise modernist background, the overwhelming majority were "culturally NU" neo-traditionalists. These youth referred to their approach to the profession of Islam as "transformative." In a similar spirit, some neo-traditionalist women— and even a few men—identified themselves as "Muslim feminists." In fact, it is noteworthy that during the late 1990s and into the 2000s the great majority of Muslim feminist activists came out of National Islamic Universities such as the Sunan Kalijaga State Islamic University rather than out of nonconfessional state universities such as Gadjah Mada University (cf. Schröter 2013; Syamsiyatun 2008; van Doorn-Harder 2006). In the heady period of progressive activism from the mid-1990s to Abdurrahman Wahid's resignation from the presidency in August 2001, a small number of students from the UIN described themselves in even more radical terms, calling themselves "left Islam" (*Islam kiri*). An even tinier percentage had spoken boldly of an Islamic and Marxist synthesis (cf. E. Prasetyo 2003). However, these latter labels—especially the "left" and "Marxist" labels—faded from the university scene with surprising speed after 2001, along with the once-glorious memories of the student activism of the anti-Suharto movement.

Zaki's junior classmate, Yayuk, had been influenced by elements of this critical discourse as well, including the global discourse of human rights as gender rights. In fact, if anything, neo-traditionalist women were even more vocal about their desire to challenge some aspects of their religious background identified as having strong social or cultural elements that rendered them open to debate. Perhaps not surprisingly, issues relating to gender were a particular focus of these debates. Yayuk, who had seven brothers and sisters, said she considered herself lucky to have been allowed to attend UIN. She came from a family in which religious education was strongly emphasized over general education, and all of her older sisters had been sent to *pesantren* to memorize the Qur'an (cf. Gade 2004a). She recounted,

> In my community, everyone is really proud of those who memorize the Qur'an, like even more than studying to become a doctor or an engineer. When you memorize the Qur'an you have to just constantly study and every second you have to go over and over the verses, to remind yourself. There's never an empty time, like when you're sitting around or watching television, you have to keep reciting the verses in your head, under your breath, so you don't forget. I didn't want to do that; I went to *madrasah* for grade school and secondary school and to a *pesantren* for religious study in the afternoons. So I felt I already had a strong background in religion. I wanted to do something different. Fortunately, my parents trusted me and allowed me to go to UIN.

Yayuk had enrolled in Faculty of Dakwah (Proselytizing/Communications) at the State Islamic University and was majoring in advising and counseling. Although she wasn't a member of the PMII, Yayuk had participated in several PMII-sponsored workshops on feminism and human rights and was involved in a campus movement working to address domestic violence. She said she viewed many of the problems facing women as cultural, not related to religion. "It's culture that has conditioned men to view themselves as superior to women; they are taught to believe they are allowed to hit their wives," she explained. "It's also lack of education. Because the Qur'an teaches us that men and women are equal before God."

Yayuk said she wanted to apply the critical ideas she had been exposed to through extracurricular student workshops and study groups to building new forms of personal relationships that would allow both partners to express their opinions and realize their potential. Like many of the female students I interviewed at the UIN, she was interested in a form of Islam more responsive to issues of gender and was looking for a marital partner who shared a similar vision. Yayuk said she was hoping to find someone willing to "move beyond the dominant discourse" to actualize new more egalitarian forms of gender relations in everyday, lived, interactions. "But change is difficult because those behaviors are supported by the community," she said. "So I have to start with myself, with my own [future] family. I want a marriage partner [*jodoh*] who will agree to a more equitable relationship and to establishing a more democratic household. The problem is finding someone who will agree with my vision. It's difficult because lots of guys don't agree with equality or feminism. They don't want to change, and the environment doesn't support change."

Yayuk, like Zaki and so many other students from the State Islamic University—and like many from Gadjah Mada—saw herself poised on the precipice of a new set of identifications. While she was not an active member of a Muslim student organization, she drew on a similar discourse and took advantage of the campus programs they offered. Like so many other young people I spoke with, she viewed Islam as a critical factor in her life but also expressed a desire to continue to develop her potential and to "actualize herself" through the cultivation of new forms of sociability and self-expression. What is more, she envisioned a future mate of her own choosing who would share these aspirations and concerns, one willing to struggle with her to create an intellectual and emotional partnership. For young people at the UIN as well as at Gadjah Mada—particularly but not only young women—the question of how to balance social and familial expectations with personal desires and aspirations loomed especially large and is a theme taken up in detail in the following chapters.

New Muslim Youth, New Varieties of Islam

Both Clifford Geertz and James Peacock were correct in identifying modern education as a key to social and psychological change in postcolonial Indonesia. However, neither foresaw the fact that modern education, including religious education, would lead to the deepening pluralization of Islamic streams (*aliran*), authority, and lifestyles. What we see among young people in Yogyakarta and elsewhere is the emergence of competing movements, groupings, and modes of sociability with very different ideas about how to be Muslim, modern, and middle class. In the face of the Islamic resurgence, reform-minded Muslim groups of various sorts have experienced a steady expansion in influence, while the proportion of the student population that identifies as nominal Muslim or *abangan* or *Islam Jawa* has dwindled, almost to the point of extinction (Ricklefs 2012). Today, when a Muslim student opts not to construct too much of her or his identity around pietistic Islamic references, he or she almost always identifies and is identified as simply "secular" rather than *abangan* or "Javanist." For those who avert an engaged Islamic self-identification in this way, the "secular" label is almost always worn defensively.

Much has changed then, over the past two generations, and nowhere more dramatically than in youth circles. If *abangan* have dwindled almost to extinction, Muslim traditionalists have not at all faded away but have instead diversified and adapted. More perhaps than any other youth segment, they have used global discourses of human rights and individual dignity to deepen and extend traditionalist Islamic normativities, not least with regard to gender and social justice. In addition to this neo-traditionalist permutation, the university youth scene has also been transformed by the arrival of a variety of Islamist or "new *santri*" groups. Although some go on to a sustained engagement with both new and old Islamic scholarship, most are drawn to a new profession of their faith with the hope of achieving ethical simplicity and rule-driven clarity in their lives, and within the larger society.

While Islamic observance has become a far greater feature of university life over the past two generations, the pluralization of its profession is just as socially significant. The "new *santri*" groups differ, indeed dramatically, in just what they see as an authentic profession of Islam. The public airing of those differences itself has become a major feature of public debate. It has unleashed an ongoing "competition in goodness" (*kompetisi kebaikan*) in which the new arrivals stake claims to normative superiority, and other groups, not least those from NU backgrounds, must respond. Not everyone of course has been swept into the normative maelstrom. In the aftermath of the political tumult of the late-Suharto (1993–1998) and the early Reformasi period (1999–2002), some students on Yogyakarta university campuses have distanced themselves from activism and any formal affiliation. Since 2009 or so, in particular, some faculty and students speak of a new spirit of "professionalism" and career-mindedness, trends deepened perhaps by the Asian economic crisis of 2007–2011. Nonetheless the Islamic tenor of campus life is insistent and palpable.

As suggested by the stories recounted above, for many young people, at the center of this pluralization of Muslim orientations lies a concern with new forms public piety, of gendered sociability, and of femininity and masculinity. As will become clear in the chapters that follow, there is another, less publicly salient but no less important trend at work in Muslim youth circles. Namely, in addition to a heightened interest in religious piety, there is also a greater desire for personal expression and self-actualization in a variety of less religiously marked social fields. No matter the depth of their religious involvement, young people—both men and women—want not only to cultivate pious Muslim selves but also to draw on popular trends and contemporary cultural and class developments in shaping new Muslim middle-class subjectivities. Within this process of pluralization and hybridization, however, it is women's roles that have been adjusted more radically. And it is women, in particular, who remain at the center of debates surrounding public piety, modesty, sexuality, and marriage.

Conceptualizing Gender

This chapter examines issues of pluralization and hybridization of youth identifications through the more careful examination of available models or paradigms of gender—what I identify here as "gender currents." By "gender current," I refer to a socially sustained normative frame for understanding and enacting some dimension of social life, in this case, gender. As evaluative frames for understanding and enacting gender relations, the concept of gender currents intersects and overlaps with what other anthropologists of Islam and of morality have referred to as moral or ethical "registers" (Schielke 2009a) or "rubrics" (Deeb and Harb 2013b). All societies sustain not one but a variety of such currents; in this sense, all human societies are ethically and normatively plural (Benda-Beckmann and Benda-Beckmann 2012; Bowen 2003; Merry 1988). Drawing on the work of Jill Matthews (1984) and R. A. Connell (2000, 2002, 2014 [1987]), the anthropologist of gender Kathryn Robinson (2009) refers to similar cultural realities as "gender orders," emphasizing their wider political entailments and arguing that together they make up the structural inventory of a society with regard to gender relations (Robinson 2009, 2). The terms "register," "rubric," and "order," however, carry the risk of implying a fixity that does not capture the fluidity of the gender conceptions among Muslim Javanese youth I describe here. I use the term "current" to underscore that fluidity and to emphasize the susceptibility of these cultural categorizations to both change and reinterpretation; they are not entirely commensurate with but rather crosscut what have been described as ethical and moral registers or rubrics.

As with the related idea of moral registers described by Samuli Schielke, the gender currents with which young Muslims grapple here in Indonesia do not comprise a neatly coherent system but exist in parallel—sometimes reinforcing, sometimes contradicting one another (cf. Schielke 2009a, S30; see also Simon 2014). They are flexible psycho-cultural representations that are more or less familiar to the members of a community, and are used to read and respond to intentions, attitudes, and emotions within a particular social context (Bennardo and de Munck 2014, 3–5; Shore 1996). In describing their lives and experiences, young people may draw on not one but several of these currents. They do so as often to critique or negate them as to embrace or affirm them. In other words, their orientations need not be consistent or unchanging over time.

My focus in this chapter is on presenting the important conceptual threads and influences that identify various understandings (currents) of Javanese gender as they emerge from young people's accounts as well as from available research on youth in Indonesia. Recognizing the plural nature of gender and morality allows us to foreground and theorize the complex subjective experience of individuals in the context of their everyday interactions. My concern in the chapters that follow will be to demonstrate how these broadly constituted but not necessarily consistent currents are engaged or, alternately, challenged by young actors in experience-near renderings of the ever-evolving construction of gendered realities expressed in patterns of sociability, sexuality, courtship, and marriage.

Four important conceptual currents can be identified in formulations of Javanese gender ideology. While I present them here as separate streams, there are elements of overlap and imbrication as well as tension and contradiction. Moreover, while the four currents in some sense "exist" in Javanese society, their influence in different times and social places has varied. The four currents are the current expressed in the Javanese kinship system and in local customs and traditions (*adat istiadat*); the aristocratic/hierarchical current associated with the Javanese courts and *priyayi* nobility; the current associated with the state (especially in its earlier, New Order incarnation) and disseminated through its programs and policies; and the Islamic current taught in the schools and in religion classes and informed by a contemporary rereading of the Qur'an and hadiths. A fifth gender current—that associated with modern (Islamic) cosmopolitanism—is taken up in detail in chapter 6.

The Complementary Current

What have come to be viewed as "traditional" conceptions of gender in Java are largely grounded in the realities of Javanese kinship and its associated concepts and practices identified—sometimes with considerable historical invention—as Javanese "tradition" or "custom" (*adat istiadat*). This basic or foundational view of gender roles tends to emphasize the complementarity or mutuality of the sexes and the reciprocal and interdependent nature of men and women. Although the complementary current is widely recognized across Javanese social groups, historically it has been more strongly associated with the rural population and with *abangan* Javanese of nominal or syncretic Muslim persuasion, rather than the aristocratic *priyayi* or the *santri* Javanese oriented toward a more textually and jurisprudentially informed profession of Islam.

According to this complementary conceptualization, both male and female roles are considered important and necessary, though not necessarily equal or socially commensurable. In a wide-ranging discussion of gender traditions across the Malayo-Indonesian world, the Malay anthropologist Wazir Jahan Karim (1995) has referred to this pattern as one of "popular bilaterality." She writes that across Muslim Southeast Asia, "the popular view that women are not the same as men and do different things does not generate a discourse that they are inferior or less important than men." Rather, "differences in power between men and women suggest differences in domains of preference, perceived as complementary rather than hierarchical" (W. J. Karim 1995, xiii–xiv; see also Andaya 2000, 235). This conception of male and female roles was traditionally reinforced by a pattern of life cycle and community rituals (*slametan*) that expressed the necessary duality and creative interdependency of male and female, seen as vital to individual and communal well-being (Andaya 2006; Beatty 2002; Hefner 1985; Peletz 2007, 2009; Reid 1988).

This ostensibly "complementary" conception of Javanese gender relations is the one with which most anthropologists in the early independence era (1950s to early 1960s) were familiar, and has been presented in rich detail in ethnographies based on research from that period (C. Geertz 1976 [1960]; H. Geertz 1989 [1961]; Jay 1969; Koentjaraningrat 1957, 1989). In her classic study of the Javanese family, Hildred Geertz (1989 [1961]) identifies Javanese kinship as a bilateral or cognatic system in which both the mother's and the father's sides of the family are given equal weight in determining relatedness and inheritance (see also Jay 1969; Koentjaraningrat 1957). Both the mother's and the father's relatives are referred to using similar kin terms and are addressed with similar terms undistinguished as to whether the relationship is through the mother's or father's side. In this system, generation and relative age are often of more significance than gender—which, linguistically speaking, is not always or necessarily marked (Keeler 1990). Although some high-status Javanese kin groups own small corporate properties related to burial grounds (*trah*), for most non-elite Javanese, kinship organization beyond the nuclear family is thoroughly non-corporate and even "optative" to a significant degree (H. Geertz 1989 [1961], 26). Relationships between kin beyond the nuclear family thus depend on individual needs, personalities, and predilections rather than on a pre-scripted and socially compulsory kinship norm.

In this Javanese current, marriage is considered a "pivotal moment" in the individual's life, a life passage replete with implications for his or her standing in the family and in the community (H. Geertz 1989 [1961], 54; H. Salim 1999, 71–74). Marriage celebrations are elaborate affairs in which the bride and groom literally become "king and queen for the day" and dress in regal garb modeled in some stylized way on the court elite. Lengthy and expensive weddings serve to reinforce both family and communal ties by engaging networks of reciprocity among kin and neighbors. Parents play an important role in spousal selection for their offspring, generally preferring matches between individuals from families with roughly equivalent social and economic status to their own (H. Geertz 1989 [1961], 54; see also Brenner 1998, 41). Although the prospective bride or groom may be understood as having the right to decline a parental suggestion,[1] acquiescing to parental wishes is not infrequently articulated as filial "repayment" for years of parental love and support (Jv. *balas budi*). On the other hand, compelling a son or daughter to marry against their will to someone they were "not meant for" (Jv. *sing dudu jodohne*) may be, and in earlier times often was, cited as a reason for marital discord and divorce.

According to this same more or less traditional Javanese current, residence after marriage is, in the long term, ideally neolocal. However, the newlywed couple may at first live with the wife's or, in some cases, the husband's parents for a period of time while accumulating the capital required to establish a household of their own (H. Geertz 1989 [1961], 55; Jay 1969, 40). In earlier generations, particularly in rural areas, the first several years of marriage were considered a trial period during which time the couple determined whether or not they would in effect stay together or divorce. First marriages, especially those arranged between very young individuals, were highly unstable, with upward of 50 percent of all marriages ending in divorce (Jay 1969, 62; G. Jones 1994a, 188).

In this non-*santri* gender current, divorce is regarded as an easy and not particularly stigmatized solution to marital problems, at least where the couple has not yet had children. Women who are divorced or widowed have considerable autonomy and are free to make their own choice of spouse. Young divorcées or widows are, however, seen as attractive and willing targets for the amorous attentions of both married and unmarried men, and for this reason are often the targets of gossip and suspicion. Most divorced women quickly remarry, but some, especially those with grown children, opt to live on their own. Divorcés and widowers, by contrast, rarely remain on their own for long, because men are seen as requiring a wife to maintain the minimal requirements of a household (H. Geertz 1989 [1961], 46; see also Brenner 1998).

The story of Inayah's parents illustrates many of these traditional, non-*santri* gender ideals as seen through the optic of marriage. When I first met her, Inayah was a student at Gadjah Mada University in the Department of English. She lived with her mother, father, and youngest brother in a modest but comfortable home in an urban neighborhood of Yogyakarta. Inayah described her parents as "regular Muslims" (*Islam biasa*), "not fanatics" (*tidak fantik*). Her father, Pak Marto, was a retired government worker (*pegawai negeri*). Her mother, Bu Ratna—a plump, attractive woman with a round face and an infectious laugh—described herself as "just a housewife" (*ibu rumah tangga saja*). Nonetheless, over the years of her marriage Inayah's mother had managed to save up enough money to open a bridal salon next to their house. She did a brisk business in the wedding season, renting out wedding costumes and decorations and styling bridal parties. Bu Ratna was widely known for her expertise in Javanese dress and makeup. As a child, Inayah always won the annual Kartini Day contest at school for the student who is best able to wear the traditional Javanese women's costume—a tightly wrapped batik sarong (Jv. *kain jarik*) and a form-fitting lacy jacket (*kebaya*)—and the elaborate formal hairstyle known as *sangul*.[2]

For most of the fifteen years that I have known her, Bu Ratna has worn a Western-style skirt and a blouse or a housedress without a head covering. At weddings, she dresses in traditional Javanese style. If the wedding party is religiously conservative, she dons a less form-fitting and more modest version of this outfit and throws a decorative shawl over her head. Only in more recent years has Bu Ratna begun to wear the headscarf more regularly. Now in family Ramadan photos she appears with her daughters and daughters-in-law, all wearing matching headscarves and long Muslim dresses.[3]

Bu Ratna told me the story of her marriage on several occasions. She did so not only for my benefit and as a comment on how much the times had changed, but also clearly as a reminder to her daughter, Inayah, of the sacrifices she (Bu Ratna) had made for her own parents. In the late 1990s and early 2000s, Inayah was in her early twenties and in the process of finishing up her undergraduate degree and contemplating marriage herself. In stark contrast to her daughter's situation, Bu Ratna's parents had arranged her marriage when she was only seventeen and not yet finished with high school. Her fiancé was twenty-six. Bu Ratna emphasized that at the time, she really didn't want to get married:

> This was in 1974 and I was still young, still a student. I wasn't thinking about marriage at that time. I felt as if my parents were forcing me. They were village people and they thought that if I waited too long I wouldn't attract a husband [*tidak laku*]. I really wanted to finish high school, but my parents said, "What are you waiting for? He's a government employee [*pegawai negeri*]. Just think what a great future you'll have." I should explain that they weren't my real parents. They were my "little" aunt and uncle. They didn't have any children of their own, so they asked my [biological] mother if they could raise me. They took me when I was six months old. They never told me I wasn't their child. When I was in my teens I found out from a neighbor. But it didn't matter. To me they were my mother and father. I was their only child. They loved me more than my own mother. They spoiled me terribly. So when my little aunt and uncle asked me to marry, I felt like I had to say yes to repay them [*balas budi*] for raising me and for loving me more than my own parents. I felt that if they told me to marry this guy and I refused, it would mean that I didn't appreciate all they had done for me. I wanted to make them happy. So I said "yes," but inside I was thinking to myself, "If it turns out I don't like him, I'll just divorce him" [peals of laughter].

Bu Ratna's attitude toward marriage is revealing. She says she agreed to marry the man her parents chose for her to repay them for her upbringing, but considered divorce as an option if things didn't turn out well. In fact, things did turn out well. The couple has had five children together and gives all evidence of having a caring and mutually supportive relationship. Now in his late sixties and retired, Inayah's father spends much of his time helping his wife with her bridal business, accompanying her to weddings, transporting chairs and ceremonial props, and setting up for events. He also helps with the housework, sweeping the house and even washing his youngest son's laundry in the hope it will allow him to devote more time to his studies.

In this complementary conception of Javanese gender roles, the marital relationship is secured by the arrival of a child. Teknonymy, whereby the new mother and father are referred to by the name of their first-born (as, for example, Bu Tri, "mother of Tri," and Pak Tri, "father of Tri"), is a common practice among Javanese and reinforces a cultural emphasis on marriage and parenthood as the bases of adult social status (H. Geertz 1989 [1961], 137; see also Beatty 2002; Keeler 1987; H. Salim 1999). Javanese view children as important sources of comfort, companionship, and support in one's old age and express piety and concern for couples who are unable to conceive. Infertility is the cause of considerable stress in family and social relations and is recognized as a legitimate cause for divorce or even polygyny.

A common solution to childlessness is the Javanese pattern of "fostering" or "borrowing" children (referred to by a variety of terms among them: Jv. *akon, among, pek, pupu;* In. *angkat, adopsi*). While there are cultural and Islamic barriers to legal adoption among Javanese, there has long been a pattern of informal caretaking of young children by a close relative for shorter or longer periods of time (Beatty 2002; see also H. Geertz 1989 [1961], 36–41; Jay 1969, 72–76). Typically a woman desiring a child will turn to her sister—sometimes requesting a child while it is still in the womb. In some cases, like that of Bu Ratna above, the arrangement is permanent. In other cases it may last only until the woman has a child of her own. In the latter case, called *memancing anak,* or "fishing for a child," the hope is that by caring for someone else's baby the woman will "relax" and can then become pregnant.

Grandparents or what is considered the equivalent, a grandmother's sister and husband, will sometimes ask to raise a young child to keep them "company" in their old age, particularly if their own children have all grown up and have moved away. In other cases, a grandmother may take on the role of mother to a grandchild simply because the child's parents are living with her and she is providing the child with most of its care while the parents are away at work. In such situations, the child may come to call the grandmother "mother" (*ibu/mbok*) and its own mother "elder sister" (*mbak/yu*); terms of address for other family members may be adjusted as well. Less often acknowledged in the literature on Java, the converse pattern also occurs. A new mother will in some cases initiate the fosterage arrangement herself, asking a female relative to take and care for her child either temporarily or permanently because she is unable or unwilling to do so.[4]

The British anthropologist Andrew Beatty has argued that Javanese practices such as widespread fosterage and adoption, terminological usages involving teknonymy, the negotiation of the Javanese speech levels and terms of address, as well as traditionally high rates of separation and divorce inject a measure of interactional flexibility and moral "relativism" into Javanese categories and relationships, including those relating to gender (Beatty 2002; see also Peletz 2009, 94).[5] Beatty identifies such practices as key to the child's development of the highly valued Javanese concept of *tepo sliro,* or the "ability to put oneself in another's place," which Javanese associate with maturity; that is, "becoming Javanese" (Beatty 2002, 480; H. Geertz 1989 [1961], 105). There is little question that the situational flexibility and ethical relativism about which Beatty and, before him, Clifford Geertz (1976 [1960]) have written were once widespread among the nominally Islamic Javanese known as *abangan.* As is clear in the life histories of contemporary youth presented in chapter 3, however, many of these more relativist Javanese practices are being challenged by new normative understandings of personhood and achievement on the part of young people, including those from families with parents who were once in the category of Javanese Islam or *abangan.* The changes are particularly apparent in the realm of family and gender relations, where older ideas of complementarity and structural flexibility have come up against state-promoted and more scripturally informed Islamic discourses. The latter focus on the establishment of small, stable, nuclear families and emphasize the biological mother's central role and responsibility in caring for and educating her children in accordance with her natural, God-given *kodrat*, or religiously sanctioned capacity (see White 2006, 296–297).

Within the complementary gender current, both sons and daughters are desired, and both are treated with great affection. In contrast to the stipulations of Islamic jurisprudence (*fiqh*), daughters inherit shares of family property equal to or sometimes even greater than those of their brothers upon the death of their parents, or prior to death, according to need. Describing this pattern, Hildred Geertz writes, "The 'real Javanese' law is that all children, male and female, inherit equally" (1989 [1961], 47; see also Jay 1969, 78; G. Jones 1994a, 11). While Javanese have long been aware of inheritance rules in Islamic jurisprudence that allocate two shares to male heirs for every one given to females, the rules have not historically been followed by most Javanese, with the exception of *fiqh*-observant *santri* Muslims and in instances where inheritance is disputed and taken before the Islamic court. More typically, Javanese parents take into consideration the particular requirements of their individual children and divide their property accordingly. This may mean that an unmarried child receives a larger share of the inheritance than an older, already-established, sibling. To avoid the squabbles and court battles over inheritance that sometimes occur after death, parents often hand over a portion of their property to their children while they are still living.[6] In a common pattern, the youngest daughter inherits the family home with the expectation that she will bring her husband to live there and will take care of her aging parents until they die (Jay 1969, 83; G. Jones 1994a, 11).[7]

Bu Ratna and her husband, for example, explained that they had already carefully divided their property (land and houses) among their five children. They had given each of their two oldest daughters portions of family rice fields in their parents' natal village when they married, since the girls' husbands had already secured housing for their young families in the capital, Jakarta. They had given their eldest son a plot of land near their own house in Yogyakarta. Although the son and his wife were, at the time, still living with the wife's parents, the assumption was that sometime in the future the couple would use the land to establish a home of their own. When their youngest daughter, Inayah, married in 2004, she and her husband moved in with Bu Ratna and Pak Marto, taking over an attached pavilion. The understanding was that the main house would become Inayah's when her parents passed away, and the pavilion would go to Inayah's younger brother, their youngest son.

Within this current, too, women are identified as playing a central role in family life and particularly in household management—a pattern that has been widely noted in the ethnographic literature (Brenner 1995; H. Geertz 1989 [1961]; Jay 1969; Keeler 1987; Sullivan 1994). Indeed, Hildred Geertz (1989 [1961], 78) goes so far as to identify the Javanese household as matrifocal (see also Schröter

2013, 13–14), and underscores what she called the "affective centrality" of the mother in family relations in general.[8] While the husband represents his family in the wider community and is identified as the family head, within the household, the wife/mother effectively manages family relations and maintains important networks with female kin. In this matrifocal pattern, Geertz writes, the woman has "more authority, influence and responsibility than her husband and at the same time receives more affection and loyalty" (H. Geertz 1989 [1961], 78–79).

As an extension of their role as family managers in this conceptual framework, Javanese women also play a pivotal economic role in their households.[9] They have the right to maintain their own property and to determine how it will be used even after marriage. Money the couple earns during their marriage, commonly known as *gono-gini* (Jay 1969, 63), is recognized as jointly owned and is divided equally between the spouses in the event of a divorce. Although more conventional Islamic norms and aspects of middle-class culture have introduced challenges to the arrangement, in this complementary gender current it is women who typically manage the household budget. In a common and often remarked-upon pattern, a Javanese husband hands over his income to his wife, who gives him spending money for cigarettes and coffee. She then takes care of the bills and daily expenditures and saves or invests whatever is left (Brenner 1995; H. Geertz 1989 [1961]; Keeler 1987; Smith-Hefner 1988a).

Bu Ratna, for example, said she had always dealt with the money in her household. It began, she explained, when the couple was newly married and lived for a time with her husband's parents. Her in-laws had insisted that their son turn over all of his money to her so that she could buy gold that could be used eventually to establish a household of their own. The pattern persisted throughout the marriage; Bu Ratna continued to manage the budget and the household. She shopped for the family's daily needs, paid the monthly bills, and was careful to put aside the remainder. In the case of large expenditures or significant events having to do, for example, with life cycle celebrations or the education of their children, she and her husband made their decisions jointly.[10]

The prevalence of this mutualistic or bilateral gender current that emphasizes women's central economic and affective role within the family and household, particularly, but not only, in non-*santri* areas of the countryside, has often been seen as evidence of Javanese women's relatively high status and autonomy (H. Geertz 1989 [1961]; Jay 1969; Reid 1988). The Malay anthropologist Wazir Jahan Karim (1995) has argued that it is in fact the "essential bilateralism" of Javanese kinship and culture that has been a key factor in protecting Javanese women against radical or permanent shifts toward gender inequality in the face of colonial occupation or patriarchal models imposed by the state or the proponents of conservative understandings of Islam. More recently, Australian anthropologist Kathryn Robinson has made a similar and compelling argument. She writes that "bilateral systems as a framework for social relationships open up a space for social practices that allow agency to women, especially in comparison to societies practicing patrilineal descent and patrivirilocal residence" (Robinson 2009, 14). Perhaps most important for the present discussion, the flexibility and relativity inherent in this Javanese current allow—under certain circumstances—for a measure of variation and even "play" in Javanese gender roles and family relations, and can indeed act as a counterpoint to more hierarchical and patriarchal conceptualizations.

The Hierarchical Current

Gender culture in Java has always been plural rather than unitary in its forms and meanings, and the complementary conceptualization of Javanese gender relations was always subject to challenge or marginalization by more insistently hierarchical currents. In the early modern history of the island, Java's traditional aristocracy and court-based elite, the *priyayi*, developed a variation on the popular Javanese gender conception but imbued it with a greater measure of patriarchal authority (see Dzuhayatin 2001; Gouda 1995; Sutherland 1979). In this hierarchical gender current, family relations are ranked and the father is recognized as the undisputed head of the household. His superior position and status are expressed and reinforced by those beneath him not through forceful demonstrations of masculinist power but through the deferential speech with which he is addressed and through the refined behavior of which the father is thought uniquely capable (C. Geertz 1976 [1960], 243–244; Smith-Hefner 1988b; Sutherland 1979). In the ideal-typical *priyayi* family, the father spends little time involved in day-to-day household chores or in intimate interactions with his children, both of which are seen as women's activities and potential affronts to elite masculine dignity (Koentjaraningrat 1989, 261). Instead his focus is on the cultivation of art, proper etiquette, and mystical practice, identified as key indices of elite status (C. Geertz 1976 [1960], 238).[11] Informed by a highly idealized model of feminine devotion, the wife's role in this gender current is to serve her husband selflessly and to sacrifice her own desires for the well-being of her family. She is, in the ideal, modest and compliant. Often described as the *konco wingking*, literally, the "friend in back," her place is appropriately secluded in the private areas of the house (Andaya 2000).[12]

It is widely recognized in the historical literature that the Dutch reinforced this hierarchal conception of gender roles and the strict division between public and domestic spheres through their colonial policies (Gouda 1995, 96; see also Stoler 1996). On the model of the middle-class Victorian family, they identified the husband as family patriarch and breadwinner and the wife as homemaker and mother.[13] This emphasis was particularly strong during the period of the late-colonial "Ethical Policy" put into place in the early twentieth century when large numbers of men were recruited to work for the Dutch as clerks and petty administrators. "As men and not women were recruited into the Dutch bureaucracy, the separation between the productive and reproductive domains in the household became all the stronger" (Dzuhayatin 2001, 257). One effect of this division of public and domestic domains was women's greater dependence on their husbands' salaries and a corresponding diminution in their autonomy. *Priyayi* women were not allowed to work except in certain reputable home-based occupations, such as gold work and batik production (Gouda 1995; Hull 1996 [1982]). A woman's employment in other enterprises was inconsistent with *priyayi* status, because extra-familial labor was regarded as a threat to her family's good name.[14]

This hierarchical current in Javanese gender relations as developed under Dutch colonialism was perhaps most vividly highlighted in the published letters of the great Javanese *priyayi* writer Raden Adjeng Kartini (1879–1904; see Kartini 1985). In correspondence with Dutch friends, Kartini lamented the fact that young *priyayi* women were not allowed to continue their educations but were secluded within the household (Jv. *dipunpingit*) by age ten or twelve and could not go out unless accompanied by an appropriate chaperone and only with permission. During their time in seclusion, they learned to be modest young ladies and proper wives. They were taught to always be in control of their behavior: to walk slowly with tiny steps, to speak softly, and to avoid opening their mouths too widely when eating or showing their teeth when laughing (Kartini 1985, 73). With regard to marriage, they were reminded *surga nunut, neraka katut* (follow [your husband] to heaven, get dragged [with him] into hell); that is, no matter what his character, a wife must always obey her husband (Tiwon 1996, 51).

So as to guard their own and their family's reputations, *priyayi* girls were typically married off at a young age, often to a man they had never met. In this sense, *priyayi* families showed a greater preoccupation with family name and honor than did their counterparts among the ordinary people, referred to in elite circles as the "little people" (*wong cilik*). Marriage arrangements were often made by the father and had very little to do with the young girl's desires or welfare but served mainly to enhance the father's status and position (see Gouda 1995, 98).[15] Even worse, once a wife had given birth to children, her husband often took a new wife, essentially replacing her.[16] In her letters to Dutch friends, Kartini denounced the practice of polygyny as "that cruel wrong" and railed against her imprisonment and impending marriage (Kartini 1985, 69; Coté 2005, 56–57). "I long to be free, to be able to stand alone, to study, not to be subject to anyone, and, above all, *never, never* to be obliged to marry" (Kartini 1985, 33–34). Kartini did marry, however, to the man chosen for her by her father. He was a well-positioned aristocrat, a regent or *bupati*, who already had three wives.[17] Less than a year after her marriage, at the age of twenty-five, Kartini died due to complications related to the birth of a son.

Priyayi women who were unhappy with their marital situation had few options. Whereas divorce rates were high among ordinary Javanese, among *priyayi* they were considerably lower (Koentjaraningrat 1989, 262).[18] Hildred Geertz writes that "*priyayis* do not disapprove of divorce as such, but they deplore any action which reveals a person's inner self as lacking in refinement and control" (1989 [1961], 138). The *priyayi* ideal of emotional self-control and refinement contrasted with their view of rural peasants (the *wong cilik*) as uncultivated and driven by worldly desires.

Despite Clifford Geertz' depiction of *priyayi* as nominal Muslims (see chapter 2) whose religious life focused on etiquette, art, and mystical practice (1976 [1960],

238), many of the more patriarchal aspects of *priyayi* gender conceptions are consistent with patriarchal interpretations of Islam. *Priyayi* drew heavily, for example, on the Muslim Javanese concept of *kodrat* to legitimate the "natural-ness" of the hierarchical gender order and women's inferior position relative to men. The Indonesian term *kodrat* (Jv. *kudrat*) connotes "God's will" or "God's omnipotence" (Echols and Shadily 1989, 302). It is related to the Arabic *qadara/qadar/qudra*, which means, similarly, "(God's) will or power" and has connotations of "fate" or "ability" (Cowan 1994, 873–874; White 2006, 278). In its Javanese usage *kodrat* provides a normative—and in particular, patriarchal—reference point for what are considered to be basic social and biological differences between the genders. According to his *kodrat*, the husband leads as well as provides for and protects his wife and children, reflecting the Islamic ideal of *nafkah*.[19] By contrast, *priyayi* women conformed to their *kodrat* by providing sexual service to their husbands, giving birth to and raising children, and assuming primary responsibility for the household management and organization. An important aspect of the *kodrat* of *priyayi* women was the imperative to uphold the honor of the family and to secure her husband's status through her modesty and sub-servient demeanor.

The hierarchical current in Javanese social relations was reinforced by the Javanese speech styles or language "levels" (Jv. *ungguh-unggah ing basa*), which indexed the nature of the relationship between the speaker and addressee and which were given especially strong emphasis in *priyayi* and otherwise elite cir-cles (Errington 1985; see also Keeler 1987). In social interactions, the lower-status speaker was required to use a more respectful speech variety to a higher-status addressee and would receive a lower (less respectful, more familiar) speech var-iety in return. Often glossed by Javanese as forms of "politeness" (In. *sopan santun*), the speech levels also indexed ideals of gender expressivity and gen-dered hierarchy. In a discussion of shifting patterns of language use (away from formal Javanese), Mbak Lis, a young lecturer in the department of Javanese language and literature at Gadjah Mada University and a scholar of court litera-ture, emphasized the gendered aspects of the speech levels and their behavioral concomitants, explaining that,

> especially for the priyayi and descendants of the courts, the woman had to speak in polite Javanese to her husband, but the husband was not required to do the same. There were also behaviors that went along with that. For example, [in the past] when a Javanese wife used formal Javanese [*kromo*] to her husband, she could not say "I want" and she could not say "no." But her husband could say "I want" [Jv. *dikersakke*] and she would have to serve him. She could not refuse. This was also true for sex. The woman could never ask directly for that. And she could not refuse her husband if he asked.[20]

Over the course of the early modern and modern period, as a Java that from the fifteenth century onward had been highly regionalized began to develop a more transregional linguistic and status culture, the speech levels and other aspects of the hierarchical current diffused outward from the court and elite urban areas. In many areas of the Javanese countryside these elements of *priyayi* culture were embraced by rural elites as a model of refinement and status and as a means of distinguishing themselves from their neighbors of lower status (Smith-Hefner 1989).[21] Despite this diffusion of elite styles into the countryside, however, the continued association of the more restrictive aspects of the hierarchical current with the Javanese courts and with urban *priyayi* has led to the observation that rural Javanese women may have more autonomy and may be treated more equally by their spouses than urban, middle-class women. The Indonesian scholar Siti Ruhaini Dzuhayatin (2001, 257) writes, "Women in peasant and poor families pay vague homage to the patriarchal idioms but then go on to exercise considerable influence in the 'non-ideological' or practical management of the family. However, the division of gender roles was, and still is, far more rigid in *ningrat* [blue blood/royal] and *priyayi* [aristocratic] families, where women are required to be the loyal backstop to their husbands." Feminist anthropologist Saskia Wieringa (2002, 62) writes similarly, "Noble Javanese women seem to have been among the most restricted in the archipelago. The freedom of movement of Javanese peasant women is generally considered to have been substantial" (see also Gouda 1995, 96). Wieringa further observes, "*Priyayi* women had no access to the expanding educational opportunities of the men of their rank, almost no access to public life and suffered from unequal marriage relations" (Wieringa 2002, 62; see also H. Geertz 1989 [1961]; Vreede-de Stuers 1960).

Today, elements of *priyayi*-inflected gender attitudes are often referred to highly critically by young urban Javanese, who describe them as "feudal" (*feodal*). However, these elite gender norms have remained an important reference point in the life histories of young people, particularly among those individuals who traced a relationship to the courts. Estu, for example, a third-year student at Gadjah Mada University whose house literally shares a wall with the palace (*kraton*), described her father as "so *priyayi*" (*sangat priyayi*). He had worked his whole life at the palace as a court retainer (*abdi dalam*). Although the pay was abysmal, he considered it an honor to serve the Sultan. Estu's mother was left to make do. Her father carried the aristocratic title *raden;* his father (Estu's paternal grandfather) had been a *raden mas*. Estu said that her father was quite insistent on the inherent superiority of men, often citing women's *kodrat*, or biological destiny, to support his view.

When I pointed out the fact that her father had nonetheless supported her pursuit of a college education and a career in the tourist industry, Estu replied, "Yes, he realizes that today with education women can be at the same level as men, but they are still not allowed to ignore their womanly responsibilities. That is, they are not allowed to act like men, and they can't forget their responsibility to care for their husband and children. Even if they achieve a high level of education, they are not allowed to just hand their children over to a maid and ignore their duties to their husband. The main thing is: a woman should never forget her *kodrat*."

Gender and the State

A modified variant of the *priyayi* conception of family relations and gender hierarchy was adopted first by the colonial and then the postcolonial state. As part of the colonial government's Ethical Policy (1901–1942), a series of new social programs were proposed to address the poverty and inequality that had developed under the earlier "cultivation system."[22] These programs included the establishment of public health and sanitation services, improved irrigation, agricultural extension services, and (limited) public education for the indigenous population, primarily aimed at children of local elites. Implementation of these projects required a more substantial colonial administration and the deeper involvement of the colonial government in village affairs (Koentjaraningrat 1989, 63, 70).[23] There was a parallel need for more Dutch-speaking Indonesians to fill the lower ranks of government bureaucracy and positions in the expanding commercial sector. Not surprisingly, it was male members of the *priyayi* class who were best positioned to take advantage of such opportunities.

One objective of Ethical Policy educational reforms was to create a group of educated natives who would be able to interface and communicate with the Dutch but would serve primarily as bureaucrats and professionals. The Dutch imagined that this new, Westernized Indonesian elite would be both grateful and cooperative and act as an inspiring example for the lower classes (Ricklefs 1993, 156; see also Gouda 1995). The stated aims of Dutch Ethical Policy educational reforms—to create a grateful and cooperative new elite and to "uplift the spirit of the masses"—did not, however, develop quite as intended. New educational opportunities produced some able and loyal officials, but the programs of state-sponsored education also brought into existence an alternative social elite that was to go on to play a central role in the anti-colonial and nationalist movements (Ricklefs 1993, 160; see also Gouda 1995; Sidel 2006). A number of these movements focused on the creation of a nationalist education. Prominent among them were the Taman Siswa (lit. "garden of students") schools whose educational philosophy would introduce a new, "neo-*priyayi*" conception of gender and family relations.

Taman Siswa was founded in the early 1920s by a Javanese aristocrat from the Yogyakartan court, Ki Hajar Dewantara. Dewantara's schools were the first to self-consciously follow the "family system" (*sistem kekeluargaan*), also known as the "*among* system" (*sistim among*), as a countercurrent to Dutch colonial regimentation. In Javanese, *among* means "to take care of, to protect," and is often used to describe the caretaking relationship of parent to child. The *among* system encouraged a relationship of closeness and affection between student and teacher that was quite different from that between Dutch or Dutch-trained teachers and indigenous students. Students in Taman Siswa schools were instructed to address their teachers in Indonesian using the kin terms *bapak* (father) and *ibu* (mother) instead of using the Dutch, Malay, or Javanese terms of address that were commonly used in other schools and implied both status and distance (Tsuchiya 1987, 114; see also Shiraishi 1997, 88). While Dutch schools emphasized compulsion, discipline, and order, Taman Siswa schools embraced an educational philosophy of "guidance and support from behind" (Jv. *tut wuri handayani*), which in the ideal allowed students to follow their own interests and develop independent personalities, under the watchful eye and with the encouragement of their teachers.[24]

In 1927 members of the Dutch-educated native elite organized a more specifically nationalist organization, the Indonesian Nationalist Party (Partai Nasional Indonesia, PNI). The organization's leader was the young Sukarno, who would go on to become Indonesia's first president. Sukarno was a graduate of the Technical Higher School in Bandung, an engineering college that would later become the Bandung Technical Institute (Ricklefs 1993, 182). In Bandung Sukarno met and grew close to Taman Siswa's founder, Ki Hadjar Dewantara. Sukarno was impressed by the educational philosophy of the Taman Siswa schools, which rejected more puritanical varieties of reformist Islam and adopted Javanese culture as the basis for a new national character. The historian Merle Ricklefs writes that the schools' philosophy appealed to Sukarno's idea of a religiously neutral nationalism. In particular the way that non–*santri priyayi* had absorbed Hindu, Buddhist, and Islamic and Western ideas into a synthesis seemed to Sukarno to be a fitting model for the Indonesian nation as a whole (Ricklefs 1993, 182).

As Indonesia's first president, Sukarno attempted to promote a form of neo-*priyayi* tradition as the dominant culture of the new republic; some of its most striking features were gendered. "Familism" was enshrined in the 1945 consti-tution and further elaborated in Sukarno's concept of guided democracy (1957–1965) when the president abolished the elected parliament and instituted a centralized, executive-driven government (Robinson 2009, 69; see also Shiraishi 1997). In this framework, the *bapak* (lit. "father") was the ultimate governmental authority, just as the father is within the family. Conversely, "the *priyayi* ideals of women as dedicated housewives became the ideal type for Indonesian women as a whole" (Dzuhayatin 2001, 258; Wieringa 2002). The irony, as Dzuhayatin points out, is that this representation of women as middle-class housewives with few other social concerns was not indigenous or Javanese at all. It was an invented tradition introduced to the archipelago by Dutch authorities only in the nineteenth century.

In fact, Indonesian women had been active participants in the struggle for national independence and had remained politically active in the early years of the republic (Blackburn 2004, 21–23; Wieringa 2002, 7; see also Steedly 2013). As Japanese authority withered in the final months of the Second World War, several large and socially engaged women's organizations emerged. Among these groups were the nonreligious Union of Women of the Indonesian Republic (Perwari); the Muslimat NU (the women's wing of Nahdlatul Ulama); the nationalist-oriented federation, Indonesian Women's Congress (Kowani); and the Communist Party–sponsored Indonesian Women's Movement (Gerwani). In the early years of Sukarno's presidency Perwari, Kowani, and Gerwani actively debated issues of women's education, marriage reform, and polygyny. Women's issues quickly became a diacritical marker in the contest between nationalists, communists, and Muslim parties, with Muslim women's organizations typically adopting more conservative positions with regard to the issue of marriage reform and polygyny and generally maintaining a low profile on issues regarded as too "political" (Blackburn 2004, 23).[25] The situation for women changed considerably, however, during the period of Guided Democracy, when Sukarno's agenda shifted to focus on nationalism and anti-imperialism and his presidency became increasingly authoritarian. Even the PKI-linked Gerwani, the most vocal of women's organizations, had to subordinate its agenda to Sukarno's nationalist and anti-imperialist project (Blackburn 2004, 24; Wieringa 2002).

When, in the aftermath of the attempted left-wing officers' coup on the night of October 1, 1965, the Indonesian Communist Party was blamed for the attempt and targeted for destruction, Gerwani was vilified and brutally suppressed as well (Wieringa 2002, 281). In her analysis of the Indonesian women's movement, *Sexual Politics in Indonesia*, Saskia Wieringa details how the young General Suharto, who took up the reins of government during the chaos following the failed coup, used a campaign of sexual slander against Gerwani to justify his takeover of the presidency from Sukarno.[26] In the process, he succeeded in linking the idea of women's political activity with sexual and moral depravity (Wieringa 2002). Wieringa views this moment as essentially ending the women's movement in Indonesia. In describing gender roles under the New Order (the regime that succeeded the Sukarno government in a prolonged transition from 1965 to 1967), she writes, "The gendered nature of this [the New Order] state is best illustrated by the forcible return of women to an Indonesian model of meek womanhood contained within a hierarchical male order" (5). In historical retrospect, however, the situation of women in New Order Indonesia was to prove more complex, and replete with cultural and developmental ironies.

Suharto's New Order reinstated the principle of the "family as basis" (*asas keluarga*), the ideology that affirmed the family as the foundation of state and society. Although in practice there was a measure of contextual flexibility to the system, the formal model was one in which Indonesian women were unambiguously subordinate to men within the family, public life, and political affairs (Robinson 1999, 237). In official pronouncements, the New Order presented a highly conservative gender ideology through its own neo-*priyayi* elaboration of the "nature"-based *kodrat wanita*. In this ideology, women were positioned in the role of the middle-class housewife selflessly serving her husband, family, and the nation (Blackburn 2004, 25). The Indonesian social commentator Julia Suryakusuma has referred to the state's identification of women with their status as housewives as an ideology of state "motherism," or *ibuism* (Suryakusuma 1996, 101; see also Dzuhayatin 2001). The converse, "fatherism," or *bapakism*, identified men as natural leaders in the public sphere as well as in the home (Blackburn 2004, 25).[27]

However vague its precise policy entailments, the New Order ideology of familism was actively disseminated via state agencies and training programs as a central component in the government's development agenda (Blackburn 2004, 25;

Shiraishi 1997). Through the Pancasila Moral Education Program (P4) citizens were inculcated with the proper views on "everything from the presidency to the status of women and wives" (Dzuhayatin 2001, 260). P4 moral education was an important aspect of the ideological training all civil servants were required to undergo; it was also a mandatory subject in the school curriculum through college (see Rudnyckyj 2010, 195–200). There were in addition two institutions targeted directly at Indonesian women that played a central role in the propagation and acceptance of the New Order's gender ideology: the PKK (Pembinaan Kesejahteraan Keluarga), or Family Welfare Movement, and the Dharma Wanita, or Women's Good Work.

Established in 1974 for non-elite women, the PKK had a pervasive presence across all of Indonesia, from the most remote mountain villages to big cities. The organization had multiple functions (Robinson 2009, 74). First and foremost was the promotion of the government's vision of development (*pembangunan*), an integral component of which was the state's conservative gender ideology. This ideology emphasized above all women's "responsibilities as custodians of the household and for bearing and nurturing the next generation of Indonesians" (Robinson 1999, 248).[28] The organization also implemented the Family Welfare Program and its many related projects in neighborhoods and villages, including important programs for maternal and child health (Robinson 2009, 248). As an outgrowth of their participation in organizing health-service stations (*pos pelayanan terpadu* or *posyandu*) that served to monitor infants and pregnant women, the PKK was especially active in promoting the state's Family Planning Program, Keluarga Berencana, or KB (Wieringa 2015, 31; see also Niehof and Lubis 2003). Established in 1968, the family planning program was viewed as one of the New Order's sterling developmental achievements, and one of the most successful family planning programs in the Muslim world. Kathryn Robinson reports that "from an average of more than six children per mother in the 1960s, total fertility fell to less than three children per mother in the 1990s" (Robinson 2009, 249). Central to the state's birth control campaign was its emphasis on the ideal of small, high-quality, nuclear families composed of no more than two children, a working father, and a stay-at-home mother and wife. The PKK embraced the state's family ideal in their programs—even if it was very far from the realities of members' own lives.[29]

The women's organization for the wives of government officials, Dharma Wanita, was founded originally under Sukarno (with an organizational precursor under the Japanese), but assumed a greatly expanded role during the New Order when membership became compulsory for all women civil servants and civil servants' wives (see Wieringa 2002, 81). The organization's objectives were to encourage women's civil service and participation in national development in accordance with their "natural" roles as wives and mothers. For the good of national development, women were expected to subordinate their own interests and careers to supporting the careers of their husbands. In both the PKK and Dharma Wanita (DW), the woman's position within the organization reflected her husband's rank and position within the government bureaucracy, not her own (Gerke 1992, 47; Sen 2002, 42; Suryakusuma 1996, 98). Women in government service whose positions ranked higher than that of their husbands, and women civil servants who did not have husbands in the civil service, were treated as anomalies. "The organization was based on an assumption that wives had free time for voluntary work and that women who themselves held public office had to find time to participate in the DW of their husbands' organizations" (Robinson 2009, 75).

Robinson argues that the New Order attempted to impose a homogenizing view of female social roles on the diversity of gender relations that actually existed. The example of Diah and her mother introduced in the previous chapter suggests the state's conception of gender roles did not completely displace but rather added another layer to Javanese gender conceptions.

Diah's family was solidly middle-class. Her father was a civil servant, a doctor; her mother was a housewife. The couple had met in college. Theirs was not an arranged marriage, but when Diah's mother married, she quit school to devote herself to her husband and family. Diah described her mother as the "submissive, devoted type" (*tipe mengabdi sekali, nurut sekali*), who, aside from her involvements in a monthly religious study group (*pengajian*) and several professional wives' organizations, spent all of her time at home. Although Diah's father had no direct ties to the court, Diah described him alternately as *jowo kolot* (old-fashioned Javanese) and *jowo banget* (really Javanese)—in this context referencing her father's orientation toward *priyayi* ideals that elsewhere she called *feodal* or "feudal." In particular, Diah's father had insisted that Diah's mother not work but stay at home and care for the household and the children and support his career.

The notion of women sacrificing for their families is consistent with neo-*priyayi* New Order gender conceptions described above. At the same time the central economic and emotional roles that Diah's mother played within the household are an aspect of the basic complementary current. Diah explained,

> It's really my dad who wants my mom in the house, in the kitchen, taking care of the kids, managing the household, arranging everything for him. Like, for instance, the issue of money. My mom is the one who is totally in charge. When my dad gets money, he just turns it over right away to my mom. He doesn't deal with it at all. My mom then gives my dad some money for his daily expenses and pays the electricity and the other bills and stuff. She takes care of absolutely everything that has to do with the household. My dad just steps in as a last resort, if for some reason my mom can't handle something. She's the emotional center [*pusat emosional*] of the family as well. She's always the one that we go to for anything, like if we have a problem or to get advice, she's the one we confide in [*curhat*]. When I was small, my dad would often travel to Bangkok or Malaysia for his work and he'd be away sometimes for month. A long time, right? But I really didn't care because we weren't close at all.

> Now that we are grown up and have moved away (except for me) my mom's bored at home all day. I feel sorry for her. She's involved in some social groups,

like Dharma Wanita and the League of the Wives of Indonesian Doctors [Ikatan Isteri Dokter Indonesia], and she attends a weekly Islamic study group [*pengajian*], but those activities don't really take up much of her time. She'd like to open a small business, but my dad won't allow her to work [*sama bapak, nggak boleh*]. The main thing as far as my dad's concerned is that he just wants her in the house and that's it.

What is confusing for Diah, she said, is that whatever her father's gender attitudes with regard to her mother, he has nonetheless insisted that his daughters all obtain advanced degrees and pursue careers. "I don't understand my dad," she said. "He continues to insist that my mom is not allowed to work, that a wife should stay at home and not work. But he really pushed all of his daughters to go as far as we possibly could in school. He told us that we should at least get our master's degrees, but if we could go higher, then all the better. If we could do the PhD, then go ahead. 'The main thing is, just don't stay at home!'"

In fact, notwithstanding official New Order gender doctrines, the reality of women's roles during the New Order was complex and fast-changing. The homogenizing and hierarchical conceptualization of gender roles that the New Order attempted to impose often contradicted the changes in women's roles and conjugal relations that resulted from the regime's development programs, not least of all those that promoted women as well as men's education. Robinson (1999, 237) writes, "In broadcasting an essentialized image of the ideal Indonesian woman as loyal wife and dutiful mother, the regime denied the transformation and diversification of women's roles that its own relentless campaign for material expansion had helped to bring about." Among the laboring classes, more and more factories were recruiting young women from rural and urban proletariat backgrounds. Indonesian education was expanding, and growing numbers of women were moving on to secondary and even tertiary levels. Others were taking up employment in the ranks of the expanding civil service. As a result of improvements in transportation and systems of communication, new, if often contradictory, images of femininity were making their way into the mass media, both from the West and from local centers of "metropolitan culture" (as Hildred Geertz called it) within Indonesia. In addition to promoting new forms of metropolitan culture, however, these same changes in Indonesian social and economic life catalyzed a *growing interest among young people in new and more normative-minded forms of gendered piety.*

Gender and Islam

Islam has had a long and historically variable influence on Javanese conceptions of gender, elements of which have already been noted in the discussion above. More recently—particularly since the decline of Suharto's New Order—important aspects of a Muslim-inflected gender current, especially as related to the roles of women, have become the focus of contestation and debate. New forms of religious piety and controversies surrounding contemporary patterns of gender and sexuality in the context of courtship and marriage are taken up in detail in chapters 6 and 7. What I offer here is a discussion of some of the most basic elements of the *santri* gender current associated with the mainstream mass Muslim organizations, the traditionalist Nahdlatul Ulama (NU) and modernist Muhammadiyah. Issues pertaining to gender within these organizations have most consistently been taken up by their affiliated women's wings, Muhammadiyah's Aisyiyah and the Nahdlatul Ulama's Muslimat NU. While there are points of contention between and even within these groups with regard to some details of interpretation and practice, and increasing generational tensions with regard to more conservative ideals, a general framework can nonetheless be discerned.

There is widespread consensus among Muslim activists and intellectuals that the historical development of Islam served to elevate the status of women, first in Arabia, and shortly thereafter across much of the Middle East (Hasyim 2006; Munir 2002; Wadud-Muhsin 1992). Whereas previously women had been treated as objects and the property of men, Islam offered women protection and important rights, including the right to own property and to inherit. Most critically with respect to the status of women, within Islam men and women are considered "equal before God." That is to say, on Judgment Day, each individual will be evaluated *as an individual* by God on the basis of his or her faith and religious practice.[30] In this regard, the Indonesian Muslim scholar Syafiq Hasyim (2006, 14) writes, "The arrival of Islam brought with it the declaration that all human beings are equal before God. . . . All are valued and treated equally before God. . . . There is only one thing that differentiates people and that is their degree of belief in God."

As Hasyim and other Muslim commentators have pointed out, however, there are other, strongly patriarchal currents in Islamic traditions, particularly within the great tradition of Islamic jurisprudence, which emphasize women's subordination to men. Although highly contested in modern times by a new generation of educated Muslim women (as well as some men), these patriarchal currents often overshadow Islam's more egalitarian gender conceptions (Mir-Hosseini 2003; see also Ali 2006). Muslim understandings of the nature of femininity and masculinity as well as male and female roles and responsibilities with regard to marriage, divorce, and inheritance are based on Islam's two scriptural sources, the Qur'an and hadith, as mediated through the wealth of commentaries found in Islamic jurisprudence, or *fiqh*.[31] An especially important source of information regarding gender roles within Islam is the *Surah An-Nisa*. *An-Nisa* means "women" in Arabic. The *Surah An-Nisa* is the chapter of the Qur'an that takes up the rights, responsibilities, and legal relations that pertain to Muslim women and, by extension, Muslim men (White 2006). It is *An-Nisa* 4, verse 34, that is most often cited as support for the idea of men's superior status:

> Men are the leaders of women, because Allah has blessed them [men] with more than women and because they [men] spend their wealth on women.

Because of this, virtuous women are those who obey Allah and restrain themselves when they are without their husbands because Allah will protect them. (Adamson 2007, 14; see also White 2006, 285)

The passage goes on to state that men have the right to discipline their wives to ensure their obedience (Munir 2002, 209):

As for those whom you fear may rebel [*nusyuz*], admonish them and banish them to separate beds, and beat them. Then if they obey you, seek not a way against them. For God is Exalted, Great. (Stowasser 1998, 33)

It should be noted that many modern Muslim scholars, not least Muslim feminists, have disputed the rendering of the Arabic original so as to authorize beating as a last resort (see Ali 2006; Wadud-Muhsin 1992). In Java, however, the central message of the passage with regard to a father and husband's authority is widely known and widely regarded as canonical. How it is understood and applied can be discerned in the comments of an elderly activist and frequent public speaker associated with the Muhammadiyah-linked women's organization Aisyiyah. Addressing a women's religious study group, Bu Uswatun made reference to this verse repeatedly in an extended discussion of the Muslim family. A slight woman in a traditional wrapped skirt (*kain*), loose long-sleeved blouse (*kebaya*), and knit cap, she explained that the husband is the recognized head of the household and final decision maker. He provides the economic support for his family and should also ideally act as a moral model and teacher to his wife and children: "In Islam, yes, according to the Qur'an, *Surah An-Nisa*, verse 34, the husband is considered the leader of the family. Why must the husband take this role? Because it is written that the husband must provide food and economic support for his family. This is his responsibility. In fact, he is the leader in multiple senses: economic, religious, as well as moral."

Conversely, the woman's most important responsibilities lie within the household as wife and mother. She manages everything to do with the domestic sphere and attends to the early socialization and education of her children. The Qur'an (2:233) stipulates that she nurse her children for two years. She is, in addition, responsible for teaching them politeness, cleanliness, and modesty. In this gender current, a woman is allowed to work outside of the house with the permission of her husband. However, because it is the husband who has foremost responsibility for meeting the economic needs of the family, the woman's income and position are viewed as merely supportive and supplementary to his. In any case, a wife may not ignore her primary duty, which is the care and management of the household, her husband, and children.

The older generation of Aisyiyah activists represented by Bu Uswatun does not view this arrangement as problematic. Most regularly emphasize the reciprocal and complementary aspects of male and female roles but interpret the difference in roles in a mutualistic and supportive way. Many cite the vivid and moving Qur'anic passage (*Surah Al-Baqarah* 2:187), "You are his garment as he is yours" (Munir 2002). Indeed, senior activists consistently prefer to highlight more egalitarian and mutualistic understandings of gender complementarity, downplaying those that would place women in a secondary position vis-à-vis men (see van Doorn-Harder 2006). Bu Uswatun was at pains to emphasize, for example, that although men are the leaders of women and heads of their households, there are important requirements of that leadership: "[Husbands] must lead with love and affection. Because the Prophet said, 'On this earth, the best men are those who are most loving to their wives.' And another hadith says, 'There are no honorable men except for those who honor women.'" In lectures to newlyweds Bu Uswatun declared that she always emphasizes the complementarity of marital roles insisting that every individual has both strengths and deficiencies (*kekurangan dan kelebihan*), but that in marriage each partner ideally completes the other (*saling mengisi*). She went on to say that although she had traveled widely for her work with Aisyiyah—giving speeches and carrying out workshops and seminars across the archipelago—she had never felt torn between her domestic duties and her public involvement—and that her husband has been consistently supportive.

This easy domestic negotiation and accommodation was not, however, everywhere the norm among the older generation of *santri* women. Bu Firza, the attractive middle-aged wife of a local Nahdlatul Ulama leader, made reference to these same gender expectations—and related tensions—in a discussion of her own marriage. The neighbor of a close friend, I met Bu Firza at her home in an urban neighborhood on Yogyakarta's outskirts. She came to the door in knee-length shorts and a matching sleeveless top. Her hair was stylishly coiffed and she was carefully made up. Sensing my confusion at her appearance, she explained that although she dressed modestly and wore a headscarf whenever she went out, when she was at home, her husband asked her to look attractive for him.

While we sampled an assortment of homemade Javanese snacks and glasses of cold orange Tang, Bu Firza recounted how when she was younger she ran a small sewing business out of her home. She enjoyed her work and especially enjoyed the extra spending money it afforded, but after a while her husband felt he was being neglected and ordered her to quit:

> My business was doing well. I had a lot of orders, but I was often exhausted from the work. Sometimes I wouldn't get to bed until really late. Finally my husband told me I had to quit. He said I was always tired and didn't pay enough attention to him. But I kept working because the economy at that time was really bad. I could make Rp 40,000 or 30,000 a month, which at that time was a lot. I used it to buy clothes for myself, or jewelry. I really enjoyed the work. In the end, my husband said, "If you keep working and don't pay attention to me, don't blame me if I look for attention elsewhere." I was afraid of what he might do, and I returned to my belief in God. "Ya Allah, as a wife, I have to obey my husband. Otherwise, he may take another wife."

Bu Firza gave up her job reluctantly. In her household, she explained, it was her husband who controlled the budget, a pattern that is relatively rare in Javanese households, but is becoming more common among observant *santri* and some members of the new middle class. Her story highlights the tensions within more normative Islamic conceptions of gender, both with regard to women's employment and with regard to the possibility of polygyny, which is allowed by Islamic law but subject to significant restrictions in Indonesia's Islamic legal compilation (see Mulia and Cammack 2007; Lindsey 2012).[32]

In the Islamic gender current important aspects of men's and women's roles are also (as in the gender current ratified by the state) expressed through the discourse of *kodrat*—understood in Java and in most of Indonesia as the divinely conceived nature of men and women.[33] The Islamic discourse of *kodrat* draws on commentary from the Qur'an and hadith to underscore the irrefutable social and biological differences between men and women.[34] It is because of their divinely conceived nature that women are destined to give birth and to care for their offspring and men are destined to be providers. For similar reasons, women are considered to be naturally passionate and emotional, while men are more rational (Brenner 1995; Peletz 1995, 1996; see also Mir-Hosseini 2003). In this view, if left uncontrolled, women's sexuality threatens the entire social order with chaos (*fitnah*); it is for this reason that pious women must cultivate modesty and sexual restraint (cf. Tucker 2008, 179, 191).

In my research and interviews over the years, I encountered few younger women who reject these *fiqh*-based conceptualizations of femininity outright, but many women struggled with their message (cf. Mona, introduced in chapter 3). Women's inherently emotional nature, and the tendency to represent emotionality as a destabilizing influence on both self and society, is often cited to support the argument that they are not suited to take on political positions and are incapable of acting as effective leaders in the public sphere. This understanding caused considerable debate in Muslim circles during the candidacy of Megawati Sukarnoputri in the 1999 presidential elections (see van Doorn-Harder 2002; van Wichelen 2010) and remains a point of tension in many conservative Muslim organizations.

Gender Currents, Ambivalence, and Interactive Constructionism

Gender theorists in the field of Southeast Asian studies, including Aiwa Ong and Michael Peletz, have convincingly argued for a view of gender conceptions in Southeast Asia as characterized by tension, ambivalence, and change. Although introduced here for the purpose of discussion as four distinct conceptual frameworks or currents, Javanese gender conceptions in fact bear a complex and mutually imbricating relationship to one another—sometimes overlapping or reinforcing, sometimes contradicting each other, and often generating profound ambivalences. These conceptions, moreover, have continued to undergo radical readjustments as a result of the great social changes that have taken place in Javanese and Indonesian society since the 1970s. These social changes include, among others, a dramatic pattern of urbanization, the growth of capitalist commerce and the media, greater physical and social mobility, and expanded educational opportunities for young women as well as young men.

One important result of these wide-ranging social changes has been the general weakening of the *santri-abangan* divide through an ongoing, unstable, but creative process of social and religious change. The process has witnessed the "Islamization" of vast areas of public and private life, including understandings of gender (see Ricklefs 2012). No less important, however, the process has also involved the reflexive modernization and cultural diversification of Indonesia's Islamic traditions. As a result of these and other developments, over the past generation the practitioners of Javanese *abangan* tradition have become noticeably more Islamic—though not necessarily *santri* in the earlier sense of that term. A result in part of years of more normative religious education in the schools, many more young Javanese now cultivate a more consciously pious lifestyle and reject those elements of *abangan* ritual tradition identified as heretical or polytheistic (*syirik*). At the same time, the emphasis on normative practice and textualism in religious education has meant that growing numbers of young people realize that, if they are to be pious Muslims, they must come to terms with legal and ethical traditions identified as Islamically normative. And, although plural and contested, some of these traditions present more conservative and patriarchal interpretations of Muslim gender roles.

At both a personal and social level, young people's response to this conflict of gender norms has been varied, to say the least. Convinced that Islam is intended to serve as an all-encompassing source of social regulations, some young people have enthusiastically embraced literalist or strict-constructionist interpretations of Islamic legal traditions, many of which in student circles are understood on the basis of a selective and greatly simplified reading of classical Islamic jurisprudence. Others, however, not least of all women, have begun to look to less narrowly selective and ostensibly textualist models of Islam and Muslim gender relations, emphasizing both a rereading of scriptural sources and a contextualization of Islam's divine commands, including those that emphasize a historical and contextual approach to the interpretation of religious texts (cf. Ali 2006; Syamsiyatun 2008; van Doorn-Harder 2006). As we shall see, mutualistic and complementary gender currents continue to exist in tension with more patriarchal and hierarchal conceptions; moreover, public debates, arguments, and affiliations cross traditionalist/ reformist divides.

In Java, as in most societies, the conceptualizations of gender into which individuals and groups are socialized are marked by certain dominant images, themes, and patterns. But gender relations are never a fixed or effectively totalizing system; gendered subjectivities and gender formations are always marked by normative cracks and fissures. Gender and its constructions are never fully prefigured or seamlessly hegemonic. Rather, actors may consciously or unconsciously choose from available alternatives even while constrained to some extent by the structural realities of power, prestige, and gendered authority in a particular time or place (see also Abu-Lughod 2000; Ortner 1997).

Equally important, gender is a cultural-psychological reality as well as a social construction. Its acquisition depends not only on discourses that happen to be dominant/available in a particular social field but also on the dispositions, aspirations, and concerns that agents "bring" to the process of their own socialization (Barth 1993; Kleinman and Kleinman 1985; Wikan 1990). Some of the latter may be so uniquely subjective or personally biographical as to offer no realistic possibility for their expression in the performed realities of everyday life. However, in other contexts, or over the course of one's life, these heretofore inarticulate social models and yearnings may be scaled up into full-blown alternatives to dominant social forms. The alternatives need not be, and often are not, explicitly "political" in form. But their influence may be significant nonetheless, introducing normative tensions and performative plurality into a gendered field that, years earlier, may have looked securely stable and normalized.

Gender Shifts

Sitting on the porch outside her parents' house, Inayah, a student in her fourth and final year studying English literature at Gadjah Mada University, observed as her mother nodded in agreement,

It's different from when my mom was young. She had to quit school and get married when she was only seventeen because her parents thought if she got much older she wouldn't be marketable [*tidak laku*] and she'd end up an old maid [*perawan tua*]. Nowadays women who marry young are laughed at, "*Kok kawin, masih muda!*" [How come she's married, she's so young!]. Women want to finish their educations first and, if possible, to work before marrying. And it's not just city people who think that way. If they can afford to, rural people send their daughters to the city to go to school, and they get married later, too.

This chapter examines shifting conceptions of gender within the context of the resurgent interest in more normative forms of Islam and new social and educational opportunities for youth. In comparing young people's accounts of family life and gender socialization with the experiences of their parents, the contrast in the life situation and aspirations of the recent generation of young women with that of their mothers is particularly striking. In an extended discussion of trends in Javanese women's education and age at first marriage, the Australian sociologist Gavin Jones describes the recent changes as a "revolution," adding that they took place after what had been half a century of stability. He writes, "The word 'revolution' is no exaggeration in describing these trends, because the changes, besides being dramatic in themselves, reflect fundamental changes in family structure, parent-child relationships, child-raising practices, and expectations of daughters" (G. Jones 1994a, 61). Most significantly, whereas in a previous generation it was common for young women to quit school at a young age to marry, often as the result of arrangements made by their elders, Javanese parents today encourage their daughters to put off marriage in order to pursue an education—even if it requires their moving away from home to do so (cf. G. Jones 2004, 2005). And although a small percentage of Javanese parents continues to see the education of their daughters as just another form of preparation for their inevitable roles as wives and mothers, young women themselves see education as unambiguously linked to employment, self-expression, and personal autonomy—albeit an autonomy defined within the parameters of family and a more normatively self-conscious Islamic piety.

College graduate with her mother, Sunan Kalijaga State
Islamic University, Yogyakarta. Photo by Watini Khairi
Syilasyafi.

In examining the shifting and contested understandings of gender among contemporary young people, I build on the broad categories of Muslim Javanese youth
introduced in earlier chapters, categories associated with Yogyakarta's Sunan
Kalijaga State Islamic University (UIN) and the nonconfessional Gadjah Mada
University (UGM). As I have suggested, this contrast overlaps loosely if imper-
fectly with that of neo-traditionalists and neo-reformists, respectively.[1] The family lives and socialization experiences of these two categories of Muslim youth

have been shaped, in each instance, by a number of widely shared social, cultural, and economic factors, all of which have combined to exercise a transformative influence on family relationships and household dynamics. An important distinction between the two groups is that the families of neo-traditionalist youth are for the most part traditionalist *santri* households in which family and gender roles are expressed in terms of religiously inflected ideals derived from traditionalist sources and reflecting the sustained influence of Javanese (cognatic) kinship and customs (*adat-istiadat, tradisi Jawa*). The parents of neo-traditionalist youth are generally more conservative with regard to gender roles and gender expectations, with distinctions between sons and daughters often made by reference to "natural" or "God-given" sexual differences based on *kodrat* (White 2006, 278–279; see chapter 4). This religious emphasis extends to schooling; many traditionalist parents emphasize religious knowledge over general education. And while these parents consistently express the hope that both their sons and their daughters will finish their schooling and obtain a college diploma, the message sent to daughters with regard to work and family is sometimes ambiguous (cf. Srimulyani 2007, 2012). A significant percentage of the young women from traditionalist households attending the State Islamic University—especially in the late 1990s and early 2000s—recount struggling with parental and community restrictions.

In contrast to the situation of neo-traditionalist youth, the family and gender dynamics experienced by students from Gadjah Mada are more varied in their forms and referents. Some of these young people come from deeply religious families, but many do not. In these families both parents and young people themselves downplay overt gender differences, particularly with regard to educational opportunity. Gender distinctions with regard to autonomy and responsibility, nonetheless, still exist. In justifying these distinctions, the parents of neo-reformist youth also make reference to the concept of religious *kodrat*. Here, however, *kodrat* is often couched within the gender discourses promoted by the New Order state and those identified with elite *priyayi* precedents. Most importantly, these parents not only express uniformly high expectations that their daughters as well as their sons will obtain a degree, they are equally consistent in their expectations that both sons *and* daughters should put their educations to work.

Traditionalist Families, Neo-traditionalist Youth

Although Indonesian society is fast changing, nearly half of the population still lives in the countryside. The percentage is slightly higher in Java, from which the majority of the students at the Sunan Kalijaga State Islamic University hail. While rural Java is anything but uniform in culture and social organization, across the countryside the ongoing process of Islamization has led many formerly *abangan* villages to abandon the community-wide and familial rituals propitiating ancestral and place spirits identified as *syirik* (polytheistic; lit. "associating or confusing that which is not God with God") by Muslim reformists (Hefner 2011; Ricklefs 2006, 2007, 2012; van Bruinessen 2013). These recently "re-Islamized" and religiously "renewed" areas of the countryside often stand side by side with villages and towns that have long been identified as staunchly Islamic. These are communities of observant *santri* in which daily life is focused on the mosque and is punctuated by the call to prayers, and where Islamic education—the institutional heart of observant Muslim communities here in Java as in so much of the world (Zaman 2002; Zeghal 2007)—is a valued and long-standing tradition.

Most young people attending the State Islamic University come from these densely populated rural areas of Java and from religious (*santri*) households that are relatively less secure economically than their counterparts from the urban Muslim middle class. While these communities are often referred to as traditionalist, I have identified the youth from these families as *neo*-traditionalist, as it is the younger generation who have most directly experienced the impact of the Islamic resurgence and recent educational and socioeconomic shifts. Significantly, many, in fact most, of these young people are the first members of their families to attend university and to receive a tertiary degree. Nonetheless, compared to neo-reformists, neo-traditionalist youth express a greater continuity in their religious orientation and affiliation with that of earlier generations; the majority has been raised in traditionalist families and communities where Islamic education in *pesantren, madrasah*, and Muslim day schools (*sekolah Islam*) was a central and defining focus of their experience and identity.

In traditionalist families, following the religious ideal of the "good and wholesome family" (*keluarga maslaha*),[2] fathers are identified as the main economic providers (*pencari nafkah*) and family heads (*kepala keluarga*). While most fathers of neo-traditionalist youth worked as farmers or ran small businesses, a good number ran their own religious schools and were also religion teachers either full- or part-time. According to this same family ideal, mothers are described and described themselves as "in the house" (*di rumah saja*) and as "household managers" (*pengatur rumah*). In fact, the social reality is often more complicated: many of these "housewives" also worked as religion teachers, ran small house-front stores, helped with their husband's businesses, or sold items on consignment. The work they perform, however, was often not immediately recognized as employment because it usually did not involve going far from home; it was neither full-time nor permanent and typically did not involve a salary.[3] Mothers' work in these families was often overlooked because of the normative expectation of the family ideal: that the father is the major provider and household head (see also Srimulyani 2012, 125–126).

In these families, fathers typically had noticeably higher levels of education than mothers. Most had graduated from a high school *madrasah* (*madrasah aliyah*); some had specialized teacher training or a few years of college. A small number had graduated from a religious university such as Yogyakarta's State Islamic University, or from one of the many Islamic Teachers' Colleges (IAIN). The overwhelming majority of fathers had, in addition, spent five or more years in a *pesantren* boarding school. Mothers had also typically received their education in religious schools, most often in a family-run *pesantren* or in a *madrasah* located not far from their house (see Azra, Afrianty, and Hefner 2007).[4] In these earlier generations, however, the normative idealization of woman as wife and mother had often displaced women's educational aspirations: a significant number of these mothers had left school to marry at a young age and had had a first child while still in their teens.

Alifa's family exemplified many of these basic traditionalist patterns of family, education, and social mobility. In 2005, Alifa was twenty years old and a second-year student at the Sunan Kalijaga State Islamic University studying Islamic law. Her parents lived in the countryside about a four-hour drive northwest from Yogyakarta. Her mother and father were both from staunchly religious, Nahdlatul Ulama (NU) backgrounds, and, following the general pattern of siblings, cousins, and neighbors, had received most of their education in *pesantren* schools. Alifa's father had completed high school in a *madrasah* (*madrasah aliyah*), but her mother had only managed to complete the equivalent of grade school before dropping out to marry. Alifa was to be the first in her extended family to graduate from college. She said,

> My parents both come from strong religious backgrounds. My dad grew up in a really orthodox area of Cirebon [West Java]. He attended a semitraditional *pesantren* that was also kind of modern. I mean, it was really religious, you know, *salafi* [that is, only offering courses in religious subjects], but they let the students play sports or study the arts. My mom's family comes from a *pesantren* background too. All of her eight younger brothers and sisters went to the same *pesantren*, and all of them graduated at least from high school [*madrasah aliyah*]. My mom was the only one who didn't finish. She only completed grade school [*madrasah ibtidaiyah*]. And then, when she was sixteen, her parents arranged her marriage to my dad.

Not only did marriage take place at a young age among earlier generations of traditionalist Javanese, the marriage itself was far more likely to have been arranged (*dijodohkan*) rather than being the result of personal choice (see G. Jones 1994a). In fact, over twice as many State Islamic University students reported that their parents' marriages had been arranged as did students from Gadjah Mada.[5] The arrangements had usually been made by parents or grandparents, with the groom's (male) kin formalizing the agreement. Parents offered a variety of reasons for these arrangements. The most frequently cited were the desire on the part of their elders to strengthen ties between families and the fear that if a daughter waited too long, she would not be "marketable" (*tidak laku*), due to her age or the possibility of a tarnished reputation.

In Alifa's parents' case, the marriage was her maternal uncle's idea. He had attended the same *pesantren* as Alifa's father. Alifa's uncle brought his classmate home to meet Alifa's grandparents with the idea of matching him up with his sister. The plan worked, and Alifa's grandfather decided to arrange the marriage. Alifa recounts,

> My mom was sixteen, and my dad was twenty-nine. I think my mom was too young to resist, and at that time girls did what their parents told them to do. My mom had put off continuing her schooling because there had been some

kind of problem in the family, and then she got this proposal. I don't think my mom felt she had a choice. It was her parents who made the decision. So she got married and didn't continue her education. Her first child came after they were married one year, when she was seventeen. My mom has never talked about how she felt about it except to say, "Aduh, if you marry young, you're old for a long time." That is, if you become a mother at age seventeen, you're a mother for a long, long time. But my mom is the kind that *"nerima,"* she just accepts whatever happens.

Firda's mother had also left school at a very young age because of an arranged marriage to a much older man. A senior classmate of Alifa soon to graduate from the State Islamic University, Firda came from a small village on the border of Central Java and East Java, about an eight-hour bus ride from Yogyakarta. Her father, who was a religious scholar and a government employee (*pegawai negeri*)—a religion teacher—was considered a particularly good "catch," and in her mother's family, Firda explained, there was a tradition of marrying off daughters at a young age. Firda's mother married at the age of twelve, dropping out of school in the process. Her father was twenty-five.

I once asked my mother, "How could you do that, mom? How could you marry at the age of twelve?" And she said it was because her father was anxious to see his daughter marry, that was the reason. My grandfather (my mother's father) was wealthy. His father (my great-grandfather) had been one of the village founders. He was a rural landowner. But he had lots of wives and lots of children, and the land was divided among them. In addition, there was a tradition in the family of selling off land in order to go on the hajj. So today the land is almost gone. But even though the family had money, there was no tradition of educating children, especially not girls. They were kept at home and expected to become farmers' wives. The boys were sent to *madrasah ibtidaiyah* [Islamic elementary school] and then to a *pesantren* for five or six years. They would marry and were expected to become farmers too.

In devout traditionalist *santri* families in particular, the long-standing pattern was for adolescent girls to be kept close to home and under parental supervision until a suitable partner could be found. Parents were concerned to protect the virtue and reputation of their daughters and the status and reputation of the family (see also Srimulyani 2012, 116). By keeping her close to home, they not only guarded their family's good name but also increased the prospects that the girl might be able to marry a man from a "good" family and with the promise of future economic security. In many traditionalist families this meant that in an earlier generation daughters would be married young, or, if they were allowed to continue their schooling, they would be sent to a nearby religious school, where it was hoped they would receive a strong moral education (cf. G. Jones 1994a; Oey-Gardiner 1991).

In their capacity as the heads of their families and as a function of their greater levels of education and religious training compared with that of their wives, fathers in these families often made important educational decisions for their children, particularly for their daughters. This pattern was common in the parental generation, and continues to be the case in many contemporary families as well. Many neo-traditionalist youth recounted that it was their fathers who decided whether they would continue their educations, and whether it would be in religious or "general" schools. In some families—such as Firda's—fathers not only chose the school but even the program of study. Firda explained,

> Because my mom had so little education, my dad was the one who gave us advice about school and decided where we would go. When I was in grade school [SD], I still lived at home with my parents. Then for middle school [*madrasah tsanawiyah*] I was sent to live with my grandmother and then to stay in a *pesantren*, where I studied the Qur'an. At first I was really homesick and I'd sometimes sneak out and walk the forty-five minutes from the *pesantren* to my grandmother's house for a visit. I attended the same schools as my brother, first *madrasah tsanawiyah* and then *madrasah aliyah*. We had maybe 50 percent general education courses and 50 percent religious study. We weren't really prepared to go on to college for serious study; it was just for our own betterment. My parents expected that my brother would come home to work in the rice fields or teach religion, and I would get married and follow my husband. Even when I got into the State Islamic University, my dad chose my major. He said, "Da, this looks good." I took that as what he wanted me to do and so I went into *tafsir hadith* [interpreting hadith].

This gender differentiation with regard to decision making in traditionalist families was not limited to fathers but extended to sons, who, once they reached adolescence, were allowed to exercise more choice in educational and other decisions than their sisters. The greater role accorded sons in decision making is an expression of the greater degree of personal autonomy and freedom of movement accorded to Javanese males more generally—both in religiously observant (*santri*) families and in the population as a whole (Blackwood 2011, 73; see also Bennett 2005, 28; H. Geertz 1989 [1961], 119). In traditionalist families, this pattern was especially evident in households that were less well off. It was not unusual, for example, for a young man to strike out on his own from a young age—particularly if his parents could not offer him much financial support. Parents often made reference to the Javanese aphorism "a man has a long stride" (In. *laki-laki, langkahnya panjang*) to mean both that it's natural for a young man to travel far from home and that—unlike a young woman—he is more easily able to escape from trouble if it arises. The greater autonomy enjoyed by sons could occasionally be a source of family friction, especially during teen years, when many boys test the limits of their newly achieved freedom of movement. Parents, however, were aware that their sons would eventually have to support a family, and most accepted, even encouraged, their sons' independence.

Ahmad, in his third year of coursework at the State Islamic University, insisted that from the age of twelve he had made his own decisions about where he would go to school. Ahmad's family was relatively well off, but he had a large

number of siblings (he was the second of seven children).[6] His father sold building materials; his mother was "just a housewife" but helped her husband with
his business. Ahmad's family was from a remote rural area of East Java, a region
with an abundance of NU-linked *pesantren*. In Ahmad's case he chose to attend
a distant *pesantren* despite his parents' expressed desire that he attend one of
the boarding schools located nearer to his home.

> The main thing for my parents was they wanted all of us to have a strong
> religious foundation. That was their first principle, that's what they told us.
> They had both spent a long time in *pesantren*, and they wanted us to have
> the same experience. They sent me to a general kindergarten and then to a
> *madrasah ibtidaiyah* for grade school. After that, they expected I would
> attend one of the *pesantren* in our area because there were so many. In the
> end I decided to follow them and enter a *pesantren*, but I was the one who
> decided where I wanted to go. I chose a *pesantren* in Ponorogo, 175 kilometers
> [a six-hour bus ride] from my home. My parents didn't agree with my choice,
> but I insisted. They wanted me to attend a place nearer to my home, but I told
> them, no, it had to be my choice. I wanted to go far from my parents, to be on
> my own. I didn't like being told what to do, even though I was only twelve at
> the time.

It was nonetheless Ahmad's father who told him he should apply to the State
Islamic University. Ahmad followed his father's advice and was accepted into
the Faculty of Ushuluddin (Theology).

Mothers in traditionalist families, although not identified as the major decision makers, nonetheless made their opinions known. Many did so through a
pattern of off-the-record backtalk (cf. Brenner 1998, 141; see also Keeler 1990).
Others offered private counsel to their children, especially to their daughters.
In particular, women who had quit school to marry at a young age could be quite
insistent that their daughters continue their educations and put off marriage
until they had received their diplomas. In contrast to the previous generation,
they viewed education as offering their daughters a form of economic security
and personal autonomy—and the possibility of supporting themselves and their
offspring should their husbands die or divorce them. Some were like Alifa's
mother, who had always regretted not finishing school and who continued to
improve herself by reading newspapers and listening to news programs on radio
and television. She had reminded her daughter from the time she was young of
the importance of education and of her desire to see Alifa "go farther and
achieve more" than she herself had been able to achieve, telling her, "you never
know what the future will bring."

In fact, one of the more striking themes of my interviews and discussions
was that *both* mothers and fathers of neo-traditionalist youth were anxious to
see their children go further and achieve more than they had. Although generally from more limited economic circumstances than the parents of Gadjah
Mada students, the parents of neo-traditionalist youth have embraced the new
middle-class ideal that education is linked to social mobility and economic success.

Unlike parents of neo-reformist youth, however, many parents of neo-traditionalist youth place a stronger emphasis on the acquisition of religious knowledge and piety (*kesalehan*) than on general education, because they believe that their children need a strong moral foundation to face the challenges of a rapidly changing world.[7] This piety-first educational principle was especially true with regard to the education of daughters who were expected to be the moral standard-bearers for the next generation. And although many parents in these families fully anticipated that their daughters would put their educations to work after graduation, there were others who assumed that in accordance with their religiously sanctioned roles and nature (*kodrat*), their daughters would "follow their husbands." From this point of view, their daughters' education was viewed as being mainly for their own improvement and to prepare them to be better wives and mothers (Srimulyani 2007, 88).

Alifa's parents told her expressly that they had sent her to school to get knowledge (*ilmu*), and that learning was "the most important thing" (cf. Parker and Nilan 2013, 88; Nilan 2009). They told her, "What's important is that you have a good education and it can be used in raising your children, or whatever. Lots of things can come from education; it doesn't have to be a job." Halimah's parents had told her much the same thing. Her family was from a rural area of Central Java that Halimah described as a "warehouse for the production of *santri*." It was an area where the religious education of young women in local *pesantren* had a long tradition and the sheltering of young women was still common. Halimah explained,

> In my family, the boys are given the freedom to choose the kind of school they want to go to, because boys will have to grow up and support a family. But the girls are all sent to religious schools. I think my parents feel that girls have to have more religious knowledge so that they follow their husbands more obediently or something. In my area, lots of girls are still put in seclusion [*dipingit*]; that is, kept inside, out of sight. So I feel lucky [to be allowed to continue on in school]. In my mind, I think, no matter what, I still have to follow what my parents say. They want me to go farther, to do better than them. They think knowledge is worth more than money. They don't really talk about work or make the connection to a career. They just say, "Remember, your first responsibility is to be a good wife, because no matter what, you'll be an example for your children."

In addition to the religious ideal of *kodrat*, traditionalist parents emphasized the traditional Javanese ideals of *nrimo* (compliance, acceptance), *ngalah* (yielding, submitting), and *ikhlas* (devotion, sacrifice) in the moral education of daughters. Reports from young women in these families reveal that they were far less likely than their brothers to directly challenge parental decisions and generally found it more difficult than their brothers to avoid patriarchal authority by making themselves scarce around the house or simply leaving. And although some girls had managed to convince their parents to allow them to attend a religious school of their choice (often one with a particularly good reputation or a family connection), most were painfully aware of the financial burden education imposed upon their parents and were grateful for the educational opportunities they had been given.

Culture and *Kodrat*

In traditionalist families, the religious education of children begins quite young and emphasizes gender difference, although important distinctions in the treatment and expectations of males and females do not begin to appear until the age of ten or twelve. Very young children typically followed the example of their mothers or (especially in the case of boys) their fathers in learning to pray and recite prayers. As soon as they are old enough, they join the neighborhood children and attend religious lessons at the mosque in the evening. On average, male and female youths from these families report as children they began to learn to read the Qur'an around age five.

By the age of eight or ten, both boys and girls were performing the five daily prayers with some regularity, and most had already begun to follow the annual Ramadan fast. According to a well-known hadith, children of this age who do not perform their prayers when reminded to do so may be beaten by their parents.[8] For parents, daily prayer is considered the most important and ethically instructive of the five religious pillars, and most place special emphasis on ensuring that their children learn at an early age to pray properly and regularly. Young people from traditionalist backgrounds recalled that when they were little the most common reason for being punished by their parents—next to quarreling with siblings—was their failure to perform their daily prayers or to attend religious classes at the mosque or *langgar* (prayer house).

In traditionalist communities, young boys are typically circumcised between the ages of ten and twelve. The operation itself is a relatively brief procedure, after which family members offer the boy small gifts of money. In some cases, the circumcision is followed by a more elaborate traditional celebration (*slametan*) that includes a feast of several courses served to large numbers of neighbors and guests. If there is this larger celebration, the family typically also offers some form of entertainment—a masked dance performance, *wayang* shadow play, or a percussionist orchestra—and the festivities may go on long into the night (see C. Geertz 1976 [1960], 51–53; H. Geertz 1989 [1961], 67). Even in the countryside, however, large and expensive celebrations of this sort have been experiencing a serious decline over the past generation. The reasons have not only to do with Islamization but also with the high cost of sponsorship and the shift of social investment away from the arts and festivities and into other types of family goods (cf. Ricklefs 2012).

Once circumcised, boys are expected to dedicate themselves more seriously to their religious studies and to regularly attend Friday prayers with the men. In fact, in some areas of the Javanese countryside circumcision is called *islaman* and the boy is described as *diislamkan*, literally, "to be made Muslim." As significant, circumcision is recognized as signaling the beginning of the young man's increased autonomy and nascent sexuality. Around this time, many boys begin spending even less time around the house and more time with friends, sneaking cigarettes and drinking coffee at the neighborhood guard post (*pos kamling*) late into the evening, and even sleeping at the mosque (see also Jay 1969, 33).[9]

At this age, by contrast, young girls begin to experience growing restrictions on their freedom of movement. Whereas at an earlier age they may have played outside in the evenings, by age ten or twelve young girls are required to come home directly after school or evening religious lessons and are not allowed to go out unless they first secure permission and are accompanied. They are also expected to more consistently wear the loose headscarf (*krudung*) and to dress modestly when outside the house. Many young women recounted rather serious arguments with parents over their desires to continue wearing jeans or culottes and T-shirts and their parents' insistence that they switch to long skirts and tunics. By this age, too, girls are expected to begin helping their mothers with household chores by sweeping, chopping vegetables, and serving guests. With regard to household chores, less is expected of boys, who, at any rate, no longer spend much free time around the family home.

Around this same time (age twelve or the beginning of middle school), many young people in traditionalist families are sent to *pesantren* boarding schools, returning to visit their parents only three or four times a year for several years thereafter (see Srimulyani 2007, 86). In Java, the great majority of these schools are affiliated with the traditionalist Muslim organization Nahdlatul Ulama. *Pesantren* are places where the traditional Islamic sciences—especially those related to the study of the Qur'an, traditions of the Prophet (hadith), and jurisprudence (*fiqh*)—are taught in a residential setting that places as much emphasis on the embodiment and performance of Islamic learning as its intellectual acquisition (Gade 2004a). Although a few are of more modern origins, the main *pesantren* texts are the *kitab kuning*, or "yellow books," most of which date from the classical and medieval Islamic periods (Dhofier 1999 [1982], xix; van Bruinessen 1990, 227).[10] Unlike Islamic reformists of modernist persuasion who justify their religious views by way of an *ijtihadic* (examination through reason) reading of scriptural sources, traditionalist Sunni Islamic scholarship draws heavily on the commentaries and writings of classical Muslim scholars, especially those identified with any of the four Sunni "schools of law" (*madhab*) recognized still today.[11]

For young children sent off to boarding schools in this manner, the experience can at first be shocking or even traumatic, marked as it is by a rather sudden immersion in a world marked by twenty-four-hour-a-day scheduling and a strict institutional hierarchy. However, the experience also provides an opportunity for youthful adventure of a sort that has long been prized in Javanese and Javo-Islamic culture, where the ideal of setting off in search of knowledge and experience (*cari ilmu, cari pengalaman*) has a long precedent.[12] In addition to obtaining knowledge and experience, there is the additionally attractive possibility of making new friends (*banyak teman*) and developing a significant degree of self-sufficiency (*berdikari*). Not all young people, however, are able to bear being separated from their families; some run away and return home. Living conditions in most *pesantren* are Spartan, and the daily schedule of prayer and religious study is rigorous (see Dhofier 1999 [1982]; Lukens-Bull 2001, 2005; Srimulyani 2007).

Ahmad, who had decided on his own at the age of twelve to attend a *pesantren* far from his home in East Java, recalled,

> Every morning at 3:00 we had to get up for *subuh* prayers, and after prayers, we had to study. We studied the *kitab*, then in the morning we went to *tsanawiyah* or to *aliyah* [for courses in general education]. The school was outside of the *pesantren*, but close by. We came back to the dormitory at 1:00 and ate and napped from 1:00 until 2:00. Then we had religious school in the afternoon in the *pesantren*. We came back to our rooms at *ashar*, and after prayers we studied again. After religious study [*ngaji*] we did *magrib* prayers and then more religious study [*ngaji*]. So our schedule of activities was full; we only rested a short while. At 10:00 at night we cooked for ourselves. We cooked and ate, cleaned up and everything until 12 midnight. We went to bed at 12 or so . . . and then got up again at 3:00 for prayers.

Although *pesantren* vary considerably—the size of school and number of *santri*, the specific religious texts that are taught, and the quality of the staff and facilities—virtually all are segregated by gender. A given school is either all-male or all-female; or, if it accepts both genders, the institution maintains a separate campus for each (Nasir n.d., 5; van Doorn-Harder 2006, 180; see also Srimulyani 2007).[13] Male and female students are always taught in different buildings or different rooms, or, if in the same room, they are kept visually separated by a sheet or curtain hung between them. Separation of the sexes continues outside of classes. Regulations vary depending on the specific *pesantren*, but in most schools young people are forbidden to interact in any substantial way with a member of the opposite sex or to be alone with a member of the opposite sex not classified as *muhrim* (that is, within the category of close kin). In Ahmad's *pesantren*, no communication whatsoever was allowed between male and female *santri*. When a *santri* happened to encounter members of the opposite sex on the way to *madrasah* or when visiting or picking up a relative, there was typically much yelling, laughing, and teasing:

> We never talked with the female *santri* in the *pesantren*. To arrange a meeting at the girl's *pesantren*, like to pick up your sister or cousin, you had to go through this really long procedure, because it was taboo for a girl to meet with a guy. If the guy was doing volunteer work at the women's dormitory, that was normal, but there were no reasons for a girl to appear at the guy's dorm. It didn't happen. If it did, all the guys would yell and holler.

> Sometimes we saw girls, like outside of the *pesantren* on our way to classes at the *madrasah* or something, and if we knew each other, like from home or it was a relative, we might say "hello" or maybe ask about school. But we didn't know anything about dating. There was no opportunity anyway. I once heard about a *santri* who tried to send letters secretly to a girl in the *pondok*, and he was caught. That guy had his head shaved. That was his punishment.

In most *pesantren,* the rules for female *santri* are considerably stricter than those for males (Srimulyani 2012, 120). Whereas a male *santri* who sends letters to or meets secretly with a girl might have his head shaved, a female *santri* caught passing letters to boys or meeting a boy is more likely to be expelled.

Not only are female *santri* taught separately from male *santri* and required to abide by stricter rules, but they are exposed to texts relating to gender roles and domestic life that most male *santri* do not study. These texts include the *'Uqud al-Lujjayn,* the *Adab al-Mu'asyarah,* and the *Qurratul 'Uyun.* Of these, Eka Srimulyani, an Indonesian scholar of Islam, writes that the *'Uqud al-Lujjayn* is the most popular and has become "the main textbook on the rights and responsibilities of a husband and wife, or marital life in general" (Srimulyani 2012, 123; see also van Doorn-Harder 2006, 167).[14] The text contains passages that glorify the unqualified submission of the wife to her husband, including passages that support the right of the husband to "educate" his wife by beating her if she goes out of the house without his permission, does not cover herself adequately in front of men who are unrelated (non-*muhrim*), or even talks with other men. Especially notable is a passage that describes a woman as being "like a slave marrying her master, or a prisoner who is helpless under someone else's power" and instructs a wife to lower her head and her gaze in front of her husband and to obey him no matter what he instructs her to do, unless it is forbidden by Islamic law (van Doorn-Harder 2006, 197; 2007).

The *'Uqud al-Lujjayn* has been criticized for its patriarchal, even misogynistic, passages by a number of Muslim scholars but most extensively by the Forum for the Study of Kitab Kuning (Forum Kajian Kitab Kuning (FK3), 2001). The team of scholars, led by Sinta Nuriyah A. Wahid, the wife of former Indonesian president Abdurrahman Wahid, contested the authenticity of the sources cited by the author of the text and argued for a more contextual interpretation of the work. The forum's revised and annotated version of the *'Uqud al-Lujjayn* is being distributed to women's *pesantren* all over Java (van Doorn-Harder 2006, 200). Replacing classical texts with revised versions, however, has never been part of the *pesantren* tradition; in fact, quite the opposite is the case: the continued study of the *kitab kuning* is the distinctive feature of the Islamic classical learning tradition. Srimulyani comments that while the original text of the *'Uqud al-Lujjayn* continues to be taught in many *pesantren,* at least some teachers now present it along with their own analysis and contextualization (Srimulyani 2012, 127).[15]

Despite ongoing efforts to address the patriarchal bias of some *pesantren* texts, female *santri* continue to be taught that they must be careful not to dress or behave in a way that would attract the male gaze and lead men to sinful thoughts. Male *santri,* conversely, are warned that women are a source of temptation and that "gazing at women is like sipping Satan's poison."[16] In virtually all *pesantren,* physical contact, touching, and even handshaking are forbidden between male and female *santri.* Both males and females become accustomed to averting their gaze in the presence of a member of the opposite sex. The result of this instruction is that interactions between the sexes tend to be marked by awkward shyness and a lack of self-confidence that do not easily dissipate even after leaving the *pesantren*. Many young people from traditionalist families, particularly young women, reported continued difficulties interacting with and talking to members of the opposite sex, making their adjustment to the cosmopolitan social life of metropolitan Yogyakarta a particular challenge.

While female students from traditionalist households report encountering multiple social and familial obstacles in the course of their life journey to the State Islamic University, most insisted that they considered themselves lucky compared with many of their friends in their home communities whose parents would not allow or could not afford to send their daughters on to college. In most cases, these young women reported that they were the first women in their families and communities to receive a college degree. They were proud of that fact and took seriously their role as models and mentors for their younger siblings.

There were, nonetheless, some neo-traditionalist women who chafed at the gender expectations placed upon them by their families and communities and struggled to have their personal aspirations realized. Nurul—introduced in chapter 3—had tried from a young age to convince her parents to allow her to attend general rather than religious schools. She had dreamt of studying in a nonreligious field such as language or political science. However, her father put more emphasis on religion than on general knowledge and wanted to keep his daughter close to home. He had enrolled Nurul in an Islamic grade school (*madrasah ibtidaiyah*) near their home and then sent her to an Islamic middle school (*madrasah tsanawiyah*) and on to an Islamic high school (*madrasah aliyah*). After graduating high school, Nurul had applied to Gadjah Mada University and was not surprised, but was nonetheless disappointed, when she did not get in. Her parents, however, were delighted and relieved when she was subsequently accepted for admission to the UIN.

As was the case in many other families of neo-traditionalist women, Nurul's mother was particularly supportive of her daughter's desire to continue her education, in part because years earlier her own educational aspirations had been frustrated. When she was seventeen and still a student in a high-school *madrasah* (*madrasah aliyah*), her marriage had been arranged to a man ten years her senior. She had agreed to the marriage on the condition that she be allowed to finish high school before setting up a household with her new husband.[17] Because of her own frustrations at having to cut short her schooling to marry, from the time her daughter was in high school, Nurul's mother had impressed upon her the importance of becoming self-sufficient and had urged her daughter to put off marriage and get her college degree first. Recognizing the uncertainties of marriage and the real possibilities of divorce or death of a spouse, she told Nurul that it would be better if she went to work and had her own income so she wouldn't have to depend on her husband: "The problem is that your husband may leave, and you'll be faced with the responsibility of supporting the household on your own. Better that you are prepared for that possibility from the beginning."

Nurul's father gave his daughter similar advice about the importance of education, but his message with regard to gender roles was more mixed. While he was proud of his daughter and supportive of her education, he continued to think of her schooling within the context of her religiously informed *kodrat* and the inevitability of her eventually assuming her core adult role as a wife and mother. According to Nurul,

> Even though he agreed to send me to college to study, my dad still clings to an ideology of *pengibuan* [motherliness]; it's still there. So the expectation that I will be first and foremost a wife and mother hasn't changed at all. It's like "Yes, you should go to college, and yes, you have a right to work, but according to your *kodrat,* you will become a mother and you have to be ready to support the career of your husband."

Although constrained by their families with regard to their educational choices and role expectations relating to the ideology of *kodrat,* Nurul and most of the other young, neo-traditionalist women I interviewed recognized the sacrifices their parents had made for them in supporting their education. These young women looked forward to helping their younger siblings get through school or to contributing to the support of their parents in their older age. They wanted to "repay the [moral] debt" (*membalas budi*) they felt they owed their parents for supporting their years of schooling. The debt is one that is understood as having both Islamic and Javanese qualities. Its Javanese elements include the sense of deep moral obligation one is expected to feel toward the parents who gave birth to and nurtured one as a child (see H. Geertz 1989 [1961], 68). The debt's more explicitly Islamic elements reference the hadith that states, "For the child who pleases his parents, Allah opens the doors to heaven. If he displeases either his mother or father, Allah will not be pleased with him, even if his parents have treated him unjustly."[18]

In contrast to some of their parents, however, very few of these young women expressed reservations about going on to use their education for the purposes of finding employment outside of the household. In response to her father's admonition that in accordance with her *kodrat* she would become a mother and should prioritize the career of her husband, Nurul argued, "I find that hard to accept. I mean, what's the use of my getting an education if I'm supposed to forget it all when I get married?"

Neo-reformist Youth and Their Families

A majority of the families of the Gadjah Mada students—that is, the families of what I am referring to as neo-reformist youth—grew up living in urban areas of Java (city wards, towns, county seats) and were relatively well off in comparison to their State Islamic University counterparts. Complicating any easy categorization, at least some of these families had moved away from the countryside only within the last generation, as a function of broader processes of urbanization and industrialization that occurred during the Suharto era. In these families the precise role of religion is considerably more varied than among the families of UIN students. A generation or two earlier, many of the elders in these families were *abangan* largely indifferent to the normative imperatives of *santri* Islam; others were moderately observant Muslims but, politically speaking, multicon-fessional nationalists largely opposed to Islamic political parties. Some believed that "Javanese Islam" could and should differ from other forms of Islam in matters of custom (*adat-istiadat*) if not worship (*ibadat*), theology (*kalam*), or jurisprudence (*fiqh*). The Islamic resurgence of the 1970s and 1980s, of course, changed all of this, with the most palpable effects being felt by a new generation of young people (cf. Ricklefs 2012; van Bruinessen 2013).

Among neo-reformist youth, less than one-quarter of those I surveyed described their parents as "religious" or "very religious," while a majority reported that their parents practiced simply "common, popular" Islam (*Islam awam*) or "regular Islam" (*Islam biasa*). Of this latter group, it was not uncommon for young people to volunteer that they viewed their parents as "insufficiently pious" or, worse yet in their eyes, still involved in traditional Javanese (*kejawen*) practices their children now regarded as no less than polytheistic (*syirik*). It is the orien-tation of the children, then, that can most aptly be described as *neo*-reformist, a result in part of their years of religious education in school, exposure to a heightened public religious discourse, and involvement in both self-study and regular religious study groups (*pengajian;* see chapter 3). Within these house-holds, shifts in family relations and gender roles have also occurred over the past generation, although the changes take a somewhat more varied form than those observed among neo-traditionalists. As is the case among neo-traditionalist youth, however, these shifts have affected the situation of young women even more dramatically than young men.

By comparison with their State Islamic University *santri* counterparts, these were families in which a higher percentage of fathers as well as mothers had some years of college education. A small number of the fathers of Gadjah Mada students had even had some years of postgraduate study. But what distinguishes these families most in comparison with the families of neo-traditionalist students is parents' unambiguous support for the education of both sons and daughters, "at least as far as an S1 (a bachelor's degree)," and their emphasis on the *economic* and social class benefits of education in addition to and even more than any ostensibly religious reward. These parents, many of whom were civil servants (*pegawai negeri*), had enthusiastically embraced the government's development narrative that education was a key to upward mobility, economic security, and middle-class status, and consistently expressed the hope that their children would surpass their own achievements (*melebihi orang tuanya*). Mothers were particularly outspoken in linking the education of daughters with greater eco-nomic independence and personal autonomy.

In the families of Gadjah Mada students, basic parental roles were in accord with the state's version of the "small prosperous" family (*keluarga sejahtera, keluarga sakinah*),[19] a model associated with the modernist Muhammadiyah and promoted by numerous government agencies under the Suharto regime (1966–1998; see Syamsiyatun 2007; van Doorn-Harder 2013; White 2006). Like the neo-traditionalists, neo-reformist young people were also inclined to identify their fathers as the "main providers of economic support" (*pencari nafkah yang pokok*) and as the heads or leaders of the family (*kepala keluarga, pemimpin keluarga*), while they referred to their mothers as household managers (*pengurus rumah tangga*) who dealt with their families' daily needs. However, unlike the mothers of neo-traditionalist youth, a significant percentage of the mothers of Gadjah Mada students were also identified as making an important contribution to household income by working outside of the home. Many were salaried civil servants or were involved in business or trade. Others worked as caterers, makeup artists, wedding organizers, or seamstresses. Working mothers were nonetheless expected to take responsibility for the supervision of the household and the care of children. In order to fulfill their dual roles (*peran ganda*), mothers of Gadjah Mada students not uncommonly relied on some form of hired help (*pembantu* [housekeepers] or *babysister* [nursemaids]),[20] in some cases taking in a series of young, distant relatives from the countryside who were given room and board and sometimes school fees in exchange for child care and housework.

In these families, marriages in the parental generation were more often the result of individual choice than parental arrangement. Parents had met each other in school or through friends, and there was typically much less of a difference between spouses both in terms of ages as well as educational level than was common among parents of neo-traditionalist students from the State Islamic University. As a result, mothers in these families had relatively more say in decision making, educational and otherwise. Although fathers still had the last word in important deliberations, many neo-reformist youth identified their mothers as the ones most involved in choosing schools and overseeing their schoolwork (cf. C. Jones 2004, 517–518).

What is more, mothers in these households were reported to be almost twice as likely to be identified as fulfilling a significant emotional role in their children's lives as mothers in traditionalist households.[21] Reflecting a pattern of matrifocality identified in early ethnographies of Java (H. Geertz 1989 [1961]; Tanner 1974), and as an extension of their role as household managers, mothers in urban middle-class families have taken on the modern tasks of psychological counseling and "stress management" for their families (see C. Jones 2004). Young women in particular described their mothers as "like friends" (*seperti teman*) and "confidants," *tempat curahan hati* (lit. "a place to pour out feelings"). Carla Jones, drawing on the work of the sociologist Arlie Hochschild (1979, 2012 [1989]), has referred to the role of women in this negotiation of sentiments within the domestic sphere as "emotion work."[22] She observes that emotional resources were one among the many kinds of resources women in the New Order were encouraged to develop in pursuit of an ideal middle-class domestic life (C. Jones 2004, 514). The state's detailed injunctions on the role of women in domestic management were reinforced by the explosion in the late 1990s and early 2000s of books, television shows, and magazines that offered married women advice on how to maintain a stress-free, harmonious, middle-class household (C. Jones 2004; see also Krier 2011).

Isti's family offered a neo-*priyayi* version of many of these basic patterns with regard to familial roles and relationships. When I first met her in 1999, Isti was a second-year student at Gadjah Mada University, studying Javanese language and literature. Her family lives in Yogyakarta in a long-established neighborhood of well-tended houses adjacent to the Sultan's palace. Isti's mother has a law degree, and her father has a degree from a technical academy. They had both been married previously and divorced. They met through family friends and married when they were both in their late thirties. Isti was born one year later and is an only child.

Isti's mother is a lecturer (*dosen*) and the dean of a law school at a university in a city about one hour from Yogyakarta. Her job requires that she spend a considerable amount of time commuting to and from work; she travels frequently to Jakarta as well. When Isti was an infant, her mother hired a trained caretaker (*babysister*) from a nearby hospital to care for her. The family also has a live-in maid—an older woman who is a distant relation—who helps with food shopping and housework. Isti's father had been a successful businessman but suffered ill health and has since retired.

Revealing her non-*santri* background, Isti describes her parents as "regular" Muslims, "not fanatic." Her mother is actually a distant relation to the Sultan's court; Isti's maternal grandmother had been a member of the Sultan's dance troupe and danced the *bedoyo* at the palace when she was young.[23] The family proudly shows off its prior courtly connections in other regards as well. Prominently displayed in the family's front sitting room is a carved wooden stand with the royal insignia of two entwined serpents. In the stand are a yellow umbrella and a spear, both sacred court heirlooms (*pusaka*; see Ricklefs 2012, 40–41; see also Daniels 2009). Isti's mother still embraces elements of Javanese court culture and belief, particularly with regard to life-cycle ceremonies, including those to which many Muslim reformists today object. On the wall next to the stand is a large framed picture of Isti as a small child of six or seven dressed in traditional Javanese dress on the occasion of her *tetesan*, or ceremonial circumcision.[24] While Isti showed me an album of photographs of the event—an elaborate affair with Javanese dancers and over three hundred guests—her mother assured me that female circumcision is merely symbolic; that is, no cutting of the clitoris or labia is involved:[25] "According to Islam, *tetesan* is just a cleansing. Javanese believe that it's the male who provides the seed [*bibit*] and the female who is the container [*bobot*]. If the egg then breaks and is fertilized [*netas*], it must later pass through the female part, so that part must be cleansed. You do that by wiping the labia with turmeric [*kunyit*]. There is no cutting at all."

My assistant, who was a friend and classmate of Isti's, broke in at this point to say that the elaborate celebration of *tetesan* was never widespread but associated only with the Javanese courts and with *priyayi* culture. If they circumcise their daughter at all, most young couples today have the procedure carried out quietly at the hospital.[26] My assistant offered the example of her two older sisters, whose daughters were both circumcised when they were infants. It was part of the "birth package" that was paid for by their husbands' employers. The package included the birthing itself as well as circumcision and ear piercing; the latter procedures had been carried out when the babies were taken in for their first physical exam at one month or forty days after birth (cf. Jaspan and Hill 1987, 13, 22; Feillard and Marcoes 1998, 357). Both of the young women agreed that having the procedure done in the hospital by a nurse or *bidan* (midwife) was "more practical" (*lebih praktis*) with regard to time and expense and that the general direction of change among new parents nowadays was toward early circumcision without any celebration.[27] Whatever its motive, the streamlining of this rite of early life passage is consistent with the growing neglect of Javanist rites of life passage as community-wide celebrations in much of Java in the aftermath of the Islamic resurgence of the 1980s and 1990s (Ricklefs 2012).[28]

Isti's relationship with her mother was visibly close and affectionate, and during our conversation she often turned to her mother for confirmation of the information she proffered. Isti said it was her mother who most often gave her advice and helped her with personal problems. It was her mother, for example, who had advised Isti to put off marriage until she had obtained her degree, telling her it would make it easier for her to later obtain employment and in the long run would allow her to maintain a more comfortable standard of living. Although Isti had a serious boyfriend, the couple had agreed that it was best to wait to get married until Isti had finished her undergraduate degree (*sarjana muda*). Isti laughed along with my assistant and said that all of their friends were putting off marriage to get their degrees. Those who married young were the exception. When such youthful marriages occurred, there was not infrequently gossip and speculation that the bride "had" to get married because she was pregnant, a condition jokingly referred to as MBA or "married because accident."[29]

Nina's mother had given her daughter similar advice about marriage and schooling, admonishing her to "[put] school first" (*kuliah dulu*) and avoid serious relationships. Nina was in her third year at Gadjah Mada and was studying farming technology. Her family lived in an industrial town to the north of Yogyakarta where her father worked for the state Department of Small Businesses and her mother was a pharmacist. Her parents had grown up in the same small Javanese town and had known each other from childhood. It wasn't an arranged marriage, although their families were close. The couple married when they were both twenty-five and had already graduated from college.

Like Isti, Nina described her parents' religion as "ordinary" or "common" Islam (*Islam awam*). They prayed and performed the Ramadan fast, she explained, but also still engaged in some *kejawen* practices such as the presentation of ritual offerings to ancestral spirits. Nina insisted that she had no interest in and even objected to her parent's performance of these practices. Like other neo-reformist students (see chapter 3), she said she had no intention of continuing these traditions once she was married and raising a family of her own:

My dad once told me that his father had been a *dukun* [a traditional ritual specialist]. My dad still does things like meditate and fast in order to do well in his work and make lots of money. And my mom puts out offerings and burns incense for the ancestors on certain nights. But from my religious education, I know things like that are *syirik* and are not allowed. Like one time my mom was menstruating and couldn't do the prayers and she told me to invite the ancestors to eat the offerings. So I told her that I would do that, but then I recited a different prayer. I asked God to forgive my mother and to forgive the sins of my ancestors and then I ate the offerings myself.

Nina recounted that throughout her childhood her parents had stressed the importance of respecting her father's position as the undisputed head of the family, using refined Javanese speech (*kromo*) to address elders, and appreciating the traditional arts. Although her parents were not the descendants of nobility, because of their appreciation for Javanese traditions, their casual attitude toward religious matters, and her father's status as a government employee, Nina's family, like Isti's, could be considered members of the new bureaucratic elite, the neo-*priyayi*. Although in the 1950s and 1960s the neo-*priyayi* were often stalwart supporters of nonreligious nationalism, the children of this generation, like Isti and Nina, are today becoming more religiously observant.

Nina also reported that she had a very close relationship with her mother, whom she described as "like a friend" (*seperti teman*). While both of Nina's parents emphasized the importance of their daughter getting a college diploma, it was her mother who had told her from the time she was young that it would be best if Nina had an income of her own so that she would not have to depend on her husband and would have more choices "if anything should happen"; that is, if her husband died or divorced her. Here in fact the issue is neither female autonomy nor egoistic individualism but a realistic assessment of the precariousness of conjugal ties and women's greater vulnerability relative to men within marriage. Nina explained, "My mom often tells me that because she works and has her own income, she isn't so dependent on my dad. Like for example, if anything should happen, she could make her own choices. We like to joke around with each other. Like once I said to her, 'What's the point of working? What if my husband is a millionaire?' And she said, 'No, you still have to work even if your husband is rich. Because it's different, you know, if you work, you won't be dependent and you can make your own choices.'"

Joking aside, Nina said she was looking forward to graduating and anxious to put her degree to work. She hoped to find a job in food manufacturing or food processing, and planned to put off marriage until she had secured a job and worked for a few years because she knew that many companies preferred to hire single women. Most importantly—and illustrating once again the socially embedded individualism characteristic of so many in the new Muslim middle class regardless of background—she was looking forward to "paying back her parents" (*membalas orang tua*) for their investment in her education, by helping to pay for the schooling of her younger brother (cf. Parker and Nilan 2013, 86): "I really want to graduate, work, and repay my parents first [before marrying]. I want to make my parents happy so that they can enjoy my success. Repaying my parents is my first priority. I think lots of young people feel that way, especially those from families without a lot of wealth. We understand how difficult it is for our parents to find the money to send us to school. So we hope to be able to repay them."

The parental emphasis on the education of daughters and the importance of daughters putting their educations "to work" in extrafamilial employment was a consistent theme, not only in families young people described as religiously "regular" or "ordinary" but also in those families identified by neo-reformist youth as "really religious" (*sangat agamis*). Tiwi, a first-year student at UGM, who described her parents as "very Muhammadiyah," reported a similar theme in her socialization:

> My parents always emphasized education. Growing up, they always treated us all the same, boys and girls. In fact, my mom once said to me, "Don't worry about learning how to cook. Just focus on your studies for now. You can learn to cook on the job after you're married." They are really democratic [*demokratis*] and never differentiated between the education of my brothers and my sisters, never. They expect all of us to get at least an undergraduate degree. If we want to go further, it's up to us, but they would support us. And of course they expect us to work; if not, they think it would really be a waste [*rugi sekali*].

Neo-reformist youth such as Tiwi regularly described their parents as "democratic" (*demokratis, sangat demokratis*) in reference to their attitudes toward the schooling of sons and daughters. In young people's usage, the term "democratic" generally carried positive connotations of "equality" and "openness," particularly, but not only, with regard to communications, attitudes, and relationships. When I asked about gender socialization, young people often assumed the question was about gender differences with regard to schooling and responded that there were "no differences" in their families. "They are just the same; that is, boys and girls are given equal education" (*Sama saja. Jadi laki-laki dan perempuan diberi pendidikan yang sama*). Indeed, in reformist families, overt gender differences are generally downplayed by comparison with traditionalist families. In more extended discussions, however, it became evident that, as in the families of neo-traditionalist youth, there are in fact distinctions made in the treatment of sons and daughters in reformist families as well—particularly with regard to household responsibilities and autonomy.

Achievement and Piety

Neo-reformist youth recounted that up until the age of eight or ten, children of both sexes are given relative freedom to play outdoors with neighbors and friends. After that age, however, girls are typically expected to begin to curtail their neighborhood activities and stay closer to home. By this age, too, they begin helping their mothers with some household chores and, most importantly, are encouraged to pay more attention to their appearance and demeanor. (cf. Bennett 2005, 48). Although most of these young women come from families and communities in which wearing the headscarf was not common except during religious activities, by age eight or ten, girls are expected to dress neatly and modestly in gender-appropriate clothing that is not too tight or revealing. However, the consensus on what constituted appropriate dress for female adolescents is generally weaker in the families of neo-reformist youth than is the case in the families of neo-traditionalists. Particularly in the 1980s and early 1990s, some youth who would eventually join the ranks of Muslim neo-reformists lived in families where the influence of Indonesian—and even East Asian and Western—pop culture was strong, and girls' dress reflected these disparate and largely nonreligious cultural currents. Although the deepening Islamic resurgence of the 2000s has done much to contain this fashion diversity, it has by no means eliminated it (cf. Bennett 2005, 49–50; C. Jones 2010)

Differences in the roles and responsibilities of males and females in the families of neo-reformist youth, as in traditionalist families, become even more apparent with adolescence—beginning around age twelve and corresponding roughly with circumcision for boys and menarche for young girls. As noted above, male circumcision is widely recognized as an important Islamic rite and is mentioned in a hadith as a sign of belonging to the Islamic community (*umat*). Young people, however, more often cited the occurrence of nocturnal emissions or wet dreams as the indicator of male adolescence or puberty (*akhil balig*) rather than circumcision. This is because young people learn in their religion classes that males who experience wet dreams must take care to undertake the appropriate ritual ablutions so that they can subsequently perform their obligatory prayers in a clean and proper fashion. Circumcision, by contrast, has no comparably specific behavioral correlate.

A generation ago, the American anthropologist James Peacock (1978b) argued that among the Muslim reformists he studied the tendency was toward the earlier circumcision of sons so as to hasten the boy's identification with the Muslim community of believers (*umat*). Many parents of neo-reformist youth, however, particularly those who identified with the modernist Muslim organization Muhammadiyah, said they felt that male circumcision was just as well done in the hospital when the child is first born without any celebration, and young people repeated this sentiment.[30] While some neo-reformist boys described their circumcision ceremonies as involving elaborate feasting and entertainment (not unlike the *slametan* celebrations described by some neo-traditionalist youth), a much larger number (and those from Muhammadiyah backgrounds in particular) described theirs as considerably streamlined and focused on Qur'anic recitation. Rather than a religious argument, the more common discourse surrounding the wisdom of early circumcision focused on practicality (*lebih praktis*) with regard to expense and social effort.

Nina, who was introduced above, said she rarely heard of lavish circumcision ceremonies for young men anymore. At most a few male neighbors are invited to the house to recite prayers together. Afterward, they are offered a simple ritual meal (*kenduren*), a portion of which is hastily eaten and then the rest of which is taken home to share with family members. "But even that is rare these days," she said. "It's more common for the boy to be taken to the *bong supit* [circumcision specialist] or to the doctor, and that's it. Just that, and there's no celebration at all. When my younger brother was circumcised, there was no meal or party. He was just taken to the *bong supit* for the procedure and then brought home. A few neighbors stopped by to see him and gave him a little money, but that was all."

There was even less of a fuss made over menarche,[31] although as in the case of neo-traditionalists, young girls learned in their religion classes about making the proper ritual ablutions after their periods to restore their bodily purity and thereby ensure that God would accept their prayers. While a small number of women said their mothers had talked with them about menstruation, most of the information they shared had to do with how to use and dispose of sanitary products. Other girls said that when they experienced their first menstrual period, they were too embarrassed to tell their mothers and instead sought out an older sister or favorite aunt to confide in. Whatever the case, around this same time mothers begin to more regularly remind their daughters that they must take special care to "protect themselves" (*menjaga diri*) and "practice self-control" (*mengendalikan diri*). The requisite measures include being in the house after evening prayers, and not going any distance away from home without permission and unless accompanied by a family member. Although there is no Javanese tradition of honor killings as is found in some areas of the Middle East and South Asia, girls are nonetheless said to "carry the family name" (*membawa nama keluarga*), and therefore their actions and demeanor are the focus of considerable familial and public scrutiny. Of course, young men are also expected to behave in a manner that does not bring shame on their families; they are nonetheless freer to go where they like, with whomever they like, and to stay out late into the night—often to the chagrin of their sisters.

As was the case among neo-traditionalist youth, neo-reformist females not only reported spending more time around the house when young than did their brothers but also reported doing a much greater array of household chores. Mothers are typically in charge of food shopping and cooking for the family, but even young girls are expected to help as needed and, as they become older, to cook for the family when their mother is away.[32] Girls also reported being expected to regularly sweep and tidy up the family home. As in the families of State Islamic University students, neo-reformist males reported that they did "outside" work, such as repairing roof tiles or fences or carrying heavy loads. In households that have some form of hired help (*pembantu*), young people of both sexes were freer to focus their time on their schoolwork. Interestingly however, it was only young women who reported performing household chores of their own volition (*atas kesadaran sendiri*) once they became conscious of the burden shouldered by their mothers or housekeepers.

Like many other neo-reformist women, Nina complained that growing up, neither of her brothers ever did anything around the house. They were free to come and go as they pleased, she said, but she was not allowed to go out after 9 p.m. and had to always report to her parents where she was and who she was with. She explained,

Growing up, we had a housekeeper [*pembantu*], and she did most of the housework. My brothers never even did their own laundry. When the housekeeper went home to her village, my mom and I did everything. Even now when I'm home from school and my younger brother has friends over, my mom will tell me to make drinks for them. "What? He can't make a drink? All you have to do is put the syrup in the water and stir." [She'll say,] "But I worry that he'll make it too sweet." It's like she worries it will poison him if it's too sweet! I don't agree with that. I think guys need to know how to do those things, how to take care of themselves.

This pattern of young men's greater freedom of movement and relative freedom from household chores was reinforced by an increasingly normativized religious instruction that identified women's roles as defined by her *kodrat,* or God-given biological nature.

In the families of Gadjah Mada students, religious education typically began later and was less intensive compared to the pattern reported by students from the State Islamic University. There is also considerably more variation in its form and substance. Like the neo-traditionalists, most neo-reformist youth indicated that as young children they first followed the example of their mothers and fathers in learning to pray (*sholat*) and recite scripture. Also similar to neo-traditionalist youth, between the ages of eight and ten both boys and girls began to more seriously observe the yearly fast during the month of *Ramadan.* On average, however, neo-reformist males reported that they began to read and study the Qur'an at age nine—four years later than was the case in traditionalist families—and began to perform the five daily prayers regularly only at age eleven.[33]

Sometime during grade school, many neo-reformist youth joined their friends at the local mosque or *langgar,* for religion lessons in the late afternoon—in those neighborhoods where a mosque or *langgar* was easily accessible. In other cases, parents hired a Muslim scholar (*guru ngaji* or *ustadz*), to give their children religious lessons in their home several days a week over a period of several years. Young people also received religious education in the schools, a required minimum of one hour a day, two days a week. Those who attend religious schools, of course, received more.

As a result of New Order educational developments and the continual upgrading of teacher training, the religious instruction compulsory in the nation's schools has become increasingly standardized. Moreover, whereas prior to the mid-1970s it was possible for students to avoid taking religion classes too seriously, class performance is now factored into the student's GPA (NEM) and therefore affects academic advancement and college acceptance. As presented in the national curriculum, Islam tends to be taught as a unitary and relatively standardized system of educational knowledge. Unlike *pesantren* schools, religious instruction in the state schools makes little if any reference to jurisprudential texts (the *kitab kuning*) or the Islamic sciences with which they are associated—Islamic sciences that, among other things, emphasize the methods and inevitable plurality of religious reasoning on many matters. By contrast, religion classes in the national curriculum emphasize the mastery of a standardized menu of religious topics as well as the proper performance of religious duties or worship (*ibadah*). The classes convey the impression that the normative and ritual requirements of Islam are uniform and universal—a lesson that was almost certainly lost on some in their parents' and grandparents' generation.

In their state-sponsored religious classes, girls are also taught that at menarche or shortly thereafter they should take up the headscarf (*jilbab*) and otherwise dress modestly so as not to attract the gaze of male strangers. They are repeatedly reminded that it is a woman's responsibility (*kewajiban*) to cover herself in order to avoid *fitnah* (chaos, disorder, in this instance as a result of being misjudged) and so as to help men keep on the moral path and away from sinful acts. Many religion teachers require that female students wear the headscarf during their religion classes and monitor students' dress outside of school as well.[34] In these classes young people are also taught categorically that interactions with the opposite sex are fraught with danger and that sex outside of marriage (*zina*) is a grave sin (*dosa besar*) and is not allowed within Islam (cf. Mir-Hosseini and Hamzić 2010; Tucker 2008). Pregnancy outside of marriage is described as a source of deep shame (*aib*) for her family (Bennett 2005, 24). Islamic law requires that the biological father of an illegitimate child acknowledge his offspring and that the father and mother marry.

On some urban high school campuses, this in-class religious instruction is supplemented by religious activities in after-school "Islamic Spirituality" clubs called Rohis (Kerohanian Islam). These clubs—which take a significantly more conservative line than that presented in students' regular religion classes—began to appear in the early 2000s with the support of university-based groups such as KAMMI and the Campus Institute for Predication (Lembaga Dakwa Kampus, LDK). The goal of the clubs is to encourage the development of a more properly Islamic atmosphere on secondary school campuses (Ahnaf 2013; Salim, Kailani, and Azekiyah 2011). Rohis activities include academic and personal mentoring and tutoring as well as after-school Qur'anic readings and prayer programs. The clubs encourage students to adopt more conservative Muslim clothing styles—the more enveloping style of *jilbab* and loose dress for girls, and ankle-length trousers and collarless tunics for boys. They also promote strict social codes akin to those found in many *pesantren,* such as restricted interaction between male and female students, no shaking of hands or touching, and gender segregation in all public events.

Among the schools that have active Rohis programs on their campuses are several of Yogyakarta's top-ranked (*favorit*) high schools; in a number of cases the schools have even adopted the club's strict dress code as school-wide policy (Salim, Kailani, and Azekiyah 2011; see also Parker 2008a). Teachers and administrators at these schools identify Islamic piety with school discipline and strong academic performance, and identified Rohis members as school leaders and moral role models (Ahnaf 2013, 181; see also Parker 2008a; Parker and Nilan 2013). They argue that those schools that adopt more conservative uniforms for their students have fewer problems with gangs or bullying, and that the club's activities enhance the school's reputation.

While some parents voiced concerns about the religious clubs' conservative message as constraining young people's freedom of expression and creativity, most said they appreciated the organizations' efforts to counter the negative influences of a popular youth culture increasingly identified with drugs, gangs, promiscuity, and pornography. Through a mentoring program (*program pembimbing*), Rohis groups are especially vigilant in policing the behaviors of their membership who are identified as "moral models" for the student body. An important focus of their programs is to alert the student body to the dangers of Western-style dating, an emphasis that speaks to parental fears surrounding premarital sex.

Education in nonconfessional, state schools is broadly coeducational. As a result, students in these schools—unlike students who attend *pesantren* schools—have extensive opportunities to observe and interact with members of the opposite sex. While some parents of neo-reformist youth view this interaction as healthy, many regard unsupervised interactions with members of the opposite sex as potentially detrimental to young people's attainment of highly valued educational aims. Most critically, in their view, relationships could possibly lead a young person to abandon his or her educational goals, thereby forfeiting the possibility of a prestigious job in the civil service or the professions and a secure hold on middle-class status.

In this regard—that is, with regard to young people's involvements with the opposite sex—the concerns of parents of Gadjah Mada students are similar to those expressed by the parents of neo-traditionalist youth. Both worry that a sexual relationship might result in their son or daughter having to leave school before obtaining their college degree or, worse yet, the shameful possibility of *zina* (sex outside of marriage). Many parents make clear their preference that their children, especially their daughters, avoid "serious" relationships, certainly until after they have finished high school, and, if possible, until after obtaining their college degrees. In the cosmopolitan atmosphere of Yogyakarta with its malls, and coffee shops, clubs, and tourist sites, that is much easier said than done.

Sex and Sociability

Despite the fact that Indonesia has been in the thick of a Muslim resurgence now for over thirty-five years, Indonesians widely assume that today's youth are far more sexually active than their predecessors in previous generations. This assumption is reinforced by sensationalist media accounts of high school call girls and sex-paged coeds, as well as by the very real evidence of a popular youth culture whose sexual behaviors seem strikingly at odds with those of their elders (cf. Parker and Nilan 2013; I. D. Utomo 2002, 2003; Webster 2016). Today in Yogyakarta, as in other modern Indonesian cities, young people can be seen at cafés, fast-food restaurants, and malls wearing tight-fitting jeans and T-shirts, holding hands, and even embracing. On Saturday nights couples park on motorcycles around the city's central square (the *alun-alun*), laughing and flirting openly. Others seek out the dim shadows of the walls around the sultan's palace, where it is possible to steal a kiss or meet in the cool darkness of the bridge embankment (*jembatan*) at Kaliurang. On the opposite side of town, the well-heeled crowd can be seen entering Western-style discos and hotel bars where the music blares, the dance floors are full, and some eagerly negotiate the purchase of ecstasy or sex. All of these behaviors, needless to say, violate "traditional" Javanese and Muslim norms and are taken as proof of the moral laxity of today's youth.

Adding to the general perception of the unprincipled licentiousness of the younger generation, beginning in the early 2000s and continuing into the present, a series of media-inflamed public moral panics have focused on the sexual behavior of Indonesia's youth (cf. Harding 2008; Kailani 2011; Lim 2013; Parker and Nilan 2013; Smith-Hefner 2006, 2009a; Webster 2016). One of the first and most sensational of these moral panics occurred in August of 2002, when the Institute for the Study of Love and Humanity, a private Muslim research group based in Yogyakarta, released a report of a survey suggesting that "free sex" (*seks bebas*) had become the norm among Yoygakarta's university students (*Straits Times* 2002; see also Smith-Hefner 2009a). The principle investigator, Iip Wijayanto, was, at the time, a twenty-three-year-old student in civil engineering at the large and well-regarded Indonesian Islamic University (Universitas Islam Indonesia, UII). A self-proclaimed "sexologist" as well as a Muslim preacher, or *da'i*, he was also the institute's executive director. Wijayanto claimed that according to his survey of female college students living in rented rooms or boarding houses in Yogyakarta, over 97 percent were no longer virgins. Of the 1,660 young women interviewed by his research team, the study reported, only forty-six said they had never had sexual intercourse; only three said they had never engaged in any form of sexual activity. Wijayanto attributed the problem to a permissive social atmosphere and weak parental control. He is quoted in the Singapore-based *Straits Times* as saying that his publishing the results of his study constituted "shock therapy" for the Indonesian public (*Straits Times* 2002; see also *Radar Jogja* 2002). Parents should wake up, he warned, to the reality of their children's widespread sexual involvements.

Wijayanto's research created an immediate uproar, not only in Yogyakarta but across Indonesia. Feminist groups, including Muslim feminists, criticized the study for focusing on women's virginity and ignoring the sexual behavior of men. Members of the academic and research community challenged Wijayanto's survey methods and statistical measurements. Even the publicity-shy wife of the Sultan of Yogyakarta, GKR Hemas, issued a public denunciation of the study, saying that it gave Yogyakarta's women a bad name and could possibly result in parents deciding against sending their daughters to Yogyakarta's schools and universities (*Kedaulatan Rakyat* 2002). Wijayanto's investigation was followed by a flurry of studies focusing on the sexual activities of Indonesian youth in other cities and towns across the archipelago. While none of these reported the dramatic figures put forward by Wijayanto, all of them claim to have identified a significant uptick in the percentage of youth who were engaging in premarital sex.[1] Over the ten years that followed his initial research, Wijayanto himself continued to conduct "scientific polls" and publish books with intentionally provocative titles on promiscuity, abortion, and moral degradation in his effort to expose the public to the depth of the youth problem. These publications include *Sex in the "Kost": Realitas dan Moralitas Seks Kaum "Terpelajar"* (Sex in the Boardinghouse: Reality and Sexual Morality of Educated Youth); *Pemerkosaan atas Nama Cinta: Potret Muram Interaksi Sosial Kaum Muda* (Rape in the Name of Love: A Disturbing Portrait of the Social Interactions of Youth); *Campus "Fresh Chicken": Menelanjangi Praktik Pelacuran Kaum Terpelajar* (Campus "Fresh Chicken": Uncovering the Practice of Prostitution among Educated Youth); and *Sex in the Kost 2: MAM Married after "Metteng"!* (Sex in the Boardinghouse 2: M.A.M. Married after Pregnant!)—all of which have undergone multiple printings.

Seen from the vantage point of these and other studies, developments in Indonesian youth culture might at first seem to offer support for Dennis Altman's thesis concerning the emergence of an increasingly globalized, homogeneous, and Western-style sexuality (Altman 2001; see also Giddens 1992). In the global marketplace of products and ideas, Altman argues, the dominant sexual styles tend to be Western—more specifically American—in the sense that the new sexual behaviors and discourses focus on the expression of individual rights and the fulfillment of personal desires. Altman further speculates, "The impetus of globalization is almost certainly to both break down existing taboos (e.g., the very high premium on premarital virginity for women) and lead to a gradual convergence of sexual behavior across different societies" (Altman 2001, 38).

Indonesian clerics and moral reformers themselves highlight the pernicious effects of Westernization on the nation's youth in their impassioned calls for moral reform to stem the libertine tide. The situation, however, is considerably more culturally complex than it at first appears. Public moral panics and sensational allegations of widespread sexual licentiousness among Indonesian youth have overshadowed the no-less-real impact of a resurgent Islam on young people's sexual understandings and behaviors. More specifically, both media accounts and Western studies of Indonesian Muslims have tended to overlook the emergence among young middle-class Indonesians of new, more self-consciously *Muslim* understandings of sexuality. That is, while in earlier generations there was a fairly well-established ethical consensus on this and related matters (such as dating, courtship, and marriage), there is today a diversity of new ethical orientations. Significantly for the argument being made here, many of those new orientations are being reconstructed with reference to more self-conscious and discursivized Muslim norms, ones that draw more heavily on explicit scripturalist (Qur'anic- and Sunnah-based) references and commentaries.

Certainly, subjectivities are by no means exhaustively constituted by culturally conveyed norms and discourses; in all subjectivity there is a complex interplay of cultural discourses, social relations, and individual personality and biography (Altman 2001; see Biehl, Good, and Kleinman 2007; Ewing 1990; Kleinman and Kleinman 1985; Ortner 2005). As we have seen in earlier chapters, discourses and the currents they draw on are multiple and shifting. But it is no less true that normative discourses play a pivotal role in youth sexuality by providing moral reference points in the lives of those who identify with the groups that convey these discourses. More specifically, these "authorized" discourses figure centrally in individual actor's and groups' conscious and unconscious deliberations regarding the range and realms of the subjectively and ethically "possible" (Foucault 1990 [1978]; Kleinman 2011; Mahmood 2005). This is particularly true with regard to Islamist and religiously scripturalist approaches to Islam.

By "scripturalist" approaches, I refer to those discourses and practices that draw explicitly and insistently on authoritative commentaries on the Qur'an and hadith to legitimate certain ethical discourses of self and society, not least by promoting the example of the Prophet as the proper model for contemporary youth. Here in Indonesia, Islamist groups such as KAMMI, Hizbut Tahrir,[2] and the MMI (Majelis Mujahidin Indonesia, Indonesian Mujahadin Council) insist that "everything is there in the text; you just have to follow it." Unlike traditionalist scholars with their long-standing emphasis on jurisprudential exegeses, or modernist scholars with their appeals to "contextual" and pluralist approaches to Islamic scriptures and ethics, Islamist groups typically present Islam as offering a simple, singular, and "complete" (*kaffah*) model for individual and social life. Although the details of the models they convey in fact vary, each of these groups presents a normative template that is said to be based on the Qur'an and Sunnah, and to alone qualify as representative of "true Islam." Each offers a model of pious perfection and social good, while cautioning that all alternatives are deviationist (*sesat*) and thereby likely to lead only to the flames of hell.

Against the backdrop of public moral panic and purported decadence and promiscuity, this chapter considers the rise of more normative and discursivized forms of Islam as they have affected the norms and practices of youth sexuality and sociability. It explores the shape and direction of recent changes and examines how they have affected the intentional practices and lived experiences that constitute contemporary subjectivities and lifestyles among the varieties of young Javanese Muslims. In this chapter I also take up in some detail the flurry of youth publications (cautionary tracts, novels, sexual advice, and self-help guides) that has exploded onto the scene since the end of the Suharto regime as well as the new styles of youth language and gender sociability that have accompanied it. While the subjective experience of desire may be discursively organized, it is nonetheless important to interrogate the practical and conceptual conditions under which different forms of desire emerge. Islamist discourses hold out the possibility of pious perfection; however the examination of young people's lives and lived experience indicates considerable ambivalence, uncertainty, and plurality in the ways in which young people draw on and enact normative ideals (cf. Deeb and Harb 2013b; Ewing 1990; Schielke 2009b).

Sexuality and the State

Contemporary debates surrounding youth sexuality in Indonesia can be fully understood only within the context of the extensive development initiatives that were put into place during Suharto's New Order. By significantly prolonging the period between the onset of puberty and marriage, New Order programs and policies, particularly those related to population regulation, marriage, and universal education, have had a direct and powerful impact on youth social and sexual behavior, influences that continue into the present.

Under Suharto's New Order, state institutions attempted to link sexuality to fertility and confine both to the bonds of legal marriage (cf. Bennett 2005, 29; see also Parker and Nilan 2013; I. D. Utomo 2002). Although Indonesia's first president, Sukarno, viewed contraception and family planning as cultural inventions designed to secure the West's imperialist domination, President Suharto heeded development experts' counsel and concluded that population control was imperative for Indonesia's long-term development. Not long after coming to office, Suharto established the National Family Planning Board and instituted a program for the mass distribution of modern contraceptives (Blackburn 2004; Niehof and Lubis 2003; Wieringa 2002). Before he did so, he took care to secure authoritative *fatwa* (a legal opinion of a Muslim jurist) in support of the country's family-planning initiatives from leading state-linked Islamic scholars (cf. Lindsey 2008).

In framing its policies, the state was constrained in the degree to which it could directly address youth sexuality not only by the concerns of leading Muslim scholars but also by the social conservatism of ordinary Indonesians. Both groups expressed the fear that making contraceptives available to unmarried youth would encourage sexual promiscuity and undermine the moral authority of the family (Dwyer 2000; see also Bennett 2005; Blackburn 2004; Parker 2008a). State-supplied contraception emphasized female methods of fertility regulation, including the IUD, the pill, implants, and sterilization. Participation in the program and access to the contraceptives it made available were strictly limited to married couples (*pasangan usia subur;* lit. "couples of fertile age"),[3] and many doctors required proof of the husband's agreement before providing a woman with birth control. Although it is not illegal for unmarried couples to use contraception, and young people can buy contraceptives in kiosks, shops, and pharmacies, even today, "the effect of the presence of this law is that many people assume that it is illegal for unmarried people to use contraception" (see also Bennett 2005; Parker 2009).

Muslim organizations endorsed abstinence and early marriage as the appropriate solutions to the problem of youth sexuality (cf. Niehof and Lubis 2003). Other state initiatives, however, effectively encouraged the postponement of marriage. The new marriage legislation enacted in 1974 established the minimum age for marriage as sixteen for women and nineteen for men. It also "enshrined the principle that the consent of both parties must be obtained prior to marriage" (Robinson and Utomo 2003, 6; see also Lindsey 2008). Perhaps even more critical—as detailed in previous chapters—were the government's educational and economic programs. The new employment opportunities in factories, the greatly expanded civil service, and the service sector served as an incentive for parents to keep their children in school with an eye to obtaining a well-paying job and a foothold in the emerging middle class.

By the end of the New Order period, growing numbers of Indonesian youth were postponing marriage to take advantage of new opportunities in secondary and higher education (G. Jones 1994a, 1994b). This pattern, coupled with what Peter Xenos (2004) of Honolulu's East-West Center has identified as a "youth bulge" in populations throughout Southeast Asia, has vastly increased the number of unmarried young people visible on Indonesian high school and college campuses, and in streets, shops, and theaters.[4] As a result of new educational and employment opportunities, which often require that young people relocate to larger cities and live in rented rooms and dormitories, Indonesian youth today have considerably more opportunities to meet and interact with members of the opposite sex on their own without direct adult oversight. It is this situation in particular that has fueled parental fears and public moral panics surrounding youth promiscuity.

Reflecting in part the social success and ethical challenge of New Order educational and social programs, it is not only parents and authorities that view the moral decay among youth as a public threat. A majority of Indonesian young people themselves cite the "erosion of personal morals" (*pemerosotan moral*), "free sex" (*seks bebas*), and "free interactions with the opposite sex" (*pergaulan bebas*) as among the most critical problems facing Indonesia today (see Parker and Nilan 2013, 105; see also Nilan et al. 2011; Parker 2009; Webster 2016). It would appear that the "Western" model of personal choice and individual freedom has been met in Indonesia with significant ethical ambivalence.

Sex and Adolescence

Notwithstanding their concerns about moral decay and free interactions with the opposite sex, in practice—which is to say in actual parental interactions with their adolescent and young adult offspring—neither the parents of neo-reformist nor neo-traditionalist youth offer much in the way of either direct sexual counsel or technical sexual information to their children, whether male or female. Despite the increasingly sexualized atmosphere of everyday life (online porno sites, the availability of "blue" films and videos, Western television programs and advertisements, and repeated public moral panics), the discussion of sex within Javanese families remains charged with anxiety and taboo (see I. D. Utomo 2002, 2003).

Most parents at best provide a highly generalized and somewhat vague ethical counsel on matters of sexuality. As they approach adolescence, young women are told simply and repeatedly to "control or safeguard themselves" (*mengenda-likan diri, menjaga diri*) in interactions with boys and not to do anything to disappoint their family ("*jangan mengecewakan keluarga*"; see also Bennett 2002; Parker 2009). The emphasis here is on individual self-discipline as well as the impact of misbehavior on family relations and social standing. Ayu, a third-year student at Gadjah Mada University and of neo-reformist orientation, described her parents as just "regular Muslims" and "not very observant." With regard to her parents and sexual counsel, she recounted, "My parents just kept telling me I had to be able to protect myself [*menjaga diri*]. They meant in my interactions with guys; you know, no sex." Her classmate, Nina, who shared a similar family background and neo-reformist outlook, explained, "My mom never talked to me or to any of us directly about sex. She would only say, 'Don't disappoint me.' Like if we were watching a film about a girl who got pregnant out of wedlock or a neighbor got into trouble and had to get married, she'd just say, 'Don't you disappoint me like that.'"

Compared to their female counterparts, male university students from Gadjah Mada reported even more discomfort at the idea of discussing sex with their parents. Andi's comments reflect what was a common theme in my discussions with young men regardless of their family backgrounds: "When I got older, I was around the house less and less, and besides, I would feel awkward discussing sex with my parents." "In my family," Agung said simply, "talk about sex is still taboo [*masih tabu*]." For their part, parents told me repeatedly that they believe that young people will "figure it out on their own" (*tahu sendiri*; H. Salim 1999), and they look to moral training in the schools and religious education to provide the rest.

Sex Education in the Schools

Sex education is not part of the official curriculum in Indonesian schools, although young people who follow the exact science (*ilmu pasti*) track in high school may study animal reproduction in their biology classes (Parker 2008a, 49; I. D. Utomo 2003; Utomo and McDonald 2009). By contrast, Indonesian education has always included an important focus on moral training. Originally, such training took the form of lessons in "character [development]," or *budi pekerti*, which, in schools in Java, was closely associated with teaching the Javanese language and speech levels, and with traditional norms of appropriate social interaction. Beginning in the late 1960s, religious instruction became a required part of the Indonesian public school curriculum, and *budi pekerti*, along with instruction in Javanese language, has been gradually phased out. In more recent years, as an effect of decentralization, some districts across Java have reintroduced Javanese language study in response to what is widely seen as a precipitous drop in youth mastery of the more formal and polite variety of Javanese and the forms of sociability associated with its use.

Rather than sex education, parents emphasize the importance of religious education in providing a strong moral foundation for their children. The trend among middle-class families since the early 2000s is to enroll young children in religious preschools or Qur'anic schools as early as age four so as to ensure that "they develop a strong moral and religious foundation while they are still young and impressionable." In Yogyakarta, these schools have become so popular that they are consistently oversubscribed, and many schools resort to choosing new students by lottery. As a result of New Order educational developments and the constant upgrading of teacher training, the religious instruction that young people receive in the nation's schools—including preschools—has become increasingly normativized (see chapter 5). It is normativized in the sense that it emphasizes that Islam is a religion of ethical norms and laws, that these norms are consistent and clear, and that it is the duty of the believer to learn and implement these regulations. Religious education in preschools, public schools, and in Muslim after-schools emphasizes the proper performance of religious duties or worship (*ibadah*). Discussion of sexuality remains largely focused on matters of ritual purity and impurity, particularly with regard to the ritual requirements of fasting, religious study, and the performance of the five daily prayers. This information is introduced relatively early (in mid- to late primary school) in abbreviated form and is repeated in increasing detail in later grades.

Sometime in the fourth or fifth year of primary school, religious education— while still focused on proper performance of religious duties—takes a more sexually explicit turn. At this time, young people are taught that sexual maturity (*aqil baliq*) is marked by the presence of wet dreams (*mimpi basah*) in boys and menstruation (*haid*) in girls (H. Salim 1999, 70; see also Bouhdiba 2004). When these events take place, and as a youth develops the other characteristics of physiological puberty, he or she is considered mature enough to be individually responsible for carrying out the required five daily prayers, attending daily religious study classes, and keeping the fast during Ramadan. Girls are likewise taught that at menarche or shortly thereafter they should take up the veil and otherwise dress modestly so as not to attract the gaze of male strangers. They are repeatedly reminded that it is a woman's responsibility (*kewajiban*) to cover herself in order to avoid *fitnah* (chaos, disorder, in this instance as a result of being misjudged) and so as to discourage men from sinning (cf. Ali 2006, 8–9).

However reluctant middle-class parents may be to discuss sexual matters, religion teachers are keenly aware that it is imperative that adolescent youth have a basic understanding of sexual impurity and the processes of ritual cleansing. Without such knowledge, a youth cannot fulfill his or her ritual obligations. In Islam, fulfillment of these ritual obligations is one of the most important standards by which individuals are evaluated on Judgment Day. Prayers that do not follow religious requirements and are not preceded by the required ablutions, for example, are carried out in a state of impurity and "do not count." Young boys are taught that they must take a thorough ritual bath (*mandi besar*) before their daily prayers if they have previously experienced a nocturnal emission (wet dream). In their religious training they learn that wet dreams are equated with actual sexual intercourse, and, as such, they require that one engage in ritual ablutions before fulfilling one's devotional obligations. The focus on wet dreams rather than circumcision as the defining indicator of male adolescence (*aqil baliq*) expresses a more textual understanding of Muslim masculine maturity. This more religiously normative view of maturation is an index of the general shift away from public celebration of life stages, once common across Java, to a focus on personal responsibility and individual devotion.

The Islamic regulations pertaining to menstruating women are more complex than those relating to male sexual emissions. In religion classes girls learn that within Islam, menstruation (*haid*) is viewed as polluting (*najis*), and that menstruating women are considered unclean. A menstruating woman may not perform daily prayers (*sholat*) or fast. She may not touch or read from the Qur'an or enter the mosque due to her unclean state. If married, she may not have sexual relations with her husband. The restrictions related to menstruation require that the girl learn to distinguish what "counts" as menstrual flow and what "counts" as illness. How many days is a cycle? When does it officially begin and when does it definitively end? In secular state schools, male and female students may or may not be separated for some of this instruction. Not only women but men, too, must be familiar with these regulations in order to fulfill their role as the (future) religious heads of their families, so that they can lead family worship, and know when sexual relations with their wives are allowed and when they are prohibited.[5]

It is telling, however, that the details of the religious instruction concerning menstruation (or wet dreams for that matter) almost never extend to a comprehensive discussion of its role in sexual reproduction. Several young female students from rural backgrounds laughed while recounting that, even though they had memorized all of the religious requirements related to *haid,* they were nonetheless shocked at their first menstruation and didn't immediately recognize what was happening. They had made no connection between their religious instruction and the actual physical experience of bleeding. They also laughed about their misapprehensions concerning male wet dreams. "Wet dreams? What was that? We heard about that from the time we were young, but it didn't concern us and we didn't really pay any attention."

In religion classes, whether in school or outside of school, young people are offered a consistent and unequivocally moral message with regard to premarital sex, one that is reiterated by the mainstream media in much the same form.[6] The moral message here moves beyond self-control and familial face to the linking of sexual behaviors to divinely sanctioned norms. The message is that sex outside of marriage is categorically forbidden within Islam; it is "fornication or adultery" (*zina*),[7] and is a "grave sin" (*dosa besar*). Often the ethical norm is given even stronger moral force by being linked to notions of divine reward and punishment. Young male students on the campus of the State Islamic University who had attended *pesantren* schools said they were warned by their teachers that "if one engages in premarital sex even one time, he will suffer in hell for forty years." Sexual promiscuity is compared to the debased and primitive behavior of animals, which are distinguished from humans by the loathsome fact that they have no shame or inhibitions. *Zina* can result in children of uncertain parentage, and therefore raises the possibility of incest.[8]

To a remarkable degree, the comments of young people in interviews and informal discussions reflected important elements of this normative Muslim view of sexuality. In fact, answers to my questions about sexuality in many cases appeared to be taken directly from a religious lesson or Friday sermon. Though not to be taken as an indication of actual practice, students widely report that they consider sexual purity (virginity) before marriage a central tenet of their faith.[9] Many refer to it as "my most basic principle." Others cite their Asian or Indonesian "values" (*nilai moral*) as keeping them from engaging in immoral behavior. Contrary to the reports of some sexual researchers, such as Iip Wijayanto, virtually all of the hundreds of female students with whom I spoke—including many I came to know quite well—said they fully expect to remain virgins up until the time they marry. "The requirements of Islam, which I have studied since childhood, teach us that sex must be confined to the legal state of marriage, said one." Another told me, "In Islam, sex outside of marriage is 'adultery' [*zina*] and a 'great sin' [*dosa besar*]."

Significantly, the great majority of the male students I surveyed also said they fully intend to remain sexually inexperienced before marriage (cf. Ford, Shaluhiyah, and Suryoputro 2007, 66). They offered reasons similar to those offered by young women—that sex outside of marriage is a "grave sin" (*dosa besar*) and is forbidden (*diharamkan*) in Islam. Other common responses from young men included "Of course I expect to be a virgin. Sex is one's honor [*kehormatan*], which must be protected and handed over complete to one's wife "; "Yes, I expect to be a virgin; I think all guys feel that way. It is a responsibility no matter how difficult"; and "Sex outside of marriage is a sin that destroys one morally. My ultimate goal is to remain 'pure' [*suci*] in the eyes of God."

Religious education in general schools (*sekolah umum*), afternoon religious classes (*pengajian*), and Muslim boarding schools (*pesantren*) have all ensured that university students, regardless of their backgrounds, have absorbed the normative ideal, "an idealized morality." Normative ideals do not, however, necessarily translate automatically or consistently into actual practice. Certainly, in the radically "untraditional" environments of cities such as Yogyakarta, there are many new and exciting opportunities for social and sexual experimentation, and not all young people are able to resist.

Modern Sociability: Cosmopolitan Cool

Rapid urbanization and the massive and ongoing social changes that have accompanied it have demanded new understandings of the self, as well as the development of new ways of interacting across ethnic, religious, regional, and gender lines. And that is just what has happened in contemporary Indonesia, in a manner that at times is surprisingly distinct from or at odds with the young public's growing familiarity with Islamic normativity.

To cite one dramatic example, in the late 1990s and early 2000s a hip new youth style called *gaul* ("sociable, hip") arrived on the scene and was visible—and audible—on campuses and in coffee shops and clubs (Smith-Hefner 2007). Cool, confident, and relaxed, *gaul* ideology encouraged flexible, open, and ostensibly "democratic"—but, in practice, thoroughly apolitical—interactions. Meta-ethnic rather than ethnically marked, *gaul* at its most basic level designates someone who is both socially at ease in and socially savvy with regard to the modern landscapes of malls, theaters, restaurants, and universities, all of which lie outside the established hierarchies and disciplines of the rural countryside. A young university student articulated what I heard from many others, that *gaul* refers to a person who is socially flexible and can both communicate and get along well with others: "*Gaul* means someone who is self-assured and good at adapting socially. A kid who can talk to older people or to people from the village or to city people or modern people is a *gaul* kid. They're 'up-to-date' [*tidak ketinggalan jaman*], developed, and 'advanced' [*maju*]. *Gaul* is modern. I think whoever or whatever is not *gaul* is just not modern."

In these and other comments, it is striking that *gaul* style, at least in its most elemental form, is described in a manner that avoids any overt challenge to new Muslim styles of youth sociability. There is neither explicit "resistance" nor tacit accommodation. Instead, *gaul* is a social style that, in its insistence on the importance of commensurability across various groups and categories of people, is normatively at odds with some of the most basic features of the more religiously conservative new Muslim sociability. As we shall see, however, the religiously unmarked nature of *gaul* has itself generated countercurrents, including those that aspire to Islamize *gaul*.

By the early 2000s Yogyakarta's bookstores were flooded with handbooks on how to cultivate the mysterious but alluring habitus of the new youth style called *gaul*. In the summer of 2005, a casual computer search in the popular Indonesian bookstore *Gramedia* identified forty-seven books with the term *gaul* in their titles, a number of which were on prominent display. In addition to stacks of Debby Sahertian's best-selling *Kamus Bahasa Gaul* (Gaul Dictionary), which first appeared in bookstores in 1999 and by 2005 had already been reprinted twelve times, other "best-selling" *gaul* tracts included Adi Kurnia's *All about Gaul!* (All about Being Social!); Wining Rohani's *Gaul Smart dengan Dunia* (Smart Socializing with the World); Wishnubroto Widarso's *Kiat Sukses Bergaul* (The Secret to Successful Social Interactions); Dina Astuti's *Gaul Ok! Belajar Ok! Cerdas Gak Berarti Kuper* (Socializing Is Okay! Studying Is Okay!

Intelligent Doesn't [Have to] Mean Unsocial); and Eileen Rachman and Petrina Omar's *Gaul: Meraih lebih Banyak Kesempatan* (Be Sociable: Take Advantage of More Opportunities). The authors of this last book, Be Sociable: Take Advantage of More Opportunities, state that *gaul* is "any activity where one has an opportunity to meet people who are interesting and to invite them to engage in a relationship" (Rachman and Omar 2004, 9). They assert furthermore that "experts" have now determined that *gaul* is the best method for achieving social success, both personal and professional. As the breathless promise of the titles indicate, *gaul* is not just about hipness and religiously nonexclusive sociability. It is also about an individualized and "smart" sociability that promises to work very well with upward social mobility: "Gaul has now become an important value/skill in everyday life as well as at work. Those who are not social (*yang tidak gaul*) are considered not really ok. Why? The impression is that they are not trendy (*tidak trendi*). This might be surprising because usually trendiness is judged by outward appearance—does he follow the latest fashion trend or not. But now gaul itself has become a measure of trendiness" (Rachman and Omar 2004, 6).

Like the new horizons of social life to which it is linked, *gaul* posits the modern individual as an ongoing project ever in need of self-making improvements. Perhaps another variation on the theme of localized "neoliberal" subjectivities, the improvements have first and foremost to do with oneself as a product and presenter (cf. Boellstorff 2005; Hoesterey 2008; 2015; C. Jones 2003; Rudnyckyj 2010). Social observers of the new Indonesian middle class have remarked that a striking characteristic of the new middle-class culture is the conviction that the future of Indonesia depends on individuals shaping themselves through self-cultivation and self-fashioning (C. Jones 2003, 190–191; Lindquist 2002). In these tracts, all individuals are described as having both strengths and limitations (*kelebihan dan kekurangan*). Here again, the ethical assessment at work in these accounts is striking for its lack of explicit religious reference, and its emphasis on achievement-oriented individuality. The point of *gaul*, it seems, is to be aware of one's own personal qualities, to learn to minimize one's limitations and "optimalize" one's strengths (*ngoptimalin bakatnya*) in social interactions. This emphasis on self-understanding and on self-development as a continuous and quasi-career-enhancing process is a central theme of the *gaul* guidebooks, described in a representative excerpt from *All about Gaul*:

Why [is it that you are less than impressive in front of people]? We could say that it happens because you maintain several negative characteristics. Or you just haven't developed a strategy to rid yourself of those characteristics . . . like egoism, stubbornness, and thinking you're always right. Everyone has an ego, but don't become egotistical; that's dangerous you know! The effects of these characteristics are simple. You become too self-confident and in the end, conceited. Or you become too self-effacing/self-conscious [minder] and in the end, overly timid. Of course other people don't like these characteristics. If you exhibit them, people will stay away from you. But you don't have to give up. *You should remember that life is a process that never ends. Everything that you are and everything that you know will continue to develop, as long as you believe that everything is a process.* (Kurnia 2005, 14–15, emphasis added)

Unthinkable or unattractive under the long-standing scheme of Javanese social style and self-presentation, with its heavy emphasis on ascribed social classifications and identification with ethnically marked communitarian categories and consumption, "knowing oneself" and the achievement of "personal style" are critical to the new *gaul* habitus. Yet, as the above quotation makes clear, self-recognition and personal style are not viewed in the modern context as something that just "happens" through interactions with one's family or natal community; they require conscious reflection, cultivation, and self-making work. And that's what the proliferation of *gaul* handbooks is about. These handbooks take as their focus not the recognition of a communal, ethnic, or specific religious identity but the cultivation of the individualized self-confidence and ego-centered social skills required for interacting outside of one's circle of family and close friends. *Gaul* orients one to a distinctive social world, but it is a world made up of upwardly aspirant expressive individuals rather than tradition-minded communities. There are striking parallels in this regard with some of the life-coaching and neoliberal influences that made their way into new schools of Islamic management, such as Ari Ginanjar's ESQ movement, which has been described in such rich detail by the anthropologist Daromir Rudnyckyj (2010). No less striking, however, is that this variety of life coaching and self-formation tends in its most elemental form to avoid all reference to the new Islamic normativity.

Thus, the authors of the new *gaul* guidebooks offer tips on how to make friends, how to be a good listener, how to express oneself, and how to make the most of one's individual abilities and talents. The small guide titled *The Secret to Successful Social Interactions* (Kiat Sukses Bergaul [Widarso 1997]), for example, suggests that the reader should always "be present" in social interactions, put the interlocutor first, and act like an equal partner in conversations rather than like a parent/elder—all skills identified as necessary in navigating the modern, socially variegated landscape. This counsel is understandable enough for anxious youth aspiring to smooth success and reassuring sociability.

The intended audience for these guidebooks are those young people eager for middle-class status, most of whom have recently arrived in urban centers in large numbers to take advantage of new educational and employment opportunities. Many of these young people are living on their own and away from close parental supervision for the first time or commuting daily to schools or work sites some distance from their homes. They are seeking out the advice of "experts" who understand their life experience and situation, a situation not shared by their parents. The guidebooks address youthful anxieties and insecurities that arise from finding oneself in new social settings, meeting new categories of people, and interacting with members of the opposite sex. The publications hold particular appeal for those in their late teens and early twenties who grew up in villages or small towns, in socially conservative or closely monitored backgrounds. Although the authors often take males as their focus, according to publishers and booksellers, as many, if not more, females than males are the buyers and consumer of these publications.

Style and Self-Expression

A key index of *gaul* style is the language through which it is expressed. *Bahasa gaul* (social language or the language of sociability) is an informal variety of Indonesian (Bahasa Indonesia)[10] that is part of a continuing shift among urban Javanese youth away from the use of Javanese and toward (more informal varieties of) the national language (cf. Oetomo 1990; Smith-Hefner 2007, 2009b; Sneddon 2003, 2006). Some refer to *bahasa gaul* as *slenk* or "slang," because of its association with trendiness and cool (*keren*) and because of its historical links with *bahasa prokem,* the cant of gangsters and criminals (Chambert-Loir and Collins 1984). Like slang, the most salient feature of *gaul* is its lexicon (cf. Eble 1996). *Gaul* borrows from English but draws most heavily from the Jakartan dialect of Indonesian to articulate an attitude of casual ease and cool urbanity and cosmopolitanism. It also incorporates elements of other informal Indonesian speech varieties—not only the cant of gangsters and criminals but also the language of the gay community (*bahasa gay;* cf. Boellstorff 2004a, 2004b) and the informal Javanese speech level known as *ngoko*—to communicate a shared social identity and sense of urbane belonging among its speakers. In its range of borrowings and its unmarked but systematic avoidance of new Islamic linguo-interactive styles, *gaul* once again signals a distinct, and largely nonreligious, worldview and social ethic.[11]

Gaul style is fast, fluent, and self-confident. It is achieved through prosody, intonation, and gesture as well as pragmatics. Its speakers adopt a characteristically playful stance often accompanied by a shrug or laughter. Words, including foreign borrowings, are clipped, contracted, and blended for effect and ease of pronunciation. Many *gaul* lexical items are acronyms that are made up of the initial letters of each of the words in a phrase. For example, *JJS* (/jejeEs/) is an abbreviation of *jalan jalan santai* (to walk around/hang out). *PD* or *pede* (/pede/) is an abbreviation for *percaya diri* (lit. "to believe in oneself; self-confident"). *HTI* (/hatei/) stands for *hubungan tanpa ikatan* (lit. "relations without [legal] connection" or "illicit sex"), also referred to as *HTS* (/hateEs/) *hubungan tanpa status* (relations without [legal] status).[12] The resulting impression is one of interactional flexibility and relaxed informality that hints at the more inclusive aspirations of a generation of speakers who came of age in the optimistic era of "[democratic] reform" (*reformasi*).

Bahasa gaul expresses a new type of youth sociability; it speaks to solidarity rather than status differentials and to a shared positive value placed on cool and occasionally ironic distancing from the formality and hierarchy of an earlier generation. Perhaps most importantly, *gaul* articulates the desire of Indonesian youth for new types of social identifications through the formulation of relationships that are more egalitarian and interactionally fluid as well as more personally expressive and psychologically individualized.

Youth publications play on *gaul*'s iconic associations to speak directly to their readers from a position of shared experience. Authors often employ key indices of *gaul* style to address their readers, calling them, for example, the equivalent of "bro" (*brur*) or "dude" (*bo, coy*) or using the personal pronouns *gue* "I," and *(e)lu* "you"[13] to signal their identification with the modern cosmopolitanism and hip youth culture associated with the capital, Jakarta. The commentary found on the back of *gaul* book covers often testify to the author's authentic youth voice and audience appeal:

> This is a young author with a characteristic (youth) style of language who has achieved a special place among his readers (Kurnia 2005).[14]

> This book is interesting and can become a guide for young people. I like this book because I don't feel like I'm being lectured to. For those of you who don't want to be confused in social interactions, I suggest you read this book (Alatas 2006).

> This book asks us to think again about how to be "gaulers." Older brother Alwi [the author], offers tips on the sociability that will make our interactions more engrossing and interesting (Alatas 2006).

This identification of the author as relatively close in age and experience to his or her audience, often taking the role of an older sibling or close friend, allows for the more direct exchange of experience and emotion referred to as *curhat*.[15] *Curhat* is an abbreviation or blending of a type that is quite common among *gaul* terms. It is composed of the words *curahan hati* (lit. "outpouring the heart" or "to pour out one's heart"). *Curhat* has taken on greater significance within the context of the explosion of Internet cafés and the popularity of chatting, which also took off in the early 2000s (Slama 2010). Internet chatting, as well as electronic texting and messaging, much of which takes place in *bahasa gaul* (Barendregt 2008; Manns 2010),[16] has posed a challenge to traditional Javanese emotional reserve and restraint in interpersonal relations. This restraint and reserve, commonly referred to as *malu*, falls disproportionately on young women who are socialized to be shy and demure—particularly in interactions with young men (Collins and Bahar 2000). A significant amount of chatting and texting in fact takes place with members of the opposite sex and is a prelude to or substitute for face-to-face encounters. Whereas young people, especially young women, might feel awkward and tongue-tied (*kurang pede* [lacking in self-confidence] or *risih* [awkward, uncomfortable]) conversing directly with a young man to whom they were attracted, online and electronic conversations allow for the exchange of confidences (*curhat*) in a safe context. It also allows for the screening of possible candidates: is he capable of *sharing* and the expression of *concern*, or not? Iconic of the *gaul* persona and style of sociability, *curhat* describes a relation of emotional closeness and trust, one that is often placed at the center of "modern" romantic relationships. It has become a kind of litmus test for an attractive and modern romantic partner (Slama 2010; see also Barendregt 2008; Nadia 2008).

Curhat is one of a number of *gaul* terms that refer to emotional or psychological states and the quality of "modern" interactions with friends and significant others (cf. Parker 2016). Adding to their cosmopolitan cachet, many of these terms are borrowed from English. They include *care* (care), *sharing* (sharing), *concern* (concerned), *support* (support), and *move on* (move on).[17] The tension with the Javanese cultural expectation of modest reserve and a certain flatness of emotion is evidenced in the fact that other borrowed "emotion" words also identified as *gaul*, including *emosi* (emotional), *sensi* (sensitive), and *individu* (individualist), tend more often than not to be used in their negative sense. (The term *individu* [individualist], for example, is often followed in youth discourse by *egois* [egotistical, selfish] and *narsis* [narcissistic, self-centered]). There are, of course, ways of expressing these concepts in Indonesian, but young people argue that the use of English borrowings allows for the expression of emotions that one might otherwise feel uncomfortable expressing in one's own language, while simultaneously underscoring the sophisticated cosmopolitanism or "coolness" of the speaker. Again, notable by comparison—particularly in light of the resurgent interest in Islam—is the absence of borrowings in *gaul* youth slang from Arabic (Smith-Hefner 2007; see also Supriyanti 2004).

Perhaps not surprisingly, the *gaul* ideal of more emotionally expressive and egalitarian relationships described by these and similar terms and particularly as indexed by the concept of *curhat* is one that is viewed as cause for alarm by those of a more deliberately normative Islamic orientation. The latter see in these forms the specter of encroaching individualism and a dilution of the Islamized sociability to which they have dedicated themselves. Yet these same Muslim youth share many of the new *gaul* youth's aspirations to a greater measure of upward mobility, nonformal sociability, and emotional expressivity. One more example of the complex imbrications at work in the new Islamic sociability, some Muslim youth have rallied to promote their own competing speech and lifestyle identity, referred to simply as *Islami*.

The term *Islami* (Islamic) is in fact used to refer to a number of different social styles. At the most general level it indexes those who cultivate Muslim piety through modest dress and demeanor and normative religious practice. It is also used to refer to the style of conservative Islamist groups that promote scripturalist or strict constructionist approaches to the Qur'an and the Sunnah of the Prophet. Groups such as the caliphate-promoting Hizbut Tahrir, the hardline MMI, and the more moderate PKS draw heavily on the Qur'an and hadith as sources of legitimation and promote the example of the Prophet as a proper role model for contemporary youth. While all *Islami* guides for youth draw on these authoritative texts for answers to the questions facing today's young people, strict-constructionist groups (those that aspire to hew particularly closely to scriptural texts) insist that pious Muslims must refrain from individualized interpretation of scripture (*ijtihad*) and instead conform to what they regard as the one and true religious interpretation of God's commands. In other words, and perhaps unintuitively for those unfamiliar with Islamic traditions, there is a process of individualization being invoked here. However, it is not that of the free-ranging "expressive individualism" celebrated in the sociology of the post-1960s West nor that of the *ijtihadic* individualism of some self-consciously "liberal" Muslim Indonesians. It is instead an individualization that seeks to free the individual from inherited culture and traditions so as to reposition that individual beneath the singular and unimpeachable authority of God's commands.

Publications written in *Islami* style include the top-selling Islamist magazines *Hidayah* (God's Guidance) and *Sabili* (Fighters for the Holy Cause) and their offshoots,[18] as well as the extensive works of the Muslim entrepreneur Abu Al-Ghifari, printed by his personal publishing house, Mujahid Press (cf. Widodo 2008). Al-Ghifari's books first appeared in the early 2000s along with the first wave of *gaul* publications. Among his fiery religious tracts are his "best-selling" *Kudung Gaul: Berjilbab Tapi Telanjang* (Trendy Headscarves: Covered but Naked); *Gelombang Kejahatan Seks Remaja Modern* (A Wave of Modern Teen Sex Crimes); and *Romantika Remaja: Kisah-Kisah Tragis dan Solusinya dalam Islam* (Teen Romance: Tragic Stories and Solutions in Islam). Like Wijayanto's books, all of these books have been published in multiple editions.[19]

As is typical of authors who write in this Islamist genre, Al-Ghifari blames the moral corruption of today's youth directly on media and consumptive flows from the West. He points to American movies and television shows, which are widely watched by Indonesian youth (offering the anachronistic examples of *Bay Watch*, *Beverly Hills 90210*, and *Melrose Place*), as contaminating young people with ideas of free sex and promiscuity as an individual right. He describes Western youth as behaving "like animals," and free sex as an extreme form of "narcissism which develops into a wandering lust that can never be satisfied, eventually becoming an insatiable sexual hunger" (Al-Ghifari 2001b, 40–41). The outcome is a condition he calls (not without his own measure of trendy hyperbole) "hypersexuality." In the case of women, he argues, hypersexuality can be understood as a type of "pathological masochism." When sexual freedom has gone too far and can no longer be controlled, the only solution, Al-Ghifari writes, is to quickly marry (Al-Ghifari 2002b, 2003a).

The works of Al-Ghifari and others writing in this genre are uniform in their condemnation of Western immorality and their appeals to young people to avoid situations that offer the temptation of illicit sex (*berzina*). Satan, these authors remind young readers, is found in all those places (cinemas, nightclubs, bars, discotheques, and malls) that create opportunities for *berkhalwat* ("illicit proximity;" i.e., being alone together with an unrelated member of the opposite sex) and lead quickly to other immoral acts, such as being too close together and holding or touching each other. The best defense is to avoid such places altogether. An even more radical course of action—that taken up by Islamist vigilantes such as Indonesia's Islamic Defenders Front (Front Pembela Islam)—is to force such places of vice (*maksiat*) to close down.[20]

Another especially popular work in this genre is Salim A. Fillah's *Islami* guide to marriage and courtship, *Nikmatnya Pacaran Setelah Pernikahan* (The Pleasure of Courtship after Marriage), which was first published in 2003, and has since been reprinted in multiple editions.[21] Like Al-Ghifari, Fillah warns young people to avoid all those situations that might lead one to sin. In this case, however, the author takes aim squarely at the *gaul*-sanctioned desire to *curhat*, or "share feelings," with a boyfriend/girlfriend. If mainstream *gaul* deftly avoids direct attacks on the new Muslim sociability, there can be no such strategic liberality in neoconservative Muslims' statements on the culture of *gaul*. Fillah argues that what may appear according to *gaul* guidelines as innocent and benign is in fact a dangerous practice that can easily lead youth into a moral and emotional abyss. He warns the reader that those who have experienced the "sharing of feelings, the lightening of worries, the giving of advice with a member of the opposite sex," make God jealous. Moreover, they set themselves up for disappointment when their later marital relationship does not equal the false pleasure of these early and immoral flirtations.[22] Instead of sharing personal thoughts and emotions with a girlfriend or boyfriend, Fillah advises his readers to "bring their troubles to God" (2003, 44)—thereby avoiding the possible sin of fornication.

In Fillah's work and in the work of others who write from a strict constructionist perspective, *gaul* terms are generally avoided. But the counterattack engagement with *gaul* sociability is striking. Rather than going down the slippery slope of the *gaul* lexicon, Fillah's and similar *Islami* works are liberally sprinkled with borrowings from Arabic. Widely used terms include *ikhwan* (a pious male/brother) and *akhwat* (a pious female/sister) and phrases such as *Bismillah* (In the name of God), *Insya'Allah* (God willing), *Astaghfirullah* (I ask God for forgiveness), and *Subhanallah* (Glory be to God). *Islami* authors typically include lengthy passages quoted directly from the Qur'an and hadith in Arabic (followed by Indonesian translations) to buttress their arguments.[23] Their young readers are directed to Qur'anic study and prayer as antidotes to contemporary problems. As with mainstream *gaul*, there is a deliberate and careful effort to lay the foundation for a new youth sociability. Unlike *gaul*, however, this sociability is ostensibly "Islamized." That is, it is intended to be deeply and systematically responsive to what are understood to be God's commands for youth sexuality and social interaction.

Sociable but Shari'a-Minded

Not all Muslim resistance to the dangers of urban immorality, however, takes such militant forms. As in so many other aspects of Indonesian Muslim youth culture, complex and creative imbrications abound. Indeed, some of this ostensibly religious resistance adopts the trappings of youth language and social style, becoming an accommodating and hybridized variety of Muslim sociability—one that is both *gaul* and *Islami*. These *gaul*-but-*Islami* authors use the vocabulary of *gaul* more liberally, if cautiously—in some cases to speak directly to their audiences (identified as confused and in need of moral uplift) in a language they understand and in others to index negative categories of youth.

Among the many books on *gaul* sociability that began to appear in the bookstores in the mid-2000s and that continue to appear on bookshelves today are those that offer an alternative, Islamic sociability—*gaul Islami* or *gaul syari'i* (shari'a-minded *gaul*). This model for a new Muslim sociability is based on a distinctive blend of Muslim piety and individual self-expression. The key difference from mainstream *gaul*, of course, is that the self-expression that is prescribed is supposed to be more systematically responsive to religious norms. The proponents of this Islamized *gaul* sociability use *gaul* speech and social styles to present their readership with an image of a Muslim sociability that is open, dynamic, and engaged but nonetheless not in contradiction with a perceived scriptural normativity. Representative works in this genre include Muhammad Najib Salim's *Zaman Gaul: Tips Menjadi Gaul bagi Remaja Tanpa Kehilangan Identitas Keislamannya* (The Gaul Era: Tips for Muslim Youth on Becoming Sociable without Losing Your Muslim Identity); Muhapi's *Gaul tapi Syar'i* (Sociable but Shari'a-minded); Thobieb Al Asyhar's *Sufi Funky: Menjadi Remaja Gaul yang Saleh* (Sufi Funky: Become a Youth Who Is Sociable and Pious); and Tethy Ezokanzo and Sinyo's *Tetap Gaul tapi Syar'i* (Staying Sociable but Pious).[24] These books, like those of more conservative Islamist authors, lament the current state of the world and its negative effects on today's youth. They earnestly and repeatedly appeal to young people to be aware of their religion and not be drawn into sin and immorality. However, rather than rejecting this new world of personal development and social mobility, they offer the believer tips for how to enter more effectively—but also ethically—into its dizzying corridors.

In *Sociable but Syariah-minded* (Muhapi 2006), for example, the author cautions his readers to avoid those situations that might draw them into sin and immorality—situations associated with certain kinds of *gaul* sociability. He encourages young people instead to focus their energies and attention on setting goals—goals imagined with self-conscious reference to Islamic normativity—and then doing their best to achieve those goals: "In this book I want to help youth to understand an era which is becoming so much more complex and more challenging, and some say, more crazy [*edan*]. *Don't get pulled into ignorance, laziness, let alone drown in the world of darkness that is immorality, that is considered gaul!*" (Muhapi 2006, vi, emphasis added).

Speaking of the propensity of contemporary youth to hang out with friends on street corners, smoking and causing trouble for passersby, Muhapi writes, "They say, 'you gotta do things like this and this, it's like *gaul* man'" (*Mereka katakan,"yang begini-ni, baru anak gaul, man"* [Muhapi 2006, 23]). Here again, the culture war with mainstream *gaul* is semantically marked and rhetorically striking. No reader can overlook the contest in play. In a similar passage, the author describes a certain type of youth, one who urges his friends, "Hey, you gotta get out and be *gaul* you know; don't stay at home and be a loser without any friends." (*Jadi orang gaul dong, jangan kuper nggak punya teman . . . jangan di rumah terus* [Muhapi 2006, 40]). His response is that socializing is something that is both enjoyable and good. But once again he seeks to Islamize the social impulse. He reminds his readers that it is important to choose friends wisely so that they add to one's understanding and vision and motivate one's faith; we should always choose companions who will encourage us to be better people, not those who encourage us to go astray.

The attempt in these *gaul Islami* texts is thus one that seeks to combine a message of personal development and disciplined achievement with repeated appeals to regulate both currents through self-conscious ethical reference to the Qur'an and hadith. Sociability is thus ethicalized by being grounded on God's commands and the model of the Prophet and his companions. In these texts, social relationships are to be carefully constrained, and the energy and emotion of youth diverted to ethically affirmative endeavors. The texts' broader message thus links personal success with a *principled* sociability (*gaul yang berprinsip*).

No less important, the message here is also that "principled sociability" is that which is grounded on religious study (*ngaji/tarbiyah*) and the ethical cultivation it allows. Instead of a sociability linked to hedonistic pleasure and consumption, principled sociability is a sociability that is responsive to and based on an understanding of the injunctions and prohibitions of Islamic normativity. Religious study is the means to obtain that knowledge. Young people are encouraged to use their free time to seek religious knowledge, including, most importantly, knowledge of Islamic law (shari'a). It is only by organizing one's free time and habitus around God's commandments that one can learn how to resist things forbidden by religion.

The model at work here, then, is not that of the self-expressive individuality celebrated in certain accounts of Western modernity. It is that of the pious believer, whose piety is defined with reference not to the expressive celebration of personal feelings or a unique and authentic self, but knowledge of God's commands:

> Sociability that is truly ok is that which is principled. . . . We have to hold on tightly to our religious principles. If our friends invite us to go against the requirements of God or to do something forbidden by our religion, we have to refuse. "Sorry, this is against my principles. I can't go along with it." But if they still press us, what do we do? [If they say,] "Oh you act so pious. Have you become an *ustadz* [religious scholar/teacher]?" If they say that, don't be surprised. Just respond, "Better to act pious than to act like a *kafir* [unbeliever]!" (Alatas 2006, 97–99).

What is of particular interest in this discourse is that, even while occasionally railing against the West, these authors do not recommend that Muslims seal themselves off from the broader social world or from the changes associated with modern globalization. The pervasive reality of cultural imbrication is recognized and, to some degree, affirmed. In fact, at times one encounters explicit and relatively "liberal" affirmations of some of the products of Western modernization. Although there are dangers associated with uncritical Westernization, we hear repeatedly, "Muslims have to keep up with the latest in order to develop and advance so that we are not left behind" (Muhapi 2006, 34).

In fact, these authors liberally quote Western figures throughout their works, urging young people to take their inspiration from people such as Henry Ford, Helen Keller, and Albert Einstein to overcome difficult odds and to make a difference in the world. Like the new Muslim celebrity preachers described by James Hoesterey (2008, 2015), these authors draw on Western psychological models from Freud to Howard Gardner to buttress their claims to modern authority while encouraging new forms of religious experience (see also Rudnyckyj 2010). Also like Hoesterey's celebrity preachers, these authors are themselves entrepreneurs who, in addition to writing books, typically write advice columns in newspapers and magazines, work as consultants, offer educational seminars, and participate in television and radio talk shows. As a result, their message of principled sociability has an influence that extends far beyond the readership of their books.

Modern Muslim Subjectivities

It was to this discourse of "principled sociability" that the young people in my interviews and ethnographic encounters constantly referred in describing the temptations of urban life and, especially, interactions with members of the opposite sex. A story recounted by Abbas, a fourth-year student at the State Islamic University is a case in point. Abbas told of how when he first arrived in Yogyakarta from his rural *pesantren*, he was drawn to Yogyakarta's night scene. He described how he was invited to join a group of young men and women who liked to frequent nightclubs and discotheques. He got to know the group well, and most of its members felt comfortable confiding in him. He discovered that both male and female members of the group were very casual about sexual encounters, and that many members of the group had been intimate. One time after an evening on the town, Abbas recounted, the whole group spent the night together. The women had the men take their clothes off so that they could measure the men's penises. Then the women took off their blouses and the men measured the women's breasts. Abbas decided it was too much for him. His conscience bothered him, he said, and he kept thinking about the teachings of a Muslim scholar (*kyai*) from his religious school. "I returned to my principles" (*Saya kembali ke princip saya*), he said. Besides, he didn't have the money to keep up with their party lifestyle. He severed his social ties with the group entirely.

"Principled sociability," "my religious principles," or "my foundational principles" came up most consistently in discussions of dating and marriage. It was, for example, widely accepted that interfaith relationships were doomed to failure because marriage between two people of different faiths would be based on differing foundational principles. The children of such unions would grow up morally confused; the marriage, it was said, would most likely end in divorce—as so often occurs, young people pointed out, in the West. At the same time,

Girls at the Ambarukkmo Plaza Mall, Yogyakarta. Photo by the author.

Saturday night on Jalan Malioboro, Yogyakarta. Photo by Claire-Marie Hefner.

marriages arranged by religious authorities even without the partners spending any time alone together beforehand would be successful because each party would hold to (and would be held to) the same foundational principles (cf. Smith-Hefner 2005). Citing one's "Islamic principles" or "most basic principles" was also the most common response in interviews to my questions about premarital sex. The response does not mean, of course, that students always abide by these principles, as the example of Abbas illustrates. Nonetheless, this new ethical register or current is widely discussed and thus socially available. No less important, it is for many Muslim youth a resonant and powerful strategy for neutralizing the uncertainties of a new and unfamiliar social environment, including the alluring temptations of Yogyakarta's bars, discotheques, movie theaters, and shopping malls.

In embracing a principled, religiously informed sociability, young people draw on widely available discourses that address and reformat major ethical challenges in their own lives. Many of these concerns have everything to do with the anxieties surround achieving and maintaining middle-class status: how to stay clear of the enticements of the urban social scene; how to avoid potentially disastrous sexual involvements; and how to stay disciplined and focused so as to finish one's university studies and obtain a diploma. Liberally sprinkled with borrowings from contemporary youth slang (*bahasa gaul*) and making major concessions to popular interest in self-expression and self-making, this principled and Muslim sociability has enough in common with mainline *gaul* so as to appear thoroughly modern and even trendy. It is a mechanism of principled integration into, not segregation from, the allures of modern social life. It is, in Patrick Haenni's terminology, a key feature of *l'Islam de marché* (Haenni 2005; see also Njoto-Feillard 2012): an Islam of the marketplace, one that accommodates rather than rejects modernity, but accommodates it on ethical terms that remake and yet restrain individual habitus—a habitus that is at once *gaul* and *Islami*, Muslim and modern.

The New Muslim Romance

As discussed in the previous chapter, one unanticipated result of the new social and educational opportunities now available to young people is that they have significantly more possibilities today for meeting and interacting with members of the opposite sex on their own and away from parental supervision. Increased opportunities for mixed-sex socializing and the range of new sociabilities associated with urban life have fueled public anxiety and raised fears that young people might engage in behaviors that compromise their own and their families' reputations. As alarming for many parents, these new social styles and sociabilities have also introduced the possibility that young people might jeopardize their educational plans and the chance of a secure foothold in the middle class. Familial anxieties and public panics have focused particular attention on the behavior of young women, who have taken up new educational and economic opportunities in disproportionate numbers. An often-cited hadith enjoins members of the Muslim *umat* to "seek knowledge as far as China." Indonesian women have heeded this admonition and are increasingly postponing marriage in order to seek knowledge through higher education;[1] they are also planning to put that knowledge to work (G. Jones 2009; Nilan 2008; Parker and Nilan 2013; A. Utomo 2014).

Most young Javanese women today—including religiously observant Muslims—see women's extrafamilial employment as both a personal necessity and an unambiguous social good. They and their parents are acutely aware of the need in today's economy for two incomes to support a middle-class lifestyle. No less important, for most women employment outside the home is viewed as a pathway to personal autonomy, in particular where marital ties and family supports may be less than certain. University women recount how their own mothers—ordinary Muslims as well as those religiously observant—repeatedly reminded them of the wisdom of a woman having her own money so that she is not dependent on the generosity of her husband and can support herself and her children if circumstances require (see chapter 5).[2]

This broader link—between education, work, and autonomy—is often expressed in parents' comments with regard to the fact that their daughters will be allowed to choose their own husbands. Bu Suharti, a high school teacher in urban Yogyakarta and mother of three daughters and one son, who described herself as an "ordinary Muslim," quite matter-of-factly stated what many other mothers of young women told me, "As for my daughters, they will choose their own husbands. We cannot choose their husbands for them; we can only offer advice. But my husband and I have given them lots of education so that they can make good decisions." The link to autonomy is clear. It is education that prepares young women to make good marital choices, and it is education that offers them the possibility of working, not only to help their husbands to support their families but also to support themselves and their children if necessary.

What is more, a woman who has her own money has the means to help out her parents or siblings if the need arises. Bu Suharti continued, "And with education they can help their husbands to support their families, not just stay home with the children, no! I feel strongly that the wife has to have her own income. That way if she wants to give some money to her younger sibling or to her parents, and if her husband disagrees, she can just say, 'I have my own money.' If she has no money of her own, he'll feel it's a drain. But if she has her own money, it's fine. She can say, 'I have my own income.'"

Many young women themselves report being painfully aware of the sacrifices their parents had made in supporting their childrens' education and state that they hope to repay the debt (*mbalas budi*) by taking over the financial burden of schooling their younger siblings or helping their parents out financially in other ways (Parker and Nilan 2013, 85–86). This ethical concern for the support of parents and siblings is to a significant degree "gendered"; that is, the theme looms far larger in the personal narratives of young women than young men:[3] "I want to work after I graduate to make my parents happy"; "I know how much my parents have sacrificed to support my education, I want to work so that I can repay their sacrifice"; "I want to be an example for my siblings, and when I graduate I plan to support their schooling."

Seen from the perspective of this social matrix, the situation of Indonesian women is strikingly different from that of the educated young women described by Fida Adely (2012) in her study of a Jordanian high school. Adely cites figures that show the school enrollment of Jordanian females is higher than that of males at all levels: primary, secondary, and tertiary (141). Unlike Indonesian women, however, many young Jordanian women stated a preference for becoming housewives who do not pursue careers outside of the home. Adley observes that higher education for Jordanian women is linked to social status and respectability, and that both are related, in turn, not to long-term career imaginings but to midterm marriage. She writes, "Although I was regularly told by Jordanians that contemporary economic circumstances demanded that a woman work, both men and women expressed ambivalence about women's labor force participation" (139).[4]

By contrast, middle-class and aspiring middle-class Javanese women repeat a now familiar refrain: that *not* to work after receiving a college degree would be a wasted investment of time and money. Statistics offered by the World Bank confirm this difference between the situation and aspiration of Indonesian women and their counterparts in the Muslim Middle East. Data for 2012 indicate that 47.6 percent of Indonesian women ages fifteen and older are employed, compared to 12.1 percent of Jordanian women in the same age group.[5] That is, among working-age females, Indonesian women are *almost four times* as likely to be employed as working-aged females in Jordan.[6] Indonesian women also stand out in comparison to Egyptian women (17.2 percent of whom work), Tunisian women (21.5 percent of whom work), and Moroccan women (23.7 percent of whom work), according to World Bank statistics for the same year.[7]

Against this gendered social and economic background, this chapter takes up new trends in courtship and marriage among educated Muslim youth and examines the anxieties created by new social mobility and economic opportunities for Indonesia's middle class. New opportunities for women in particular have led to what is widely perceived as a "marriage crisis," or what some have referred to as a "marriage squeeze" (G. Jones 1994a, 122–125; G. Jones and Yeung 2014, 1579–1580; A. Utomo 2014). This widely observed and, for most women, deeply unsettling phenomenon refers to the difficulties many educated young women face in finding partners due to an imbalance in the number of available men or to young women putting off marriage for "too long" and aging out of the marital market. Facing a narrowing pool of marriageable men, educated women scramble to identify a partner who is willing to negotiate work and family roles within the context of a "modern," companionate marriage. Women's life histories indicate that many have had to adjust both their strategies and their expectations in their search for a suitable spouse.

Contemporary trends in courtship and marriage among educated youth are a response to these shifting realities. These trends include on the one hand increasingly—and in some estimations, alarmingly—long courtship and engagement periods as well as larger and more elaborate middle-class Javanese weddings. In contrast to these trends is a more limited but nonetheless growing phenomenon among some more normatively conservative Muslim young people: the decision to forego courtship (*pacaran*) and premarital familiarization entirely and to marry according to newly prescribed *Islami* models—models that involve the surrender of individual choice of marital partner to a recognized religious authority (Smith-Hefner 2005). These latter models include shorter or nonexistent engagements and more modest wedding celebrations that emphasize Muslim elements over traditional ones. As with other aspects of the new *Islami* sociabilities, the models are also illustrative of a distinctive pattern of individuality within modernity, one that is morally embedded rather than self-constructively "free."

Getting Serious

Although increasing numbers of Indonesian young people are postponing marriage in order to pursue an education or employment, they have hardly abandoned it. Within Indonesian Islam, and as is the case in other Muslim majority countries, there is a powerfully felt "marital imperative" (cf. Adely 2012, 125; G. Jones 1994a, 61; Singerman 2007, 5). Marriage is strongly enjoined by Islam (Ali 2006; Bouhdiba 2004),[8] but for ordinary Muslims it is also an important marker of social maturity; any who opt not to marry face social stigmatization (Parker 2008a, 23). There is a widespread assumption that those who do not marry are in fact defective or incomplete (*tidak sempurna*). Even homosexuals in Indonesia feel strong social pressures to enter into hetero-sexual unions and produce offspring so as to take up an identifiable position within Javanese social life and graduate from the category of "unmarried youth" (Blackwood 2010; Boellstorf 1999, 2005; McNally, Grierson, and Hidayana 2015).

In a pioneering study of young Javanese women who took up factory jobs in rural Java in the early 1980s, Diane Wolf reported similarly that increased education, social mobility, and employment opportunities had not diminished young women's intention to marry (Wolf 1992, 211). Indeed, this is one realm in which mainline Javanese-Muslim sexual ethics has long shown a notable im-brication with scripturally based Islamic ethics. Religion teachers and schol-ars insist based on Qur'anic sources; there is "no monkery in Islam" (cf. Ali 2006, 6).[9] Young people regularly identify marriage as a religious requirement (*kewajiban*) as well as a deeply felt moral obligation to their parents (*balas budi*). Virtually all of the young people whom I came to know over the years—including those who did not regard themselves as particularly religious—reported they both expected and looked forward to marrying.

Youth commentary on the necessity and normalcy of marriage is borne out by large scale statistical trends. The Australian demographers Gavin Jones and Bina Gubhaju (2008, 3) describe Indonesia as following the pattern of "universal marriage," defined as a country where less than 5 percent of women are still single in their late forties. In Indonesia in 2005, they write, only 2 percent of Indonesian women ages 45 to 49 were never married (G. Jones and Gubhaju 2008, 11). Although this pattern has shifted in many areas of South and South-east Asia, and may shift with later generations in Indonesia as well,[10] marriage is still taken for granted by the vast majority of Indonesian youth. According to this near-universal norm, women who reach their mid-twenties and are not yet married are considered "old maids" (*prawan tua*), and anxious concern is expressed over their "marketability" and, in particular, their declining fertility.

Marriage goes hand in hand with childbearing, and the normative expecta-tions that surround childbearing also show a surprising measure of overlap or ethical consensus between those who regard themselves as casual in their re-ligious observance and those who regard themselves as strict Muslims. Children are referred to as "gifts" (*anugrah*) and "blessings" (*berkat*) from God that bring good fortune (*rejeki*) to their parents. Young people from all back-grounds regularly volunteer, "If I'm ready to get married, I'm ready to have a child." Newlyweds anticipate producing a "fruit of their love" (*buah hati*) as quickly as possible. If, after several months of marriage they have not yet made a happy announcement, people begin to ask if something is the matter.

Although Javanese parents warn their daughters to avoid relationships that could interfere with their studies and possibly keep them from obtaining their degrees, the fear of never marrying is a source of considerable anxiety for young women as well as for their parents. As their daughters approach their twenties and are close to attaining their educational goals, many parents are willing—even delighted—to accept a relationship with a young man from a good background and with good future prospects who is "serious" in his intentions. In fact, across religious backgrounds, if a young woman does not have a serious boyfriend at graduation or soon after, family members begin pressing her to find someone.

Not only parents but young people themselves emphasize the distinction between "serious" and "not serious" relationships. Nonserious relationships do not quite matter; they are "just playing around" (*main-main saja, having fun saja*),[11] and they may involve individuals who are not in the long view candidates for marriage. By the time they are in college, however, most women—and the majority of young men—insist that they are only interested in a serious relationship that could possibly "lead to matrimony" (*yang menuju ke jenjang perkawinan*). Those young women who find they are approaching graduation without a "serious" partner express nervous apprehension.[12]

A serious candidate has ideally already finished his own education and has secure employment or the promise of secure employment, some form of transportation, and possibly a place for the newlyweds to live—although many young couples in fact live with one or the other set of parents until they are ready to establish a household of their own. It goes almost without saying that, as far as parents are concerned, whether they are "ordinary" Muslims or strictly observant, any potential candidate for their daughter must be Muslim. Although two generations ago mixed marriages between Christians and Muslims were tolerated in some Javanese Muslim families, in recent years, attitudes in most Muslim circles have changed dramatically. Young women reiterated the same religious requirement, echoing what is taught in schools and religion classes and supported by the 1974 marriage legislation: that marriage outside of one's religion inevitably results in discord and a "broken home" (e.g., divorce; cf. Lindsey 2012, 75; Parker, Hoon, and Raihani 2014).[13]

Young women's accounts of their efforts to balance academic ambitions with marital aspirations, however, revealed how even the best-laid plans often lead to emotional as well as ethical challenges. Ismi, a third-year student and an acquaintance of one of my research assistants from Gadjah Mada, detailed the repeated frustrations she experienced in her attempts to maintain a serious relationship while completing her undergraduate degree at Yogyakarta's Muhammadiyah University (Universitas Muhammadiyah Yogyakarta, UMY). Although Ismi is neo-reformist in orientation, similar frustrations emerged in the stories of young women across Muslim backgrounds.

Ismi is a slight young woman with an oval face accentuated by a carefully arranged and securely pinned chiffon headscarf. She wore to our meeting a fashionable long polka-dot skirt with a matching tunic and closed-toe shoes with flesh-colored stockings. It was an outfit that identified her as religiously observant but trendy at the same time. Although only twenty-one, Ismi, like many middle-class female students I spoke with, had carefully mapped out a life plan for herself that included education, work, and most importantly marriage:

My plan was by age twenty I would have a serious boyfriend who I was sure I would marry. That was my plan. And I would get married at age twenty-two or twenty-three, or at the latest age twenty-five if I go on to get a master's degree. The maximal age when I have to be settled is by age twenty-seven. That's because, you know, women have a fertile period [*masa suburnya*], and if I reach age thirty and haven't yet gotten pregnant, any pregnancies will be high risk. . . . . Well, I met my boyfriend when I had just turned twenty, so I was completely on target. I was twenty and I had my serious boyfriend. I was exactly on my target.

Although Ismi was from a reformist Muslim background, the style of "life planning" in which she was engaging here is in fact common among university students. It is, in other words, a trademark of the new Muslim middle class. Designed to allow a balance among several aspirational ambitions, life plans like Ismi's tend to be especially notable among young middle-class Muslim women intent on combining family life with out-of-home employment. As it turned out, however, despite her well-laid plans, Ismi's boyfriend had ended their relationship of almost two years just five weeks before our interview. Ismi was emotionally devastated and was still struggling to come to terms with her situation. It had been a serious relationship. She had fully expected that they would get married and that their stable relationship would facilitate her progress along the path of combining piety and professionalism, family life, and employment.

Her boyfriend was enrolled in a military academy in another city, and so the couple had not been able to see each other very often. It was, in Ismi's words, a

Couple on the beach, Parangtritis, Special Region of Yogyakarta. Photo by the author.

Couple studying together, Sunan Kalijaga State Islamic University, Yogyakarta. Photo by Claire-Marie Hefner.

"long-distance relationship" (in *gaul* youth slang, *LDR*). Once a month or so his school had allowed him to have visitors, and Ismi would go to see him and stay with a girlfriend. Otherwise the two just exchanged text messages or chatted on the phone. But there were limits to their personal communications as well. Academy regulations allowed the couple to talk or meet only on Saturdays and Sundays. In fact, Ismi recounted, there were lists of military rules they were required to follow, including the type of restaurants they were allowed to eat at (only formal restaurants, no roadside food stalls), the sorts of transportation they could take (only taxis or private cars, no motorbikes), and the style of clothes she could wear (wives and girlfriends were allowed to wear the headscarf; however, much more fashionably put together Muslim ensembles than those Ismi wore to school were expected at official events). She explained,

> I was willing to adjust to all those requirements. I even bought new clothes! But it didn't matter. In the end he left me for the daughter of a general; that's what I heard. I was totally traumatized. I was so depressed that I completely stopped eating and drinking. I just stayed at home in my room and only came out to pray. I didn't even want to go back to school. After one week in my room like that, my mom asked my religion teacher [*ustadz*] to come and talk with me. He told me not to worry. He said everyone is certain to have a life partner [*jodoh*]. We don't know when or where we will meet him, but it is certain that we all have one. That doesn't mean we can be passive, we have to do our best and take care of ourselves, improve ourselves. "Our *jodoh* is a

reflection of ourselves. People who are good get a *jodoh* who is good, and people who are bad get a *jodoh* who is bad."

Ismi had to readjust her well-made life plans. She decided that rather than worrying about finding someone to marry, she would focus instead on finding a "graduation companion/partner" (*pendamping wisuda*); that is, she hoped to find someone in the coming year who would be by her side at graduation, and she would try not to think about the rest. "Now I just want to start with the target of graduation and finding a 'graduation partner'" she said, "and then I'll move on to the next target."

Despite the trauma of her breakup, and despite the fact that the difficulties she experienced had reaffirmed her commitment to a serious profession of Islam, Ismi still considered *pacaran* an important way to get to know someone before marrying. She was adamant, in fact, about her right to choose her own partner, and rejected the possibility of relinquishing that right either to her parents or to a religious official: "No, I'd never do that. It's my life, so the decision is up to me." There is nothing immoral about having a boyfriend, she argued; it is much better to discover that you don't like someone while you are just boyfriend and girlfriend (*pacar*) than after you are married.

Ismi was quite conscious, however, of the moral debates surrounding dating, and had a clear though not unnuanced ethical sense of the social and sexual boundaries of *pacaran*, ideas she had absorbed from her Islamic teachers and religion classes:

We are taught in our religion classes that it's not allowed to touch a boy. In Islam, it's not allowed. And especially touching or hugging each other with feelings of desire, it's not allowed. I mean, you're not even supposed to shake hands with men—though it's okay for me. They teach us that it's the girl's responsibility to put the brakes on. And they say things like, if a woman just shows her foot a little bit, it can be a problem because the guy can't control his desire. But I think it has to be the guy's responsibility, too, to control himself. And if a guy told me he fell in love with a woman because he saw her ankle, I wouldn't believe him.

In these and other examples, it is interesting to see how, even as they embrace ostensibly Islamic norms on opposite-sex friendship, many youth adjust the norms in a manner that reflects their own understanding of gender realities. In this case, for example, even while accepting her religious teachers' dictum that it is a young woman's responsibility "to put the brakes on," Ismi tweaks the ethical principle in a manner that allows it to reflect her own sense of mutualism and equality: guys should learn to control their desire as well. Like many of her educated age- and gender-mates, Ismi sought to strike a more equitable balance on these and related issues, even while recognizing a gender-differentiated element of female responsibility.

While Ismi expressed clear limits with regard to sex, she said she had discovered in discussions with her housemates that some of the girls had rather different understandings.[14] Some argued, for example, that French kissing and touching above the waist (though over the clothes) were acceptable. Ismi didn't agree. "The problem is that if we do that, then it leads to stimulation and more serious problems, so it's better not to do it," she explained. According to Ismi, most of her closest friends were like her and were fairly conservative in their views regarding sex; they drew the line at holding hands, hugging, and kissing. She and her girlfriends had also informally agreed to monitor and support each other's behaviors by keeping a close check on each other's relationships and by offering encouragement and reminders (cf. Bennett 2005, 74)

Given this mutual monitoring, it came as a complete surprise to Ismi to discover that one of her girlfriends had recently gotten pregnant out of wedlock:

It was just like three months ago. She came to me crying and asking my forgiveness. I had no idea what she was talking about. Then she said, "I'm pregnant." Oh my God, I never imagined that! I really couldn't believe it. She said that she and her boyfriend were in love and that he wanted to marry her, but she didn't want to force him into marriage. She said she wasn't ready to be pregnant; she was still taking classes. Of course she was thinking about her parents. What would they do? Would they throw her out? How could she take care of a baby, run a household, and go to school?

Things quickly became complicated as Ismi learned that her girlfriend had decided to abort the baby.[15] She had come to Ismi to enlist her help.

She told me she had already bought the medicine. I don't know where she got it, but it was some kind of very strong medicine, two kinds actually. You mix them with water and then drink them, first one and then the other. She asked me to be there when she did it. The problem was that once she drank the second medicine, they said she could possibly fall unconscious. She was afraid to do it alone in case she didn't wake up. But I was thinking, if she didn't wake up people might think that I had killed her. I would be responsible if I was with her. I didn't want to be a murderer! And if she aborted and I helped her, it would be a double sin, my sin and her sin.

Ismi said she had no idea what she should do. She told her friend that she would help her, because she didn't have another plan. She needed time to think. So she asked her to wait to take the medicine until the following Monday because her girlfriend always went home on the weekends to see her parents. "If she did it on Monday, I told her, it would be over by Tuesday and she'd have plenty of time to recover before going home again. I was stalling, you know, because I really didn't know what to do. And then when Monday came, I told her we had to wait until my morning classes were over and I had done my *dhuhur* prayers at 12:00. So she agreed to wait until I was finished with my prayers before taking the first medicine." But Ismi didn't go to classes, instead she got on her motorcycle and left for her girlfriend's parents' house. "Oh my God! I'll never forget it" she said. "Halfway there, my tire blew out and I was forced to stop at a mechanic's shop. I kept thinking, has she taken the first medicine? Would she do it without me? I got a text message from her, 'Is, are you coming? I've taken the first medication.' Oh God, my heart was pounding. Her parents' house was still thirty minutes away."

Somehow Ismi made it to her friend's home, and as soon as she arrived she told her friend's parents that their daughter was five weeks pregnant and was going to abort the fetus.

> I just told them right away, "Your daughter is five weeks pregnant." They were of course in shock and crying. They couldn't believe it. But they thanked me for telling them. Then I told them that she planned to abort the fetus and had already taken the first medicine. So they just left me there and rushed out to borrow the neighbor's car. And by the time I got back to my boarding house, they were already there with their daughter. It turned out that she really had taken some medicine, but thanks be to God it was only a sedative.

These events all took place on a Monday. That Wednesday, Ismi said, she heard from a classmate that her friend was married.

Ismi repeated what I had heard from many other young people, that use of contraceptives is not common among young couples. Indonesian doctors regularly refuse to prescribe birth control for unmarried women (and even in the case of married women may ask for proof of their husband's approval).[16] Although condoms are easily available at pharmacies and corner kiosks, many young women say they would be too embarrassed (*malu*) to purchase one, pointing out the possibility that the seller or another customer might recognize them. Moreover, if a young woman were to have a condom available and to provide it to her partner prior to sex, it would be an indication that she had planned to have sex, thereby calling her reputation into question. Men are still expected to be the more active partners in relationships, and women are the ones who should "put the brakes on."[17] Other forms of contraception, such as the pill, are perilous to one's health and unreliable, because without a doctor's prescription one cannot be certain of the proper dose. What is more, many young women, and some young men, said they believe condoms and other forms of contraception can have a negative effect on a woman's fertility by "drying out the uterus," so it is best not to use any form of birth control before one is married and has had a first child. What this means is that young couples who do have sex most often rely on withdrawal or other risky practices to avoid pregnancy (see also Bennett 2005, 35).

Parents not uncommonly tell their daughters, and sometimes even their sons, that if they were to get pregnant or to get someone pregnant while still in school, they would no longer receive any economic or other form of support. In fact, a young woman who becomes pregnant out of wedlock—like Ismi's friend—is quickly married in order to "cover up the disgrace/shame" (*menutupi aib*). The family of the young woman enlists the help of friends and relatives to identify the father of the child, and considerable pressure is placed on the couple to marry. The situation then dictates against the young woman continuing her schooling. There is, of course, the initial embarrassment of the pregnancy itself and the gossip that it engenders. Then once the baby arrives, the young mother is expected to maintain the household as well as take care of her husband and the baby, while her husband shoulders the responsibility of supporting his new family financially. Even if the parents of the young couple do not withdraw their economic support, continuing school would be difficult if not impossible for the young woman. If there is support for one member of the couple to continue their schooling, it is more often the young man who goes on with his studies because of his role as the expected family provider (cf. Bennett 2005, 24).

"There Is No Dating in Islam"

The contemporary pattern of extended schooling and longer courtships and the new possibilities for illicit premarital sex they afford would have presented serious ethical challenges to Javanese Muslims even if their religiosity and levels of observance had not changed since the 1980s. But the shift in schooling, mixed-sex socializing, and urban life has been rendered all the more ethically challenging because these changes have coincided with an Islamic resurgence that, in addition to raising questions about the place of Islam in public life, has also sought to bring social and sexual relations into a greater measure of conformity with norms and behaviors deemed "Islamic."

Since the collapse of the New Order, Muslim conservatives have stepped to the fore in public debates and vigorously promoted polygyny (*poligami*) and early marriage (*nikah dini*) as solutions to what they view as a moral crisis among today's Muslim youth. Among the cacophony of Islamist voices that arose in the early 2000s was that of Puspo Wardoyo, a popular and vocal supporter of polygyny (and the owner of a well-known chain of fried chicken restaurants; see Brenner 2006; Nurmila 2009; van Wichelen 2009). Wardoyo appeared frequently in public forums to argue that the taking of multiple wives by Muslim men would radically reduce premarital sex, extramarital affairs, and prostitution by addressing men's greater libidinal requirements. Wardoyo held up his own life as an example of how polygyny can be successful. He was often pictured in newspapers and magazines surrounded by his four smiling, veiled wives, each of whom manages one of his fried chicken restaurants located in various cities throughout Java.[18] Wardoyo and other proponents of polygyny voice support for the loosening of Indonesian laws on marriage to allow early marriage (*nikah dini*) and unofficial marriage (*nikah sirrih/nikah dibawah tangan*) without parental permission.[19] They argue that young people should be allowed, even encouraged, to marry before finishing their college degrees, because these alternative forms of marriage would facilitate the taking of multiple wives and prevent immoral premarital relationships from occurring during long engagements.

Wardoyo and other Islamist commentators who support polygyny and early marriage cite scriptural references in support of their cause: "O, you young men! Whoever is able to marry should marry, for that will help him to lower his gaze and guard his modesty" (Al-Bukhari 62:4); and "And if you fear that you may not be just to the orphans, then you may marry whom you please of the women: two, and three, and four. But if you fear you will not be fair, then only one" (Qur'an 4:3). The same or similar arguments are made by Islamist groups such as the caliphate-promoting Hizbut Tahrir, the hardline Majelis Mujahidin, and the Muslim-Brotherhood influenced Prosperous Justice Party (PKS) and its loose affiliate, KAMMI. These organizations, too, insist that Indonesia's moral crisis can be resolved in one and only one way: by tethering one's subjectivity and sexuality to the firm mooring of the Qur'an and the hadith. While varying in many ways on the details of their respective political and social programs, these groups offer a view of gender socialization, courtship, and marriage that allows little space for interpretation, based as it is on the claim that scripture is immutable, and that its meanings are not subject to widely divergent interpretation.

Even for young people not directly involved in campus *dakwah* (predication) groups or conservative Muslim organizations, popular versions of the Islamist view with regard to dating and marriage are widely disseminated through television and radio talk shows, *sinetron* (television serial dramas) and films,[20] as well a variety of print media.[21] By 2005, youth publications that had focused more narrowly on the cosmopolitan style of sociability known as *gaul* had been pushed aside on bookstore shelves by tracts that focused more insistently on the social and personal dangers of dating (*pacaran*) and other forms of premarital familiarization. Among the more recent of these titles are *Bawa Aku ke Penghulu* (Take Me to the Religious Authority) by Jasmine Asyahida; *Menikah Saja* (Just Marry) by Said Rosyadi and Armyta D. Pratiwi; *Jangan Jatuh Cinta!* (Don't Fall in Love!) by Setia F. Kholid and Ina Agustina; *Pacaran No Way! Why?* (Dating No Way! Why?) by Ahmad Masrul; and *Tausiyah Cinta: No Khalwat until Akad* (Tausiyah Love: No Being Alone Together until Married) by @tausiyahku—all of which take up the same refrain: that dating is sinful and marriage is the best solution.[22]

A particularly popular publication in this anti-dating genre is Salim A. Fillah's guide to courtship and marriage, *The Pleasure of Courtship after Marriage* (*Nikmatnya Pacaran Setelah Pernikahan*), introduced in the previous chapter. First published in 2003 and thus a forerunner of the genre of "no dating" tracts, by October of 2012 this book had undergone its seventeenth print run. The normative discourse presented by Fillah addresses the controversy surrounding courtship and dating by asserting the answer is simple when one uses Islam as one's guide: in Islam there is no such thing as *pacaran*, or dating; there is only *ta'aruf* (meeting for the purpose of engagement). Any premarital familiarization that is not conducted for the purposes of marriage is classified as sinful and thus strictly contrary to God's plan. Fillah explains, "There is never love in relationships that are outside of legal marriage. There is only lust and adultery" (Fillah 2003, 27). And, in a similar vein, "Islam advocates a solution to love and lust and that is: marriage. It is a tie that makes acceptable what was previously [prior to marriage] taboo" (22).

The message of authors of Islamist inclination, then, is clear and unambiguous: young people should avoid relationships with the opposite sex; if one is already in such a relationship, one should break it off immediately or quickly marry. Fillah, moreover, chides those parents who allow their children to date because they consider it "modern" and argue that their children "understand the limits of their interactions." His message is moralizing and condemnatory: "Dating constitutes adultery" (Fillah 2003, 27–28). He cites a verse from the *Surah Al Isra'* to underscore his point: "And do not approach fornication. Truly adultery is a heinous act and a wretched road" (*Al Isra'* 32, cited in Fillah 2003, 26). The idea that we should not approach fornication, Fillah writes, means that we should avoid putting ourselves in all tempting situations: "Everything that might lead to adultery is also forbidden"; "Allah prohibits fornication and orders us to marry" (2003, 25).

Unacquainted and Yet Engaged

Of course, if one does not date or even place oneself in situations where one might interact with members of the opposite sex for the purposes of getting to know them better, the question arises of how then to find someone to marry—and not just any someone but the *right* someone. The solution proposed by *Islami* authors such as Fillah is to enlist the services of a *dakwah* organization or other religious group to identify a suitable mate, with the result that there is not the least possibility of inappropriate interactions taking place.[23] Islamist associations here are intended not to "make democracy work," as Robert Putnam et alia (1993) might suggest with regard to civil-society associations, but to promulgate and police a proper Islamic sexuality.

Early in my research I met Kustiyah, a twenty-five-year-old writer and graduate of Gadjah Mada University. Kustiyah's experience offers one example of how one can marry with little or no premarital familiarization. At the time of our first interview in 2002, Kustiyah had just recently married. She dressed in neo-reformist style, with a rather enveloping headscarf pinned under her chin, a stylishly cut but not too fitted brown jacket, and a matching long skirt, with flesh-colored socks and shoes, not sandals. Kustiyah had grown up in a small town outside Solo, Central Java. She came from a family with vaguely Muhammadiyah-reformist leanings, but pointed out that when she was young her family was not particularly religious. She took up the veil as a teenager when she moved to Yogyakarta for secondary school. While studying literature at Gadjah Mada University she became involved in *dakwah* religious outreach activities through the campus mosque. Through these activities she became convinced that Islam offers a "comprehensive" (*kaffah*) answer to all social and ethical matters, including courtship and marriage.

Kustiyah declared that she had married without ever having once been alone with her fiancé. She explained that there are several ways to arrange such a relationship, but in her case, she had used a go-between from her student *dakwah* organization to get to know her future husband. "The go-between would always accompany us, whenever we met. I actually knew my fiancé; that is, we had attended different schools but belonged to the same organizations, and we would occasionally run into each other at events between schools. So I had seen him and knew something about him. At a certain point he decided that he was ready to marry. I had come to the same decision. I was ready to marry, too."

Her husband didn't propose immediately. He waited for a while so that the two could get to know each other. They had several long discussions together, but the intermediary was always present. Kustiyah explained, "My future husband made his intentions clear through the intermediary, and I indicated that I was interested. Only at that point did he go to my parents and, thanks be to God, they agreed. I think the whole process took only about two months. It didn't take long, because our vision and our principles are the same and because we were both ready to marry."

Kustiyah stressed that they never overstepped the bounds of Islamic law. Before they married, she said, they never touched, "not even a kiss on the cheek, not even the touch of one finger." "People misunderstand," she said. "They ask, 'How can marriage work if you don't know the man?' But interacting with men is allowed. It's only those interactions which might lead to desire which are not."

Kustiyah said that not only was her courtship *Islami* style but her wedding was as well. There was, for example, no traditional ritual meal (*slametan*) to which neighbors and family were invited (see C. Geertz 1976 [1960], 62). Such festival meals, Kustiyah insisted, frequently include the making of offerings to family and guardian spirits, all of which are "polytheistic" (*syirik*) and thus not allowed within Islam. Furthermore, she added, such rituals are "too complicated and just not practical." Also *Islami* style, the male and female wedding guests were seated in different sections of the reception room, separated by a rattan screen. The bride and groom were separated as well. Moreover, the bride and groom dressed in "regular clothes" rather than in royal garb, as is traditional in Javanese wedding ceremonies (C. Geertz 1976 [1960], 57). Kustiyah said she wore a long, white gown, and a white headscarf decorated with gold embroidery and flowers; her female wedding assistants all wore uniforms consisting of matching long-sleeved tunics, long skirts, and headscarves. Her husband wore a Muslim-style collarless jacket and loose pants and an innovative "Baghdad-style" hat.[24] Finally, she said, the focus of the ceremony was reading from the Qur'an rather than the traditional Javanese speeches and rituals that emphasize the ideals of harmony, fertility, and cooperation. She described the overall atmosphere of the ceremony as being "more like a religious study session [*pengajian*] than a wedding."[25] As these and other details illustrate, the social imaginary to which Kustiyah's marriage appealed was no longer that of a "traditional" Javanese Muslim wedding, with its stylistic references to Muslim courts and sultanic styles and rituals focused on fertility and cosmic harmony (C. Geertz 1976 [1960]; Pemberton 1994). The imaginary was instead that of an ostensibly Islamic rite, purified (it was hoped) of un-Islamic references.

For others who are anxious to marry but have no available prospects, religious organizations are often willing to identify a candidate for them (cf. Widiarti 2010). Mona, the KAMMI leader from Gadjah Mada University first introduced

Wedding couple, Yogyakarta. Photo by Claire-Marie
Hefner.

in chapter 3, explained that KAMMI has a committee that will facilitate the
process of finding a marriage candidate for its members and will supply chaperones for meetings so that the couple can get together and come to a decision
without ever being alone with one another. An individual simply submits his or
her "biodata" to the committee when he or she feels ready to marry. Biodata
typically include information such as a candidate's age, height and weight, educational level, employment, home address, and telephone number as well as a brief
statement of their personal aspirations and some indication of what they are
looking for in a partner; it is usually accompanied by a passport-style photo. The
committee then uses the data to identify someone who is a good match in terms

of personal profile, family background, life goals, and religious commitment. Matches are usually made with individuals from within the organization. In these and other ways, the selection process looks thoroughly modern—and indeed "rationalized" in a Weberian way to be in conformity with a singular social norm. The difference with other, "modern" matchmaking services, of course, is that this one places a priority on religiosity in the pairing.

Mona said she herself expected to use this approach. She said she was looking for a partner who shared her "mission and vision"; that is, someone who was equally committed to a life of religious activism and struggle. But she also confided that she didn't think she would ever find that person on her own, and at twenty-three she was "already old" (*sudah tua*) and would soon be considered an "old maid" (*prawan tua*). Mona's parents, who lived in Jakarta, expected her to make her own decisions about marrying; she said she would never rely on them anyway to make a choice for her, as their level of religiosity and lifestyle were quite different from her own.

Mona explained something I often heard from other young women contemplating "marriage without dating": "When you marry quickly like that without *pacaran* beforehand, we say that you *pacaran* after marrying. My friends all say that it's more beautiful, more romantic, than if you already know the person before marriage. It's a surprise, like 'What's his favorite color? What dishes does he like?' It's all a big surprise." I asked her how she could be certain that it would always be a positive surprise. Mona's answer emphasized the security of marrying within the framework of Islamic law (cf. Dwyer 2001). The assumption here is that God's law adds an element of certainty and security that human whim cannot. She told me, "It's always a positive surprise because in Islam you are protected by the rules. There are clear rights and responsibilities for both husband and wife. Those are basic principles which have to be followed. In Islam you're not allowed to hurt each other. When we hurt another person, we have sinned. So if you marry within Islam, each partner supports the other and they grow in faith together." What is interesting in this passage—and much less notable in many Islamist men's comments on the same matter—is the way in which Mona links conformity to Islamic marital norms to a decidedly "modern," even liberal measure of spousal equality: "In Islam you're not allowed to hurt each other . . . each partner supports the other." In other words, these women are confident that, sheltered by scripture and the shared commitment to recognize and abide by the rights and responsibilities set out by Islam, they will be safeguarded against masculinist excesses and can come to equitable agreement with their husbands.[26] This is not an interpretation with which either all traditionalist or Islamist scholars would agree. But this "equity twist" is in fact quite common in young Islamist women's commentaries on the ethics of spousal relations, and shows that even neoconservative Muslim ethics is to some degree in dialogue with new, broadly "liberal" ethical registers.

Young people from neo-traditionalist backgrounds are often more comfortable turning to a religious leader, such as a *kyai* or *ustadz* from their *pesantren* or religious study group (*pengajian*), to help them in finding a marriage partner.

The process, however, is much the same. In all cases the emphasis is on the candidates being serious in their intent; that is, "ready to marry" and willing to move forward quickly, without spending any unchaperoned time together "dating." Adi's experience illustrates the procedure while underscoring a difference between the young men in my survey who had turned to Muslim matchmaking services, as compared to young women who had taken a similar route to marriage. In the case of young men, it seemed that a larger percentage had turned to these services as a way to turn around a decidedly impious and occasionally even promiscuous life.[27] This was certainly true of Adi.

Adi was a graduate of the State Islamic University (UIN), who was completing his master's degree at the Indonesian Islamic University (UII) at the time of our initial interview in 2004. He had been a member of the mainstream (i.e., non-Islamist) Islamic Students' Association (Himpunan Mahasiswa Islam, HMI) and an activist in the pro-democracy movement in the 1990s. Although he had attended a *salafi* boarding school up through high school,[28] he averred that he had let his religious convictions slide at university, where he enjoyed reading and debating politics, religion, and radical social theory. As an undergraduate at the State Islamic University, Adi had experienced for the first time close and unchaperoned contact with women. Initially, he said he found the experience deeply unsettling, but in his second year of undergraduate study and in a radical departure from his conservative *pesantren* training, he had decided he would socialize with women the "modern way." He would have "multiple girlfriends, go out on dates, have physical relations, and all the rest."

Gaunt with protruding eyes, Adi is not handsome by any conventional measure. Nonetheless, he was highly regarded as an intellectual and a writer. Graced with these qualities, he had no trouble finding girlfriends; most were attractive and intelligent fellow activists also involved in campus politics.[29] Several of these relationships became quite serious. One had even approached marriage. The mother of the young woman in question, however, was adamantly opposed to the relationship. Her daughter had a proposal from another man who had a much more promising future. When Adi's girlfriend announced to her parents that she would run away with Adi if they did not agree to the relationship, her mother threatened to kill herself. In a final dramatic gesture, the mother actually slit her wrists with a paring knife in front of the young couple and had to be rushed to the hospital. Two days later, the parents had rented out their house in Yogyakarta and moved the family to Jakarta so that their daughter would be as far away from Adi as possible.[30]

By the late 1990s, Adi was approaching twenty-eight years old. As Suharto struggled to stay in power, Adi began to see his fellow activists put in jail one by one. Others had gone underground. Searching for some comfort and stability, Adi decided to marry the *Islami* way, quickly and without *pacaran*. He went to his *kyai*, the religious teacher with whom he had previously studied, and asked him to find a young woman who would agree to marry him. Adi said he was surprised when his teacher called him the very next day and told Adi to come see him; he had three possible candidates.

[Adi laughs] I had no idea it would happen so quickly. I went there that evening and there were three women—not just their photos, but in the flesh. They were all in headscarves, just regular, you know, and my teacher told me I should talk to them, like *ta'aruf*, talk to them with the intention of choosing one. We read some verses from the Qur'an and talked for a while and after that they left. Then my *kyai* turned to me, "Okay, which one do you choose?" I didn't really know which to choose. They all were similar. The only difference was that one was more talkative. So I told him I thought maybe [I would choose] the one who talked the most. But because of my religious training, I really couldn't answer for myself. I handed the final decision over to him. I asked him, which one in his estimation would be best for me? Which one would complement my character? So we settled on the talkative one, Ani.

Actually Ani and I didn't exactly decide to marry right away. We weren't allowed to meet, but we corresponded, we wrote letters back and forth for a year. And after a year of corresponding I went to her parents and we discussed the marriage. Then I told my own parents, but my mother refused.

Adi explained that his mother was hoping for a daughter-in-law with more education. Ani had only a three-year diploma (a D3). His mother wanted a daughter-in-law with at least a BA (*sarjana muda*), and preferably a career woman.

Adi continued,

I realized then there were class differences that I hadn't thought about. I come from a family of only two children; Ani comes from a family of nine. To my parents this meant there would be too many relatives we would have to help out, too many siblings to put through school or to help find work. But most importantly, I was only in my second semester of my MA program. My parents said they wouldn't agree to my marrying before I had completed my graduate work. It was a big deal to them because I was the first in my family to get a college degree and would be the first to get an MA. They brought up the example of my uncle who married and never finished his BA. "He married before he graduated and had to depend on his parents. His parents invested all that money in his education and he didn't finish." They kept saying, "If you don't finish your degree, you won't have a secure future!" That really frightened them, even more than Ani's background.

But the more Adi's parents resisted, the more determined Adi became to go through with the marriage. Because his parents refused to contribute anything to the wedding, Adi offered Ani's family all the money he had for the celebration, which was only Rp. 300,000, or roughly US $30.00. The wedding was small (*seadanya*). The couple read from the Qur'an and then there was a simple meal.

Ani, not surprisingly, had a slightly different perspective on the whole process. She came from a family that by her account were not very normative-minded and in fact had been opposed to her own religiosity. She described her parents as *wong awam,* a term that she translated as "just regular Muslims." Her father had been embarrassed when she decided to wear the headscarf and was initially upset at her involvement in *pengajian* religious study.

She told me,

At that time, I was seriously involved in a *pengajian* study group. The teacher happened to be Adi's *kyai.* So my teacher told me my friends and I were going to meet this guy and that he was interested in marriage, just that. There were three of us, all in our early twenties. So, okay, none of us was worried about it. It was just a meeting. But in our religious circle [*halaqah*] we are taught that whoever proposes first, there is a kind of requirement that you not refuse, unless there is something really negative about the guy that would keep you from accepting. And I believed that. My religious convictions were very strong. I didn't believe in dating, but I had a friendship with someone back home for a long time. So I just broke it off, even though I knew he would be upset with me. I just sent him a letter saying I was going to marry someone else on this date, just that.

Despite their early resistance to their daughter's religiosity, Ani's parents accepted her choice of marital partner. They had already "lost" one of Ani's older sisters, who had run away to marry a young man from a radical (underground) Muslim group; they did not want to lose another daughter by refusing to go along with her decision. They were willing to accept Adi's religious background, but the normative landscape that figured most prominently in their assessment of their daughter's choice of partner was informed by considerations of security and social mobility; they recognized Adi came from a solidly middle-class family and had a good education. They gave their daughter their blessings but told her they could afford only a small wedding, no more.

Adi's parents also begrudgingly gave the couple their blessings. However, as an expression of their displeasure at Adi's decision to marry despite their expressed disapproval, the day after the wedding celebration, they sent Adi's rebellious younger sister to live with the newlyweds. Adi complained that she came and went at all hours and watched television at full volume whenever she was home. What is more, she ignored all of Adi's efforts to rein her in. Later, when Ani became seriously ill during her first pregnancy, her own family was unable to help the young couple financially; Adi's family refused.

Adi and Ani's experience highlights the fact that those who marry by religious arrangement (*ta'aruf*) may risk the future support of their parents if the parents feel their right to approve of their son's or daughter's choice of partner has been ignored. But Ani and Adi's example aside, by far the majority of the parents of young people who had married by *ta'aruf* said they were quite willing to accept the higher moral authority of the religious official or group and were happy their children's marriage would have a solid foundation based on religious principles. And as is often the case, once Ani and Adi provided Adi's family with a grandchild, family tensions diminished considerably.

Matchmaking Services, Morality, and Muslim Subjectivities

By 2010, there were multiple groups and organizations that had sprung up around Yogyakarta offering matchmaking services that encouraged young people who were serious about marrying to marry quickly with a minimum of premarital familiarization. These services included monthly "mass matchmaking events" (*perjodohan masal, ta'aruf masal*) advertised in local newspapers. Some of these events are sponsored by religious organizations, others by concerned parties—local religious leaders or private individuals who had successfully gone through the matchmaking process and wanted to help others achieve the same pious and happy outcome.[31] Although it is not necessarily their primary motivation, these services also address the concerns of many young Muslim women who have put off marriage to pursue their educations and, as a result, find their marital options rapidly narrowing. These mass meetings attract a much larger and more diverse group than the university-based *dakwah* organizations and are less tightly controlled; nonetheless, the concept is similar. The ads for the services that appear in local newspapers emphasize the importance of seriousness of intent and the sincere desire to marry quickly on the part of participants. Some organizations offer chaperones to allow the couple to meet for the purposes of negotiating marriage, others offer a safe, public, supervised place to meet. There are even organizations that enlist pious and affluent donors willing to cover the wedding costs for couples who decide to marry quickly. A few of these sponsors go so far as to offer couples all-expenses-paid honeymoon trips to Singapore.

Nindy, a graduate of Gadjah Mada University in child psychology, had found her husband through one of these mass matchmaking events (*ta'aruf masal*). A former classmate of one of my research assistants, Nindy lived in the southernmost section of Yogyakarta with her elderly aunt and uncle. When we met in the summer of 2012, Nindy was wearing a light-colored headscarf pinned modestly under her chin, long pants, and a tunic. She was tall and slim, and had a pretty face and a gentle manner. Her two-year-old daughter, Lita, toddled in and out of the room as we talked. Nindy described her aunt and uncle as just "regular Muslims," though they and Nindy appeared decidedly reformist in orientation. The elderly aunt had recently returned from making the hajj to Mecca and was wrapped from head to toe in austere white robes that were a contrast with her black-framed glasses. She called out to her grand-niece Lita from the next room, encouraging her to stop playing with my tape recorder and come eat a snack.

Nindy worked as a teacher's aide in a school for children with disabilities and had taken the test to become a civil servant (*pegawai negeri sipil*). She did not seem to be the type of young woman who would have any problem attracting a marriage partner. However, she was thirty-five when she turned to matchmaking services, an age considered to be "well past the standard for marriage." She was, in addition, by her own account almost painfully shy and lacking in self-confidence (*kurang pede*). In fact, she said, she hadn't planned on attending the mass matchmaking event at all and had only gone along because her cousin had signed her up and had even filled out the form for her.

The event was a mass matchmaking event sponsored by the Bureau of Religious Affairs (Kantor Urusan Agama, KUA) to the south of the city in the subdistrict of Sewon in the regency of Bantul and was similar to matchmaking events that I attended in the summers of 2013 and 2014. Nindy said that when she and her cousin arrived, there were already hundreds of people gathered in the courtyard. She estimated that there were significantly more women than men in the crowd; maybe as many as 150 females and only 100 males. There was a welcoming committee whose members greeted each of the guests and helped those who had not yet filled out the biodata form. The information sheets were then collected into two books, one for men and one for women. At the end of the meeting, all of the participants would be given access to the biodata of the other participants. There was also a team of students from Yogyakarta Muhammadiyah University who had volunteered to fix participants' hair and do their makeup. A doctor took participants' blood pressure and asked questions about hypertension and diabetes.

Nindy explained the procedure as follows:

Not long after we arrived, the organizer requested that everyone gather in an empty pavilion for personal introductions. He gave a short speech, reminding everyone that the event was only for those who were serious [about marriage] and not just having fun, and that he hoped we would all move quickly and marry. He told us that the KUA Sewon [Sewon's Bureau of Religious Affairs] had a 40 percent success rate—40 percent of their participants had actually gotten married! Then he led a brief prayer. After that, each of us stood up, one by one, and gave our name and said something about ourselves and what we were looking for. There were lots of women in their thirties like me, but there were also some younger people, and of course lots of widows and widowers. A few women had even brought along their children or had come with their parents for moral support.

Nindy said that when asked to tell the group what they were looking for, most of the younger "single" women—that is women who had never married and were in in their twenties or thirties—said more or less the same thing. Most explained that they wanted a man with at least the same level of education as themselves, a steady job, around their age or maybe a little older, and of the same faith. When it was her turn to stand up, Nindy was too embarrassed to say anything different. Afterward when the participants were divided into smaller groups and urged to use the opportunity to get to know one another, she was still too shy to say much of anything. A number of men approached her to chat, she said, but she could not find the words to respond.

In the days and weeks following the meeting, Nindy began to receive phone calls and text messages from interested men who had made note of her telephone number from the book of collected biodata. One of those men was Hermawan, the man she would eventually marry. Nindy refers to him with the teknonym "Lita's father" in her description of how they met each other and married.

> The man who became my husband, Lita's father, actually called and texted me several times, but I was always too busy to meet with him. A friend that I worked with happened to see his text message and said, "Why don't you meet with him? Who knows, he could be your *jodoh*." So finally I told him that I would meet him at the mall at Malioboro in the late afternoon. When I was going to leave the house, two other candidates [from the *ta'aruf* event] showed up unexpectedly for a visit. Lita's father texted me, "I'm here at the mall, where are you?" I had to explain that I had guests and I told him I would try to get away as soon as I could. So I was late for our first meeting and he almost gave up but in the end we met and ate together and did our Isha'a prayers in the *mushollah* in the mall.

> I don't know why, but I felt something, some compassion or sympathy for him right away. He said he was serious about marriage, and I thought, I'm old enough, I'm ready to marry, so why not? Maybe this really is my *jodoh*. My aunt said, "Well, let your uncle investigate him first." It turns out my husband had a job selling office supplies at a store just five minutes from my house. So my aunt and uncle went to the store and pretended to be interested in buying a printer. He thought they were just regular customers. "Please have a seat. What are you looking for? Is there something you'd like to buy?" My uncle and aunt were satisfied with the way that he spoke and how he treated them. They came home afterward and said that it seemed he had good morals and a good character.

Nindy was thirty-five at the time; her future husband was thirty-three. Nindy had a college degree; Hermawan had only a grade school education. He had quit school when he was twelve because his father had died and the family did not have the money for him to continue. Instead he had gone to work as a handyman to help support his younger siblings. He had postponed his own marriage because he wanted to see his younger siblings marry first and had helped to pay for their wedding expenses. Now he was free of his obligations and could marry; his siblings were all married and had families. He had a steady, though modestly paying job in the office supply store.[32] Nindy and Hermawan's wedding ceremony (*nikah*) was held just two weeks after the couple's first meeting at the mall. Their daughter was born ten months later.

Too Educated to Marry

Young women like Nindy have turned to Muslim matchmaking services as a strategy for marriage in a marital market straining under the weight of new social and ethical pressure. The pressure has multiple sources. It comes from the proponents of the new Islamic normativity, who seek to bring courtship and marriage into conformity with far stricter notions of premarital contact and sociability. It also comes from families anxious about their children's futures, especially about daughters at risk of sexual impropriety or surpassing the socially acceptable age for marriage. Finally, the pressure arises from young people themselves, who are trying desperately to balance new educational and economic opportunities with the desire to marry and establish families of their own. The latter pressure is greater for young women than it is for young men. Young women see themselves as having less control over their choices than do men. They realize that young men have greater freedom than they do in the sense that it is still young men who are typically the ones to signal their interest and initiate relationships, while women are still expected to wait to be approached.[33] But women also feel under pressure because those who have delayed marriage to pursue an education are painfully aware of their narrowing window of fertility.

Marital pressure on young women is heightened by the popular misapprehension of a population imbalance—the widespread belief that Indonesian women far outnumber men.[34] In fact, there *is* an imbalance in the ratio of females to males, but one that exists largely within the ranks of educated single females relative to *educated* single males. The Australian demographer Gavin Jones (2009, 19, 22–23) makes a similar observation based on broader statistical trends that indicate that the marriage market is particularly tight for well-educated women who are looking for equally well-educated partners. What Jones refers to as "the marriage squeeze" is a result of the fact that many Javanese men still tend to marry someone younger and less well-educated than themselves, creating a dearth of available candidates for those well-educated women "at the top" (see also A. Utomo 2014, 1689–1690; Nilan 2008, 76). It is a pattern exacerbated by the concern expressed by many men that a woman with more education or experience will place herself "above her husband" in the relationship.[35]

Mahmudah, a graduate of the State Islamic University currently pursuing an MA, is one of those women who are "at the top" educationally and experientially. Although Mahmudah is unusual in some respects, her situation nonetheless shares many features with that of other well-educated neo-traditionalist women in my study. Mahmudah is a tiny figure with a round face and a huge smile. When I met her in 2013, she was thirty-three years old and said that she had been actively searching for a marriage partner for the past five years. The result of a complicated family situation (she had been "adopted" by her aunt and uncle but not informed of that fact until she was in her twenties), Mahmudah had been on her own since she came to Yogyakarta for university at the age of nineteen. She supported herself by teaching in a religious boarding school and by working several years in Saudi Arabia as a tutor, nanny, and maid.

While in Saudi Arabia Mahmudah had grown accustomed to dressing in "Saudi style"; she wore a long brown robe and long brown headscarf that reached all the way below her hips. It is a style of dress that is not common in Indonesia and unusual even among neo-traditionalists. Because of her conservative dress, Mahmudah said she tends to attract men who are looking for a religiously conservative wife who will take on a subservient position within the marriage. To her dismay, several men who had approached her with marriage propositions were in fact looking to take a second wife. Mahmudah, like the majority of the women in my study and regardless of their religious background, made it clear that she has no interest in a polygynous relationship;[36] on the contrary, she was looking for someone who viewed marriage as a partnership and was willing to share family responsibilities. She had discovered, however, that finding someone with the desired qualifications was difficult, and was particularly challenging given her age and level of education.

> Where I'm from, a *gadis* [young girl] is maybe up to twenty or twenty-one years old. If by age twenty-five she hasn't yet married, she's considered "unmarketable," an old maid, or not normal. That's how villagers think almost everywhere across Indonesia—and not just villagers. I mean I spent a lot of time in a *pesantren* where the students were from all over Indonesia, and I heard the same thing. When they asked how old I was and I said [at that time] twenty-five, and I wasn't married yet, they all said, "If I were twenty-five and not yet married I'd be ashamed [*malu*] to go home, and everyone would say I wasn't marketable [*tidak laku*]."

Mahmudah expressed her frustration over her repeated attempts (and failures) to find a match. But it had not diminished her desire to marry. "Of course I want to marry! Doesn't everyone?"

The difficulties Mahmudah faced in negotiating marriage were multiple. She explained that in moving away from her village to the city for school and then abroad to work, she had essentially "lost her community." That is, when she returned to her parents' home after her various travels, her cohort of friends and neighbors, among whom she might otherwise have found a match, had all married and already had children. So the possibility of her marrying someone with whom she had grown up or gone to grade school or secondary school was small to none. And the male students in her classes were now all much younger than she was. "I keep trying," she told me, "but I have difficulty thinking who I could be with. Now in my MA classes at UIN, most of the students are twenty-one, twenty-two, . . . twenty-three is like the oldest. And they all say 'Wow, whoever gets you later will really be happy!' But what they're really thinking is 'It's not possible that you are ever going to find anyone.' I've lost my community."

Repeated attempts to meet with eligible young men, especially those recommended by her friends and colleagues as possible candidates for marriage, have made Mahmudah more realistic about her options and increasingly willing to make compromises. She admits that while she was initially hoping to find someone who shared her same level of education, she no longer feels that it's critical, so long as he is flexible and willing to compromise. But she's found that too many men find her educational status and experience intimidating and quickly withdraw their interest once they learn about her achievements. This masculinist anxiety figured frequently in my interviews: many men fear that a woman with more education and experience than themselves will be the one to take the lead in making family decisions and will leave their husband without any power.

Mahmudah confided,

I'm really serious [about wanting to marry], and I'm not picky. Maybe I used to be. Like when I got my BA, I felt I really had to have someone with a BA. But now I don't think it's a problem. What's important is that we can connect. We can talk and come to an agreement about things. And we can work together as a team. [If he's less educated] it's no problem. We can improve things as we go along in the process of getting to know each other. But lots of guys just back down when they find out about my education and experience. They say they feel I'm too far above them. Like the guys at home feel inferior because I've been living so long in Yogya on my own and I've been abroad, and I've traveled and I have so much education. They wonder if I would be happy as their partner because they haven't done anything like that. They feel inferior [minder]. They say, "Later, if we marry, I'll be behind and you'll be in front making the decisions and I won't be able to do anything at all."

But that's not how it would be. We have to each complement the other [kita harus saling melengkapi] and to work together as a team. "There will be moments when I'm in front and moments when you are in front. How could it ever be that I would be the one to lead prayers? Not possible! But maybe in the education of our children, I would know more and I would lead there." They always reply, "I'm just not sufficiently self-confident."

In the summer of 2014, Mahmudah told me she was considering a young man whose biodata had been supplied to her by the friend of a friend. They had been corresponding for a couple of weeks. Initially, Mahmudah said, she was hopeful. He looked nice in his picture. He indicated that he was serious and wanted to marry quickly. But she was put off by the fact that he did not seem to be completely honest about himself:

He asked that we exchange a couple of pages about ourselves. He sent me his pages, but he only wrote about the good things. Like "I pray five times a day, I read the Qur'an, I go to the mosque, I play badminton twice a week, if there's a soccer game, I play soccer." It's like he's perfect. But what's important to me is honesty. I'm prepared to describe both my strengths and my imperfections [kelebihan dan kekurangan]. I think if you're going to build a relationship, it has to be like that. I want to know whether his way of thinking fits with mine and whether we click or not. Then we can continue the discussion, because a husband is a partner, and together we're a team. It's as if he wants to present himself as a serious Muslim, which is a positive for me, but I wonder if he is one of those recent converts to Salafism—Hizbut Tahrir or Jema'ah Tabligh. Because I don't agree with those Muslims who always position women far behind. I don't want that kind of relationship, the kind where the husband doesn't allow his wife to work. I have to be realistic. I have two sets of parents because I was adopted. So if my husband won't allow me to work, then what? My birth mother is divorced, and my adoptive parents have no one but me to depend on.

It slowly became clear to Mahmudah that the young man wanted to negotiate marriage without ever meeting, arguing that their relationship would be purer and "more perfect" (*lebih sempurna*) that way. Mahmudah was insistent that they discuss things face to face, saying, "He thinks it's 'more perfect' [*lebih sempurna*] to marry without ever meeting. But he only presents his good side in his messages. It's all good. Nothing bad. It's like viewing a house by only looking at the living room. But, you know, every house has a bathroom!" The negotiations were stalled. The longer he resisted Mahmudah's request that they meet face to face, the more Mahmudah began to suspect that something was wrong. "What is he hiding from me?"

The challenges of the marriage market have led at least some educated women to adopt more enterprising strategies in pursuing a match. Fika, a recent graduate of Gadjah Mada and a lecturer in the Faculty of Religious Education (Tarbiyah) at Yogyakarta's Muhammadiyah University, laughingly described herself as "rather aggressive" in her pursuit of a husband. Now in her early thirties, Fika has an MA and has plans to go on to pursue a PhD, possibly abroad. She dresses in neo-reformist style in a tightly pinned headscarf, a long skirt, and a long-sleeved tunic. She is pretty and vivacious. She says she first saw her future husband at a seminar where he was one of the presenters, and was immediately attracted to him. At the end of his talk, she asked him for his contact information, using the excuse that she was working on a similar topic for her MA thesis. Afterward, she let all of her friends know that she was interested in him. She stalked him on Facebook. She enlisted a colleague to tell him she was interested. "[Laughs] I was actually what you might call aggressive. My mom always said if you have a goal and you just keep quiet, you won't achieve it. My mom warned me, 'Because you have so much education, guys will feel nervous approaching you. So you have to open the way.'"

When none of her efforts seemed to work, Fika finally messaged him asking if she could borrow a book for her MA thesis. He responded that he would bring it right over. Things moved quickly from there. He brought the book to her house and they immediately "clicked."

Fika recounts, smiling,

We really only met one or two times. The first was the seminar and the second was when he dropped by my house with the book. The third time he asked me to a movie. And after the movie we had something to eat. While we were eating, he said he was looking for a marriage partner [*jodoh*], and I said I was too. And that's when he said, "I really like you. I'd like to meet your parents. Would that be okay?" And I said, "Sure, go ahead."

So he came to my house to meet my parents and talk [*nembung*].[37] He told them "I'm serious. I like your daughter, and I'm serious. Is that okay with you?" In fact, my dad had already asked my brother to check him out beforehand. So when they met he only said, "Mbak Fika is already twenty-six and it's time for her to marry. So you need to talk with your own parents if you're really serious." [Laughs] You know, here, if a daughter is older than twenty-five, her parents are really worried, and I was almost twenty-seven at that time.

The speed with which couples make marital decisions can be dizzying—especially if the woman is "older" (that is, over twenty-five) and anxious about her dwindling possibilities and plummeting fertility. Fika and her now-husband decided they were serious about each other after meeting only twice, and married within three months of coming to an agreement. At the time, Fika was twenty-six, almost twenty-seven, and working on completing her MA. There was no dating involved, only meetings to make the marriage arrangements. In fact, Fika said, the wedding celebration would have taken place even sooner, but the couple had to secure the agreement of the groom's older sister, who had not yet married.[38]

In making the decision to marry, Fika, like Nindy and Mahmudah, emphasized above all else the importance of both partners being "serious" (*serius*) and ready to marry quickly. Of course, they all agreed that it is best if the man has some form of income, preferably a steady job or the promise of a future job. However, in the case of women with educational credentials and employment, the willingness to make a commitment and move quickly to marriage are mentioned more often than the man's educational level or economic situation. In many cases, young women have had to adjust their marital requirements to consider men who have fewer years of schooling, less than secure incomes, and are even several years younger than themselves.[39] All this, too, is part of the new economy of Muslim courtship and marriage.

Despite the considerable difficulties many educated women encounter in finding a partner, very few say they would consider asking their parents to arrange a marriage for them. Whereas just a generation or two ago, the majority of marriages in Indonesia were parentally arranged, today the percentage of arranged marriages has dropped precipitously (G. Jones 1994a, 2004). And yet, although young women are insistent about finding a partner on their own, a surprising number report they have never had a boyfriend.[40] There is a familiar if problem-generating pattern to their plight: many of these women report that they put off having a relationship in order to pursue their educations or to work—a pattern many of their parents endorsed. Many describe feeling awkward (*canggung, kaku*) and nervous (*grogi, gugup*) around eligible, unmarried men. This is especially true of women who have absorbed the message of their Islamic teachers, who warn that interactions with unrelated members of the opposite sex can easily lead to sinful thoughts and interactions (*zina, dosa besar*) and should be avoided. Many thus endorse the admonition heard in conservative and mainline, if not liberal, Islamic circles, that "there is no dating in Islam—only *ta'aruf*" (meeting for the purpose of deciding whether or not to marry).

The New Muslim Romance

At a time when social and educational developments have led to the prolongation of the period of premarital singlehood, and when social mobility has created new opportunities for unsupervised encounters between members of the opposite sex, some young Muslims in Indonesia have found a solution to the marital problem in a course of action that they see as submitting to an ethical imperative larger than themselves. These young people eschew premarital familiarization as sinful and urge a radically shortened period of courtship or even no courtship at all. And while the majority of Indonesians now accept the "modern" right of individual choice of marital partner, many of these youth turn to matchmaking services that narrow the field by screening candidates to ensure their religious credentials and suitability. Modern notions of liberal autonomy, relatively speaking, merge here with a tightly regulated moral economy to embed individuals exercising genuine agency within the constrained and sacralized universe of Islamist normativity. Elements of the "socially constructed liberal model of self," however, have not entirely vanished from this process— but have reemerged in new religious forms. Displacing but not replacing the role of the family in marital decisions is the religious community with its Islamic authorities. The latter base their prescriptions on a careful if inevitably perspectival reading of the Qur'an and hadith. In so doing, these new authorities offer a clear and specific set of moral guidelines, ones that, in their eyes, displace the imperfect authority of family and ethnic custom with the perfection of God's law.

This shift in the economy of sexual normativity represents a radical change from other incipient trends apparent in the Indonesian middle classes in the 1980s. At that time, researchers reported that they saw that long courtship and extended engagement periods were giving rise to new options, and a new sense of individualized sexual autonomy. The trend was most apparent in the growing incidence of "Western-style" dating, and according to some sources, heightened rates of premarital sex—evidence of the erosion of a Javanese sense of self that is highly social in nature, and a shift to one that is increasingly interiorized and individualized (see Eves 2007).

It is clear that the latter sexual trend has not come entirely to a halt. However, what is also clear is that in the intervening years the marital economy has undergone a small if still unfinished normative revolution. One of the revolution's most distinctive features has been the arrival on the campus scene of a small army of Islamic sex counselors, pamphleteers, and anti-promiscuity activists. Using mosque services, study groups, and the exemplary model of their own daily lives, these activists have succeeded at taking up a commanding if still far from hegemonic position in Yogyakarta's youth scene. From that perch, they have struggled tirelessly to reorient their generation mates toward a less individualistic and more unitarily pietistic model of sexuality and sociability. In this process, and in their promotion of "more Islamic" wedding celebrations that exclude elements identified as non-Islamic, Islamist marital agents have assumed some of the authority previously reserved for Indonesian parents.

Indeed, as some of my examples make clear, the shift in the economy of sexual normativity at work in these circles combines some of the features of generational rebellion and individualistic choice that we often associate with the sexual revolution in the West but with a rather different focus and outcome (cf. Parker 2008a). Quite unlike their Western liberal counterparts, the shift taking place in Islamist circles in Indonesia uses the energy of youthful rebellion and individual agency not to set the individual adrift in a sea of like-minded, autonomy-minded individuals, but to re-embed the individual and her sexuality within a new, chosen, religious community. For those drawn into this new economy of sexual normativity, the discursive authority of this chosen religious community is sufficient to deflect parental, community, and ethnocultural pressures. In that process it has created "a new Muslim romance."

Conclusion

Islamizing Intimacies

I first met Ismail in June 2015 as my research was entering its final phases. He was a quiet and neatly dressed nineteen year old who had just finished his first year at Gadjah Mada University in cultural studies. He is thus among the most recent cohort of university students in my fifteen-year study. Ismail's life experience illustrates many of the arguments that have cut across the chapters of this book and underscores their continuing relevance for Muslim Javanese youth. Particularly prominent in Ismail's account are the themes of pluralization and contestation of religious currents and identifications. Through his continuing efforts to reflexively engage and reconcile competing concerns, Ismail, like so many of the young people presented throughout this book, is actively involved in an ongoing process of weighing multiple and often competing ethical aspirations, not least with regard to the ideals and practices of gendered intimacy.

Ismail comes from a strongly religious Nahdlatul Ulama (NU) family. He is representative of the group I have identified throughout this book as neo-traditionalist. His family lives in a subdistrict of East Java. His father teaches in a government religious school, and his mother is a midwife. Both of his parents have university degrees. (His father has a BA from an Islamic university; his mother has a three-year diploma.) Ismail has one younger brother who is still in high school. Ismail says he owes his academic achievements and his acceptance into Gadjah Mada University to his mother, who has prayed for his every success. He comments that he is always conscious of her expectations, even now that he is far away from home and living on his own: "I truly believe that 'heaven lies beneath the feet of one's mother.' In Islam we say 'the blessings of our mother are the blessings of Allah.'"[1] Ismail's mother was the one who prayed and fasted on his behalf when he competed in a district-wide debate contest in his final year of high school. It was because of her efforts, Ismail says, that he won first place in the competition and was accepted directly into UGM.

Ismail had attended general schools in his hometown for grade school and middle school. But his parents felt strongly about the importance of his receiving a rigorous religious education, and for high school they sent him to a private religious school, a *madrasah*. The *madrasah* was in a regency of East Java some distance from his home and too far to commute, so Ismail boarded in the school dormitory, which was run much like a *pesantren*. He was awakened every morning at 4 a.m. by the *adzan* call to prayers; religious study began at 6 a.m. Students who did not get up would receive an electric shock to jolt them out of sleep. Classes and school activities continued until 10:00 at night.

Ismail's teachers at the *madrasah* were Muhammadiyah-leaning in their religious orientation and, over time, Ismail found himself shifting his religious identity from Nahdlatul Ulama to Muhammadiyah. He said he explained his decision to his parents, and they were not alarmed: "In my opinion, everything that has to do with religion is part of like a restaurant menu. And I can pick what best suits me.[2] So I told my parents, 'You know mom, I feel like I'm sort of more in the direction of Muhammadiyah.' And when it was Ramadan, I asked her, 'May I have permission to begin fasting on this day?'[3] And my parents gave me their permission."

His religious studies had also led Ismail to reassess some of his previous practices. He recounted how in his community when a young person was facing a particular challenge, it was common to kneel before one's mother and wash her feet as a symbol of filial love and respect. The wash water was then drunk as a way to imbibe her blessing. Ismail had done this himself before leaving home for his boarding school and recalled how his mother was so touched by his gesture that she cried. A few years later, however, when he prepared to leave for university, he simply kneeled before his seated mother and bowed his head to ask her blessing. He explained that his religious education had taught him that the custom of drinking the wash water of teachers and elders was not a part of Islam but merely a local custom (*adat*); bowing at his mother's knees was a sufficient demonstration of his respect and filial piety.

But Ismail's religious evolution did not end there. Once settled in Yogyakarta, with its overwhelming religious and ethnic diversity, and once immersed in his coursework in cultural studies, Ismail was surprised to find himself slowly drifting back toward his Nahdlatul Ulama roots. He said he felt that NU was more flexible and open to a greater diversity of practices than he had found in his experience with Muhammadiyah. He explained that in his *madrasah* he had been a member of a Rohis club[4] and that during his first semester at Gadjah Mada he had continued his participation with a campus Muslim-Brotherhood–inspired *tarbiyah* group (see Bubalo and Fealy 2005; Machmudi 2008b). He had followed its weekly *pengajian* sessions and had joined in several of its campus activities. After a while, however, he decided the group was too exclusive and narrow-minded. A few weeks into his second semester at UGM, then, he stopped answering *tarbiyah* members' telephone calls reminding him of their meetings. He said he found himself enjoying Yogyakarta's plural culture and did not want to limit his interactions with people from a diversity of backgrounds.

Notwithstanding these whirlwind changes, Ismail has not turned himself into a secular liberal. He remains especially cautious in his interactions with women. His mother had asked him not to date before finishing his university studies, and, now in his second year of his coursework at Gadjah Mada, he continues to honor her request. He explains that he views romantic relationships as time-consuming and distracting. Moreover, he adds, having a girlfriend can easily lead to unanticipated and unwelcome consequences, including of course, premarital sex (*zina*). He thus prefers to keep his attention focused on his studies and to maintain his spiritual and emotional equilibrium. He explained,

> In Islam, love is normal; it's something natural [*fitrah*]. But what is important is being able to control love. The problem is the line between love and lust [*nafsu*] is very thin. If, for example, I have a girlfriend and we're not yet married, it's like the line between love and lust is 50–50; that is, equal. But according to our religion, love is part of religious observance, as long as it's part of a process leading to marriage. That's why I'm reluctant to have a girlfriend before I'm ready to marry. Because right now I can't differentiate between love and lust. But when I'm officially married, love and lust will be one and the same. And when I have sex with my wife, it will be a part of my religious observance, and even an act that is rewarded by God.

Although Ismail expressed some nervousness about marriage, his concern has more to do with preparing himself mentally and financially to take on the responsibilities and support of a family, rather than concerns about finding the perfect match. While he finds "feminine women with long, shiny hair" particularly attractive, he says he would like to have a wife who wears the headscarf.[5] Her level of education is unimportant, because he is willing to provide instruction. He admits he has never had a girlfriend and explains that when he is ready to marry he plans to follow *ta'aruf,* but on his own initiative; he does not think he will turn to a Muslim organization or religious teacher to find a partner for him. After making his intentions clear to a young woman and receiving her agreement, he will marry quickly without dating. The main thing, he says, is to never be alone together before the marriage is official.

Ismail is one of several millions of young Indonesians who have moved from rural and provincial areas of Java to urban and cosmopolitan centers since the mid-1980s in order to pursue higher education. In the process he, like so many others, has experienced the opportunities and enticements of the modern city as well as the diversity and plurality of social and cultural forms—all of which have required his moral attention and reflexive engagement (Giddens 1991; see also Deeb and Harb 2013a; Nilan 2006). It was the British sociologist Anthony Giddens who identified the process of self-reflexivity as central to identity formation within the context of a "late modernity" defined by globalized capitalism, the privatization of services, and the information revolution. Giddens describes the process as both fluid and dynamic, one in which the individual simultaneously shapes and is shaped by modern institutions and social forces (Giddens 1991, 2). For many contemporary Indonesian youth, self-reflexivity involves the scrutiny not only of one's own beliefs and practices but also, increasingly, those taken for granted by earlier generations (cf. Nilan 2006). In some cases, of course, the effect of such scrutiny is simply to reinforce long-held habits and understandings. In other cases, however, new or hybrid lifeways and ethical commitments emerge. *Ta'aruf,* for example—that is, chaperoned meetings for the purposes of discussing marriage—is not a completely new practice but has long existed in a closely related form in *santri* communities where religious teachers (*kyai* or *ustadz*) would not uncommonly play a role in finding an appropriate match for their students (Wafiroh 2016; see also Dhofier 1999 [1982]).[6] The contemporary hybridic practices of *ta'aruf* also build on the Javanese courtship tradition known as *ngapel* in the insistence on careful oversight of the young couple and controlled interactions within a secure space. A modern accommodation, however, is the emphasis young people place on making their own choice of marital partner rather than acquiescing to the decision of elders— even if that choice is to enlist the aid of a go-between—and the overt and widespread acknowledgment of the ideal of *ta'aruf* ("there is no dating in Islam") by referring to normative scriptural sources[7]—even by youth who nonetheless choose to date.

Slowly but surely, through these and other reflexive processes, many of the traditions and practices once deemed fully Javanese and authentically Islamic are being recategorized and rejected as un-Islamic or insufficiently Islamic. Young people like Ismail consistently report that the long-esteemed ritual meals known as *slametan*—which Clifford Geertz (1976 [1960]) decades ago identified as the very heart of Javanese Islam—actually violate religious teachings and are wasteful and unnecessary, even *syirik*.[8] Circumcision, once an important community-wide celebration of life passage (for both male youth and their parents), is today being reconstructed as a small, private affair undertaken without entertainment and feasting but instead focused on prayer and recitation. For increasing numbers of people, the procedure is now done as a matter of course at the hospital shortly after birth. Marriage ceremonies, similarly, have been recreated by many young couples to minimize traditional court themes and to emphasize instead Islamic elements.

In these culture shifts we see evidence of the continuing erosion of Javanese *abangan*-ism and of syncretic *kejawen* forms in favor of those understood as sanctioned by scripture, which is to say the Qur'an and hadith. We also see a significant if not total blurring of the distinction between Muhammadiyah "modernists" and Nahdlatul Ulama "traditionalists." In Yogyakarta and across most of Indonesia, a new Muslim youth is coming of age, and bringing with it a new understanding of Islam, Muslim social life, and relational intimacy.

Plural Culture and Ambivalent Selves

There is no simple linear pattern to these changes. In this ongoing process of reflexive engagement and subjective rationalization, young people draw on multiple and often competing social forms and ethical aspirations. The foregrounding of one cultural current or ethical register over another shifts and changes depending on context and the life experience of the individual. To adequately account for this process requires a conception of culture that admits complexity, discordances, and ambivalence.

A pioneer of the variationist approach to ethnographic study, Fredrik Barth (1993) emphasized both the distributional and interconnected aspects of culture by positing the existence of multiple "traditions of knowledge" within any given society. While they are shaped in part by what Barth described as shared local "concerns," these knowledge traditions are never entirely consistent or integrated, as many cultural and symbolic anthropologists in previous generations once assumed. Nor are they immediately or completely available to all members of a group (Barth 1993, 340–341). Recent frameworks for the analysis of culture proposed by cognitive and psychological anthropologists show parallels to Barth's model but emphasize the moral and ethical experience of cultural complexity and variation. These studies have introduced anthropologists to concepts such as "moral models" and "cultural models" in their attempts to capture the variability and inconsistency in all ethical systems (see D'Andrade and Strauss 1992; Quinn 1996; Shore 1996). In a similar vein, anthropologists of religion have spoken of "moral rubrics" or "moral registers" (Deeb and Harb 2013b; Schielke 2009b) when referring to the multiple and sometimes contradictory sets of ideals and values that compete for young people's attention, and which ultimately orient their everyday lives. In all cases, the analytic frameworks introduced by anthropologists over the past generation emphasize not only cultural variety but also the relative availability of spaces for negotiation and contextualization—as well as for the individual's experience of doubt, paradox, or contradiction (see also McIntosh 2009; Simon 2014).

In his work on the moral lives of young Cairene Egyptians, Samuli Schielke writes that moral registers, as "modalities of moral speech and action," allow for the recognition and influence of competing social forces and ethical aspirations, including those emanating from religious, familial, institutional, and political social spheres. These clusters of ideals or values provide guidelines for an individual's actions in a given situation or social field but are not determinative of an actor's reflection or social practice in any exhaustively scripted way (Schielke 2009b, 166–167). Rather, because of their multiplicity, the registers give rise to inner conflicts, contradictions, and inconsistencies in moral experience, selfhood, and practice. The coexistence of varied motivations, goals, and identities can and often does converge to create moral ambivalences (Schielke 2009a, S29–S32; Shore 1990). Ambivalent youth may then attempt to negotiate a competing and complex set of moral registers or rubrics in order to develop strategies of action in different spheres of their social life (Deeb and Harb 2013a, 2013b; Schielke 2009a; Quinn 1996). As Gregory Simon has noted with regard to Minangkabau Muslims in West Sumatra, "Tensions between values and experiences follow" actors who move across social spheres, and for individuals to make sense of such ethical and aspirational plurality requires they engage in an active process of "work and reflection" (Simon 2014, 5–16).

We see a similar process at work among Muslim Javanese youth. However, what is perhaps most noteworthy in the case of the young people at the center of the present study is that, despite the plurality, fluidity, and ambivalence evident in young people's accounts, this process of engaging and negotiating diverse moral currents is often also accompanied by an ongoing and rather insistent normativization with regard to what are seen as Islamic rules and values.

Among young people in particular there is a powerful and pervasive desire to bring ever broader domains of personal and societal life into alignment with what are regarded as supererogatory religious norms—even if, as is indeed the case in Indonesia as in other Muslim-majority society, the precise contours of those norms remain hotly contested.

For the many Javanese youth who, unlike Ismail, did not grow up in pious *santri* families, this engagement with and concern for normative Islam has been informed by years of standardized religious education in schools as well as in after-school religious study. The consistency with which young people reference that instruction in their descriptions of personal ethical deliberations (even among those who do so only to distance themselves from it) speaks to the far-reaching influence and efficacy of that state-sponsored religious instruction, most of which was introduced into the national school system only in the early years of the New Order period (Hefner 2009b; Machmudi 2008a).

Further reinforcing the trend toward a heightened and self-reflexive normativization of social and personal life have been the continuing efforts of the small but highly organized networks of conservative *dakwah* or *tarbiyah* groups as well as religious study circles (*halaqah*) that have been a growing and active presence on college and high school campuses, especially since the late 1990s (Hasan 2010, 2012; Machmudi 2008a, 2008b). Most young people do not in fact become active members of such organizations; of those who do, many behave like Ismail, and cycle in and out of these groups and activities with developments in their own lives. Although few in number, these *dakwah* organizations have nonetheless had a disproportionate impact on Indonesian youth and society over the past two generations. Their members have become visible exemplars of a new and more culturally oppositional Islamic morality on campus and in public life. Their dress, their interactional styles, and their innovations with regard to courtship and intimacy serve as regular and insistent public reminders of a normative religious ideal to which more mainstream Muslim organizations, as well as ordinary Muslims, have had to respond.[9] Although many Muslim youth have reservations about these groups, *dakwah* activists' presence on campus and in the city is broadly felt, and significant elements of their religious appeals and programs have made their way into mainstream religious education and discourse. Many of their members have become vocal and influential figures in conservative Muslim political groups such as the moderately Islamist Prosperous Justice Party (PKS), as well as the even more influential Council of Indonesian Ulama (MUI; see Gillespie 2007; Hasyim 2015; Ichwan 2013). Others have attempted to insert themselves into more mainstream Muslim organizations such as Nahdlatul Ulama and Muhammadiyah, contributing in the first decade of the new millennium to what Martin van Bruinessen (2013) has referred to as the "conservative turn" in Indonesian Islam.

Dakwah activists have also been important contributors to Indonesia's burgeoning youth literature, a significant portion of which is pietistic in nature. Religious tracts and pocket books reiterate familiar normative themes in a form that is attractive to young people confronting a multitude of modern choices and looking for life counsel and encouragement. Like young people elsewhere in the Muslim world, Indonesian youth are not immune to the desire to be sociable and on trend. Much of the youth literature that has emerged since the early 2000s speaks to young people's desires to be not only pious but also cool and cosmopolitan (*gaul Islami* or *gaul syari'i/syar'i*).

The recently published how-to guide *Tetap Gaul tapi Syar'i* (Staying Sociable but Pious) by Tethy Ezokanzo and Sinyo (2015) is yet another example of the continuing appeal of this genre of life-coaching religious literature. As is the case in the *gaul Islami* youth literature discussed in chapter 6, the authors speak directly to their young readership by relying on elements of popular youth slang (*bahasa gaul*) to index their relaxed and up-to-date attitude. At the same time, their advice is buttressed and legitimated by regular references to scriptural sources, especially the Qur'an and hadith.

A chapter titled *"Zina Mata"* (Adultery via the Eyes) offers a now-recognizable discussion of the dangers of the male gaze:

> The habit of *"cuci mata"* [lit. "refreshing the eyes" (by staring at someone attractive of the opposite sex)] really doesn't seem like a big deal, but the fact is that just by staring at someone we can begin to be attracted to them. The habit of staring can also give rise to feelings of sexual desire, which may or may not be accompanied by feelings of love. And eventually, staring has the effect of making people want to have sexual relations. . . . You know, the imagination of young men is truly remarkable, especially with regard to things having to do with sex. That's why Islam strongly advises us to guard our gaze. Because the gaze is the first step towards zina. (Ezokanzo and Sinyo 2015, 82)

The passage is followed by the relevant Qur'anic verse: "And don't you approach zina. For truly zina is a vile and wicked act" (*Surah Al-Isra'* 17:32).[10]

In a chapter titled *"Awas PHP"* ("Beware of Those Who Give False Hope"),[11] the authors address the familiar topic of the dangers of dating. They offer the story of Dewi, a young woman who is dizzy with excitement because a handsome and popular classmate, Dewa, has asked her to be his girlfriend. Dewi shows her friend Mia a message she received from Dewa on WhatsApp, professing his love. Mia laughs and shows Dewi a similar message from the same young man on *her* phone asking *her* to be his girlfriend. Dewi is heartbroken. Mia tells her friend, "Wow, you've been led on; you've become a victim of PHP! Actually, you should be thankful you didn't fall into that creep's trap," Mia continues. "Courageous guys don't talk about love or invite you to date them, but come directly to talk with your dad and ask to marry you. . . . So don't think about dating if you aren't ready to marry. What is dating [*pacaran*] anyway? It's just a version of PHP, don't you know. But when you marry, it's official, right? And there's a contract" (Ezokanzo and Sinyo 2015, 97–98).

The authors go on to offer familiar advice about the importance of focusing on studying and working hard to achieve one's goals and ensure a happy yet pious future. Young women should wait to marry until they have completed their studies, they argue, and only consider a young man who is truly serious about nurturing a future together in the context of legal marriage. They end their discussion with the usual admonition, "Say no to dating [*pacaran*]!" (Ezokanzo and Sinyo 2015, 99). It is a message heard with striking regularity across growing swaths of young Muslim Indonesians.

Negotiating Islam, Negotiating Gender

As emphasized throughout this book, a critical focus of the debates surrounding normative forms of Islam has to do with gender roles and with the proper Islamic form of intimate relationships. Preparing oneself mentally and materially for marriage, identifying an appropriate "soul mate" (*jodoh*), marrying, and raising a family are viewed by young people and their parents as central to larger and ongoing projects of self-improvement and social mobility characteristic of the new Muslim middle class (cf. C. Jones 2003; Nilan 2008). However, and especially for women, finding an appropriate marriage partner has become increasingly fraught, not least within the current context of rapid social and educational change and new forms of class and gender mobility (G. Jones 2004, 2005, 2009; A. Utomo 2014). As Indonesian women have put off marriage in order to pursue higher levels of education and a greater measure of economic security, many have found it difficult to secure an attractive match. Women in particular emphasize their desires for a modern, companionate marriage and a more equitable marital relationship in which their spouse is an active partner and parent.[12] Here, too, one finds evidence of the ongoing negotiation of varied moralities of intimacy.

I have argued that the ambivalences and challenges of balancing religiously normative injunctions and romantic and social concerns in the context of courtship and marriage have intensified in recent years, especially for university-educated women. A dramatic example of these challenges emerges from the story of Febriyanti (Yanti for short), an accomplished young woman I have known for close to a decade. Yanti is a thirty-one-year-old lecturer in psychology at Gadjah Mada University, where she is also pursuing a master's degree. She lives in a southern neighborhood of Yogyakarta with her parents and two younger brothers. Her father works in a government office, and her mother is a grade school teacher. She describes her parents as "Javanese Muslims/secular Muslims" (*kejawen/Islam sekuler*); nonetheless, they emphasized religious education for their children and sent them to Muhammadiyah schools so that they would have a strong academic and religious foundation. For these and other reasons, Yanti falls squarely in the ranks of those I have described in this book as "neo-reformist."

Yanti, who is pleasant and (by her own admission) just a bit plump, wears a headscarf that is pinned under her chin and covers most of her ample chest—a physical trait that, she observes, has caused her no small embarrassment since middle school. Although Yanti was required to wear the headscarf in middle school and high school as part of her school uniform, she made the decision to wear it consistently only when she was twenty-five. When she first made the commitment, she reports, she did not go out of her house for a week. She wanted to "try it out," she said, in order to be certain that she was able to accept the consequences and adjust her behavior appropriately. She thought in particular about how she would have to moderate herself in debates with men, how she would have to be more willing to give in (*ngalah*) even when she knew she was right. Although unstated, an additional and likely critical consideration in Yanti's decision to take up the headscarf seems to have been her desire to cement a relationship with a young man, someone who was at the time of our initial meeting "just a friend."

Yanti describes herself as having been a tomboy growing up, someone who had never paid much attention to her appearance and who enjoyed challenging the male students in her classes. She had many male friends in middle school and high school, but none of them were boyfriends (*pacar*). In fact, it was not unusual for her male friends to rely upon her as a confidant and facilitator in negotiating their relationships with other young women. As she approached the age of twenty-five, however, Yanti says she became increasingly aware that she needed someone to talk to, "a life partner." He didn't have to be handsome, she says, because "appearances can be worked on." But he did have to have at least the same level of education as Yanti herself so that they could exchange ideas, discuss important decisions, and share their life project together. Although she is not comfortable with the label feminist, Yanti, like most of the educated, middle-class Javanese women in my study, aspires to a modern companionate marriage and a more equitable marital relationship. She recounted her indignation at her mother's and grandmother's insistence that she perform routine household chores such as sweeping and cooking, while much less was expected of her younger brothers. And she was quick to point out the critical economic role her mother had always played in their family and what she considered the lack of recognition and appreciation her mother's efforts received from her husband and in-laws. Although Yanti's father was a strong supporter of Yanti's continuing education, it was her mother's example that Yanti took to heart. She explained,

> My father's family always relied heavily on my dad, but at a certain point he just couldn't provide them the same level of support as he had previously. Still, they just kept asking him for more. Then my grandmother got sick and had to be hospitalized and needed almost $4,000 for medical procedures. And my dad's family all came to my dad expecting him to pay for it. He paid all that he could, but it wasn't enough. His siblings didn't contribute anything. *Alhamdulilah* my mom never quit working even when we were little. And she was somehow able to find the extra money to cover the rest of my grandma's bills and managed to keep us in school and everything. In my opinion, my mom is a really strong woman.

As Yanti approached age twenty-five, her parents, especially her mother, had also begun to press her more insistently to marry, regularly inquiring as to whether there was anyone "special" among her male friends. But when Yanti made it clear that she planned to continue her education and reminded her parents that she was already able not only to support herself but also to assist in paying for her younger brothers' schooling as a result of her teaching and research projects, they stopped pressuring her. She did not tell them that in fact she already had a possible marriage candidate in mind but that she and the young man had not yet made a commitment to marry.

A year later, the couple announced their relationship to their respective families. Yanti's fiancé, Maman, was also finishing a master's degree. He is a part-time management consultant and works on intermittent projects. Yanti describes him as a chain smoker and a workaholic. She says he is not particularly handsome and generally doesn't care about how he looks. And yet, because he comes from a strong NU background and is also a religious scholar, he attracts the attention of young women, a cause for some concern on Yanti's part.

In the first two years of their relationship, Maman was often ill. It was, in Yanti's estimation, a result of his working too hard and too late into the night, a lack of attention to eating properly, and a failure to follow the advice of his doctor. Yanti began to care for him, to make certain he paid more attention to his health and diet, and to monitor his medications. She cooked his favorite dishes and brought them to his house or office. When he developed an abscess from an infection that would not heal, Yanti was the only one he would allow to clean and dress it. Here Yanti took a calculated risk in coming by Maman's office regularly and even dropping by his rental unit in the evening to care for him physically in this way. She braved constant gossip and rumors concerning her reputation. On more than one occasion, she confronted young women who challenged her suitability for Maman and attempted to entice him away from her. She brushed aside my questions concerning the religious injunctions against premarital intimacy (*khalwat*). She was hedging her bets, confident that the relationship would end in marriage.

Here it is important to underscore, as Samuli Schielke does, that, ethically and experientially speaking, Muslims are never "just Muslims" (Schielke 2009b). And religiously normative registers are not the only registers on which young people draw in making life decisions, including marital ones. Young people inhabit worlds that are structured by institutions and circumstances that inspire aspirations and ambivalences the cultural logic of which is not just Islamic in any simple or exhaustive way but which, somehow, ultimately becomes part of an ethically and aspirationally complex life led by individuals who self-identify as Muslim. Yanti was painfully aware of her advancing age and was self-conscious about her weight and what she perceived as a narrowing field of educated candidates. She had invested considerable time and effort into her relationship with Maman and was reluctant to start the process all over again with someone else.

It is not certain that Yanti has gambled wisely. Although she is anxious to marry, the couple has encountered multiple challenges from both sides of their families that have resulted in repeated postponements of the marriage day. Yanti has had to adjust her expectations and has begun to express a more practical view of marriage and of romantic love. At our last meeting she explained her position, saying, "I've become more realistic [about love and marriage]. I once told my boyfriend, 'It's possible that I could marry someone I don't love. Because what I need is a partner who can walk with me into the future. Not just because of love, because love can evaporate.' It's not that I don't believe that a relationship can work based on love alone. But love is not enough. You may love each other but you don't work together. So you have to be realistic. That's how I feel."

A similar gamble had not paid off for one of Yanti's close friends, Rita. Rita came from a background not unlike Yanti's, though her family identified with "neither NU nor Muhammadiyah." Rita described her parents' religious orientation as *netral*, or "neutral." They were devout, Rita said, but not fanatic. Rita had attended public schools, and although in principle she was not supposed to date, she had had several boyfriends in high school, "one after the other" (*ber-ganti-ganti*). According to Rita, however, none of those relationships was serious.

Rita was particularly good at math, and when she graduated from high school, she went on to study economics in a private business college. It was during her first semester of coursework that Rita fell head over heels in love with a classmate who was three years her senior. It was a serious relationship. He said he loved her too.

Then, as Rita describes it, "tragedy struck." She got pregnant. Although they had been seeing each other only for a semester, Rita assumed that if anything like that happened, her boyfriend would marry her. When she told him she was pregnant, he initially agreed to do just that and announced his decision to his parents. However, when his family looked into Rita's background and discovered that she had had several boyfriends in the past, they decided Rita was a "bad girl" (*anak buruk*). His parents refused to give the couple their blessing.

Rita and her boyfriend made plans to run away together. But false rumors began to circulate that Rita had been seeing someone else at the same time as her current boyfriend and that the baby was not his.[13] When she arrived at the designated place and time for their elopement, her boyfriend was not there. In fact, he had simply disappeared. "Just like that," Rita said, "he dropped out of school and left town, and nobody knew where he went." Rita was brokenhearted but also angry. Her parents were angry, too, and told their daughter that they would never allow her to marry him no matter what the case.

Rita's parents pressured her instead into marrying an acquaintance she did not love. Munawir knew about Rita's former boyfriend and her situation, nonetheless he told Rita that he loved her and wanted to marry her and would consider the child his own. Rita hesitated but was moved by his sacrifice. She was seven months pregnant and her parents were urging her to accept his proposal. Several weeks passed before Rita finally agreed. The couple married quickly. Two weeks later, the baby, a boy, was born prematurely; a short time later, he died. Rita said,

I really didn't love Munawir and I didn't want to marry him, but I pitied my parents and I felt like I had no choice. After the baby died, I felt indebted to him for agreeing to marry me in my situation, so I stayed with him. And then, you know, after some time, I started to care for him. Five years after we married, I became pregnant with our first child. That was the beginning of my husband's cheating. And five years after that, when I got pregnant again, my husband cheated on me again. This time, he left me and wanted to move in with his girlfriend. My parents convinced him to come back, but he told me, "You and I are wrong for each other. It will never work out."

Now Rita finds herself locked in a loveless marriage, one in which her husband ignores her and continues to have affairs with other women, justifying his behavior by referring to Rita's "immoral past." Other than buying occasional treats for their children, Rita says her husband provides the family with no economic support. When she once dared to ask him for money to pay the household bills, he taunted her, "Why don't you ask your former boyfriend for money?" She has never asked her husband for money again. It is here that we see evidence of an important shift in the circumstances of a growing number of middle-class Muslim Javanese women. Although her education had been interrupted by her pregnancy, Rita has managed to secure a steady job as an accountant and in fact provides the bulk of the economic support for her family. She is deeply unhappy but has not yet decided whether to ask her husband for a divorce. Nonetheless, divorce is an option, in part because she knows she can support herself and her family on her own.

As discussed in detail in chapter 7, the situation for middle-class Indonesian women is quite different from that reported in some other Muslim countries, particularly in the Arab Middle East (cf. Adely 2012, 138; Ghannam 2013, 13; Singerman 2007, 14, 17). Far more than is the case with their counterparts in Jordan or Egypt, growing numbers of Indonesian women have taken advantage of new educational opportunities and are going on to pursue employment outside of the home, both before and after marriage. Following the advice of their mothers, young women have gone to work not only so as to contribute to the support of their families and a desired middle-class lifestyle but also with an eye to maintaining an important element of leverage and autonomy within their marital relationships. It is a development that at times has run squarely into more traditional gender expectations, expectations that remain more widespread among middle-class Muslim males than among young Muslim women.

The sociologist Arlie Hochschild (2012 [1989]) has discussed a not-dissimilar shift in women's roles and in marital relations in the United States with the large-scale movement of women into the workplace beginning in the 1980s. She describes the tensions that arose and continue to exist in many American families over the reconfiguration of gender roles, particularly with regard to the allocation of household tasks and child care in families in which women who work outside the home often end up working a "second shift" at home. It is a tension that Hochschild links directly to rising rates of marital dissatisfaction (2012 [1989], 207–208). Hochschild writes, "The entrance of men into industrial labor increased men's power but did not destabilize the family; the entrance of women into employment has increased women's power somewhat but is also linked to the rise in divorce" (12).

The increase in the number of working women in Indonesia may be playing a similar role in the rising divorce rate in Indonesia. Demographic studies have shown that, in part as a result of the 1974 marriage law (which raised the age of first marriage to sixteen for women and nineteen for men, and tightened the requirements surrounding divorce and polygyny), divorce rates, which had always been extremely high among Javanese Muslims, fell significantly (Heaton, Cammack, and Young 2001; G. Jones 1994a; O'Shaughnessy 2009). More recent studies suggest, however, that divorce rates are now again on the rise (Cammack and Heaton 2011; Dommaraju and Jones 2011; G. Jones 2004). This seems to be particularly true for educated, middle-class women, who not only have higher expectations of their marital companions but have also the economic wherewithal to leave if these expectations are not met.

An interesting exception to this developing pattern involves those relationships based on *ta'aruf* and following strict religious limitations of premarital familiarization and intimacy. Initial reports suggest that rather than less stable, these relationships are *more* stable (Ardhianita and Andayani 2005; Wuryandari, Indrawati, and Siswati 2010). Based as they are on a strict interpretation of Islamic tenets, it may be that participants come into the relationship with clearer expectations with regard to marital roles and responsibilities, having negotiated important aspects of such expectations prior to marriage. Whether the husband will allow his wife to work, who will care for the children, and where the couple will live after marriage—topics such as these are typically discussed during chaperoned premarital meetings. What is more, women who have married in this way argue that in marrying by religious arrangement and acknowledging their husband's leadership role, they are secure in the knowledge they are protected by the rules of Islam. These women feel they are shielded from masculinist excesses by the constraints imposed by religious rules and can negotiate equitable compromises with their husbands by invoking the authority and guidance of Islamic norms.

Islamizing Intimacies

Regardless of background, and by comparison with the attitudes and aspirations of earlier generations, the education and social mobility of contemporary Javanese youth have generated a series of far-reaching social and ethical challenges to traditional Javanese understandings of gender and family life. Young women in particular struggle to reconcile their desires for education and employment with their hopes for more equitable and emotionally expressive gender relations within a stable, companionate marriage. They express concern with not only securing membership in the new Indonesian middle class but also with balancing a more self-conscious (self-reflexive) and *chosen* piety with new and more individualistic projects for self-actualization and personal development. Across socioeconomic groupings and irrespective of the depth of their religious engagement, Javanese youth—male *and* female—struggle to cultivate pious Muslim selves while simultaneously drawing on popular trends and contemporary cultural developments to express and shape new Muslim middle-class subjectivities (Fealy 2008; C. Jones 2007; Parker and Nilan 2013; Nilan 2008). The fact that this new orientation is affecting students whose parents and grandparents might have once adhered to radically opposed views of gender, politics, and Islamic piety offers further evidence of the blurring of the *santri-abangan* divide in a post–New Order Indonesia.

This book has described the profound social and ethical changes that have taken place in Javanese and Indonesian society as seen from the perspective of the lives of young people most deeply involved in its transformation. Although some studies of contemporary Islam and of Muslims in Indonesia highlight a single or dominant ethical or political current, what is so striking when viewing these changes from the perspective of Muslim youth is that these changes have actually been multidimensional, deeply pluralistic, and, on certain critical social matters, highly contested. Among growing numbers of Muslim youth—not least middle-class educated youth—one encounters a pervasive and acutely felt desire to take a more active and comprehensive role in the observance of one's faith. This change is sometimes described as a deepening "piety," but while it does involve piety and is therefore subjective and personal, it also has enormous implications for social and public life.

At the same time, even as they seek a more participatory and personally responsive profession of their faith, many among these new Muslim youth aspire to lifestyles and relationships that at least in some of their contours resemble those of educated youth in other, non-Muslim areas of the world. They seek social and personal relationships characterized by a greater measure of informality and intimacy than was typical of the friendships and marital ties of their parents and grandparents. They seek—and this notably includes young women—a personal freedom that also expresses itself through a heightened aspiration for employment outside of the home, not least because the daily interactions and professional achievements that such employment offers have themselves become a measure of personal worth. In the realm of intimacy and sexuality, the changes have been no less far-reaching as young people have enthusiastically embraced their right to choose their own spouse and have negotiated the process through which they will do so. Yet, once again, the scale and cultural content of these changes make clear that what is operative in the realm of personal and intimate fulfillment is not properly characterized by any single term like "individualization," "sexual liberation," or even deepening "Islamic piety." The changes in lifeways and subjectivities these young people are experiencing have aspects of all of these things, but in complex coimbrication. The precise details and course of the changes typically remain to be determined by the individual or couple in dialogue with the social and religious groupings with which they most closely identify.

Through all its complex nuances and variations, however, what is clear is that the youth reformation underway in contemporary Java, and at least some other parts of the Muslim world, involves a heightened emphasis on individuality and personal fulfillment as well as social embedding in a richly ethical Muslim community. The individualism that is apparent in contemporary youth narratives is not, then, the "Western-style" individualism assumed to emerge hand in hand with neoliberalism and railed against by Islamists as corrupting Muslim youth. It is, rather, an embedded individualism—an embedded *autonomy*—that is responsive to social and familial responsibilities, and a broader, if endlessly debated, religious good. In a word, then, these youths are young Muslims, new Muslims—aspirationally mobile, yet seeking to remain ethically grounded in a world ever in flux.

Chapter 1: Approaching Java in a Time of Transitions

1. I had first conducted research in rural East Java (Tengger) as a graduate student between 1978 and 1980; in 1985, I returned to East Java for another eight-month project. During those earlier field stints I came to Yogyakarta every few months to visit friends and colleagues, to report on my research to fellow researchers at Gadjah Mada University, and to consult with local Javanese scholars.

2. There has been considerable commentary on the rise in popularity of the headscarf in Indonesia (Brenner 1996; Ida 2008; Parker 2008a; Smith-Hefner 2007; van Wichelen 2010). Equally remarkable, but less often noted, has been the even more rapid shift to the wearing of pants on the part of women, explained as being simply "more practical."

3. My earlier research (1978–1980) had focused on issues of language and identity in the rural highlands of East Java among the Hindu Javanese population known as Tengger (Smith-Hefner 1981, 1983, 1987, 1989). My 1985 study looked at language and gender socialization, comparing Javanese families in the Hindu highlands with those in mostly Muslim Malang (Smith-Hefner 1988a, 1988b, 1989). A key point of comparison in this latter work concerned the growing influence of the Islamic resurgence, still in its early phases, on the once casual religious behavior of Malang's Muslim middle class.

4. Projected from 2010 national census data, the population of the city of Yogyakarta is estimated to be over 400,000. The surrounding regencies or *kabupaten* (Bantul, Sleman, Gunung Kidul, and Kulon Projo) that make up the "Special Region of Yogyakarta" bring the population total to an estimated 3.6 million.

5. According to World Bank estimates, Indonesia's population was 252,812,245 in 2014, World Bank: Data, "Population, Total," accessed July 15, 2015, http://data.worldbank.org.

6. Indonesians themselves use the term *modernis* (modernist) when referring to the Muhammadiyah's religious style.

7. The percentage is higher in the city proper than in surrounding regencies and does not take into account the considerable number of Christian students who come to Yogyakarta for secondary and tertiary study (see Indiyanto 2013).

8. On the growth, politics, and pluralization of Indonesia's middle class, see Dick 1985; Gerke 2000; Hefner 1993; Heryanto 1999, 2003, 2011; Tanter and Young 1990; van Klinken and Berenschot 2014.

9. Political analyses of this period and its aftermath include Aspinall 2005; Hefner 2000; Schwarz and Paris 1999; and van Dijk 2001.

10. Many authors have detailed the New Order gender ideology, among them Blackburn 2004; Brenner 2005; Robinson 1999; Sullivan 1994; Tickameyer and Kusujiarti 2012; Wieringa 2002.

11. Early exceptions are James Peacock's (1978b) *Muslim Puritans: Reformist Psychology in Southeast Asian Islam* and Saya Shiraishi's (1997) *Young Heroes: The Indonesian Family in Politics.*

12. There have, in addition, been several Indonesian publications on youth with a focus on Islam and political activism, among them Azca, Margono, and Wildan 2011; Azca and Rahadianto 2012; Kailani 2012.

13. The shift to the use of *mbak* (older sister) and *mas* (older brother)—though limited in scope—is another interesting barometer of the times. The more traditional terms of address for older individuals, *bu* (mother) and *pak* (father), are markers of greater age as well as status, whereas *mbak/mas* (older sister/brother) are used to address individuals relatively closer in age and status to oneself. At least some young people framed the shift in more political terms, emphasizing the less formal, more intimate and "democratic" connotations of the shift to "older sister/brother." Others indicated that the shift reflected a new sensitivity to aging, in particular (but not only) on the part of some women: "Oh, don't call me *bu*. I'm not that old, you know. Just call me *mbak!*" In either case, the result is a shift toward greater intimacy and general status leveling.

14. Holding up the actions of others as models (both positive and negative) for public comment and evaluation in this way is actually a common strategy used by parents and teachers in socializing appropriate behavior in young people and is a strategy that young people also use among themselves. Zane Goebel, in an extended discussion of the accommodation of migrants to Javanese village life (Goebel 2010), identifies a similar process in the analysis of "discourses of sameness and difference" and their role in establishing categories of personhood and identifying acceptable forms of social relations.

15. On new and emerging Indonesian middle-class subjectivities from somewhat different vantage points, see Boellstorff 2004a, 2005; George 2010; Hoesterey 2012; C. Jones 2003; Rudnyckyj 2010.

16. Although I interviewed a small number of Christian Javanese youth and even some non-Javanese, the focus of my research was on varieties of Muslim Javanese youth.

17. "Kampus Profil: Universitas Gadjah Mada" (Campus Profile: Gadjah Mada University), accessed August 4, 2016, http://www.kampus-info.com.

18. On the varieties of Javanese Islam see Beatty 1999; Daniels 2009; C. Geertz 1976 [1960]; Ricklefs 2006, 2007; Stange 1992. On the new Sufism in contemporary Indonesia, see Howell 2001, 2007, 2012; van Bruinessen 2007.

19. There is a large and growing literature that takes up the issue of Islamism in Indonesia. Cf. Barton 2005; Bubalo and Fealy 2005; Hasan 2006; Hilmy 2010; Machmudi 2008a; Platzdasch 2009; A. Salim 2008.

20. Although moral panics and debates over youth sexuality have occasionally touched on homosexuality and LGBT rights, these issues are overshadowed by an overwhelming focus on heterosexual concerns. It should be noted that in Indonesia homosexuality is not illegal at the national level; nonetheless, it is widely considered unacceptable within both conservative and mainline Muslim communities. In addition, as scholars of Indonesian gender Tom Boellstorf, Sharyn Graham Davies, and Helen Pausacker have emphasized, hardline Islamist groups in the post-Suharto era have attempted to portray LGBT discourses as "Western" and antithetical to Islam. Publicly declaring oneself gay or lesbian or coming out to one's family is still not common among young people, and there remains overwhelming pressure on youth, regardless of sexual orientation, to marry in heterosexual unions (see Bennett and Davies 2015; Blackwood 2010, 2015; Boellstorff 2003, 2005; Davies 2007, 2010; McNally, Grierson, and Hidayana 2015; Pausacker 2013). Not surprisingly, among the Muslim youth in my study, respondents presented their worldview and their concerns as unabashedly heteronormative. Focused as it is on the core concerns of the Muslim youth among whom I did research, then, the present study does not take up LGBT issues in significant detail.

21. This literature includes Adely 2012; Ahmed 1992; Ask and Tjomsland 1998; Blackburn, Smith, and Syamsiyatun 2008; Deeb 2006; Mahmood 2005; Mernissi 1975, 1991; Mir-Hosseini 1999; Peletz 2007; Wadud 2006.

22. See works by Brenner 2005; Syamsiyatun 2008; van Doorn-Harder 2006, 2007; Wieringa 2002; White and Anshor 2008.

Chapter 2: Islam, Youth, and Social Change

1. For statistics on population and religious affiliation, see World Bank Country Data, "Indonesia," accessed December 30, 2016, http://data.worldbank.org; World Factbook, "Indonesia," accessed December 30, 2016, https://www.cia.gov; and Indiyanto 2013.

2. The Indonesian terms *madrasah* and *pesantren* may be confusing to scholars of Islam, because in many areas of the Muslim world both types of schools are known as "madrasa" (see Hefner 2009a, 22).

3. On the heightened contact with the Middle East see Laffan 2003; on the growing emphasis on Islamic law and jurisprudence in the *pesantren* curriculum, see Hefner 2009a, 2009b; van Bruinessen 1995.

4. In the nineteenth and twentieth centuries, a small number of nominally Islamic Javanese also converted to Christianity (Aritonang and Steenbrink 2008; Guillot 1981; Ricklefs 2007; Steenbrink 2015).

5. On the form and functions of *slametan*, see C. Geertz 1976 [1960], 126–130; but compare Ricklefs 2006; Woodward 1989.

6. The roles of *haji* and *kyai* overlap but are not synonymous. Most, but not all, *kyai* have made the hajj; not all *haji* choose to become *kyai.* On *kyai* and *ulama*, see C. Geertz 1976 [1960], 134.

7. It is important to emphasize that the *santri* and *abangan* communities were not opposed or socially distinct on all matters; in fact, there were areas of ritual overlap between the two communities (cf. Lukens-Bull 2005). Although many *abangan* did not engage in congregational prayer or pay religious alms (*zakat*), most nonetheless circumcised their male children, were married in an Islamic ceremony (the *nikah*) performed by a recognized religious official (*modin*), and buried their dead in an Islamic manner and with Islamic prayers. In these and a number of other ritual events, the *abangan* did not separate themselves in any absolute way from *santri* Islam or Islamic officials. In fact, they depended upon individuals of *santri* background to recite the Arabic language prayers required for the performance of Islamic rituals, prayers in which most *abangan* in the 1950s and early 1960s were not well-versed (cf. C. Geertz 2000).

8. "Of all the reforms the modernists introduced, the idea of schools designed on a Western model was probably the most bitterly resented by the *kolot*, and the most strongly resisted; for by striking at the *pondok* [*pesantren*] system such schools were striking at the very roots of *kijaji* [*kyai*] power. But time, youth, and the 'spirit of the age' were on the side of the modernists; and by careful construction of their program they were able to weaken the effectiveness of the accusation of being 'infidel' which the *kijajis* [*kyai*] had traditionally directed at colonial 'native schools' and now turned upon them" (C. Geertz 1976 [1960], 184).

9. Although his *Religion of Java* ended on an uncertain note, Geertz also implied that some secular-modern updating of the traditions of tolerance and religious syncretism he associated with the *abangan* would likely remain the dominant mode of religiosity and sociability among Indonesian Muslims.

10. Geertz writes, "The *slametan* is the Javanese version of what is perhaps the world's most common religious ritual, the communal feast, and, as almost everywhere, it symbolizes the

mystic and social unity of those participating in it. Friends, neighbors, fellow workers, relatives, local spirits, dead ancestors, and near-forgotten gods all get bound, by virtue of their commensality, into a defined social group pledged to mutual support and cooperation" (C. Geertz 1976 [1960], 11; see also Woodward 1989).

11. The experience of emotional shock or disequilibrium—the result, for example, of scolding young children or not giving in to their demands—was thought to lead to illness and thus to be avoided.

12. From the perspective of non-reformists, such practices are not merely entertainments but manners or styles of habituated sociability and cultural reflection thought to be critical to the shaping of Javanese sociability itself.

13. The anthropologist Andrew Beatty argues that Javanese cultural practices like child-lending which involve "changing places" express and support a conceptual and moral relativism that is highly valued by Javanese (Beatty 2002, 439).

14. Peacock writes in a footnote, "Only three sons of the entire sample of Jogja [Yogya] respondents were reported to attend *pesantren*, compared to 34 respondents who themselves attended" (1978b, 66).

15. CIA World Factbook notes that in 2010, 44 percent of the population was urban, "East and Southeast Asia: Indonesia," accessed September 7, 2012, https://www.cia.gov; today, over 50 percent of the country's population is urban.

16. Young women were also paid significantly less than men, on the assumption that they did not have to support a family. The anthropologist Diane L. Wolf found that in rural Semarang in north Central Java, where she conducted fieldwork with female factory workers, young women's wages were not even sufficient to cover their monthly expenses (Wolf 1992).

17. Six years of primary education was made compulsory for all children in the mid-1970s; in 1993 Suharto announced a universal target of nine years of education to be achieved by the year 2004, later pushed back to 2009 due to the effects of the Asian Economic Crisis (Jones and Hagul 2001, 213). On the Indonesian educational system, see also Johnson, Gaylord, and Chamberland 1993.

18. Today female students comprise a slight majority of the students studying in *pesantren* boarding schools (Hefner 2009b, 63; Oey-Gardiner 1991).

19. Jackson and Parker (2008, 25) indicate that 91.5 percent of *madrasah* are private, citing Departamen Agama (Department of Religion) statistics.

20. By 2011 the middle class, as defined by an annual household income of $3,000, had reached fifty million (21 percent of the population) and was projected to triple that number by 2015 ("Indonesian Schools More Cheating, or Else! Scandals in the Classroom," *Economist*, July 21, 2011, https://www.economist.com/asia/2011/07/07/more-cheating-or-else).

21. A key illustration of this sanitized and depoliticized take on Indonesia's ethnic diversity is offered by the national amusement park Taman Mini Indonesia Indah (Beautiful Indonesia in Miniature), constructed in the early 1970s in the country's capital, Jakarta. Here, each of Indonesia's thirty-four provinces is depicted by a distinctive house style with inhabitants in regional dress engaged in regional traditions. Ethnic or cultural variation within provinces is downplayed in the amalgam of architectural and decorative features presented as a model of the province as a whole (Guinness 1994, 271; see also Pemberton 1994).

22. In the early post-Suharto period, Confucianism would be added to the list, although its equal status is not fully recognized in all Indonesian provinces.

23. Notwithstanding the coercive nature of the New Order programs, a significant number of Indonesians, including Indonesian Muslims, found principles of public ethics in the Pancasila with which they could agree; there is currently a Pancasila revival occurring in Indonesia that emphasizes its foundational principles.

Chapter 3: Varieties of Muslim Youth

1. According to the university's official website, in 2016 the enrollment was fifty-five thousand. Universitas Gadjah Mada, "Tentang UGM" (About UGM), accessed October 15, 2016, http://ugm.ac.id.

2. According to the Indonesian population census of 1990, of those Indonesians over fifteen years of age, only 3 percent of men and 1 percent of women reported some level of postsecondary education (G. Jones 1994a, 32).

3. "Favorite schools," or *sekolah favorit*, are those most highly ranked according to national end-of-year test scores. The most highly ranked schools are public schools, and public schools are generally considered by parents and students alike as the most desirable not only because of their academic rigor but also because it is assumed they provide a "general" education that will lead to secure employment.

4. At the college level, students take the National Selection Exam for State Universities (Seleksi Nasional Masuk Perguruan Tinggi Negeri, SNM-PTN, formerly, UMPTN).

5. Only a handful of male students and even fewer female students reported having attended an Islamic boarding school (*pesantren*) during their elementary or secondary education. In most cases these were in fact *pesantren kilat*, or "lightening *pesantren*," which offered three- or four-day religious study programs during the Ramadan holiday.

6. This is slowly changing as religious schools (*pesantren, madrasah*, and Muslim day schools) continue to upgrade their curriculum and introduce more secular subjects. Until the late Suharto period, however, those who graduated from the religious system were not allowed to sit for the general university admission exam (the UMPTN/ SNM-PTN) but were channeled into the state Islamic institutes.

7. R. Murray Thomas writes, "Over the 1979–1984 period, more than 14 million primary school handbooks for teachers and students were distributed by the Ministry of Religion, and 6,716 teachers and teacher aides were trained. In 1983–84, over 3.5 million religious teachers were in pre-service or in-service training programs, and 6,000 primary-level *madrasah* buildings were rehabilitated. At the junior-secondary level, 16,000 teachers were in training and 6.6 million textbooks and items of equipment were distributed" (1988, 907).

8. *Pengajian* religious study takes a variety of forms. *Pengajian Qur'an* (lit. "Qur'anic study") refers to the elementary study of Arabic script so as to allow for the reading and reciting of the Qur'an. Many young children engage in this type of *pengajian* in the late afternoons in their neighborhood mosque or prayer house (*musholla, langgar*). Alternately, a religion teacher may be invited to the home for the same purpose. Other types of *pengajian* take the form of religious study groups that meet on a regular weekly or monthly schedule and are led by a recognized religious scholar. Study may focus on a religious text or texts or more generally address issues of how to live a religious life.

9. As Dale Eickelman and Jon Anderson (1999b), C. W. Watson (2005), and others have argued, a key feature of the Islamic resurgence has been an explosion in the availability and study of inexpensive Islamic literature. See also Charles Hirschkind's (2006) study of Islam in Egypt and the proliferation and use of religious tapes.

10. Some young women reported that some middle and high school religion teachers gave high marks only to those female students who wore the headscarf consistently both inside and outside of the classroom.

11. All names are pseudonyms. In addition, some noncritical details of students' life histories have been changed or collapsed so as to obscure the identity of the respondents.

12. As if to underscore her lack of interest in such traditions and ceremonies, Diah misidentifies the *tingkeban*, which is typically done when a woman is seven months pregnant with her

first child; the *pitonan,* when the baby is seven months old; and the *selapan,* which is done when the baby is thirty-five days old (cf. C. Geertz 1976 [1960], 38).

13. The decision to allow public high school students and government workers to wear the *jilbab* to school and work (SK No. 100/C/Kep/D/1991) was issued by the Department of Education and Culture on February 16, 1991, and was meant to take effect in July 1991. Even after its announcement, however, many school districts and government offices were slow to implement the new regulation.

14. In the years after the fall of Suharto in 1998, most Javanese parents came to realize that veiling did not negatively affect their daughters' friendships, employment opportunities, or marriage prospects, and many came to view veiling as a positive phenomenon, expressive of a young woman's deeper understanding of the requirements of her faith. In fact, several previously disapproving mothers whom I interviewed in 1999 and 2000 insisted in later discussions that they had been "awakened" (*tergugah*) by their daughters' example. As a result, they had begun serious study of Islam, and in some cases had taken up the veil themselves (see Smith-Hefner 2007).

15. Machmudi argues that the Suharto regime's repression of both modernist and traditionalist groups and their subsequent shift away from political to more cultural activities focusing on education, social work, and predication, enabled the groups to interact with each other and to develop overlapping social networks. Religious education provided by the schools aided in this process by emphasizing neither NU nor Muhammadiyah affiliation but rather foundational beliefs and practice (Machmudi 2008b, 73, 77).

16. In a survey I conducted in 1999 of one hundred Gadjah Mada students across faculties, I found that nearly one-quarter of UGM students identified their religious formation in some way with Muhammadiyah, while 10 percent indicated an affiliation with NU.

17. In the late 1990s and early 2000s, a minority wing in the Muhammadiyah had sought to curb what they regarded as the excessively purifying impulses of some within their organization and to signal their respect for ethnic traditions—including *wayang*—as long as these were clearly identified as "traditions" (*tradisi*) and made no claim to being "religion" (*agama*) (see Daniels 2009, especially chapter 5, "Muslim Puritans, Cultural *Dakwah* and Reformation").

18. This is not a complete list of the Muslim organizations on campus but includes those most often referenced by students in my survey and interviews. For a more complete list, see Saluz 2009.

19. On Madjid's role in HMI politics, see Kersten 2015, 118–119.

20. See Aspinall 2005 for a more detailed political analysis of student organizations and activism during this period.

21. The acronym MPO stands for Majelis Penyelamat Organisasi, or the "Assembly to Secure/Rescue the Organization."

22. Under the leadership of Eggy Sudjana, the HMI-MPO became a major Islamist opponent of the Suharto regime. However, in the final years of the Suharto administration, and in a move that astonished many former MPO activists, Sudjana reconciled with the regime and for a period of time became an ally opposed to the pro-democracy movement, accusing it of being leftist- and Christian-dominated (see Albar and Kurniawan 2009; Aspinall 2005).

23. In some other parts of Indonesia, including, for example Makasssar, South Sulawesi (which was shaken by the ethnoreligious clashes in nearby areas of eastern Indonesia between 1999 and 2003), both the HMI and the HMI-MPO adopt more self-consciously Islamist positions on national matters (cf. Albar and Kurniawan 2009).

24. The Lembaga Dakwah Kampus Jema'ah Shalahuddin, or JS, is a campus *dakwah* (propagation) organization affiliated with Gadjah Mada that has a reputation as being rather conservative.

25. Smoking is tolerated but is considered *makruh* (disapproved, offensive).

26. In Indonesia, the Tarbiyah Movement tended not to place much emphasis on the later and more radical of Qutb's writings, and, in recent years, the movement's focus has turned to works by Turkish and Egyptian writers emphasizing the compatibility of Islam with electoral democracy (Machmudi 2008b).

27. However, in subsequent national elections, and despite forecasts of great electoral growth, the PKS has consistently polled just under 8 percent of the national voice (Hamayotsu 2011).

28. Aceh in northwestern Sumatra is the only province in Indonesia that has formally adopted public legislation (known in that province as *qanun*) that attempts to implement a form of shari'a law inclusive of the shari'a's criminal sanctions. Elsewhere in Indonesia in the aftermath of the New Order period, a number of provinces, districts, and municipalities have implemented "regional regulations" (*peraturan daerah*, or *perda*) intended to enforce "shari'a-inspired" ethical prescriptions with regard to a narrow range of noncriminal matters, including women's dress, alcohol consumption, and Qur'anic study (see Buehler 2016; Bush 2008). Aceh's special status on shari'a legislation reflects its turbulent and in some regards unique modern history. The late president Abdurrahman Wahid (r. 1999–2001) granted Aceh special autonomy in 2001 in an attempt to end a long-standing separatist insurgency (A. Salim 2008). The province took steps to begin the implementation of a more comprehensive assortment of shari'a laws not long afterward. In 2014 the law was extended to non-Muslims who are subjected to shari'a law for violations not already covered by the criminal law code. Punishment in the form of public floggings is imposed for violations such as selling alcohol, gambling, illicit proximity between unmarried members of the opposite sex (*khalwat*), which includes dating, adultery, homosexuality, and immodest dress (see Feener 2013, 2015; Feener, Kloos, and Samuels 2015; Lindsey 2012).

29. This emphasis on bottom-up and gradualist rather than top-down and immediate societal reform is a trademark feature of moderate Islamist groups, as well as others that scholars such as the Swiss political scientist Patrick Haenni (2005) have called "post-Islamist."

30. Along similar lines, Rachel Rinaldo describes women's larger project within the PKS as that of developing a "pious activating agency" that will "guide their struggle for a nation infused with Islamic values" (2013, 112).

31. Cf. Machmudi 2008a, 2008b.

32. To ensure that young women do not have to rely on males for rides to and from classes or work, KAMMI has been quite active (and successful) in its campaign to support alternative modes of city transportation in the form of additional bus lines and expanded schedules.

33. Of the eighteen state Islamic institutions of higher education (IAIN) in Indonesia, five in the early 2000s expanded their programs to become state Islamic universities (UIN), offering professional and general degrees as well as training in Islamic disciplines; Yogya's IAIN was second among the IAIN to make this transition. Three additional IAIN have more recently joined the ranks of Indonesia's state Islamic universities.

34. In 2006 the city experienced a major earthquake and the school's cement block structures were severely damaged. Although the mosque was spared, many university buildings showed visible, gaping cracks in their foundations, and others had collapsed entirely. With assistance from the Islamic Development Bank, the university has subsequently not only been rebuilt but considerably expanded. Today the campus is a model of modern, attractive, Muslim-style architecture.

35. Young Muslim scholars of NU background have themselves taken note of and celebrated this remarkable blending of traditionalist scholarship with modern forms of higher education, including the social sciences and humanities. For a striking illustration and analysis of this neo-traditionalist confidence, see Salim and Ridwan (1999) and Rumadi (2015).

36. Forty-two percent of State Islamic University students in my interviews and surveys were members of the PMII; 12 percent were members of the HMI; and 12 percent were involved in the IMM.

37. An LSM (Lembaga Swadaya Masyarakat) is an Indonesian nongovernmental organization.

38. A portion of PMII's membership had also become active in the research and publishing group LKiS. LKiS, or Lembaga Kajian Islam dan Sosial (Institute for Islamic and Social Studies), is described as "a Yogyakarta-based NGO with an NU-leaning constituency" (van Bruinessen 2013, xvii).

Chapter 4: Conceptualizing Gender

1. The right to decline a parental match was enshrined in the 1974 Marriage Act. It also set the minimum age for marriage at sixteen for females and nineteen for males, protected women from forced marriage, and attempted to address gender inequalities in divorce (Robinson 2009, 84–85; see also Cammack, Young, and Heaton 1996).

2. Raden Adjeng Kartini is an Indonesian national heroine whose birthday, April 21, is celebrated as a national holiday. On Mother Kartini Day (Hari Ibu Kartini), young schoolgirls dress in traditional costume in her honor, and competitions are held to determine who is the best model of Javanese womanliness (see Sears 1996b, 37).

3. Inayah herself resisted taking up the headscarf until 2013, when, under pressure from her own daughters, she began wearing the headscarf, joining the rest of the women in her family.

4. This may occur in cases where the mother is very young and still in school or working, or has had the child out of wedlock. It may also occur when a young divorcée marries again and fears her new husband will not accept her child from a previous marriage.

5. The well-known anthropologist of Southeast Asian gender, Michael G. Peletz, has argued that these and similar social structural and domestic variables found throughout much of Southeast Asia give rise to sentiments and dispositions that have historically supported a measure of gender pluralism (Peletz 2007, 51; Peletz 2009; see also Andaya 2006).

6. Although this practice is also common in some North African Muslim societies, it is discouraged in mainstream Islamic jurisprudence (cf. Tucker 2008).

7. While it is possible that a son might inherit the family home and bring his wife to live there and take care of his elderly parents, it seems to be a less common pattern. As several parents explained, "I prefer my daughter stay with me because she knows how to cook the things I like and I would feel less restrained in asking her to do things for me."

8. Carla Jones (2004), drawing on Arli Hochschild's (1979) work, describes this as the "emotion work" performed by women in Javanese households.

9. Observers differ, however, as to whether the role that Javanese women play in household management enhances their power or authority within the family or is in fact linked to their more worldly and less spiritual nature—and lesser prestige (cf. Brenner 1995; Djajadiningrat-Nieuwenhuis 1992; Keeler 1990). Both Norma Sullivan (1994) and Diane Wolf (1996) argue that the issue is not who manages the household or budget or even who contributes to it, but who makes the important decisions regarding expenditures or investments. On this debate over women's complementary gender roles, see also Schröter 2013, 7–8.

10. Nonetheless, Bu Ratna emphasized that their relationship was one of harmony (harmonis, rukun), not complete equality, and that, in the case of important decisions, her husband's word was final.

11. Here we see evidence that patriarchy takes widely differing cultural forms, not least of all with regard to male "distinction" and the whole question of masculine refinement (cf. Brusco 2010; Martin 2001).

12. The historian Barbara Andaya observes that between the seventeenth and eighteenth centuries as Muslim Southeast Asians came into greater contact with the Islamic heartlands, increasing numbers of upper-class women took up physical seclusion. Andaya argues that female seclusion provided a powerful means of demonstrating difference in rank, setting elite women apart from ordinary folk (2000, 253).

13. Elizabeth Locher-Scholten writes that the effects of this European "cult of domesticity" were most strongly felt among the *priyayi* and Christian converts, and much less among rural women (2000, 43).

14. Djajadiningrat-Nieuwenhuis points out that in the postcolonial period, the situation of the *priyayi* changed dramatically. In many cases husbands' jobs had ceased to exist and it was necessary for wives to earn all or part of the income (1992, 42; see also Brenner 1998).

15. This was true at least prior to 1918, when schooling became more common for *priyayi* girls and the practice of seclusion (Jv. *pingit*) was largely abandoned (see Tiwon 1996, 5; Koentjaraningrat 1989, 245).

16. Historically, polygyny was more common among *priyayi* than among rural *abangan* (H. Geertz 1978 [1961], 131; Koentjaraningrat 1989, 139). Among *priyayi* men, large numbers of children and multiple wives were a source of status and a symbol of their prosperity (Koentjaraningrat 1989, 259). A poignant example of this pattern is offered by Pramoedya Anata Toer in his story of a young village girl married off to a Javanese regent only to be replaced by a more "suitable" wife after giving birth to her first child; see *The Girl from the Coast* (Toer 2002).

17. Although Kartini has been held up as a national heroine and role model for Indonesian women by the state, under the New Order, her struggles against forced marriage and in support of the education of women were overshadowed by her identification as a self-sacrificing mother and symbol of femininity and "motherliness" (*keibuan*) (see Tiwon 1996; Wieringa 2002).

18. On marriage patterns among *priyayi* see also H. Geertz 1989 [1961], 60. For a detailed analysis of the history of divorce trends in Indonesia see G. Jones 1994a; see also Cammack, Donovan, and Heaton 2007.

19. Gavin Jones (1994a, 13) defines the Islamic principle of *nafkah* as "the obligation of husband to provide adequate food, housing, and clothing for his wife; failure to provide maintenance is grounds for divorce under Islamic law" (see also White 2006; Cammack, Donovan, and Heaton 2007).

20. Here, too, *priyayi* gender conceptions are consonant with patriarchal interpretations of Islam. A well-known and widely cited passage from the hadith states, "If a man calls his wife to his bed and she does not come to him, the angels will curse her until morning," (Al-Bukhari and Muslim; see Ali 2006, 11).

21. There was, however, great regional variation seen in this pattern. For example, in the Banuymas region of west Central Java, as well as parts of the *pasisir* (north coast area) and much of the eastern salient, nonstandard variants of Javanese remained widespread. These variants often placed much less emphasis on hierarchy and status differences and more on simple social distance among non-familiars (Smith-Hefner 1989).

22. The Dutch introduced the cultivation system, or *cultuurstelsel*, in the 1830s. It was a system of forced cultivation using native labor. Under the cultivation system the colonial government produced and exported tropical cash crops, among them, most notably, coffee, sugar, and indigo. The Dutch used the *priyayi*—native regents (*bupati*) and their subordinates—to organize the cooperation of the necessarily large Javanese labor force, allowing them to also exact labor for their own purposes (Ricklefs 1993, 119–120).

23. In this regard, the well-known political historian of Southeast Asia, Benedict Anderson, writes, "In the 19th Century, as the European powers revved up their economic activities and bureaucratic administration in the colonies, there was a tremendous increase in the need

for native administrators, 'armies of clerks', who to be useful had to be bilingual, capable of mediating linguistically between the metropolitan nation and the colonized peoples" (1983, 106).

24. The complete motto is *ing ngarsa sung tulada, ing madya mangun karsa, tut wuri handayani;* that is, the teacher should "be a positive example in front [of the class], generate ideas and excitement in the middle [among students], and give encouragement and direction from behind."

25. In this regard, Wieringa writes, "The non-Islamic women's organizations had always opposed the Islamic organizations on the issue of marriage reforms, so the relationship between Gerwani and the Islamic groups was strained from the outset" (2002, 251).

26. Army sources reported that Gerwani women danced naked and tortured the kidnapped generals who were brought to the Halim Air Force Base, known as Lobang Buaya (Crocodile Pit). In the state's version of events, the women sliced at and castrated the generals, whose bodies were then thrown into a deep well (Wieringa 2002, 301–317).

27. Suharto himself took great pride in referring to his role as *bapak pembangunan,* the "father of [Indonesian] development" (Robinson 2009, 70).

28. The PKK promoted the five duties of the Indonesian woman (the *panca dharma wanita*) as producer of the nation's future generations, wife and faithful companion to her husband, mother and educator of her children, manager of the household, and citizen (Sen 2002, 36, first cited in Hull 1996 [1982]).

29. Widely hailed as one of the most successful population programs in the world, critics have noted the coercive methods used in some instances, particularly, but not only, in rural areas (see Dwyer 2000).

30. Based on the passage from the Qur'an that is loosely translated as "Allah favors not man, or woman, but whoever is most pious" *Al-Hujarat* 49:13 (see Adamson 2007, 13).

31. Adamson (2007, 16) writes, "The widespread belief throughout the Muslim world that the Qur'an and Hadith define men as superior is supported by classical interpretations (*tafsir*) of the religious texts. Contemporary scholars argue that classical *tafsir* must be re-read as historically biased and contingent." See also Barlas 2002; Engineer 1992; Mernissi 1991; Munir 2002; Wadud-Muhsin 1992.

32. Those restrictions include the requirement that the husband seek permission from a religious court. To obtain permission of the court, he must provide evidence that he is able to support an additional wife and will treat her fairly. He must also secure the permission of his existing wife or wives (Nurmila 2009, 1).

33. In neighboring Malaysia the salient term is *fitrah,* meaning "disposition, intuition, insight, common sense" (White 2006, 278).

34. Sally White writes that "underlying both terms [*kodrat* and *fitrah*] is biological essentialism; women's difference is defined by her biology, and on the basis of this difference, she has a role in society that differs from that of men and that is predetermined, immutable and self-evident" (2006, 278).

Chapter 5: Gender Shifts

1. My use of the terms "neo-traditionalists" and "neo-reformists" is meant to emphasize the shift in self-consciousness and reflexivity with regard to religious understandings and identifications among recent generations of Muslim Javanese youth in comparison with earlier generations of Muslim Javanese.

2. Within NU circles this family ideal is referred to as the *keluarga maslaha* (van Doorn-Harder 2006, 226–228). The corresponding family ideal within Muhammadiyah is

the *keluarga sakinah* (the harmonious family)" a version of which was adopted by the New Order state as the *keluarga sejahtera* (prosperous family) (see also Wieringa 2015)

3. The exception were those mothers who, as religion teachers in state supported *madrasah* or Muslim day schools, were civil servants (*pegawai negeri*) under the Department of Religion.

4. Eighty-five percent of Indonesia's *pesantren* are located in rural areas of Indonesia (Azra, Afrianty, and Hefner 2007, 179), and 50 percent of *madrasah* students (many *madrasah* are attached to *pesantren*) are children of farmers or laborers (182).

5. In my survey of two hundred families of UIN and UGM students, 44 percent of State Islamic University students reported their parents' marriages had been arranged, compared to only 19 percent of Gadjah Mada students.

6. The families of students from the State Islamic University were typically larger than those from Gadjah Mada. UIN students often joked that their parents had followed KB (*keluarga besar*, or "big family"). The joke is that normally the acronym KB stands for *keluarga berencana* (family planning). This changed dramatically in the following generation.

7. In emphasizing the importance of a religious education, these parents told their children, "If you are pious [Jv. *wong soleh*], then it's easy to make a living. If you are pious, it's not possible that God would ever abandon you."

8. The hadith in question is "Instruct your children to *sholat* when they are seven years old and when they are ten, hit them if they do not perform their prayers and separate their bed [from yours]" (H. R. Ahmad and Abu Dawud, cited in Adhim 2003, 19, translated from Indonesian).

9. While girls in traditionalist communities also undergo circumcision, no neo-traditionalist woman made mention of any ceremony marking the event, insisting that the procedure was secret and simply involved a pinprick, or in some cases "wiping of the labia with turmeric" at around age six or seven, or even younger.

10. "Yellow books" refers to the color of the paper on which the books were written when they were brought from the Middle East in the early twentieth century (van Bruinessen 1990, 227).

11. In Indonesia, the law school most widely studied in traditionalist circles is that of the legal scholar Imam Shafi'i (767–782 CE). Although scholars from all schools of law are studied in state Islamic colleges and universities, the Shafi'i *madhab* is still the main focus of study in Indonesian *pesantren* (see van Bruinessen 1990).

12. Although its authenticity is questioned by some Muslim scholars, in discussions of education, many people cite the hadith "Seek knowledge even if you have to go as far as China, for seeking knowledge is a duty on every Muslim."

13. This is despite the fact that gender-segregated education is not directly required by the Qur'an (the Prophet himself, as well as his wife, are reported to have taught mixed-sex groups) but a historical outcome of more general Islamic values (Srimulyani 2012, 116; see also Azra 2003).

14. The *'Uqud al-Lujjayn* was composed in the nineteenth century by Imam Nawawi al-Bantani, a Muslim scholar who spent years studying and teaching in the Middle East but originated from Banten, the westernmost province of Java (see Fealy, Hooker, and White 2006, 42; White 2006).

15. See van Doorn-Harder 2006 and White 2006 for a discussion of the continuing debates over the interpretation of the *'Uqud al-Lujjayn*.

16. In Indonesian, *Memandang wanita seperti menghirup racun syaitan* (Claire-Marie Hefner, personal communication, August 25, 2009).

17. There were a number of references to the pattern of marriage with delayed consummation (In. *kawin gantung*) in stories of traditionalist parents, often related to the very young age of

the bride. Gavin Jones (1994a, 60) reports that Javanese are characterized by greater delays in consummation than any other major group in the Malay world.

18. The hadith in question is attributed to Ibn Abbas: "For any Muslim who has two Muslim parents and who goes to them every morning obeying their requests, Allah opens two doors to heaven. If he has one parent, Allah opens one door to heaven for him. If he displeases either of them, Allah will not be pleased with him until that one parent of his is pleased with him. And someone asked: 'Even when they are unjust to him?' He answered: 'Even if they are unjust.'" *Islamic Voice,* "How to Repay the Debt We Owe to Our Parents," *Adab Al-Mufrad* 1:7, accessed July 25, 2013, http://islamicvoice.com.

19. In a survey of two hundred university students (one hundred attending UGM and one hundred attending the State Islamic University), families of Gadjah Mada students were smaller on average than families of State Islamic University students by 1.3 children (UGM families averaged 2.8 children; UIN families averaged 4.1).

20. The term *babysister* (babysitter, nursemaid) seems to be a conflation of the English term "babysitter" and the Indonesian *suster,* meaning "sister/nurse/nun," a borrowing from Dutch. In Indonesia, trained nannies often come out of hospital programs.

21. Equally interesting, in my survey of two hundred university students, 34 percent of students from Gadjah Mada identified their mothers as "the dominant one in the family," whereas only 24 percent of those from the State Islamic University did.

22. Carla Jones writes, "By 'emotion work' I refer to the exchange of gestures of deference, affection, gratitude or emotional sacrifice in a domestic economy" (2004, 510; see also Hochschild 1979, 2012 [1989]).

23. The *bedoyo* is a sacred dance associated with the palace (*kraton*) of Yogyakarta. It is marked by the slow, elegant (*alus*) movements of the dancers (see Ricklefs 2012, 42).

24. *Tetes/tetesan* is the high Javanese (*kromo inggil*) term for female circumcision. As a verb it can mean "to hatch" or "to cut, snip" (Horne 1974, 614). Andrée Feillard, in an unpublished manuscript surveying available sources on female circumcision in Indonesia, writes of Javanese *tetesan* that "the midwife or healer made a minor cut, prick, scratch, or rubbing to the clitoris or the labia minora, or both" (n.d., 8). Isti's elaborate ceremony was unusual; most women could not recall their circumcisions, which were done when they were very young and without any celebration.

25. While most women reported having had the procedure when they were too young to remember, those who underwent the procedure somewhat later (between the ages of six and eight) recalled a "pin prick." Elsewhere in Indonesia, however, the procedure can be more invasive (Feillard and Marcoes 1998).

26. Feillard (n.d., 7) writes that the age at which female genital cutting is performed has generally been coming down over time as more "orthodox" forms of Islam have prevailed.

27. Both young women also insisted that absolutely no cutting is involved.

28. While elaborate celebrations such as Isti's are rare today, Feillard and Marcoes (1998) argue that the practice of female circumcision in Indonesia has become more widespread in Indonesia in the wake of the Islamic resurgence. Linda Rae Bennett (2005, 55) writes similarly that female circumcision is seemingly universal among the current generation of young women in Lombok, in contrast to earlier generations of women. Saskia Wieringa (2015, 33) explains that female genital cutting was actually banned in Indonesia 2006, however when in 2010 the Ministry of Health circulated a publication to health care providers with instructions for performing medically safe female circumcision, it was taken as permission to undertake the procedure.

29. Pregnancy outside of marriage, however, is hardly a joking matter for the young woman involved, not to mention her family, for whom it was a source of tremendous shame (*aib*) (see also Bennett 2005, 24).

30. Some Muslim social organizations have responded to these concerns by organizing mass circumcisions (*khitan massal*) for boys in urban neighborhoods in Yogyakarta and surrounding areas.

31. This confirms David Gilmore's observation that cross-culturally femininity tends to be ritually unmarked because in contrast to masculinity it is more often perceived as occurring "naturally" (Gilmore 1990).

32. Many young people (both male and female) stated flatly that "men don't cook." Some young men reported that they knew how to make simple dishes such as fried rice or instant noodles for themselves and would do so if they didn't like what their mother had cooked or if nothing had been prepared, but none reported cooking for their families.

33. In my survey of one hundred UGM students (equally divided between males and females), 8 percent of males and 5 percent of females reported that they still did not pray regularly, a pattern supported by interviews.

34. Some students complained that only the students who wore the headscarf consistently in class and outside of class as well were given high marks.

Chapter 6: Sex and Sociability

1. Much of this sensationalist research, like Wijayanto's, suffered from imprecise methodologies and faulty statistical analyses. Other more methodologically rigorous studies have presented rather different findings. Iwu Dwisetyuani Utomo's survey of 344 high school students and 174 university students in Jakarta found that 1.4 percent of youth ages 15–19 and 10.8 percent of youth ages 20–24 reported having engaged in "petting with intercourse" (I. D. Utomo 2002, 221). Augustina Situmorang's (2001, 2003) survey of 875 unmarried youth ages 15–24 in the city of Medan found that 18 percent of single youth (9 percent of females and 27 percent of males) reported having had sex. More recent studies report similar figures for youth sexual involvement—with men and non-Muslims reporting slightly higher levels of sexual activity than women and non-Muslims (cf. Ford, Shaluhiyah, and Suryoputro 2007). Given that premarital sex is not socially accepted, the real percentage of sexually active youth is likely higher than reported; however, it is unlikely it is anywhere near the figures cited by Wijayanto.

2. In July 2017, the Indonesian government banned Hizbut Tahrir for conducting activities that contradict the state ideology of Pancasila and to protect the unity of the state. The group has vowed to challenge the decision in the courts; see "Hizb ut-Tahrir Indonesia Banned 'To Protect Unity,'" *Aljazeera*, July 19, 2017, http://www.aljazeera.com.

3. The restriction is spelled out in the Family Welfare Law, Undang-Undang No. 10/1992, which states, "Family planning services are only to be provided to married couples" (Parker 2008a, 48).

4. The Indonesian scholar Mohammad Iqbal Ahnaf (2013) cites statistics from the Government Census of 2010, indicating that over 60 percent of Indonesia's population at that time was under the age of forty, and that of this group, 32.3 percent were between the ages of fifteen and thirty-nine.

5. On the details of purification in Islam as it applies to both men and women, see Bouhdiba 2004, chapter 5, "Purity Lost, Purity Regained" (43–57).

6. The majority of popular Indonesian youth magazines, even those that are not explicitly religious, reinforce this message as well (cf. Handajani 2008; Parker and Nilan 2013).

7. Mir-Hosseini and Hamzić define *zina* as "any illicit sexual activity outside of marriage in Muslim contexts, including adultery and fornication" (2010, 7); see also, Ali 2006, chapter 4, "Prohibited Acts and Forbidden Partners" (56–74).

8. Describing *zina* as the "antithesis" of *nikah* (marriage)," Bouhdiba notes there are at least twenty-seven verses devoted to it in the Qur'an (Bouhdiba 2004, 15).

9. Recognizing my position as a foreign anthropologist and an older woman and given the sensitivity of the topic, I did not expect that young people would necessarily be forthcoming or completely truthful in talking about their own sexual experiences. What was particularly striking however, is that even among the young people whom I got to know well, and even among those who acknowledged they had engaged in sex outside of marriage, agreement on the religious norm of *kesucian* "purity/virginity" remained strong.

10. More precisely, *gaul* is a continuum of informal varieties of Indonesian that incorporate various combinations and larger or smaller percentages of the linguistic elements identified as *gaul*.

11. *Bahasa gaul*, as it is represented in most *gaul* dictionaries and recognized by most young people, contains no Arabic borrowings.

12. Other common *gaul* acronyms include *ABG* (/abege/) (adolescent), from *anak baru gede* (lit. "a child just recently big/mature"), *PHK* (/pehaka/), from *putus hubungan kekasih* (to break up with one's girl/boyfriend), and *PDKT* (/pedekate/), from *proces pendekatan dan perkenalan* (the process of approaching/getting to know someone).

13. *Gue* (I) and *(e)lu* (you) are borrowings from *bahasa Betawi* and are identified with informal Jakartan Indonesian.

14. *Ini penulis muda dengan gaya bahasa yang khas dan telah dapat tempat tersendiri di kalangan pembaca.*

15. In a process of abbreviation also called blending, *curahan hati* "the outpouring of feelings" becomes *curhat*.

16. *Bahasa gaul* is the language not only of Internet chatting but also of Facebook, WhatsApp, and instant messaging (SMS). In addition to handy *gaul* pocket dictionaries, such as that of Moammar Emka (2007), there are also plenty of handbooks of the latest *gaul* expressions that assist one in locating just the right word or phrase (see Dianawati 2005; Natalia 2007).

17. Other *gaul* terms for emotional states/characteristics based on borrowings from English include *sensi* (sensitive), *bete* (bad tempered/annoyed), *tempra* (tempermental), and *jaim* (insecure/obsessed about image).

18. The publication of *Sabili* stopped in 2013 but has since been replaced by *Sabiliku Bangkit*.

19. Other publications by Al-Ghifari include *Remaja dan Cinta: Memahami Gelora Cinta Remaja dan Menyelamtkannya dari Berhala Cinta* (Teens and Love: Understanding the Thrill of Teen Love and Safeguarding them from Its Idolization); *Pacaran Yang Islami, Adakah?* (Muslim Dating, Is There Such a Thing?); and *Selingkuh, Nikmat yang Terlaknat* (Cheating, a Damning Pleasure).

20. Since the overthrow of the Suharto regime in May 1998, cafés, bars, nightclubs, and discotheques, as "sites of immorality" (*tempat maksiat*), have been the targets of repeated attacks, not least of all by the nationally organized militia known as the Islamic Defenders' Front (Front Pembela Islam); cf. I. Wilson 2008.

21. In 2012, the book was in its seventeenth edition.

22. According to Fillah these kinds of relationships also have negative consequences for personality development. "You think you are trying to understand each other through emotional sharing, but that's not what happens! Each of you is trying to appear better than you really are. . . . In fact, each of you is busy creating a [false] advertisement to entice a buyer." In putting one's efforts into "false advertising," one wastes time that could be used in more constructive pursuits. Moreover, relying on someone else to help solve one's problems impedes the development of independent thinking and self-reliance (Fillah 2003, 39–40).

23. At top nonsectarian high schools, conservative *Islami* extracurricular clubs called Rohis work to strengthen Islamic faith and practice among students (see chapter 5). These clubs circulate their own *Islami* word lists and encourage their members to use them rather than *gaul* forms. These word lists are borrowed completely from Arabic.

24. They also include the works produced by the group Lingkar Pena (Writers' Network). Lingkar Pena is a community of young writers who produce inspirational religious short stories, articles, and novels. Although authors are free to write whatever they wish, their work is Islamically oriented but speaks to the desire of young Muslims to be cool (see Kailani 2012; Widodo 2008).

Chapter 7: The New Muslim Romance

1. In 2014, according to UNESCO statistics, 82.47 percent of Indonesian young people were attending secondary school, and women's enrollment had essentially caught up with men's (at 99 percent gender parity). UNESCO Institute for Statistics, "Education, Indonesia," accessed March 2, 2017, http://data.uis.unesco.org. World Bank statistics for the year following (2015) indicate that at the tertiary level, women's enrollment (at 32.8 percent) had surpassed men's (at 29.4 percent). World Bank Gender Data Portal, "Indonesia," accessed March 12, 2017, http://datatopics.worldbank.org.

2. As among Malays in neighboring Malaysia (Ong 2010 [1987]; Peletz 1995), Javanese women have relatively few illusions about the reliability of male partners over the long term (G. Jones 2009, 16; see also Brenner 1995; Keeler 1990).

3. This is in part a reflection of men's greater autonomy. In addition, as they reach their mid-twenties, young men are generally expected to be thinking about putting aside money with an eye to eventual marriage and setting up a household of their own (see G. Jones 2005, 23).

4. Unlike women in some parts of the Muslim world, young women and elder parents cannot look to an extended family or lineage-based grouping for social and material support. As has long been the case in Java, the cognatic/bilateral system of Javanese kinship creates a small web of kindred ties, but these are of highly circumscribed social and economic importance (H. Geertz 1989 [1961]; W. J. Karim 1995; Schröter 2013). Most Javanese, and especially most educated Javanese women aspiring to a position in the middle class, are keenly aware that their own and their elder parents' well-being may well depend in the long run on their own efforts.

5. The World Bank website notes that the percentages offered are based on the employment-to-population ratio; that is, the proportion of a country's population that is employed. "In this survey ages 15+ are considered as the 'working-age population.' Employment refers to work for a public or private employer involving remuneration in wages, salary, commission, tips, piece rates, or pay in kind." World Bank, "Employment, Indonesia," accessed August 21, 2014, http://search.worldbank.org.

6. Social demographer Ariane J. Utomo, citing the BPS-Statistics Indonesia (Indonesia's Central Bureau of Statistics), offers an even higher figure for Indonesian female labor force participation—57 percent in 2000—up from 32 percent in 1971 (A. Utomo 2014, 1688).

7. World Bank, "Employment," accessed August 21, 2014, http://search.worldbank.org.

8. Citing Muslim, hadith IV:98, Bouhdiba writes, "It is 'highly recommended to marry.' It is a pleasure, but it is also a duty" (2004, 89). See also Ali (2008, 6): "Key Islamic texts present marriage, and sex within it, as a natural and desirable part of human life."

9. Bouhdiba, citing authoritative sources, writes, "Those who live as celibates are the worst kind; those who die celibate are the lowest of the low" (2004, 90).

10. See G. Jones and Gubhaju (2008, 3, 6) and G. Jones (2005).

11. "Just playing around" (*main-main saja*) does not carry the same sexual connotations the expression has in English.

12. Young men also feel the pressure to marry, but as in other spheres, they are accorded somewhat more leeway in such matters. By their mid- to late twenties, however, many young men begin to feel the pressure (and desire) to marry as well.

13. The requirement of "sharing the same faith" (*seiman*) was echoed by men as well, with the notable exception of the small number who indicated they were willing to marry a non-Muslim woman "in order to convert her." Indonesian law actually remains unclear on the issue of interreligious marriage, but most young people assume it is not legal. On the law and popular understandings relating to interreligious marriage, see Fealy and Hooker 2006a; Lindsey 2012; Seo 2013.

14. Ismi's housemates were all Muslim and all wore the headscarf, she said, but they attended a variety of different private and professional schools.

15. Abortion is illegal in Indonesia unless the mother's life is at risk or in cases of rape. It is considered a "grave sin" in Islam, similar to murder (see Bennett 2005, 106; White 2006, 336–339). Nonetheless, individuals can be found who are willing to provide abortifacients, both natural and pharmaceutical, for a price. The reliability of these preparations varies greatly, as does the medical knowledge of the supplier. One young man told me he sold his motor scooter to buy abortion pills for his pregnant girlfriend. He said he was given eight pills, four of which his girlfriend was to take orally, and the others she was instructed to take vaginally, one every four hours. After each insertion, the couple was instructed to engage in coitus to ensure that the medicine would enter the uterus. The efficacy of the procedure was never tested, as the young woman decided that she would have the child, and the couple married.

16. The medical anthropologist Linda Rae Bennett writes, "By law, women who access public family planning services for the first time must present their marriage certificate before an initial consultation" (2005, 35). Even married women may be told that it is best to wait to use birth control until they have produced a first child.

17. A widely circulating discourse on women who engage in premarital sex is "If she agreed to have sex with you, then how can you think she hasn't had sex (or won't have sex) with others?"

18. The various articles from local magazines and newspapers that comprise Wardoyo's polygyny campaign are compiled in a xeroxed format with a cover titled *Kiat Sukses Poligami Islami* (The Secret to Successful Polygyny the [True] Muslim Way) (Wardoyo n.d.). "Basically our aims are similar to those of the feminist activists," Wardoyo claimed in a personal interview in the summer of 2002. "We want to extend the protection of legal marriage [in the form of polygamy] to women who would otherwise be illegal mistresses engaging in sinful acts in adulterous relationships."

19. See also Abu Al-Ghifari's *Pacaran yang Islami, Adakah?* (Muslim Dating, Is There Such a Thing?) and Mohammad Fauzil Adhim's *Indahnya Pernikahan Dini* (The Beauty of Early Marriage).

20. The enormously popular film *Ayat-Ayat Cinta* (Verses of Love, 2008)—reportedly viewed by over four million theatergoers in the first week of its release—was seen by many as offering support to Wardoyo's pro-polygyny campaign. Most young viewers overlooked the film's subtle critique and instead regarded it as one of the first Indonesian films that offered a sympathetic and modern take on an explicitly Muslim love story (cf. Heryanto 2014, 30; see also Brenner 2011; Hakim 2010; Heryanto 2011).

21. See chapters in Andrew Weintraub's (2011) volume *Islam and Popular Culture in Indonesia and Malaysia* by Barendregt, Brenner, Heryanto, Ishadi, and Krier; see also Heryanto 2014; Hoesterey 2012; Hoesterey and Clark 2012; Sofjan 2013.

22. As one indication of how widespread this "anti-dating" discourse has become, during a visit to a friend in Yogyakarta in the summer of 2015, her ten-year-old daughter decided to entertain us with a spontaneous speech on the "dangers of dating." Reciting the familiar possibilities of ruining the reputation of one's family and dropping out of school, she punctuated each stanza with "and that is why, mothers and fathers, you should never allow your children to *pa-car-an!*"

23. A similar guide written specifically for religious activists is Asri Widiarti's *Unacquainted and yet Engaged: The Complete Guide to the Marriage Process for Religious Activists (Tak Kenal maka Ta'aruf: Panduan Lengkap Proses Ta'aruf Hingga Pernikahan Aktivis Dakwah).*

24. Wedding fashions on the model of the Middle East (but retaining elements of earlier Javanese fashion as well) are in fact now ubiquitous in women's magazines and among youth.

25. Although "Muslim style," Kustiyah's wedding celebration was far from small and austere. There were fifteen hundred guests at the celebration sponsored by her parents, and seven hundred at a later celebration sponsored by the parents of her husband. And although there were no traditional entertainments such as *wayang* (shadow puppet theater) or classical Javanese dance, there were two popular and quite lively Muslim singing groups that took turns playing throughout the evening.

26. A similar argument has been made by Bernice Martin (2001) regarding Pentecostal women in Latin America. See also Elizabeth E. Brusco 1995.

27. A similar pattern is evidenced among some pop stars, actors, or singers—male and female—who may publicly announce a radical change of heart and the decision to turn their life around by embracing a more conservative Muslim lifestyle.

28. Not to be confused with the Saudi-influenced Salafiyyah movement, a *pesantren salaf* in the Indonesian context is an Islamic boarding school that does *not* offer courses in general or secular learning but is instead dedicated to the study of the traditional Islamic sciences (especially Islamic jurisprudence, *fiqh*) as transmitted in the *kitab kuning* (see van Bruinessen 1994; see also Lukens-Bull 2001).

29. Although male activists were known for their unkempt appearance, rumpled clothes, and heavy smoking, their aura of radicalism attracted women interested in intellectual types.

30. Such behavior on the part of disapproving parents is rather (to say the least) extreme but indicative of the fact that, while relinquishing their right to choose a spouse for their offspring, parents nonetheless can and do make clear their feelings regarding their children's choices. The refusal of parents to offer their blessings on a union is often (though not always) sufficient cause for a son or daughter to break off a relationship.

31. Believers are enjoined by God to facilitate the marriage of righteous others. Helping others to marry is an act of piety. "The Qur'an says explicitly: 'Marry the spouseless among you and your slaves and handmaidens that are righteous; if they are poor, God will enrich them of His bounty,'" Qur'an XXIV "Light," 32:356 (Bouhdiba 2004, 90).

32. It was a position that would normally require at least a high school education. Nindy explained that the store owner was unusual in that she stressed honesty and hard work on the part of her employees and had decided to give Hermawan a chance based on his references. Sales positions, however, are not particularly well-paid.

33. Some young men dispute this, arguing that the man may be the one to first signal his interest but it's up to the woman to accept or refuse.

34. The greater number of women relative to men who typically show up at mass matchmaking events only reinforces this belief.

35. Along similar lines, G. Jones writes, "Women's growing financial independence and autonomy in other areas of life has posed major issues for the self-image of many men" (2005, 23).

36. These types of proposals, typically made via text message, were surprisingly common and often quite blunt: "My name is X. I saw you at a religious meeting yesterday. I am serious about marrying. If you are interested, please reply."

37. *Nembung* means to ask permission or make a request.

38. *Dilangkahi adike* means "to be stepped over by a younger sibling." Siblings are supposed to marry in order of age, oldest first. If a younger sibling wants to marry before an older sibling, they must secure their older sibling's permission first. The older sibling is allowed to make a request in return for granting permission. The request could be a fancy watch or a new shirt, or even a car. It could also simply be something symbolic. Of course, it's always possible that an elder might refuse to give permission. This often happens if they have a love interest and are planning to marry, in which case they might insist that their wedding take place first.

39. In this regard, A. Utomo writes, "Although the explicit preferences for women to marry older men continue to dominate young people's ideals on spouse qualities, . . . [i]nterestingly, the proportion of women marrying someone of higher education is declining, and conversely, the proportion of women 'marrying down' is rising" (2104, 1702).

40. As many as 30 percent of the women I interviewed said they had never had a serious relationship.

Chapter 8: Conclusion

1. The Prophet Muhammad said, "Paradise lies at the feet of your mother" (*Sunan al-Nasa'i*, 25: 20), "Sunnah.com," accessed June 20, 2018, https://sunnah.com/nasai/25/20; "The pleasure of the Lord lies in the pleasure of the parent. The anger of the Lord lies in the anger of the parent" (*Adab Al-Mufrad* 1: 2), "Sunnah.com," accessed June 20, 2018, https://sunnah.com/adab/1/2.

2. It goes without saying that the choices on the menu are all varieties of Islam. Nonetheless, the fact that Ismail sees this process not as one of simply accepting of his parents' religious understanding and practice but as the weighing of moral alternatives is yet another example of the reflexive process evidenced across so many Muslim Javanese youth.

3. Muhammadiyah and Nahdlatul Ulama rely on different sources to calculate the beginning of Ramadan, so the first day of fasting for their members often differs slightly.

4. Rohis after-school religious study clubs began to appear in the early 2000s at many high schools in Yogyakarta. The goal of the clubs is to encourage the development of a more conservative religious atmosphere on secondary school campuses (Ahnaf 2013; Salim, Kailani, and Azekiyah 2011; see chapter 5).

5. He notes, however, that while he used to imagine that he would insist that his wife wear the headscarf, as a result of his discussions with friends and classmates at Gadjah Mada, he now realizes that the decision is her own to make.

6. In this regard, Dhofier writes, "The student must show his complete respect and obedience to his teacher, not because of an absolute surrender to his teacher, who is regarded as having authority, but because of the student's belief in his teacher's sanctity; the teacher is a channel of God's grace for his student in this world and in the hereafter" (1999 [1982], 61).

7. Those scriptures include "Not one of you who are believers should meet a woman alone unless she is accompanied by a relative [*mahram*] because whenever a man is alone with a woman, Satan is the third among them" (H. R. Ahmad, cited in Ezokanzo and Sinyo 2015, 99). And "Say to the believing men that they should lower their gaze and protect their private parts. This is more pure for them. Indeed Allah is well-aware of what they do. And say to the believing women that they should lower their gaze and guard their modesty; that they should not display their beauty and ornaments except what (must ordinarily) appear thereof; that they should draw their veils over their bosoms and not display their beauty; and that they should not strike

their feet in order to draw attention to their hidden ornaments. O ye Believers! Turn ye all together towards Allah, that ye may attain Bliss." (*Surah Al-Nur* 24: 30–31), "Islam's Women: Jewels of Islam," accessed June 20, 2018, http://www.islamswomen.com/articles/rulings_on_women_in_society.php.

8. Many contemporary Muslim youth avoid the term *slametan* altogether in favor of the more Islamically inflected designation *kenduren*. *Kenduren* from *kenduri* (from Persian/Hindi) also refers to a ritual meal, but the focus is typically on the recitation of Islamic prayers and blessings.

9. See chapter 3 for details on the role of these groups in campus life.

10. "Dan, janganlah kalian mendekati zina. Sesungguhnya, zina adalah suatu perbuatan yang keji dan suatu jalan yang buruk" (*Surah Al-Isra'* 17: 32) (Ezokanzo and Sinyo 2015, 84).

11. PHP is *bahasa gaul* for *pemberi harapan palsu,* meaning "giver/giving false hope"; that is, "to lead someone on."

12. "Equitable" but not necessarily "equal." Most of the women in my study insist that men's and women's roles and responsibilities are not commensurate, and that each has a different function in society and in marital relationships based on basic biological differences (*kodrat*).

13. This is a common pattern in situations like Rita's, and a risk women take in engaging in sexual relations before marriage.

Abdillah, Masykuri
  1997   *Responses of Indonesian Muslim Intellectuals to the Concept of Democracy (1966–1993).* Hamburg: Abera Network.
Abu-Lughod, Lila
  2000   *Veiled Sentiments: Honor and Poetry in a Bedouin Society.* Berkeley: University of California Press.
Adamson, Clarissa
  2007   "Gendered Anxieties: Islam, Women's Rights, and Moral Hierarchy in Java." *Anthropological Quarterly* 80 (1): 5–37.
Adely, Fida
  2012   *Gendered Paradoxes: Educating Jordanian Women in Nation, Faith, and Progress.* Chicago: University of Chicago Press.
Adhim, Mohammad Fauzil
  2003   *Indahnya Pernikahan Dini* (The Beauty of Early Marriage). Jakarta: Gema Insani Press.
Ahmed, Leila
  1992   *Women and Gender in Islam: Historical Roots of a Modern Debate.* New Haven, CT: Yale University Press.
  2014   *A Quiet Revolution: The Veil's Resurgence, from the Middle East to America.* New Haven, CT: Yale University Press.
Ahnaf, Mohammad Iqbal
  2013   *Contesting Morality: Youth Piety and Pluralism in Indonesia.* Pluralism Working Paper No. 10. Yogyakarta, Java: Center for Religious and Cross-Cultural Studies (CRCS), Gadjah Mada University, Yogyakarta, Indonesia.
Al Asyhar, Thobieb
  2005   *Sufi Funky: Menjadi Remaja Gaul yang Saleh* (Funky Sufi: Become a Young Person Who Is Gaul and Pious). Jakarta: Gema Istani.
Alatas, Alwi
  2006   *Bikin Gaulmu Makin Gaul: Kiat Bergaul yang Asyik dan Oke* (Make Your Socializing More Sociable: The Secret to Great Socializing That's Still Acceptable). Jakarta: Hikma Press.
Alatas, Alwi, and Fifrida Desliyanti
  2002   *Revolusi Jilbab: Kasus Pelarang Jilbab di SMA Negeri Se-Jabotabek, 1982–1991* (The Jilbab Revolution: The Prohibition of Headscarves in State Schools in the Jabotabek Region, 1982–1991). Jakarta: Al-I'tishom.
Albar, Suryo, and Randi Kurniawan
  2009   "Dialektika HMI-MPO Sebagai Gerakan Kritis di UGM" (Dialectics of the HMI-MPO as a Critical Movement at UGM). In *Dynamics of Islamic Student Movements: Iklim Intelektual Islam di Kalangan Aktivis Kampus,* edited by Claudia Nef Saluz, 3–32. Yogyakarta, Indonesia: Resist Book.
Alfian, M.
  1989   *Muhammadiyah: The Political Behavior of a Muslim Modernist Organization under Dutch Colonialism.* Yogyakarta, Indonesia: Gadjah Mada University Press.

Al-Ghifari, Abu

2001a   *Kudung Gaul: Berjilbab Tapi Telanjang* (Trendy Headscarves: Covered but Naked). Bandung, Indonesia: Mujahid Press.

2001b   *Gelombang Kejahatan Seks Remaja Modern* (A Wave of Modern Teen Sex Crimes). Bandung, Indonesia: Mujahid Press.

2002a   *Romantika Remaja: Kisah-Kisah Tragis dan Solusinya dalam Islam* (Teen Romance: Tragic Stories and Their Solutions in Islam). Bandung, Indonesia: Mujahid Press.

2002b   *Remaja dan Cinta: Memahami Gelora Cinta Remaja dan Menyelamtkannya dari Berhala Cinta* (Teens and Love: Understanding Teen Love and Safeguarding Them from the Love of [Teen] Idols). Bandung, Indonesia: Mujahid Press.

2003a   *Pacaran Yang Islami, Adakah?* (Muslim Dating, Is There Such a Thing?). Bandung, Indonesia: Mujahid Press.

2003b   *Selingkuh, Nikmat yang Terlaknat* (Cheating, a Damning Pleasure). Bandung, Indonesia: Mujahid Press.

Ali, Kecia

2006   *Sexual Ethics and Islam: Feminist Reflections on Qur'an, Hadith, and Jurisprudence.* Oxford: Oneworld Publications.

al-Otaibi, Abdullah, and Pascal Ménoret

2010   "Rebels without a Cause? A Politics of Deviance in Saudi Arabia." In *Being Young and Muslim: New Cultural Politics in the Global South and North,* edited by Linda Herrera and Asef Bayat, 77–94. New York: Oxford University Press.

Altman, Dennis

2001   *Global Sex.* Chicago: University of Chicago Press.

Andaya, Barbara Watson

2000   "Delineating Female Space: Seclusion and the State in Pre-Modern Island Southeast Asia." In *Other Pasts: Women, Gender, and History in Early Modern Southeast Asia,* edited by Barbara Watson Andaya, 231–253. Honolulu: CSEAS, University of Hawai'i at Mānoa.

2006   *The Flaming Womb: Repositioning Women in Early Modern Southeast Asia.* Honolulu: University of Hawai'i Press.

Anderson, Benedict

1983   *Imagined Communities: Reflections on the Origin and Spread of Nationalism.* London: Verso.

2006 [1972]   *Java in a Time of Revolution: Occupation and Resistance, 1944–1946.* Jakarta: Equinox Publishing.

Anis, Muhammad Yunus, and Yahya

2009   "Dinamika PMII: Komisariat Gadjah Mada dalam Menjawab Tantangan Zaman" (Dynamics of the PMII: Responding to the Challenges of the Age). In *Dynamics of Islamic Student Movements: Iklim Intelektual Islam di Kalangan Aktivis Kampus,* edited by Claudia Nef Saluz, 53–74. Yogyakarta, Indonesia: Resist Book.

Anwar, Syafi'i

1995   *Pemikiran dan Aksi Islam Indonesia: Sebuah Kajian Politik Tentang Cendeki-awan Muslim Orde Baru* (Thought and Action in Indonesian Islam: A Political Study of New Order Muslim Scholars). Jakarta: Paramadina.

Ardhianita, Iis, and Budi Andayani

2005   "Kepuasan Pernikahan ditinjau dari Berpacaran dan Tidak Berpacaran" (Marital Satisfaction of Those Who Dated Before Marriage and Those Who Did Not). *Jurnal Psikologi* 32 (2): 101–111.

Aritonang, Jan S., and Karel A. Steenbrink, eds.
2008   *A History of Christianity in Indonesia.* Vol. 35. Leiden: Brill.

Ask, Karin, and Marit Tjomsland, eds.
1998   *Women and Islamization: Contemporary Dimensions of Discourse on Gender.*
        London: Berg Publishers.

Aspinall, Edward
2005   *Opposing Suharto: Compromise, Resistance, and Regime Change in Indonesia.*
        Stanford, CA: Stanford University Press.

Astuti, Dina
2005   *Gaul Ok! Belajar Ok! Cerdas Gak Berarti Kuper* (Socializing Is Okay! Studying
        Is Okay! Intelligent Doesn't [have to] Mean Unsocial). Depok, Indonesia: PT
        Kawan Pustaka.

Asyahida, Jasmine
2014   *Bawa Aku ke Penghulu* (Take Me to the Religious Authority). Yogyakarta,
        Indonesia: Buku Pintar.

Atkinson, Jane M., and Shelly Errington, eds.
1990   *Power and Difference: Gender in Island Southeast Asia.* Stanford, CA: Stanford
        University Press.

Azca, M. Najib, and Oki Rahadianto, eds.
2012   "Pemuda, Agensi dan Reformasi" (Youth, Agency, and Reform). Special issue of
        Jurnal Studi Pemuda (Journal of Youth Studies) 1 (1). Yogyakarta, Indonesia:
        Gadjah Mada University Press.

Azca, M. Najib, Subando Agus Margono, and Lalu Wildan
2011   *Pemuda pasca Orba: Potret Kontemporer Pemuda Indonesia* (Post New Order
        Youth: A Portrait of Contemporary Indonesian Youth). Yogyakarta, Indonesia:
        Youth Studies Centre, Fisipol Gadjah Mada University.

Azra, Azyumardi
2003   "Dalam Sejarah Pendidikan Islam: Tidak Ada Segregasi Laki-Laki dan
        Perempuan" (In the History of Islamic Education: There Is No Segregation of
        Men and Women). *Suara Rahima* 7 (3): 9–13.

Azra, Azyumardi, Dina Afrianty, and Robert W. Hefner
2007   "Pesantren and Madrasa: Muslim Schools and National Ideals in Indonesia."
        In *Schooling Islam: The Culture and Politics of Modern Muslim Education,*
        edited by Robert W. Hefner and Muhammad Qasim Zamin, 172–198. Prince-
        ton, NJ: Princeton University Press.

Azzahida, Wida
2016   *Pintar Mencari Jodoh* (Smart in Looking for a Partner). Jakarta: Bhuana Ilmu
        Populer.

Bachtiar, H. W.
1973   "The Religion of Java: A Commentary." *Majalah Ilmu-Ilmu Sastra Indonesia* 5
        (1): 85–118.

Bagir, Zainal Abidin
2013   "Defamation of Religion Law in Post-Reformasi Indonesia: Is Revision Possible?"
        Australian Journal of Asian Law 13 (2): 1–16.

Barendregt, Bart
2008   "Sex, Cannibals, and the Language of Cool: Indonesian Tales of the Phone and
        Modernity." *Information Society* 24 (3): 160–170.
2011   "Pop, Politics, and Piety: *Nasyid* Boy Band Music in Muslim Southeast Asia."
        In *Islam and Popular Culture in Indonesia and Malaysia,* edited by Andrew
        N. Weintraub, 235–256. New York: Routledge.

Barlas, Asma
  2002   *"Believing Women" in Islam: Unreading Patriarchal Interpretations of the Qur'an.* Austin: University of Texas Press.
Barth, Fredrik
  1993   *Balinese Worlds.* Chicago: University of Chicago Press.
Barton, Greg
  1995   "Neo-Modernism: A Vital Synthesis of Traditionalist and Modernist Islamic Thought in Indonesia." *Studia Islamika* 2 (3): 1–75.
  2005   *Jemaah Islamiyah: Radical Islamism in Indonesia.* Singapore: National University of Singapore Press.
Beatty, Andrew
  1999   *Varieties of Javanese Religion: An Anthropological Account.* Cambridge: Cambridge University Press.
  2002   "Changing Places: Relatives and Relativism in Java." *Journal of the Royal Anthropological Institute* 8 (3): 469–491.
Benda-Beckmann, Franz von, and Keebet von Benda-Beckmann
  2012   "Identity in Dispute: Law, Religion, and Identity in Minangkabau." *Asian Ethnicity* 13 (4): 341–358.
Bennardo, Giovanni, and Victor C. De Munck
  2014   *Cultural Models: Genesis, Methods, and Experiences.* New York: Oxford University Press.
Bennett, Linda Rae
  2002   "Modernity, Desire, and Courtship: The Evolution of Premarital Relationships in Mataram, Eastern Indonesia." In *Coming of Age in South and Southeast Asia,* edited by Lenore Manderson and Pranee Liamputtong, 96–112. Richmond, UK: Curzon.
  2005   *Women, Islam, and Modernity: Single Women, Sexuality, and Reproductive Health in Contemporary Indonesia.* New York: Routledge.
Bennett, Linda Rae, and Sharyn Graham Davies
  2015   "Introduction." In *Sex and Sexualities in Contemporary Indonesia: Sexual Politics, Health, Diversity, and Representations,* edited by Linda Rae Bennett and Sharyn Graham Davies, 1–25. New York: Routledge.
Berkey, Jonathan P.
  2003   *The Formation of Islam: Religion and Society in the Near East, 600–1800.* Cambridge: Cambridge University Press.
Biehl, Joao, Byron Good, and Arthur Kleinman, eds.
  2007   *Subjectivity: Ethnographic Investigations.* Berkeley: University of California Press.
Blackburn, Susan
  2004   *Women and the State in Modern Indonesia.* Cambridge: Cambridge University Press.
Blackburn, Susan, Bianca J. Smith, and Siti Syamsiyatun, eds.
  2008   *Indonesian Islam in a New Era: How Women Negotiate Their Muslim Identities.* Clayton, Australia: Monash Asia Institute, Monash University Press.
Blackwood, Evelyn
  2010   *Falling into the Lesbi World.* Honolulu: University of Hawai'i Press
  2011   *Tombois and Femmes: Defying Gender Labels in Indonesia.* Jakarta, Indonesia: The Lontar Foundation.
  2015   "Lesbian Subjectivities: Butch, Femme, and Andro from the New Order to Reformasi Era Indonesia." In *Sex and Sexualities in Contemporary Indonesia:*

SexualPolitics, Health, Diversity, and Representations, edited by Linda Rae Bennett and Sharyn Graham Davies, 220–233. New York: Routledge.

Boellstorff, Tom

1999   "The Perfect Path: Gay Men, Marriage, Indonesia." *GLQ: A Journal of Lesbian and Gay Studies* 5 (4): 475–509.

2003   "Dubbing Culture: Indonesian Gay and Lesbi Subjectivities and Ethnography in an Already Globalized World." *American Ethnologist* 30 (2): 225–242.

2004a   "Gay Language and Indonesia: Registering Belonging." *Journal of Linguistic Anthropology* 14 (2): 248–268.

2004b   "Authentic, of Course!": Gay Language in Indonesia and Cultures of Belonging." In *Speaking in Queer Tongues: Globalization and Gay Language*, edited by William Leap and Tom Boellstorff, 164–181. Champaign: University of Illinois Press.

2005   *The Gay Archipelago: Sexuality and Nation in Indonesia*. Princeton, NJ: Princeton University Press.

Bouhdiba, Abdelwahab

2004   *Sexuality in Islam*. London: Saqi Books.

Bowen, John R.

1991   *Sumatran Politics and Poetics: Gayo History, 1900–1989*. New Haven, CT: Yale University Press.

2003   *Islam, Law, and Equality in Indonesia: An Anthropology of Public Reasoning*. Cambridge, MA: Cambridge University Press.

Brenner, Suzanne A.

1995   "Why Women Rule the Roost: Rethinking Javanese Ideologies of Gender and Self-Control." In *Bewitching Women, Pious Men: Gender and Body Politics in Southeast Asia*, edited by Aiwa Ong and Michael G. Peletz, 19–50. Berkeley: University of California Press.

1996   "Reconstructing Self and Society: Javanese Muslim Women and 'the Veil.'" *American Ethnologist* 23 (4): 673–697.

1998   *The Domestication of Desire: Women, Wealth, and Modernity in Java*. Princeton, NJ: Princeton University Press.

2005   "Islam and Gender Politics in Late New Order Indonesia." In *Spirited Politics: Religion and Public Life in Contemporary Southeast Asia*, edited by Andrew C. Willford and Kenneth M. George, 93–118. Ithaca, NY: Cornell University Southeast Asia Program, Cornell University.

2006   "Democracy, Polygamy, and Women in Post-'Reformasi' Indonesia." *Social Analysis* 50 (1): 164–167.

2011   "Holy Matrimony? The Print Politics of Polygamy in Indonesia." In *Islam and Popular Culture in Indonesia and Malaysia*, edited by Andrew N. Weintraub, 212–234. New York: Routledge.

Brusco, Elizabeth E.

1995   *The Reformation of Machismo: Evangelical Conversion and Gender in Colombia*. Austin: University of Texas Press.

Bubalo, Anthony, and Greg Fealy

2005   *Joining the Caravan?: The Middle East, Islamism and Indonesia*. Paper No 5. Alexandria, NSW: The Lowy Institute.

Bubalo, Anthony, Greg Fealy, and Whit Mason

2008   *Zealous Democrats: Islamism and Democracy in Egypt, Indonesia and Turkey*. Alexandria, NSW: Lowy Institute for International Policy.

Buehler, Michael
 2016   *The Politics of Shari'a Law: Islamist Activists and the State in Democratizing Indonesia.* Cambridge: Cambridge University Press.
Bush, Robin
 2008   "Regional Sharia Regulations in Indonesia: Anomaly or Symptom?" In *Expressing Islam: Religious Life and Politics in Indonesia,* edited by Greg Fealy and Sally White, 174–191. Singapore: Institute of Southeast Asian Studies.
 2009   *Nahdlatul Ulama and the Struggle for Power within Islam and Politics in Indonesia.* Singapore: Institute of Southeast Asian Studies, National University of Singapore.
Cammack, Mark
 2003   "Indonesia's 1989 Religious Judicature Act: Islamization of Indonesia or Indonesianization of Islam?" In *Shari'a and Politics in Modern Indonesia,* edited by Arskal Salim and Azumardi Azra, 96–124. Singapore: Institute of Southeast Asian Studies.
Cammack, Mark E., Helen Donovan, and Tim B. Heaton
 2007   "Islamic Divorce Law and Practice in Indonesia." In *Islamic Law in Contemporary Indonesia: Ideas and Institutions,* edited by Michael R. Feener and Mark E. Cammack, 99–127. Cambridge, MA: Harvard University Law School.
Cammack, Mark, and Tim Heaton
 2011   "Explaining the Recent Upturn in Divorce in Indonesia: Developmental Idealism and the Effect of Political Change." *Asian Journal of Social Science* 39 (6): 776–796.
Cammack, Mark, Lawrence A. Young, and Tim Heaton
 1996   "Legislating Social Change in an Islamic Society–Indonesia's Marriage Law." *American Journal of Comparative Law* 44 (1): 45–73.
Chambert-Loir, Henri, and James T. Collins
 1984   "Those Who Speak *Prokem.*" *Indonesia* 37:105–117.
Collins, Elizabeth Fuller, and Ernaldi Bahar
 2000   "To Know Shame: Malu and Its Uses in Malay Societies." *Crossroads: An Interdisciplinary Journal of Southeast Asian Studies* 14 (1): 35–69.
Connell, R. W.
 2000   *The Men and the Boys.* Berkeley: University of California Press.
 2002   *Gender.* Cambridge: Polity Books.
 2014 [1987]   *Gender and Power: Society, the Person, and Sexual Politics.* New York: John Wiley & Sons.
Coté, Joost
 1995   *On Feminism and Nationalism: Kartini's Letters to Stella Zeehandelaar, 1899–1903.* Clayton, Australia: Monash Asia Institute.
Cowan, J. Milton, ed.
 1994   *The Hans Wehr Dictionary of Modern Written Arabic.* Urbana, IL: Spoken Language Services.
Cribb, Robert, ed.
 1990   *The Indonesian Killings of 1965–1966: Studies from Java and Bali.* Clayton, Australia: Centre of Southeast Asian Studies, Monash University.
d'Andrade, Roy G., and Claudia Strauss, eds.
 1992   *Human Motives and Cultural Models.* Cambridge: Cambridge University Press.

Daniels, Timothy
  2009   *Islamic Spectrum in Java*. Burlington, VT: Ashgate Publishing Company.
Davies, Sharyn Graham
  2007   *Challenging Gender Norms: Five Genders among Bugis in Indonesia*. Belmont,
          CA: Wadsworth Publishing Company.
  2010   *Gender Diversity in Indonesia: Sexuality, Islam, and Queer Selves*. New York:
          Routledge.
Deeb, Lara
  2006   *An Enchanted Modern: Gender and Public Piety in Shi'i Lebanon*. Princeton,
          NJ: Princeton University Press.
Deeb, Lara, and Mona Harb
  2013a   *Leisurely Islam: Negotiating Geography and Morality in Shi'ite South Beirut*.
          Princeton, NJ: Princeton University Press.
  2013b   "Choosing both Faith and Fun: Youth Negotiations of Moral Norms in South
          Beirut." *Ethnos* 78 (1): 1–22.
Dhofier, Zamakhsyari
  1999 [1982]   *The Pesantren Tradition: A Study of the Role of the Kyai in the
                Maintenance of the Traditional Ideology of Islam in Java*. Tempe:
                Program for SEA Studies, University of Arizona.
Dianawati, Ajen
  2005   *Seabreg SMS Gaul* (A Bunch of Gaul Texts). Jakarta: GagasMedia
Dick, Howard W.
  1985   "The Rise of a Middle Class and the Changing Concept of Equity in Indonesia:
          An Interpretation." *Indonesia* 39:71–92.
Djajadiningrat-Nieuwenhuis, Madelon
  1992   "Ibuism and Priyayization: Path to Power?" In *Indonesian Women in Focus:
          Past and Present Notions*, edited by Elsbeth Locher-Scholten and Anke Niehof,
          43–51. Leiden: KITLV Press.
Dommaraju, Premchand, and Gavin W. Jones
  2011   "Divorce Trends in Asia." *Asian Journal of Social Science* 39 (6): 725–750.
Dwyer, Leslie K.
  2000   "Spectacular Sexuality: Nationalism, Development and the Politics of Family
          Planning in Indonesia." In *Gender Ironies of Nationalism: Sexing the Nation*,
          edited by Tamar Mayar, 25–64. New York: Routledge.
  2001   *Making Modern Muslims: Embodied Politics in Urban Java, Indonesia*. PhD
          thesis, Princeton University.
Dzuhayatin, Siti Ruhaini
  2001   "Gender and Pluralism in Indonesia." In *The Politics of Multiculturalism:
          Pluralism and Citizenship in Malaysia, Singapore, and Indonesia*,
          edited by Robert W. Hefner, 253–267. Honolulu: University of
          Hawai'i Press.
Eble, Connie
  1996   *Slang and Sociability: In-Group Language among College Students*. Chapel Hill:
          University of North Carolina Press Books.
Echols, John M., Hassan Shadily, John U. Wolff, and James T. Collins
  1989   *Kamus Indonesia-Inggris: An Indonesian-English Dictionary*. Jakarta: Penerbit
          PT Gramedia.
Economist
  2011   "Missing BRIC in the Wall: Indonesia's Middle Class." July 21.

Effendy, Bahtiar
    2004   *Islam and the State in Indonesia.* Athens: Ohio University Press.
Eickelman, Dale F., and Jon W. Anderson, eds.
    1999a   *New Media in the Muslim World: The Emerging Public Sphere.* Bloomington:
        Indiana University Press.
Eickelman, Dale F., and Jon W. Anderson
    1999b   "Redefining Muslim Publics." In *New Media in the Muslim World:*
        The Emerging Public Sphere, edited by Dale F. Eickelman and Jon W. Anderson,
        1–18. Bloomington: Indiana University Press.
Eickelman, Dale F., and James Piscatori
    2004 [1996]   *Muslim Politics.* Princeton, NJ: Princeton University Press.
Emka, Moammar
    2007   *Kamus Gaul Hare Gene!!!* (Contemporary Gaul Dictionary). Jakarta:
        GagasMedia.
Engineer, Asghar Ali
    1992   *The Rights of Women in Islam.* New York: Saint Martin's Press.
Errington, J. Joseph
    1985   *Language and Social Change in Java: Linguistic Reflexes of Modernization in a*
        Traditional Royal Polity. No. 65–66. Athens: Ohio University Press.
    1999   *Shifting Languages: Interaction and Identity in Javanese Indonesia* (Studies in
        the Social and Cultural Foundations of Language, No. 19). Cambridge:
        Cambridge University Press.
Eves, Richard
    2007   "Billy Graham in the South Seas." In *Asian and Pacific Cosmopolitans: Self*
        and Subject in Motion, edited by Kathryn Robinson, 103–127. Basingstoke, UK:
        Palgrave Macmillan.
Ewing, Katherine P.
    1990   "The Illusion of Wholeness: Culture, Self and the Experience of Inconsistency."
        Ethos 18 (3): 251–278.
Ezokanzo, Tethy, and Sinyo
    2015   *Tetap Gaul tapi Syar'i* (Staying Sociable but Pious). Solo, Indonesia: Tiga
        Ananda.
Fealy, Greg
    2007   "Hizbut Tahrir in Indonesia: Seeking a 'Total' Islamic Identity." In *Islam and*
        Political Violence: Muslim Diaspora and Radicalism in the West, edited by
        Shahram Akbarzadeh and Fethi Mansouri, 151–164. London: IB Tauris.
    2008   "Consuming Islam: Commodified Religion and Aspirational Pietism in
        Contemporary Indonesia." In *Expressing Islam: Religious Life and Politics in*
        Indonesia, edited by Greg Fealy and Sally White, 15–39. Singapore: Institute of
        Southeast Asian Studies.
Fealy, Greg, and Greg Barton
    1996   *Nahdlatul Ulama, Traditional Islam, and Modernity in Indonesia.* Clayton,
        Australia: Monash Asia Institute.
Fealy, Greg, and Virginia Hooker, eds.
    2006a   *Voices of Islam in Southeast Asia: A Contemporary Source Book.* Singapore:
        Institute of Southeast Asian Studies, National University of Singapore.
Fealy, Greg, and Virginia Hooker
    2006b   "Interactions: Global and Local Islam; Muslims and Non-Muslims." In *Voices*
        of Islam in Southeast Asia: A Contemporary Sourcebook, edited by Greg Fealy
        and Virginia Hooker, 411–473. Singapore: Institute of Southeast Asian Studies.

Fealy, Greg, Virginia Hooker, and Sally White

2006   "Indonesia." In *Voices of Islam in Southeast Asia: A Contemporary Sourcebook*, edited by Greg Fealy and Virginia Hooker, 39–50. Singapore: Institute of Southeast Asian Studies.

Fealy, Greg, and Katharine McGregor

2010   "Nahdlatul Ulama and the Killings of 1965–66: Religion, Politics, and Remembrance." *Indonesia* 89:37–60.

Fealy, Greg, and Sally White, eds.

2008   *Expressing Islam: Religious Life and Politics in Indonesia.* Singapore: Institute of Southeast Asian Studies.

Feener, R. Michael

2007   *Muslim Legal Thought in Modern Indonesia.* Cambridge: Cambridge University Press.

2013   *Shari'a and Social Engineering: The Implementation of Islamic Law in Contemporary Aceh, Indonesia.* Oxford: Oxford University Press.

2015   "State Shari'a and Its Limits." In *Islam and the Limits of the State: Reconfigurations of Practice, Community and Authority in Contemporary Aceh*, edited by R. Michael Feener, David Kloos, and Annemarie Samuels, 1–23. Leiden: Brill.

Feener, R. Michael, David Kloos, and Annemarie Samuels, eds.

2015   *Islam and the Limits of the State: Reconfigurations of Practice, Community and Authority in Contemporary Aceh.* Leiden: Brill.

Feillard, Andrée

n.d.   "Islam and Female Genital Cutting in Southeast Asia: The Weight of the Past." Unpublished manuscript, 22 pp.

1995   *Islam et Armée dans l'Indonésie Contemporaine: Les Pionniers de la Tradition.* Paris: L'Harmattan.

1997a   "Traditionalist Islam and the State in Indonesia." In *Islam in an Era of Nation-States: Politics and Religious Renewal in Muslim Southeast Asia*, edited by Robert Hefner and Patricia Horvatich, 129–156. Honolulu: University of Hawai'i Press.

1997b   "Indonesia's Emerging Muslim Feminism: Women Leaders on Equality, Inheritance, and Other Gender Issues." *Studia Islamika* 4 (1): 83–111.

1999   "The Veil and Polygamy: Current Debates on Women and Islam in Indonesia." *Moussons* 99:5–27.

Feillard, Andrée, and Rémy Madinier

2011   *The End of Innocence? Indonesian Islam and the Temptation of Radicalism.* Honolulu: University of Hawai'i Press.

Feillard, Andrée, and Lies Marcoes

1998   "Female Circumcision in Indonesia: To 'Islamize' in Ceremony or Secrecy." *Archipel* 56 (1): 337–367.

Feith, Herbert

2007   *The Decline of Constitutional Democracy in Indonesia.* Singapore: Equinox Publishing.

Fillah, Salim A.

2003   *Nikmatnya Pacaran Setelah Pernikahan* (The Pleasure of Courtship after Marriage). Yogyakarta, Indonesia: Pro-U Media.

Ford, Nicholas J., Zahroh Shaluhiyah, and Antono Suryoputro

2007   "A Rather Benign Sexual Culture: Socio-sexual Lifestyles of Youth in Urban Central Java, Indonesia." *Population, Space and Place* 13 (1): 59–76.

Forum Kajian Kitab Kuning (FK3)

2001   *Wajah Baru Relasi Suami Istri: Telaah Kitab 'Uqûd al-Lujjayn* (The New
        Face of Husband-Wife Relations: A Study of the *'Uqûd al-Lujjayn*).
        Yogyakarta, Indonesia: LKis Yogyakarta with The Ford Foundation and FK3.

Foucault, Michel

1990 [1978]   *The History of Sexuality: An Introduction.* Translated by Robert Hurley.
              New York: Random House.

Gade, Anna M.

2004a   *Perfection Makes Practice: Learning, Emotion, and the Recited Qur'ān in
        Indonesia.* Honolulu: University of Hawai'i Press.

2004b   "Motivating Qur'anic Practice in Indonesia by 'Competing in Goodness.'"
        Journal of Ritual Studies 18 (2): 24–42.

Geertz, Clifford

1971 [1968]   *Islam Observed: Religious Development in Morocco and Indonesia.*
              Chicago: University of Chicago Press.

1976 [1960]   *The Religion of Java.* Chicago: University of Chicago Press.

2000   "Religion and Social Change: A Javanese Example." In *The Interpretation of
        Cultures,* 142–169. New York: Basic Books.

Geertz, Hildred

1989 [1961]   *The Javanese Family: A Study of Kinship and Socialization.* Prospect
              Heights, IL: Waveland Press.

George, Kenneth M.

2010   *Picturing Islam: Art and Ethics in a Muslim Lifeworld.* Malden, MA: Wiley
        Blackwell.

Gerke, Solvay

1992   "Indonesian National Development Ideology and the Role of Women."
        Indonesia Circle 21 (59–60): 45–56.

2000   "Global Lifestyles under Local Conditions: The New Indonesian Middle
        Class." In *Consumption in Asia: Lifestyle and Identities,* edited by
        Beng-Huat Chua, 135–158. New York: Routledge.

Ghannam, Farha

2013   *Live and Die Like a Man: Gender Dynamics in Urban Egypt.* Stanford, CA:
        Stanford University Press.

Giddens, Anthony

1991   *Modernity and Self-Identity: Self and Society in the Late Modern Age.*
        Stanford, CA: Stanford University Press.

1992   *The Transformation of Intimacy.* Stanford, CA: Stanford University Press.

Gillespie, Piers

2007   "Current Issues in Indonesian Islam: Analyzing the 2005 Council of
        Indonesian Ulama Fatwa No. 7 Opposing Pluralism, Liberalism and
        Secularism." *Journal of Islamic Studies* 18 (2): 202–240.

Gilmore, David D.

1990   *Manhood in the Making: Cultural Concepts of Masculinity.* New Haven, CT:
        Yale University Press.

Goebel, Zane

2010   *Language, Migration, and Identity: Neighborhood Talk in Indonesia.*
        Cambridge: Cambridge University Press.

Gouda, Frances

1995   *Dutch Culture Overseas: Colonial Practice in the Netherlands Indies,
        1900–1942.* Amsterdam: Amsterdam University Press.

Gregg, Gary S.
2007   *Culture and Identity in a Muslim Society.* Oxford: Oxford University Press.
2012   "Multiple Identities and Their Organization." In *Navigating Multiple Identities: Race, Gender, Culture, Nationality, and Roles,* edited by Ruthellen Josselson and Michele Harway, 13–38. Oxford: Oxford University Press.

Guillot, Claude
1981   *L'Affaire Sadrach: Un Essai de Christianisation à Java au XIXe Siècle.* Paris: Editions de la Maison des Sciences de l'Homme.

Guinness, Patrick
1994   "Local Society and Culture." In *Indonesia's New Order: The Dynamics of Socio-economic Transformation,* edited by Hal Hill, 267–304. Honolulu: University of Hawai'i Press.

Haenni, Patrick
2005   *L'Islam de Marche: L'Autre Revolution Conservatrice.* Paris: Seuil.

Hakim, Lukman
2010   "Conservative Islam Turn or Popular Islam? An Analysis of the Film *Ayat-ayat Cinta.*" *Al-Jami'ah: Journal of Islamic Studies* 48 (1): 101–128.

Hamayotsu, Kikue
2011   "The End of Political Islam? A Comparative Analysis of Religious Parties in the Muslim Democracy of Indonesia." *Journal of Current Southeast Asian Affairs* 30 (3): 133–159.

Handajani, Suzie
2008   "Western Inscriptions on Indonesian Bodies: Representations of Adolescents in Indonesian Female Teen Magazines." *Intersections: Gender and Sexuality in Asia and the Pacific* 18 (October), http://intersections.anu.edu.au.

Harding, Claire
2008   "The Influence of the 'Decadent West': Discourses of the Mass Media on Youth Sexuality in Indonesia." *Intersections: Gender and Sexuality in Asia and the Pacific* 18 (October), http://intersections/anu/edu.au.

Hasan, Noorhaidi
2006   *Laskar Jihad: Islam, Militancy, and the Quest for Identity in Post-New Order Indonesia.* Ithaca, NY: Southeast Asia Program Publications, Southeast Asia Program, Cornell University.
2010   "The Drama of Jihad: The Emergence of Salafi Youth in Indonesia." In *Being Young and Muslim: New Cultural Politics in the Global South and North,* edited by Linda Herrera and Asef Bayat, 49–63. Oxford: Oxford University Press.
2012   "Islamist Party, Electoral Politics, and Da'wah Mobilization among Youth: The Prosperous Justice Party (PKS) in Indonesia." *Journal of Indonesian Islam* 6 (1): 17–47.

Hasanudin, Muhammad, and Kartika Nurrahman
2009   "KAMMI: Membentuk Lapis Inteligensia Muslim-Negarawan" (KAMMI: Forming Muslim Politician-Intellectuals). In *Dynamics of Islamic Student Movements: Iklim Intelektual Islam di Kalangan Aktivis Kampus,* edited by Claudia Nef Saluz, 165–180. Yogyakarta, Indonesia: Resist Book.

Hassan, Riaz
2003   *Faithlines: Muslim Conceptions of Islam and Society.* Oxford: Oxford University Press.

Hasso, Frances
2010   *Consuming Desires: Family Crisis and the State in the Middle East.* Stanford, CA: Stanford University Press.

Hasyim, Syafiq

2006   *Understanding Women in Islam: An Indonesian Perspective.* Jakarta: Solstice.

2015   "Majelis Ulama Indonesia and Pluralism in Indonesia." *Philosophy & Social Criticism* 41 (4–5): 487–495.

Hatley, Barbara

1994   "Cultural Expression." In *Indonesia's New Order: The Dynamics of Socio-economic Transformation,* edited by Hal Hill, 216–266. Honolulu: University of Hawai'i Press.

Hatley, Ron

1984   "Mapping Cultural Regions of Java." In *Other Javas Away from the Kraton,* edited by Ron Hatley, Jim Schiller, Anton Lucas, and Barbara Martin-Schiller, 1–32. Clayton, Australia: Monash University.

Hatley, Ron, Jim Schiller, Anton Lucas, and Barbara Martin-Schiller

1984   *Other Javas Away from the Kraton.* Clayton, Australia: Monash University.

Headley, Stephen C.

2004   *Durga's Mosque: Cosmology, Conversion, and Community in Central Javanese Islam.* Singapore: Institute of Southeast Asian Studies.

Heaton, Tim B., Mark Cammack, and Larry Young

2001   "Why Is the Divorce Rate Declining in Indonesia?" *Journal of Marriage and Family* 63 (2): 480–490.

Hefner, Robert W.

1985   *Hindu Javanese: Tengger Tradition and Islam.* Princeton, NJ: Princeton University Press.

1990   *The Political Economy of Mountain Java: An Interpretive History.* Berkeley: University of California Press.

1993   "Islam, State, and Civil Society: ICMI and the Struggle for the Indonesian Middle Class." *Indonesia* 1:1–35.

2000   *Civil Islam: Muslims and Democratization in Indonesia.* Princeton, NJ: Princeton University Press.

2009a   "The Politics and Cultures of Islamic Education in Southeast Asia." In *Making Modern Muslims: The Politics of Islamic Education in Southeast Asia,* edited by Robert W. Hefner, 1–54. Honolulu: University of Hawai'i Press.

2009b   "Islamic Schools, Social Movements, and Democracy in Indonesia." In *Making Modern Muslims: The Politics of Islamic Education in Southeast Asia,* edited by Robert W. Hefner, 55–105. Honolulu: University of Hawai'i Press.

2011   "Where Have All the Abangan Gone? Religionization and the Decline of Non-standard Islam in Contemporary Indonesia." In *The Politics of Religion in Indonesia: Syncretism, Orthodoxy, and Religious Contention in Java and Bali,* edited by Michel Picard and Remy Madinier, 71–91. New York: Routledge.

Heryanto, Ariel

1999   "Identity Politics of Indonesia's New Rich." In *Culture and Privilege in Capitalist Asia,* edited by Michael Pinches, 159–187. New York: Routledge.

2003   "Public Intellectuals, Media, and Democratization: Cultural Politics of the Middle Classes in Indonesia." In *Challenging Authoritarianism in Southeast Asia: Comparing Indonesia and Malaysia,* edited by Ariel Heryanto and Sumit K. Mandel, 25–48. New York: Routledge.

2008   *Popular Culture in Indonesia: Fluid Identities in Post-Authoritarian Politics.* Edited by Ariel Heryanto. New York: Routledge.

2011   "The New Middle Class and Islam in Indonesian Popular Culture." In *Islam and Popular Culture in Indonesia and Malaysia,* edited by Andrew N. Weintraub, 60–81. New York: Routledge.

2014   *Identity and Pleasure: The Politics of Indonesian Screen Culture.* Singapore: National University of Singapore Press and Kyoto University Press.

Heryanto, Ariel, and Nancy M. Lutz

1988   "The Development of 'Development.'" *Indonesia.* 46:1–24. Ithaca, NY: Cornell Southeast Asian Program Publication.

Hill, Hal

1994   "The Economy." In *Indonesia's New Order: The Dynamics of Socio-economic Transformation,* edited by Hal Hill, 54–122. Honolulu: University of Hawai'i Press.

Hilmy, Masdar

2010   *Islamism and Democracy in Indonesia: Piety and Pragmatism.* Singapore: Institute of Southeast Asian Studies.

Hirschkind, Charles

2006   *The Ethical Soundscape: Cassette Sermons and Islamic Counterpublics.* New York: Columbia University Press.

Hochschild, Arlie R.

1979   "Emotion Work, Feeling Rules, and Social Structure." *American Journal of Sociology* 85 (3): 551–575.

2012 [1989]   *The Second Shift: Working Families and the Revolution at Home.* With Anne Machung. New York: Penguin.

Hoesterey, James B.

2008   "Marketing Morality: The Rise, Fall and Rebranding of Aa Gym." In *Expressing Islam: Religious Life and Politics in Indonesia,* edited by Greg Fealy and Sally White, 95–112. Singapore: Institute of Southeast Asian Studies.

2012   "Prophetic Cosmopolitanism: Islam, Pop Psychology, and Civic Virtue in Indonesia." *City and Society* 24 (1): 38–61.

2015   *Rebranding Islam: Piety, Prosperity, and a Self-help Guru.* Stanford, CA: Stanford University Press.

Hoesterey, James B., and Marshall A. Clark

2012   *"Film Islami:* Gender, Piety and Pop Culture in Post-authoritarian Indonesia." *Asian Studies Review* 36 (2): 207–226.

Horne, Elinor Clark

1974   *Javanese-English Dictionary.* New Haven, CT: Yale University Press.

Howell, Julia Day

2001   "Sufism and the Indonesian Islamic Revival." *Journal of Asian Studies* 60 (3): 701–729.

2007   "Modernity and Islamic Spirituality in Indonesia's New Sufi Networks." In *Sufism and the "Modern" in Islam,* edited by Martin van Bruinessen and Julia Day Howell, 217–240. Vol. 67. London: I. B. Tauris.

2012   "Sufism and Neo-Sufism in Indonesia Today." *RIMA: Review of Indonesian and Malaysian Affairs* 46 (2): 1–24.

Hull, Terence H., and Gavin W. Jones

1994   "Demographic Perspectives." In *Indonesia's New Order: The Dynamics of Socio-economic Transformation,* edited by Hal Hill, 164–168. Honolulu: University of Hawai'i Press.

Hull, Valerie L.
 1996 [1982] "Women in Java's Rural Middle Class: Progress or Regress?" In *Women of Southeast Asia,* edited by Penny Van Esterik, 78–95. Dekalb: Northern Illinois University Press.
Ichwan, Moch Nur
 2013 "Towards a Puritanical Moderate Islam: The Majelis Ulama Indonesia and the Politics of Religious Orthodoxy." In *Contemporary Developments in Indonesian Islam: Explaining the "Conservative Turn,"* edited by Martin van Bruinessen, 60–104. Singapore: Institute of Southeast Asian Studies.
Ida, Rachmah
 2008 "Muslim Women and Contemporary Veiling in Indonesian *Sinetron.*" In *Indonesian Islam in a New Era: How Women Negotiate Their Muslim Identities,* edited by Susan Blackburn, Bianca J. Smith, and Siti Syamsiyatun, 47–67. Clayton, Australia: Monash University Press.
Indiyanto, Agus
 2013 *Agama di Indonesia dalam Angka: Dinamika Demografis Berdasarkan Sensus Penduduk 2000 dan 2010* (Indonesian Religion in Statistics: The Dynamics of Demography Based on the Population Census of 2000 and 2010). Yogyakarta, Indonesia: CRCS e-book.
Ishadi, S. K.
 2011 "Negotiating Mass Media Interests and Heterogeneous Muslim Audiences in the Contemporary Social-political Environment of Indonesia." In *Islam and Popular Culture in Indonesia and Malaysia,* edited by Andrew N. Weintraub, 21–45. New York: Routledge.
Jackson, Elisabeth, and Lyn Parker
 2008 "'Enriched with Knowledge': Modernization and the Future of Islamic Education in Indonesia." *RIMA: Review of Indonesian and Malaysian Affairs* 42 (1): 21–53.
Jamhari, and Fuad Jabali
 2002 *IAIN dan Modernisasi Islam di Indonesia.* Ciputat, Indonesia: Logos Wacana Ilmu.
Jaspan, Helen, and Lewis Hill
 1987 *The Child in the Family: A Study of Childbirth and Child-Rearing in Rural Central Java in the Late 1950s.* Hull, UK: Centre for South-East Asian Studies, University of Hull.
Jay, Robert R.
 1969 *Javanese Villagers: Social Relations in Rural Mojokuto.* Cambridge, MA: MIT Press.
Johnson, Karin, Wendy Gaylord, and Gerald Chamberland
 1993 *Indonesia: A Study of the Educational System of the Republic of Indonesia.* Washington, DC: World Education Series Publication, USAID.
Jones, Carla
 2003 "Dress for *Sukses:* Fashioning Femininity and Nationality in Urban Indonesia." In *Re-orienting Fashion: The Globalization of Asian Dress,* edited by Sandra Niesson, Anne Marie Leshkowich, and Carla Jones, 185–214. London: Berg Publishers.
 2004 "Whose Stress? Emotion Work in Middle-Class Javanese Homes." *Ethnos* 69 (4): 509–528.
 2007 "Fashion and Faith in Urban Indonesia." *Fashion Theory* 11 (2–3): 211–231.

2010a   "Materializing Piety: Gendered Anxieties about Faithful Consumption in Contemporary Urban Indonesia." *American Ethnologist* 37 (4): 617–637.

2010b   "Images of Desire Creating Virtue and Value in an Indonesian Islamic Lifestyle Magazine." *Journal of Middle East Women's Studies* 6 (3): 91–117.

Jones, Gavin W.

1976   "Religion and Education in Indonesia." *Indonesia* 22:19–56. Ithaca, NY: Cornell University Southeast Asia Program Publications.

1994a   *Marriage and Divorce in Islamic South-east Asia.* Kuala Lumpur: Oxford University Press.

1994b   "Demographic Perspectives: Labour Force and Education." In *Indonesia's New Order: The Dynamics of Socio-economic Transformation,* edited by Hal Hill, 145–178. Honolulu: University of Hawai'i Press.

2004   "Not 'When to Marry' but 'Whether to Marry': The Changing Context of Marriage Decisions in East and Southeast Asia." In *(Un)tying the Knot: Ideal and Reality in Asian Marriage,* edited by Gavin W. Jones and Kamalini Ramdas, 3–56. Singapore: Singapore University Press.

2005   "The 'Flight from Marriage' in South-east and East Asia." *Journal of Comparative Family Studies* 1 (1): 93–119.

2009   "Women, Marriage and Family in Southeast Asia." In *Gender Trends in Southeast Asia: Women Now, Women in the Future,* edited by Theresa W. Devasahayam, 12–30. Singapore: Institute of Southeast Asian Studies.

Jones, Gavin W., and Bina Gubhaju

2008   "Trends in Age at Marriage in the Provinces of Indonesia." ARI Working Paper Series No. 105, 29 pp. Singapore: ARI, National University of Singapore.

Jones, Gavin W., and Peter Hagul

2001   "Schooling in Indonesia: Crisis-Related and Longer-Term Issues." *Bulletin of Indonesian Economic Studies* 37 (2): 207–231.

Jones, Gavin W., and Wei-Jun Jean Yeung

2014   "Marriage in Asia." *Journal of Family Issues* 35 (12): 1567–1583.

Kailani, Najib

2011   "Kepanikan Moral dan Dakwah Islam Populer" (Moral Panic and Popular Islamic Proselytizing). *Analisis* 11 (1): 1–16.

2012   *"Forum Lingkar Pena* and Muslim Youth in Contemporary Indonesia." *RIMA: Review of Indonesian and Malaysian Affairs* 46 (1): 33–53.

Karim, Abdul Gaffar

2009   "Nuansa Hijau di Kampus Biru: Gerakan Mahasiswa Islam di UGM" (Green Nuance on a Blue Campus: Islamic Student Movements at UGM). In *Dynamics of Islamic Student Movements: Iklim Intelektual Islam di Kalangan Aktivis Kampus,* edited by Claudia Nef Saluz, xvii–xxiii. Yogyakarta, Indonesia: Resist Books.

Karim, Wazir Jahan

1995   "Bilateralism and Gender in Southeast Asia." In *"Male" and "Female" in Developing Southeast Asia,* edited by Wazir Jahan Karim, 35–74. Oxford, UK: Berg Publishers.

Kartini, Raden Adjeng

1985   *Letters of a Javanese Princess.* Translated by Agnes Louise Symmers. Boston, MA: University Press of America.

Kedaulatan Rakyat

2002   "Soal Penelitian Virginitas Mahasiswi: GKR Hemas: 'Saya tak percaya.'" (The Issue of Research on Coed Virginity: GKR Hemas: "I Don't Believe It"), August 11.

Keeler, Ward

   1987   *Javanese Shadow Plays, Javanese Selves.* Princeton, NJ: Princeton University Press.

   1990   "Speaking of Gender in Java." In *Power and Difference: Gender in Island Southeast Asia,* edited by Jane M. Atkinson and Shelly Errington, 127–152. Stanford, CA: Stanford University Press.

Kersten, Carool

   2016   *Islam in Indonesia: The Contest for Society, Ideas, and Values.* London: Hurst & Company.

Kholid, Setia Furqon, and Ina Agustina

   2013   *Jangan Jatuh Cinta!* (Don't Fall in Love!). Sumedang, Indonesia: Rumah Karya Publishing.

Khosravi, Shahram

   2008   *Young and Defiant in Tehran.* Philadelphia: University of Pennsylvania Press.

Kim, Hyung-Jun

   1998   "The Changing Interpretation of Religious Freedom in Indonesia." *Journal of Southeast Asian Studies* 29 (2): 357–373.

Kleinman, Arthur

   2011   "Introduction." In *Deep China: The Moral Life of the Person,* edited by Arthur Kleinman, Yunxiang Yan, Jing Jun, and Sing Lee, 1–35. Berkeley: University of California Press.

Kleinman, Arthur, and Joan Kleinman

   1985   "Somatization: The Interconnections in Chinese Society among Culture, Depressive Experiences and the Meanings of Pain." In *Culture and Depression: Studies in the Anthropology and Cross-Cultural Psychiatry of Affect and Disorder,* edited by Arthur Kleinman and Byron J. Good, 429–490. Berkeley: University of California Press.

Kloos, David

   2018   *Becoming Better Muslims: Religious Authority and Ethical Improvement in Aceh, Indonesia.* Princeton, NJ: Princeton University Press.

Koentjaraningrat, R. N.

   1957   *A Preliminary Description of the Javanese Kinship System.* New Haven, CT: Yale University, Southeast Asia Studies.

   1989   *Javanese Culture.* Singapore: Oxford University Press.

Krier, Sarah E.

   2011   "Sex Sells, or Does It? Discourses of Sex and Sexuality in Popular Women's Magazines in Contemporary Indonesia." In *Islam and Popular Culture in Indonesia and Malaysia,* edited by Andrew N. Weintraub, 123–144. New York: Routledge, Taylor & Francis.

Kuipers, Joel C.

   1998   *Language, Identity, and Marginality in Indonesia: The Changing Nature of Ritual Speech on the Island of Sumba.* Studies in the Social and Cultural Foundations of Language 18. Cambridge: Cambridge University Press.

Kuipers, Joel C., and Askuri

   2017   "Islamization and Identity in Indonesia: The Case of Arabic Names in Java." *Indonesia* 103 (April): 25–49.

Kurnia, Adi

   2005   *All about Gaul!* Bandung, Indonesia: Simbiosa Rekatama Media.

Kuru, Ahmet T.
    2009   *Secularism and State Policies toward Religion: The United States, France, and Turkey.* New York: Cambridge University Press.

Laffan, Michael F.
    2003   *Islamic Nationhood and Colonial Indonesia: The Umma below the Winds.* London: RoutledgeCurzon.
    2011   *The Makings of Indonesian Islam: Orientalism and the Narration of a Sufi Past.* Princeton, NJ: Princeton University Press.

Liddle, R. William
    1996   "The Islamic Turn in Indonesia: A Political Explanation." *Journal of Asian Studies* 55 (3): 613–634.

Lim, Merlyna
    2013   "The Internet and Everyday Life in Indonesia: A New Moral Panic?" *Bijdragen tot de Taal-, Land- en Volkenkunde* 169:133–147.

Lindquist, Johan
    2002   "The Anxieties of Mobility: Development, Migration and Tourism in the Indonesian Borderlands." PhD diss., University of Stockholm, Sweden.
    2004   "Veils and Ecstasy: Negotiating Shame in the Indonesian Borderlands." *Ethnos* 69 (4): 487–508.

Lindsey, Timothy
    2008   *Indonesia, Law, and Society.* Edited by Timothy Lindsey. Leichhardt, Australia: Federation Press.
    2012   *Islam, Law, and the State in Southeast Asia.* Vol. 1, *Indonesia (Islam and the Law in Southeast Asia).* New York: I. B. Tauris.

Locher-Scholten, Elsbeth
    2000   *Women and the Colonial State: Essays on Gender and Modernity in the Netherlands Indies, 1900–1942.* Amsterdam: Amsterdam University Press.

Luhrmann, Tanya M.
    2006   "Subjectivity." *Anthropological Theory* 6 (3): 345–361.

Lukens-Bull, Ronald A.
    2001   "Two Sides of the Same Coin: Modernity and Tradition in Islamic Education in Indonesia." *Anthropology and Education* 32 (3): 350–372.
    2005   *A Peaceful Jihad: Negotiating Identity and Modernity in Muslim Java.* New York: Palgrave.
    2013   *Islamic Higher Education in Indonesia: Continuity and Conflict.* New York: Springer.

Machmudi, Yon
    2008a   *Islamising Indonesia: The Rise of Jemaah Tarbiyah and the Prosperous Justice Party (PKS).* Canberra, Australia: ANU e-press.
    2008b   "The Emergence of *New Santri* in Indonesia." *Journal of Indonesian Islam* 2 (1): 69–102.

Mackie, Jamie, and Andrew MacIntyre
    1994   "Politics." In *Indonesia's New Order: The Dynamics of Socio-economic Transformation,* edited by Hal Hill, 1–53. Honolulu: University of Hawai'i Press.

Madrid, Robin
    1999   "Islamic Students in the Indonesian Student Movement, 1998–1999: Forces for Moderation." *Bulletin of Concerned Asian Scholars* 31 (3): 17–32.

Mahmood, Saba
    2003   "Ethical Formation and Politics of Individual Autonomy in Contemporary
            Egypt." *Social Research* 70 (3): 837–866.
    2005   *The Politics of Piety: The Islamic Revival and the Feminist Subject.* Princeton,
            NJ: Princeton University Press.

Makdisi, George
    1981   *The Rise of Colleges: Institutions of Learning in Islam and the West.* New York:
            Columbia University Press.

Mandaville, Peter
    2007   "Globalization and the Politics of Religious Knowledge: Pluralizing Authority
            in the Muslim World. *Theory, Culture, Society* 24 (2): 101–115.

Manderson, Lenore, and Pranee Liamputtong
    2002   *Coming of Age in South and Southeast Asia: Youth, Courtship, and Sexuality.*
            Richmond, VA: Curzon.

Manns, Howard
    2010   "Indonesian Slang in Internet Chatting." In *Studies in Slang and Slogans*, edited by
            S. T. Babatunde, A. Adetunji, and M. Adedimeji, 71–99. Munich: Lincom Europa.

Martin, Bernice
    2001   "The Pentecostal Gender Paradox: A Cautionary Tale for the Sociology of
            Religion." In *The Blackwell Companion to the Sociology of Religion*, edited by
            Richard K. Fenn, 52–66. Malden, MA: Blackwell Publishers.

Masrul, Ahmad
    2015   *Pacaran No Way! Why?* (Dating No Way! Why?). Jakarta: PT Gramedia.

Matthews, Jill J.
    1984   *The Historical Construction of Femininity in Twentieth-Century Australia.*
            Sydney, Australia: George Allen & Unwin.

McIntosh, Janet
    2009   *The Edge of Islam: Power, Personhood, and Ethno-Religious Boundaries on the
            Kenya Coast.* Durham, NC: Duke University Press.

McNally, Stephen, Jeffrey Grierson, and Irwan Martua Hidayana
    2015   "Belonging, Community, and Identity: Gay Men in Indonesia." In *Sex and
            Sexualities in Contemporary Indonesia: Sexual Politics, Health, Diversity, and
            Representations*, edited by Linda Rae Bennett and Sharyn Graham Davies,
            203–219. New York: Routledge.

Mernissi, Fatima
    1975   *Beyond the Veil: Male-Female Dynamics in Modern Muslim Society.*
            Bloomington: Indiana University Press.
    1991   *The Veil and the Male Elite: A Feminist Interpretation of Women's Rights in
            Islam.* New York: Perseus Books Publishing.

Merry, Sally E.
    1988   "Legal Pluralism." *Law & Society Review* 22 (5): 869–896.

Mir-Hosseini, Ziba
    1999   *Islam and Gender: The Religious Debate in Contemporary Iran.* Princeton, NJ:
            Princeton University Press.
    2003   "The Construction of Gender in Islamic Legal Thought and Strategies for
            Reform." *Hawwa* 1 (1): 1–28.

Mir-Hosseini, Ziba, and Vanja Hamzić
    2010   *Control and Sexuality: The Revival of Zina Laws in Muslim Contexts.* London:
            Women Living Under Muslim Laws.

Muhapi
2006   *Gaul Tapi Syar'i* (Sociable but Shari'a-Minded). Jakarta: Penerbit Karya Ilmu.
Mulia, Siti M., and Mark E. Cammack
2007   "Toward a Just Marriage Law: Empowering Indonesian Women through a
    Counter Legal Draft to the Indonesian Compilation of Islamic Law." In *Islamic
    Law in Contemporary Indonesia: Ideas and Institutions,* edited by R. Michael
    Feener and Mark E. Cammack, 128–145. Cambridge, MA: Harvard Law School,
    Islamic Legal Studies Program.
Mulkhan, Abdul Munir
2010   *Kiai Ahmad Dahlan: Jejak Pembaruan Social dan Kemanusiaan* (Kyai Ahmad
    Dahlan: Traces of Social Renewal and Humanitarian). Jakarta: Kompas Books.
Munir, Lily Zakiyah
2002   "'He Is Your Garment and You Are His . . .': Religious Precepts, Interpretations,
    and Power Relations in Marital Sexuality among Javanese Muslim Women."
    Sojourn: Journal of Social Issues in Southeast Asia 17 (2): 191–220.
Nadia, Asma
2008   *Chat for a Date.* Yogyakarta, Indonesia: Lingkar Pena.
Nakamura, Mitsuo
1983   *The Crescent Arises over the Banyan Tree: A Study of the Muhammadiyah
    Movement in a Central Javanese Town.* Yogyakarta, Indonesia: Gadjah Mada
    University Press.
Nasir, Mohamad Abdun
n.d.   "The Islamic *Pesantren* Discourses on Gender and Sexuality in Contemporary
    Indonesia." Unpublished manuscript. 30 pp.
Natalia, Livia
2007   *Kamus Istilah Gaul SMS* (A Dictionary of Gaul for Text Messaging). Jakarta:
    GagasMedia.
Niehof, Anke, and Firman Lubis
2003   *Two Is Enough: Family Planning in Indonesia under the New Order, 1968–1998.*
    Leiden: KITLV Press.
Nilan, Pam
2006   "The Reflexive Youth Culture of Devout Young Muslims in Indonesia." In
    Global Youth? Hybrid Identities, Plural Worlds, edited by Pam Nilan and
    Carles Feixa, 91–110. London: Routledge.
2008   "Youth Transitions to Urban, Middle-Class Marriage in Indonesia: Faith,
    Family and Finances." *Journal of Youth Studies* 11 (1): 65–82.
2009   "The 'Spirit of Education' in Indonesian Pesantren." *British Journal of Sociology
    of Education* 30 (2): 219–232.
Nilan, Pam, Lyn Parker, Linda Bennett, and Kathryn Robinson
2011   "Indonesian Youth Looking towards the Future." *Journal of Youth Studies* 14 (6):
    709–728.
Nishimura, Shigeo
1995   "The Development of Pancasila Moral Education in Indonesia." *Southeast Asian
    Studies* 33 (3): 303–316.
Njoto-Feillard, Gwenaël
2012   *L'Islam et la Réinvention du Capitalisme en Indonésie.* Paris: Karthala.
Noer, Deliar
1973   *The Modernist Muslim Movement in Indonesia, 1900–42.* New York: Oxford
    University Press.

Noor, Farish A.

2011   "The Partai Keadilan Sejahtera (PKS) in the Landscape of Indonesian Islamist Politics: Cadre-Training as Mode of Preventive Radicalisation?" Working Paper. Singapore: S. Rajaratnam School of International Studies.

Nurmila, Nina

2009   *Women, Islam, and Everyday Life: Renegotiating Polygamy in Indonesia.* London: Routledge.

Ochs, Elinor, and Bambi Schieffelin

2001   "Language Acquisition and Socialization: Three Developmental Stories and Their Implications." In *Linguistic Anthropology: A Reader,* edited by Alessandro Duranti, 263–301. New York: Wiley-Blackwell.

Oetomo, Dede

1990   "The *Bahasa Indonesia* of the Middle Class." *Prisma* 50 (September): 68–79.

Oey-Gardiner, Mayling

1991   "Gender Differences in Schooling in Indonesia." *Bulletin of Indonesian Economic Studies* 27 (l): 57–79.

Ong, Aihwa

2010 [1987]   *Spirits of Resistance and Capitalist Discipline: Factory Women in Malaysia.* New York: SUNY Press.

Ong, Aihwa, and Michael G. Peletz

1995   "Introduction." In *Bewitching Women, Pious Men: Gender and Body Politics in Southeast Asia,* edited by Aihwa Ong and Michael G. Peletz, 1–17. Berkeley: University of California Press.

Ortner, Sherry B.

1997   "Gender Hegemonies." In *Making Gender: The Politics and Erotics of Culture,* 139–172. Boston, MA: Beacon Press.

2005   "Subjectivity and Cultural Critique." *Anthropological Theory* 5 (1): 31–52.

O'Shaughnessy, Kate

2009   *Gender, State, and Social Power in Contemporary Indonesia: Divorce and Marriage Law.* Oxford: Routledge.

Osman, Mohamed Nawab Mohamed

2010   "The Transnational Network of Hizbut Tahrir Indonesia." *South East Asia Research* 18 (4): 735–755.

Parker, Lyn

2008a   "To Cover the Aurat: Veiling, Sexual Morality and Agency among the Muslim Minangkabau, Indonesia." *Intersections: Gender and Sexuality in Asia and the Pacific* 16 (March), http://intersections.anu.edu.au.

2008b   "Theorising Adolescent Sexualities in Indonesia—Where 'Something Different Happens.'" *Intersections: Gender and Sexuality in Asia and the Pacific* 18 (October), http://intersections.anu.edu.au.

2009   "Religion, Class and Schooled Sexuality among Minangkabau Teenage Girls." *Bijdragen tot de Taal-, Land-en Volkenkunde / Journal of the Humanities and Social Sciences of Southeast Asia* 165 (1): 62–94.

2016   "Pouring Out One's Heart: Close Friendships among Minangkabau Young People." In *Youth Identities and Social Transformations in Modern Indonesia,* edited by Kathryn Robinson, 94–112. Leiden: Brill.

Parker, Lyn, and Linda Bennett, eds.

2008   "Body, Sexuality and Gender among Contemporary Indonesian Youth." *Intersections: Gender and Sexuality in Asia and the Pacific* 18 (October), http://intersections.anu.edu.au.

Parker, Lyn, Chang-Yau Hoon, and Raihani
    2014   "Young People's Attitudes towards Inter-ethnic and Inter-religious Socializing, Courtship and Marriage in Indonesia." *South East Asia Research* 22 (4): 467–486.

Parker, Lyn, and Pam Nilan
    2013   *Adolescents in Contemporary Indonesia.* New York: Routledge.

Pausacker, Helen
    2013   *Morality and the Nation: Pornography and Indonesia's Islamic Defenders Front.* PhD diss., University of Melbourne.

Peacock, James L.
    1978a   *Purifying the Faith: The Muhammadijah Movement in Indonesian Islam.* Menlo Park, CA: Benjamin/Cummings Publishing.
    1978b   *Muslim Puritans: Reformist Psychology in Southeast Asian Islam.* Berkeley: University of California Press.

Peletz, Michael G.
    1995   "Neither Reasonable nor Responsible: Contrasting Representations of Masculinity in a Malay Society." In *Bewitching Women, Pious Men: Gender and Body Politics in Southeast Asia,* edited by Aihwa Ong and Michael G. Peletz, 76–123. Berkeley: University of California Press.
    1996   *Reason and Passion: Representations of Gender in a Malay Society.* Berkeley: University of California Press.
    2007   *Gender, Sexuality, and Body Politics in Modern Asia.* Ann Arbor, Michigan: Association for Asian Studies.
    2009   *Gender Pluralism: Southeast Asia since Early Modern Times.* New York: Routledge.

Pemberton, John
    1994   *On the Subject of "Java."* Ithaca, NY: Cornell University Press.

Platzdasch, Bernhard
    2009   *Islamism in Indonesia: Politics in the Emerging Democracy.* Singapore: Institute of Southeast Asian Studies.

Porter, Donald
    2002   *Managing Politics and Islam in Indonesia.* New York: Routledge.

Prasetyo, Eko
    2003   *Islam Kiri: Jalan Menuju Revolusi Sosial* (Leftist Islam: The Road to Social Revolution). Yogyakarta, Indonesia: Insist Press.

Prasetyo, Wiwid
    2013   *Bismillah, Saya Mantap Menikah . . .* (In the Name of Allah, I Am Ready to Marry . . .). Yogyakarta, Indonesia: Semesta Hikmah.

Putnam, Robert D., with Robert Leonardi and Raffaella Y. Nanetti
    1993   *Making Democracy Work: Civic Traditions in Modern Italy.* Princeton, NJ: Princeton University Press.

Quinn, Naomi
    1996   "Culture and Contradiction: The Case of Americans Reasoning about Marriage." *Ethos* 24 (3): 391–425.

Rachman, Eileen, and Petrina Omar
    2004   *Gaul: Meraih lebih Banyak Kesempatan* (Gaul: Take Advantage of More Opportunities). Jakarta: Gramedia Pustaka Utama.

Radar Jogja
    2002   "Iip Wijayanto, direktur LSC & K: 'Silakan Bikin Penelitian Tandingan.'" (Iip Wijayanto, Director of LSC & K: "Please Do Comparative Research"). August 4.

Rakhmat, Andi, and Mukhamad Najib

2001   *Gerakan Perlawanan dari Masjid Kampus* (The Opposition Movement from the Campus Mosque). Surakarta, Indonesia: Purimedia.

Ramage, Douglas E.

1995   *Politics in Indonesia: Democracy, Islam, and the Ideology of Tolerance.* New York: Routledge.

Reid, Anthony

1988   *Southeast Asia in the Age of Commerce, 1450–1680.* Vol 1, *The Land below the Winds.* New Haven, CT: Yale University Press.

Ricklefs, Merle C.

1993   *A History of Modern Indonesia since c. 1300.* Stanford, CA: Stanford University Press.

2006   *Mystic Synthesis in Java: A History of Islamization from the Fourteenth to the Early Nineteenth Centuries.* Norwalk, CT: Eastbridge Press.

2007   *Polarising Javanese Society: Islamic and Other Visions, c. 1830–1930.* Singapore: Institute of Southeast Asian Studies, National University of Singapore.

2008   *A History of Modern Indonesia since c. 1200.* 4th ed. Stanford, CA: Stanford University Press.

2012   *Islamisation and Its Opponents in Java: A Political, Social, Cultural, and Religious History, c. 1930 to the Present.* Honolulu: University of Hawai'i Press.

Rif'an, Ahmad Rifa'i

2014   *Jomblo Sebelum Nikah* (Single before Married). Jakarta: PT Elex Media Komputindo.

Rinaldo, Rachel

2013   *Mobilizing Piety: Islam and Feminism in Indonesia.* New York: Oxford University Press.

Robinson, Kathryn

1999   "Women: Difference versus Diversity." In *Indonesia Beyond Suharto: Polity, Economy, Society, Transition,* edited by Donald K. Emmerson, 237–261. Armonk, NY: M. E. Sharpe.

2009   *Gender, Islam, and Democracy in Indonesia.* New York: Routledge.

2016   *Youth Identities and Social Transformations in Modern Indonesia.* Edited by Kathryn Robinson. Boston, MA: Brill.

Robinson, Kathryn, and Iwu Dwisetyani Utomo

2003   "Introduction: Youth, Sexuality, and Personal Life in Indonesia." *RIMA (Review of Indonesian and Malaysian Affairs)* 37 (1): 5–16.

Robinson, Kathryn, Iwu Dwisetyani Utomo, and Christine Campbell, eds.

2003   Special edition on *Youth, Sexuality, and Personal Life in Indonesia, RIMA (Review of Indonesian and Malaysian Affairs)* 37(1).

Rohani, Wining

2004   *Gaul Smart dengan Dunia* (Social Smarts for Interacting with the World). Yogyakarta, Indonesia: Gloria Graffa.

Roosa, John

2006   *Pretext for Mass Murder: The September 30th Movement and Suharto's Coup d'état in Indonesia.* Madison: University of Wisconsin Press.

Ropi, Ismatu

2012   "The Politics of Regulating Religion: State, Civil Society and the Quest for Religious Freedom in Modern Indonesia." PhD diss., Australian National University, Canberra, Australia.

Rosyad, Rifki
2007   A Quest for True Islam: A Study of the Islamic Resurgence Movement among the Young in Bandung, Indonesia. Canberra, Australia: ANU e-press.
Rosyadi, Said, and Armyta D. Pratiwi
2016   Menikah Saja (Just Marry). Jakarta: Qultum Media.
Rudnyckyj, Daromir
2010   Spiritual Economies: Islam, Globalization, and the Afterlife of Development. Ithaca, NY: Cornell University Press.
Rumadi
2015   Islamic Post-traditionalism in Indonesia. Singapore: Institute of Southeast Asian Studies.
Sahertian, Debby
1999   Kamus Bahasa Gaul (Dictionary of Bahasa Gaul). Jakarta: Pusaka Sinar Harapan.
Saifuddin, Achmad Fedyani, and Irwan Martua Hidayana
1997   Seksualitas Remaja (The Sexuality of Adolescents). Jakarta: Pustaka Sinar Harapan and The Ford Foundation.
Salim, Arskal
2008   Challenging the Secular State: The Islamization of Law in Modern Indonesia. Honolulu: University of Hawai'i Press.
Salim, Hairus
1999   Menjadi Perempuan: Studi Kasus dalam Masyarakat Jawa Islam (Becoming Woman: A Case Study from Muslim Java). Jakarta: LSPPA and the Ford Foundation.
Salim, Hairus, Najib Kailani, and Nikmal Azekiyah
2011   Politik Ruang Public Sekolah: Negosiasi dan Resistensi di SMUN di Yogyakarta (Politics in the Public Schools: Negotiation and Resistance in Public High School in Yogyakarta). Monograph Series on Practicing Pluralism. Yogyakarta, Java: Center for Religious and Cross-Cultural Studies (CRCS), Gadjah Mada University.
Salim, Hairus, and Muhammad Ridwan, eds.
1999   Kultura Hibrida: Anak Muda NU di Jalur Kultural (Hybrid Culture: NU Youth in the Cultural Channel). Yogyakarta, Indonesia: LKiS.
Salim, Muhammad Najib
2004   Zaman Gaul: Tips Menjadi Gaul bagi Remaja Islam Tanpa Kehilangan Identitas Keislamannya (The Era of Gaul Sociability: Tips for Muslim Youth on How to Be Gaul without Losing Your Muslim Identity). Yogyakarta, Indonesia: Diva Press.
Saluz, Claudia Nef, ed.
2009   Dynamics of Islamic Student Movements: Iklim Intelektual Islam di Kalangan Aktivis Kampus. Yogyakarta, Indonesia: Resist Book.
Schielke, Samuli
2009a   "Being Good in Ramadan: Ambivalence, Fragmentation, and the Moral Self in the Lives of Young Egyptians." Journal of the Royal Anthropological Institute 15 (S1): S24–S40.
2009b   "Ambivalent Commitments: Troubles of Morality, Religiosity and Aspiration among Young Egyptians." Journal of Religion in Africa 39 (2): 158–185.
2015   Egypt in the Future Tense: Hope, Frustration, and Ambivalence before and after 2011. Bloomington: Indiana University Press.

Schröter, Susanne

2013　"Gender and Islam in Southeast Asia: An Overview." In *Gender and Islam in Southeast Asia: Women's Rights Movements, Religious Resurgence, and Local Traditions,* edited by Susanne Schröter, 7–54. Leiden: Brill.

Schulz, Dorothea

2011　*Muslims and New Media in West Africa: Pathways to God.* Bloomington: Indiana University Press.

Schwarz, Adam, and Jonathan Paris, eds.

1999　*The Politics of Post-Suharto Indonesia.* New York: Council on Foreign Relations Press.

Sears, Laurie J.

1996a　*Fantasizing the Feminine in Indonesia.* Edited by Laurie Sears. Durham, NC: Duke University Press.

1996b　"Introduction: Fragile Identities." In *Fantasizing the Feminine in Indonesia,* edited by Laurie J. Sears, 1–44. Durham, NC: Duke University Press.

Sen, Krishna

2002　"Indonesian Women at Work: Reframing the Subject." In *Gender and Power in Affluent Asia,* edited by Krishna Sen and Maila Stivens, 35–62. London: Routledge.

Seo, Myengkyo

2013　"Falling in Love and Changing Gods: Inter-religious Marriage and Religious Conversion in Java, Indonesia." *Indonesia and the Malay World* 41 (119): 76–96.

Shiraishi, Saya S.

1997　*Young Heroes: The Indonesian Family in Politics* (Studies on Southeast Asia, No. 22). Ithaca, NY: Cornell University Press.

Shore, Bradd

1990　"Human Ambivalence and the Structuring of Moral Values." *Ethos* 18 (2): 165–179.

1996　*Culture in Mind: Cognition, Culture, and the Problem of Meaning.* Oxford: Oxford University Press.

Sidel, John Thayer

2006　*Riots, Pogroms, Jihad: Religious Violence in Indonesia.* Ithaca, NY: Cornell University Press.

Simon, Gregory M.

2014　*Caged on the Outside: Moral Subjectivity, Selfhood, and Islam in Minangkabau, Indonesia.* Honolulu: University of Hawai'i Press.

Singerman, Diane

2007　*The Economic Imperatives among Youth in the Middle East.* Middle East Youth Initiative Working Paper 6. Washington, DC: Wolfensohn Center for Development, the Brookings Institute and Dubai School of Government.

Situmorang, Augustina

1999　"Family Planning for Indonesian Unmarried Youth: Views from Medan." *Development Bulletin* 47:33–35.

2001　"Adolescent Reproductive Health and Premarital Sex in Medan." PhD diss., Australian National University.

2003　"Adolescent Reproductive Health in Indonesia." *STARH Program. Jakarta: Johns Hopkins University,* accessed April 23, 2014, http://citeseerx.ist. psu.edu .

Slama, Martin

2010   "The Agency of the Heart: Internet Chatting as Youth Culture in Indonesia."
        Social Anthropology 18 (3): 316–330.

Smith-Hefner, Nancy J.

1981   "To Level or Not to Level: Codes of Politeness and Prestige in Rural Java." In
        *Proceedings from the Chicago Linguistics Society Parasession on Language and
        Behavior, 17th Regional Meeting*, 211–217. Chicago: University of Chicago Press.

1983   *Language and Social Identity: Speaking Javanese in Tengger*. PhD diss.,
        University of Michigan, Ann Arbor.

1987   "Cara Tengger: Notes on a Non-standard Dialect of Javanese." In *Studies in
        Austronesian Linguistics*, edited by Richard McGinn, 203–233. Athens: Ohio
        University Press.

1988a   "Women and Politeness: The Javanese Example." *Language in Society* 17 (4): 535–554.

1988b   "The Linguistic Socialization of Javanese Children in Two Communities."
        Anthropological Linguistics 30 (2): 166–198.

1989   "A Social History of Language Change in Highland East Java." *Journal of Asian
        Studies* 48 (2): 257–271.

1999   *Khmer American: Identity and Moral Education in a Diasporic Community*.
        Berkeley: University of California Press.

2005   "The New Muslim Romance: Changing Patterns of Courtship and Marriage
        among Educated Javanese Youth." *Journal of Southeast Asian Studies* 36 (3):
        441–459.

2006   "Reproducing Respectability: Sex and Sexuality among Muslim Javanese
        Youth." *RIMA (Review of Indonesian and Malay Affairs)* 40 (1): 143–172.

2007   "Javanese Women and the Veil in Post-Soeharto Indonesia." *Journal of Asian
        Studies* 66 (2): 389–420.

2009a   "'Hypersexed' Youth and the New Muslim Sexology in Contemporary Java."
        Review of Indonesian and Malay Affairs 43 (1): 209–244.

2009b   "Women, Language Shift, and Ideologies of Self in Indonesia." *Journal of
        Linguistic Anthropology* 19 (1): 57–77.

Sneddon, James N.

2003   *The Indonesian Language: Its History and Role in Modern Society*. Sydney:
        University of New South Wales Press.

2006   *Colloquial Jakartan Indonesian*. Vol. 581. Pacific Linguistics, Research School
        of Pacific and Asian Studies. Canberra: Australian National University.

Sofjan, Dicky

2013   *Religion and Television in Indonesia: Ethics Surrounding Dakwatainment*.
        Geneva, Switzerland: Globethics.net.

Srimulyani, Eka

2007   "Muslim Women and Education in Indonesia: The *Pondok Pesantren*
        Experience." *Asia Pacific Journal of Education* 27 (1): 85–99.

2012   *Women from Traditional Islamic Educational Institutions in Indonesia:
        Negotiating Public Spaces*. Amsterdam: Amsterdam University Press.

Steedly, Mary M.

2013   *Rifle Reports: A Story of Indonesian Independence*. Berkeley: University of
        California Press.

Steenbrink, Karel

2014   *Catholics in Indonesia, 1808–1942: A Documented History*. Vol. 2, *The
        Spectacular Growth of a Self-Confident Minority, 1903–1942*. Boston, MA: Brill.

Stoler, Ann L.
   1996   "A Sentimental Education: Native Servants and the Cultivation of
           European Children in the Netherlands Indies." In *Fantasizing the Feminine
           in Indonesia,* edited by Laurie J. Sears, 71–91. Durham, NC: Duke University
           Press.
Stowasser, Barbara
   1998   "Gender Issues and Contemporary Qur'an Interpretation." In *Islam, Gender,
           and Social Change,* edited by Yvonne Y. Haddad and John L. Esposito, 30–44.
           New York: Oxford University Press.
Straits Times
   2002   "Free Sex the Norm among Yogyakarta's Varsity Students." August 7.
Stange, Paul
   1992   *Religious Change in Contemporary Southeast Asia.* Cambridge: Cambridge
           University Press.
Sullivan, Norma
   1994   *Masters and Managers: The Study of Gender Relations in Urban Java.*
           St Leonards, Australia: Allen and Unwin.
Supriyanti, Nanik
   2004   *Penggunaan Bahasa Gaul dalam Majalah Remaja* (The Use of Bahasa Gaul in
           Teen Magazines). Bachelor's thesis, Gadjah Mada University, Yogyakarta,
           Indonesia.
Suryakusuma, Julia
   1996   "The State and Sexuality in New Order Indonesia." In *Fantasizing the Feminine
           in Indonesia,* edited by Laurie J. Sears, 92–119. Durham, NC: Duke University
           Press.
Sutherland, Heather
   1979   *The Making of a Bureaucratic Elite: The Colonial Transformation of the Javanese
           Priyayi.* Singapore: Heinemann Educational.
Syamsiyatun, Siti
   2007   "A Daughter in the Indonesian Muhammadiyah: Nasyiatul Aisyiyah Negotiates
           a New Status and Image." *Journal of Islamic Studies* 18 (1): 69–94.
   2008   "Women Negotiating Feminism and Islamism: The Experiences of Nasyiatul
           Aisyiyah, 1985–2005." In *Indonesian Islam in a New Era: How Women
           Negotiate Their Muslim Identities,* edited by Susan Blackburn, Bianca J. Smith,
           and Siti Syamsiyatun, 139–166. Clayton, Australia: Monash University Press.
Tanner, Nancy
   1974   "Matrifocality in Indonesia and Africa and among Black Americans." In
           Woman, Culture, and Society, edited by Michelle Rosaldo and Louise Lamphere,
           129–156. Stanford, CA: Stanford University Press.
Tanter, Richard, and Kenneth Young, eds.
   1990   *The Politics of Middle Class Indonesia.* Monash, Australia: Monash Asia
           Institute.
Tausiyah (@tausiyah)
   2013   *Tausiyah Cinta: No Khalwat Until Akad* (Tausiyah Love: No Being Alone
           Together until Married). Jakarta: QultumMedia.
Taylor, Jean Gelman
   2003   *Indonesia: Peoples and Histories.* New Haven, CT: Yale University Press.
Thomas, R. Murray
   1988   "The Islamic Revival and Indonesian Education." *Asian Survey* 28 (9): 897–915.

Tickamyer, Ann R., and Siti Kusujiarti

2012 *Power, Change, and Gender Relations in Rural Java: A Tale of Two Villages.* Athens: Ohio University Center for International Studies.

Tiwon, Sylvia

1996 "Models and Maniacs: Articulating the Female in Indonesia." In *Fantasizing the Feminine in Indonesia,* edited by Laurie J. Sears, 47–70. Durham, NC: Duke University Press.

Toer, Pramoedya Anata

2002 *The Girl from the Coast.* New York: Hyperion.

Tsing, Anna L.

1993 *In the Realm of the Diamond Queen: Marginality in an Out-of-the-Way Place.* Princeton, NJ: Princeton University Press.

Tsuchiya, Kenji

1987 *Democracy and Leadership: The Rise of the Taman Siswa Movement in Indonesia.* Honolulu: University of Hawai'i Press.

Tucker, Judith E.

2008 *Women, Family, and Gender in Islamic law.* Vol. 3. Cambridge, UK: Cambridge University Press.

Utomo, Ariane J.

2014 "Marrying Up? Trends in Age and Education Gaps among Married Couples in Indonesia." *Journal of Family Issues* 35 (12): 1683–1706.

Utomo, Iwu Dwisetyani

2002 "Sexual Values and Early Experiences among Young People in Jakarta." In *Coming of Age in South and Southeast Asia: Youth, Courtship and Sexuality,* edited by Loraine Manderson and Pranee Liamputtong, 207–227. Richmond, UK: Curzon Press.

2003 "Reproductive Health Education in Indonesia: School versus Parents' Roles in Providing Sexuality Information." *RIMA (Review of Indonesian and Malaysian Affairs)* 37 (1): 107–134.

Utomo, Iwu Dwisetyani, and Peter McDonald

2009 "Adolescent Reproductive Health in Indonesia: Contested Values and Policy Inaction." *Studies in Family Planning* 40 (2): 133–146.

van Bruinessen, Martin

1990 "Kitab Kuning: Books in Arabic Script Used in the Pesantren Milieu: Comments on a New Collection in the KITLV Library." *Bijdragen tot de Taal-, Land-en Volkenkunde* 146 (2/3): 226–269.

1994 "Pesantren and Kitab Kuning: Maintenance and Continuation of a Tradition of Religious Learning." In *Texts from the Islands: Oral and Written Traditions of Indonesia and the Malay World,* edited by Wolfgang Marschall, 121–145. Bern: University of Bern, Institute of Ethnology.

1995 "Shari'a Court, Tarekat and Pesantren: Religious Institutions in the Baten Sultanate." *Archipel* 50:165–200.

2007 "Saints, Politicians and Sufi Bureaucrats: Mysticism and Politics in Indonesia's New Order." In *Sufism and the "Modern" in Islam,* edited by Martin van Bruinessen and Julia Howell, 92–112. London: IB Tauris.

2008 "Traditionalist and Modernist Pesantren in Contemporary Indonesia." In *The Madrasa in Asia: Political Activism and Transnational Linkages,* edited by Farish Noor, Yoginder Sikand, and Martin van Bruinessen, 217–246. Amsterdam: Amsterdam University Press.

2013   "Introduction: Contemporary Developments in Conservative Islam: Explaining the 'Conservative Turn' of the Early 21st Century." In *Contemporary Developments in Indonesian Islam: Explaining the "Conservative Turn,"* edited by Martin van Bruinessen, 1–20. Singapore: Institute of Southeast Asian Studies.

van Dijk, Kees
2001   *A Country in Despair: Indonesia between 1997 and 2000.* Leiden: Brill.

van Doorn-Harder, Nelly
2002   "The Indonesian Islamic Debate on a Woman President." *Sojourn: Journal of Social Issues in Southeast Asia* 17 (2): 164–190.

2006   *Women Shaping Islam: Reading the Qur'an in Indonesia.* Urbana: University of Chicago Press.

2007   Reconsidering Authority: Indonesian *fiqh* Texts about Women." In *Islamic Law in Contemporary Indonesia: Ideas and Institutions,* edited by R. Michael Feener and Mark E. Cammack, 27–43. Cambridge, MA: Harvard University Press.

2013   "Polygamy and Harmonious Families: Indonesian Debates on Gender and Marriage." In *Gender and Islam in Southeast Asia: Women's Rights Movements, Religious Resurgence, and Local Traditions,* edited by Susanne Schröter, 55–71. Leiden, Boston, MA: Brill.

van Klinken, Gerry
2007   *Communal Violence and Democratization in Indonesia: Small Town Wars.* Abingdon, UK: Routledge.

van Klinken, Gerry, and Ward Berenschot, eds.
2014   *In Search of Middle Indonesia: Middle Classes in Provincial Towns.* Leiden: Brill.

van Leeuwen, Lizzy
2005   *Lost in Mall: An Ethnography of Middle Class Jakarta in the 1990s.* PhD diss., University of Amsterdam.

Van Niel, Robert
1984   *The Emergence of the Modern Indonesian Elite.* Dordrecht, Holland / Cinnaminson, NJ: Foris Publications.

van Wichelen, Sonja
2006   "Contesting Megawati: The Mediation of Islam and Nation in Times of Political Transition." *Westminster Papers in Communication and Culture* 3 (2): 41–59. London: University of Westminster.

2009   "Polygamy Talk and the Politics of Feminism: Contestations over Masculinity in a New Muslim Indonesia." *Journal of International Women's Studies* 11 (1): 173–188.

2010   *Religion, Politics, and Gender in Indonesia: Disputing the Muslim Body.* New York: Routledge.

Vreede-de Stuers, Cora
1960   *The Indonesian Woman: Struggles and Achievements.* The Hague: Mouton.

Wadud, Amina
2006   *Inside the Gender Jihad: Women's Reform in Islam.* London: Oneworld Press.

Wadud-Muhsin, Amina
1992   *Qur'an and Woman.* Kuala Lumpur, Malaysia: Penerbit Fajar Bakti.

Wafiroh, Nihayatul
2016   "Women's Agency in Arranged Marriages within the Context of *Pesantren.*" PhD diss., Gadjah Mada University, Yogyakarta, Indonesia.

Wahid, Din

2014 "Nurturing the Salafi Manhaj: A Study of Salafi Pesantrens in Contemporary Indonesia." PhD diss., Utrecht University, Utrecht, the Netherlands.

Wardoyo, Puspo

n.d. *Kiat Sukses Poligami Islami: Pengalaman Puspo Wardoyo dan Empat Istrinya* (Secrets to Successful Polygamy in Islam: The Experience of Puspo Wardoyo and His Four Wives). Yogyakarta: private publication.

Watson, C. W.

2005 "Islamic Books and their Publishers: Notes on the Contemporary Indonesian Scene." *Journal of Islamic Studies* 16 (2): 177–210.

Webster, Tracy Wright

2016 "The Ongoing Culture Debate: Female Youth and *Pergaulan* (*Bebas*) in Yogyakarta, Indonesia." In *Youth Identities and Social Transformations in Modern Indonesia,* edited by Kathryn Robinson, 218–237. Boston, MA: Brill.

Weintraub, Andrew N.

2011 *Islam and Popular Culture in Indonesia and Malaysia.* New York: Routledge.

Wessing, Robert

1997 "A Princess from Sunda: Some Aspects of Nyai Roro Kidul." *Asian Folklore Studies,* 317–353.

White, Sally

2006 "Gender and the Family." In *Voices of Islam in Southeast Asia: A Contemporary Sourcebook,* edited by Greg Fealy and Virginia Hooker, 273–352. Singapore: Institute of Southeast Asian Studies.

White, Sally, and Maria Ulfah Anshor

2008 "Islam and Gender in Contemporary Indonesia: Public Discourses on Duties, Rights, and Morality." In *Expressing Islam: Religious Life and Politics in Indonesia,* edited by Greg Fealy and Sally White, 137–158. Singapore: Institute of Southeast Asian Studies.

Widarso, Wishnubroto

1997 *Kiat Sukses Bergaul* (The Secret to Successful Social Interactions). Yogyakarta, Indonesia: Kanisius.

Widiarti, Asri

2010 *Tak Kenal maka Ta'aruf:Panduan Lengkap Proses Ta'aruf Hingga Pernikahan Aktivis Dakwah* (Unacquainted and yet Engaged: The Complete Guide to the Marriage Process for Religious Activists). Solo, Indonesia: Era Adicitra Intermedia.

Widodo, Amrih

2008 "Writing for God: Piety and Consumption in Popular Islam." *Inside Indonesia* 93 (August–October), http://www.insideindonesia.org/writing-for-god.

Wieringa, Saskia

2002 *Sexual Politics in Indonesia.* New York: Palgrave Macmillan.

2015 "Gender Harmony and the Happy Family: Islam, Gender and Sexuality in Post-reformasi Indonesia." *South East Asia Research* 23 (1): 27–44.

Wijayanto, Iip

2003a *Sex in the "Kost": Realitas dan Moralitas Seks Kaum "Terpelajar"* (Sex in the Boardinghouse: Reality and Sexual Morality of Educated Youth). Yogyakarta, Indonesia: Tinta Press.

2003b   *Pemerkosaan atas Nama Cinta: Potret Muram Interaksi Sosial Kaum Muda* (Rape in the Name of Love: A Disturbing Portrait of the Social Interactions of Youth). Yogyakarta, Indonesia: Tinta Press.

2003c   *Campus "Fresh Chicken": Menelanjangi Praktik Pelacuran Kaum Terpelajar* (Campus "Fresh Chicken": Uncovering the Practice of Prostitution among Educated Youth). Yogyakarta, Indonesia: Tinta Press.

2004   *Sex in the Kost 2: MAM Married after "Metteng"!* (Sex in the Boardinghouse 2: M.A.M. Married after Pregnant!). Yogyakarta, Indonesia: The Iip Wijayanto Press.

Wikan, Unni

1990   *Managing Turbulent Hearts: A Balinese Formula for Living.* Chicago: University of Chicago Press.

Wilson, Chris

2008   *Ethno-Religious Violence in Indonesia: From Soil to God.* London: Routledge.

Wilson, Ian D.

2008   "'As Long as It's *Halal*': Islamic *Preman* in Jakarta." In *Expressing Islam: Religious Life and Politics in Indonesia,* edited by Greg Fealy and Sally White, 192–210. Singapore: Institute of Southeast Asian Studies.

Wolf, Diane L.

1992   *Factory Daughters: Gender, Household Dynamics, and Rural Industrialization in Java.* Berkeley: University of California Press.

1996   "Javanese Factory Daughters: Gender, the State, and Industrial Capitalism." In *Fantasizing the Feminine in Indonesia,* edited by Laurie J. Sears, 140–162. Durham, NC: Duke University Press.

Wolff, John U., and Soepomo Poedjosoedarmo

1982   *Communicative Codes in Central Java.* Ithaca, NY: Southeast Asia Program, Cornell University.

Woodward, Mark

1989   *Islam in Java: Normative Piety and Mysticism in the Sultanate of Yogyakarta.* Ann Arbor, MI: Association for Asian Studies.

World Bank

2008   *The Road Not Traveled: Education Reform in the Middle East and North Africa.* Washington, DC: World Bank Publications.

Wuryandari, Mya, Endang Sri Indrawati, and Siswati

2010   "Perbedaan Persepsi Suami Istri Terhadap Kualitas Pernikahan antara yang Menikah dengan Pacaran dan Ta'aruf" (Differences in Husbands' and Wives' Perceptions of the Quality of their Marriages based on Dating and *Ta'aruf*). Research Report, 28 pgs. Fakultas Psikologi, Universitas Diponegoro.

Xenos, Peter

2004   "The Social Demography of Urban Youth in Southeast Asia." Paper for a panel titled "Youth and Sexuality in Southeast Asia," Association for Asian Studies Annual Meeting, San Diego, California.

Zaman, Muhammad Qasim

2002   *The 'Ulama in Contemporary Islam: Custodians of Change.* Princeton, NJ: Princeton University Press.

Zeghal, Malika

2007   "The 'Recentering' of Religious Knowledge and Discourse: The Case of al-Azhar in Twentieth-Century Egypt." In *Schooling Islam: The Culture and Politics of*

Modern Muslim Education, edited by Robert W. Hefner and Muhammad Qasin Zaman, 107–130. Princeton, NJ: Princeton University Press.

Zuhdi, Muhammad

2006   "Modernization of Indonesian Islamic Schools' Curricula, 1945–2003." *The International Inclusive Education Colloquium: Critical Analyses of Inclusive Education Policy: An International Survey.* Part 2. Special issue of *International Journal of Inclusive Education* 10 (4–5): 415–427.

National Family Planning Board, 124.
See also Keluarga Berencana
Nationalist Party, Indonesian (PNI), 24, 84
nationalists (secular), 24. See also aliran
National Selection Exam for State
Universities (SNM-PTN), 191nn4, 6
nembung, 204n37
neoliberalism, 131, 186
neo-priyayi, 83, 87, 114
neo-reformists, 96, 109–110, 196n1; style,
168. See also youth, neo-reformist
neo-traditionalists, 96, 98–109, 165, 196n1.
See also youth, neo-traditionalist
newlyweds, 73
New Order, 8, 9, 10, 20, 24, 25, 31;
development programs, 85, 86;
educational expansion, 32, 34, 124; ethnic
traditions, 34–35, 190n21; gender policies,
85, 124, 187n10; last decades, 38; policies
on sexuality, 124–125; program impact on
marriage patterns, 124; religious
education and, 118, 127, 177
new santri, 40, 48, 59, 63, 70.
NGO (nongovernmental organization), 11.
See also LSM
ngoko (informal Javanese language
register), 133
Nilan, Pam, 9
normativity, Muslim, 65, 123; marriage and,
164. See also ethics; Islamic resurgence

offerings (to spirits), 45, 47, 113–114, 156.
See also abangan; spirits
old maid (prawan tua), 146, 158, 166
Ong, Aiwa, 92

pacaran. See dating
Pancasila (Five Principles of Indonesia's
National Philosophy), 35, 36; asas
tunggal, 36, 52; Moral Education
Program, 86; revival, 190n23, 199n2
paramilitaries, 6, 25
parenthood, importance of, 75, 173. See also
kinship; marriage
parents: reformist, 110–115; religion, 204n2;
rituals of respect, 173; sexual education
and, 126; traditionalist, 98–104
Partai Keadilan Sejatera (PKS, Prosperous
Justice Party), 55, 135, 177; national

elections and, 193n27; on polygyny, 154;
women and, 193n30
patriarchal: authority,109; bias, 107
patriarchy, 194n11; Islam and, 195n20.
See also gender; men; women
Pausacker, Helen, 188n20
Peacock, James, 20, 26, 187n11, 190n14; on
child socialization, 27–29
pegawai negeri (civil servants), 3, 23, 32, 42,
47, 162; jobs, 61; reformist parents and,
110, 120; wives of, 86–87
Peletz, Michael, 92, 194n5
pembantu (hired help), 111, 112, 117, 118
pemuda. See youth
pengajian (religious study group), 43, 45, 49,
51, 158, 161; forms of, 191n8; neo-reformists
and, 110; traditionalists and, 64
peran ganda (dual role), 111
Pergerakan Mahasiswa Islam Indonesia
(PMII, Indonesian Muslim University
Student Movement), 37, 40, 51; at UIN,
66–69
Perwari (Union of Women of the
Indonesian Republic), 84
pesantren (Muslim boarding school),
20, 21, 23, 33, 42, 129, 140, 189nn2, 8,
197n4; curriculum, 33, 105, 189n3;
female students, 33, 190n18; gender and,
106, 197n13; kilat, 191n5; male students,
33; salaf, 64, 203n28; traditionalists and,
61. See also education; madrasah
piety, 50, 51, 124, 138, 184, 185. See also
kesalehan
PKI. See Communist Party, Indonesian
PKK (Pembinaan Kesejahteraan Keluarga),
86; panca dharma wanita, 196n28
pluralization, 8, 39; gender, 71, 79, 194n5;
religious, 70
PMII, Indonesian Muslim University
Student Movement. See Pergerakan
Mahasiswa Islam Indonesia
polygyny (poligami), 76, 84–85, 166,
196n32, 202nn18, 20; since the New
Order, 153; among priyayi, 80, 195n16
population: imbalance, 165; urban,
190n15. See also Indonesia, population;
Yogyakarta, population
prayer, 106, 118, 167, 199n33; Friday, 104;
purification, 199n5. See also sholat

About the Author

NANCY J. SMITH-HEFNER is associate professor in the Department of Anthropology at Boston University. She has written extensively on issues of gender, sexuality, language, and education in Southeast Asia, as well as among Southeast Asian immigrants in the United States. Her first book, *Khmer-American: Identity and Moral Education in a Diasporic Community*, examined issues of personhood and morality among Cambodian refugees in New England. Her recent research and publications have focused on issues of piety, subjectivity, and sexuality among Muslim Javanese youth and have been featured in *Journal of Asian Studies, Journal of Southeast Asian Studies, Journal of Linguistic Anthropology*, and *Review of Indonesian and Malay Affairs*.